The BIG Book of ABA Programs

Michael M. Mueller, Ph.D., BCBA-D

Ajamu Nkosi, Ph.D., BCBA-D

Copyright © 2010 by Stimulus Publications, Inc.
ALL RIGHTS RESERVED

Based on the ABLLS®-R Copyright 2006 by Behavior Analysts Inc. Used by permission.

No part of this book may reproduced, stored in a retrieval system, or transmitted in any form or by any means, electronic, mechanical, photocopying, microfilming, or otherwise, without written permission from the publisher.

Stimulus Publications
2470 Windy Hill Road
Suite 300
Marietta, Georgia, 30067
www.stimuluspublications.com

"Stimulus Publications" is a registered trademark of Stimulus Publications, Inc.

ISBN: 978-09823782-4-3

Printed in the United States of America

The BIG Book of ABA Programs is dedicated to the thousands of caring individuals who have given their lives to teaching children with special needs. You perform small miracles every day. These gifts of progress you bring to children are measured in tiny increments away from the spotlight of worthy recognition. You give hope to the children and families who need it most.

The BIG Book of ABA Programs

Chapter Number	Chapter	Page
1	Introduction and Orientation to The BIG Book of ABA Programs.............................	1
2	ABA Programs Compatible with ABLLS®-R Domain A...	15
3	ABA Programs Compatible with ABLLS®-R Domain B...	27
4	ABA Programs Compatible with ABLLS®-R Domain C...	55
5	ABA Programs Compatible with ABLLS®-R Domain D...	113
6	ABA Programs Compatible with ABLLS®-R Domain E...	141
7	ABA Programs Compatible with ABLLS®-R Domain F...	161
8	ABA Programs Compatible with ABLLS®-R Domain G...	187
9	ABA Programs Compatible with ABLLS®-R Domain H...	233
10	ABA Programs Compatible with ABLLS®-R Domain J...	283
11	ABA Programs Compatible with ABLLS®-R Domain K...	305
12	ABA Programs Compatible with ABLLS®-R Domain L...	315
13	ABA Programs Compatible with ABLLS®-R Domain M...	347
14	ABA Programs Compatible with ABLLS®-R Domain N...	359
15	ABA Programs Compatible with ABLLS®-R Domain P...	371
16	ABA Programs Compatible with ABLLS®-R Domain Q...	379
17	ABA Programs Compatible with ABLLS®-R Domain R...	397
18	ABA Programs Compatible with ABLLS®-R Domain S...	437
19	ABA Programs Compatible with ABLLS®-R Domain T...	449
20	ABA Programs Compatible with ABLLS®-R Domain U...	457
21	ABA Programs Compatible with ABLLS®-R Domain V...	483
22	ABA Programs Compatible with ABLLS®-R Domain W...	495
23	ABA Programs Compatible with ABLLS®-R Domain X...	503
24	ABA Programs Compatible with ABLLS®-R Domain Y...	509
25	ABA Programs Compatible with ABLLS®-R Domain Z...	541

CHAPTER 1

Introduction and Orientation to

The BIG Book of ABA Programs

As Soon As Possible

When early learning and language deficits are first noticed in young children with autism and other developmental delays, parents and teachers generally wait as long as they can before taking action. This wait period can oftentimes be too long to take advantage of very early learning opportunities. When early developmental concerns become evident, caregivers need to act fast to ensure not another day is spent without intensive instruction. When early action is taken in schools, homes, or in a clinic setting, the best results and outcomes are possible. Children with Autism Spectrum Disorders need intensive, research-based, effective, help *As Soon As Possible*.

The Rationale For The BIG Book Of ABA Programs

In Schools: Helping students in schools requires teachers, behavior analysts, administrators, attorneys, various other professionals, and parents to gather in IEP meetings. The meetings are oftentimes contentious, the parties disagreeable, and the meetings are sometimes hours long. During the IEP meeting, when goals need to be written, a collective sigh comes over the group because the tedious and time-consuming tasks of writing goals, deciding how to record data, deciding which materials to use, how to prompt, and how to organize the student's instructional program have to be completed. Many times in such meetings, comments are made about how badly professionals need a book that will make their lives and jobs so much easier during the IEP process. "Why can't there just be a big book that already has all of these goals written out?" is a question heard frequently during the IEP process.

In Homes: Providing intensive instruction to students in home programs requires many different skills, usually provided by two different types of teachers. A less educated and less experienced teacher typically provides the actual instruction while a more senior, better educated, more experienced, and more expensive teacher typically chooses new programs, develops baseline procedures and prompting strategies, decides how data will be collected, develops data sheets, graphs, and searches for materials to use while teaching. Because early intervention programs used in most homes around the world are based on steps in the skills assessment called the Assessment of Basic Language and Learning Skills Revised (ABLLS®-R), questions are often asked about why it takes so much time to do the things supervising teachers do every day. Parents often find themselves asking, "Wouldn't it be easier and cheaper if there was a big book containing all of these different programs so we wouldn't need to spend so much money?"

Helping students in both settings, and hearing different concerns from both settings with the same solution led to the development of The BIG Book of ABA Programs. In schools, hours of IEP time is no longer required to choose appropriate instructional goals. In homes, hours of expensive service developing and writing appropriate instructional goals are no longer required. The BIG Book of ABA Programs provides the solution to all these common problems.

Everything After The ABLLS®-R

After the ABLLS®-R is completed, The BIG Book of ABA Programs is used to turn assessment results into initial learning programs. For each teachable step in the ABLLS®-R, an ABA program can be customized to fit the instructional needs of the student whose skills were just assessed. The BIG Book of ABA Programs contains an IEP goal for each teachable step of the ABLLS®-R. A teacher, behavior therapist, or parent simply conducts the ABLLS®-R and then selects ABA instructional programs from The BIG Book of ABA Programs to start teaching.

Permissions For Use Of The BIG Book Of ABA Programs

The BIG Book of ABA Programs is designed to be used repeatedly with certain restrictions. For a teacher working with children in a school setting, The BIG Book of ABA Programs is designed to be used for all the students in your classroom. For behavior analysts, The BIG Book of ABA Programs is designed to be used with all the children you serve. For parents providing therapy, The BIG Book of ABA Programs is designed to be used to help educate the children in your family. The BIG Book of ABA Programs contains more than 500 ABA programs and each is customizable and useful for multiple students. Within the guidelines listed here, The BIG Book of ABA Programs can be photocopied endlessly to suit your needs. Any other use, copying, or sharing is strictly prohibited.

Why We Like The ABLLS®-R So Much

As a skills assessment tool, we, like so many other behavior analysts, behavior therapists, teachers, and parents who help children with autism, use the ABLLS®-R on a daily basis and find tremendous value in its use. It is easy to conduct and easy to score. From the results, it is easy to choose starting points for ABA instruction. It is easy to gauge progress. It can be used multiple times. It is thorough in its list of developmentally progressive skills. It is widely accepted as *the* developmental skills inventory for children with early language and learning deficits, and children with autism.

What is ABA?

Applied Behavior Analysis (ABA) is an umbrella term similar to the way we use "Pasta." When you go to an Italian restaurant and you see the list of pasta options, you see Long Pasta options such as Spaghetti, Angel Hair, Vermicelli, Bucalini, Ziti, and possibly dozens of others. From these dozens of Pasta types, come hundreds of variations once all the sauce combinations are mixed and matched—tomato-based sauces, cheese based sauces, olive-oil based sauces, spicy sauces, meat sauces, etc. It would be hard to choose any one from many possible combinations and characterize it as accurately representing "Pasta" as a whole. Angel Hair with clams in a white-wine sauce looks nothing like Macaroni and Cheese even though both are "Pasta" in the broad sense.

ABA is a broad term that covers hundreds of procedures, methods, and systems. ABA shares similarities, but no one procedure within ABA can accurately represent the field as a whole. *Applied* Behavior Analysis is a scientific field devoted to understanding socially significant behaviors. It is the applied component of the laboratory-based field of Behavior Analysis. So, what then, is Behavior Analysis? Behavior Analysis is synonymous with "Behavioral Psychology," "Operant Learning," and the "Experimental Analysis of Behavior." Behavior Analysis is the study of the behavior of organisms. It focuses on why organisms of all shapes, sizes, and species behave in certain ways. Behavior analysis answers: Why do organisms do things in one context and not in another? How can we control different behaviors? How can we prevent certain behaviors from occurring and teach new behaviors? Behavior Analysis is devoted to answering such questions. Applied Behavior

Analysis has taken the answers to such questions provided by Behavior Analysis and *applied* those answers to human problems. For instance, as these answers pertain to children, ABA answers questions that include: How can we get teen drivers to obey speed limits and wear seat belts? How can we decrease graffiti in school bathrooms? How can we save lives taken by accidental gun play? How can we keep children from going in the cars of strangers? How can we keep kids in schools? How can we teach language to children with autism? The specific answers to all these questions may seem different, but each can be answered through ABA.

As we look at similar questions and answers within the context of teaching young children with autism and other developmental delays, we find the same things. That is, the answers are each within the field of ABA, but the precise structure, look, and feel are quite different because of the vastness of the field itself. Throughout modern culture, certain names are attached to things that then come to represent a variety of similar things. For example, a "Frisbee™" represents any number of flying disks. A "Band-aid™" comes to represent bandages of all shapes and sizes. "ABA" in the special needs community has come to represent a small number of procedures aimed at teaching young children in a structured, data-based, and effective manner. Although this is not a technically accurate representation of the field at large, it has come to denote a certain meaning in the popular language that permeates clinic, hospital, school, home, and community-based instructional programming for young children. It is too imbedded in our modern lexicon to change.

What then, has "ABA" come to mean in the context of teaching young children with autism? ABA in this context is a collection of teaching strategies, a collection of behaviorally based instructional methods that share similar features. This collection of teaching strategies includes what is referred to as "Discrete Trials Teaching," "Discrete Trials Instruction," "Discrete Trials Therapy," Lovaas Therapy," "Incidental Teaching," "Natural Environment Teaching," "Verbal Behavior Analysis," "Verbal Behavior Therapy," "Verbal Behavior," "Coaching," and "Pivotal Response Training." Some of these labels for ABA instruction are absolutely indistinguishable from others while some labels for procedures vary only slightly in the setting in which a student is taught, the behaviors or responses targeted, or by the way in which learning opportunities are arranged. Nevertheless, each of these strategies relies on the same underlying principles and is effective by the same underlying processes. All are "ABA." All are empirical and behaviorally-based teaching procedures. All are instructional methods.

It is very important to keep in mind that ABA in this context is a teaching approach. As such, the child is a student, and the person teaching is a teacher. Regardless of what you teach, you are in fact teaching. Regardless of the age of the child, the child in this context is in fact a student learning new skills. To highlight and keep the instructional focus squarely in front of everything else, we will refer to the learner as a "student" and to the person teaching as a "teacher." The teacher then might be a formally trained behavior analyst, a paraprofessional working in a school, a school teacher, a parent, a behavior therapist, or anyone else including professionals from other disciplines such as a speech and language therapist, an occupational therapist, or a physical therapist.

ABA instructional methods share a few common features. First, to teach a student a new skill, you have to tell the student what it is you want them to do. This initial instruction or cue, is sometimes referred to as a "Discriminative Stimulus" or "Sd" for short. All ABA instruction starts with this cue. Second, each instructional method shares a brief evaluative period in which you decide whether or not the student did what you told them to do. Third, if the student did what you told them to do, a potent reinforcer is delivered so they are more likely to do the same thing the next time they are asked. Fourth, if the student did not do what you told them to do, a prompting procedure is used to teach the student what to do the next time he or she is told to do the same thing.

That's it! No mystery! No magic! ABA is simply good teaching. What makes this approach work better than any other approach to educating children with autism is the consistency, repetition of learning opportunities, and high rates of reinforcement.

There are several different prompting strategies that can be used to teach a student. In general, all prompting strategies fall into one of two categories: Errorless learning strategies or Trial-and-Error learning strategies. Both categories are ABA. Both contain several specific prompting sequences that are very effective. Not all strategies and methods are perfect in every situation for every student. Very little, if anything in education is one-size fits all and there are pros and cons to prompting strategies like there are with everything that pertains to students with autism. Errorless learning strategies, although very effective, will not be discussed in The BIG Book of ABA Programs because of the difficulty of teaching new teachers to implement the strategies with high integrity. Errorless learning strategies for the teaching of students with autism are far more difficult to manualize, more difficult to learn, more difficult to implement consistently from session to session, more difficult to implement consistently across teachers, and require far more teacher judgment in their use. Because of the limitations and difficulties in acquiring mastery over Errorless strategies, we recommend their use only after a teacher becomes well-versed and confident in the use of Trial-and-Error methods and the ABA teaching routine in general.

Trial-and-Error strategies typically follow a "least-to-most" pattern of prompting. The least-to-most sequence starts with the least intrusive prompt and moves to a more intrusive prompt as the sequence progresses. Although there are prompting strategies that can contain 5, 6, or even 7 different prompts, the most commonly practiced and most widely researched prompting hierarchy is the 3-step prompting sequence. The "3-step" is incredibly powerful and widely used in many different contexts. In ABA instruction, it is the easiest to learn, the easiest to generalize, the easiest to implement with a high degree of integrity and is very effective. The 3-step is sometimes referred to as a "Tell, Show, Do" approach and keeping this phrase in mind while implementing ABA programs can be quite helpful. How the 3-step approach is used to teach motor and verbal responses is explained in detail in the following pages.

Baseline

Before you begin teaching with 3-step prompts, it is important to get a baseline level of behavior. "Baseline" simply means a current pre-teaching level of accuracy on whichever skill you might teach. Baseline is what the student can do before ABA teaching begins. Baseline is used as a measure from which to gauge teaching progress. We can consider teaching with ABA successful if the outcomes are such that the student can do more than before the teaching occurred. Knowing the current pre-teaching level of performance is the only way to understand the effects of the teaching process.

Baseline trials are not teaching trials. Baseline is purely evaluative and answers the very basic question of, "What can my student do before I start teaching?" Because baseline is not teaching, there are no prompting procedures and no reinforcement. You simply tell the student to do something and evaluate whether or not they do it. If they can already demonstrate a high level of performance on that skill, there is no reason to use ABA to teach the skill. If the student does not demonstrate an acceptably high level of performance, teaching using ABA should follow.

The 3-Step Prompt for Motor Responses

The 3-step begins with telling a student to do something. In general, this initial demand (or cue) should be very simple, stated directly, and repeated word for word throughout instruction. For example, "Match," "Sort," "Put with same," "Give me…," "Touch the…" etc. are all common initial cues for a variety of learning programs. In The BIG Book of ABA Programs, the initial cue is spelled out for the teacher, thus alleviating the need to create the most appropriate cues from program to program. The first prompt is a verbal demand for the student to engage in a certain response. You are telling the student to do something. You then must give the student a chance to do it. A 5-second wait period allows the teacher to decide whether or not the student engaged in the desired behavior. If the student demonstrated the correct response, that response is enthusiastically praised and a reinforcer is delivered. If the student did not engage in the correct response (either demonstrated an incorrect response or did nothing at all) the second prompt is delivered. The second prompt in the 3-step is a model prompt. The model prompt demonstrates the correct response to the student, or in some way shows the student how to respond. This model prompt is delivered with a second verbal prompt in which you are again telling the student to do something. Now, because the student was shown what to do, they are more likely to do it. This teaching step is very effective. If the student demonstrates the correct response after it was modeled, the response is enthusiastically praised and a reinforcer is delivered. If the student does not demonstrate the correct response, the third and final step of the prompting sequence is presented. The third step is physical guidance. Physical guidance is sometimes referred to as "hand-over-hand" teaching. This step ensures the student engages in the correct response because the teacher physically guides the student to perform the correct response. The student was initially given a verbal cue to perform a task. If they did not perform the task, the student was shown how to do it and given a second opportunity to perform the task. If the student still did not perform the task correctly, they are physically guided through the correct action. For all motor responses (any response that does not require a verbal response) the 3-step ensures that the student will eventually engage in the correct response. In The BIG Book of ABA Programs, the exact words to say and actions to take for each step of the prompting sequence are given for each program.

Let's look at a couple of examples.

First, let's look at an example in which the goal is to teach the student to receptively identify common objects. For receptive identification programs, the teacher says the name of an object and the student should identify that named object. In this example, let's assume a cup is chosen as the target object to teach. A cup and ball are placed in front of the student. The teacher says, "Touch cup" (verbal prompt). If the student's first response within 5 seconds is to touch the cup, the teacher provides enthusiastic praise and delivers a reinforcer. If the student touches the ball or does not touch either object, the *teacher* touches the cup and again says, "Touch cup" (model prompt). If the student's first response is touching the cup within 5 seconds after the model prompt, the teacher praises enthusiastically and delivers a reinforcer. If the student touches the ball or does not touch either object, the teacher takes the student's hand and touches the student's hand to the cup again saying, "Touch cup" (physical prompt).

In the cup example, the student was given 5 seconds to touch the cup before touching the ball. The student is *NOT* given 5 seconds to *eventually* touch the cup. This is an important point. If a student is given 5 seconds to eventually touch the cup, the student has enough time to touch all the objects given as choices. The goal is to teach the student to touch the cup first, when "Touch cup" is given as the cue. Allowing the student to touch the ball and then the cup before receiving a reinforcer might teach the student that "Touch cup" means to touch the ball, then the cup whereas you only want the student to learn to touch one object, the cup, when told "Touch cup." Touching the incorrect object, the ball, automatically triggers the next prompt regardless of when the incorrect touch occurred. For example, if the cue, "Touch cup" is given and the student reaches out and touches the ball, the teacher instantly places the student's hand away from the ball and presents the model prompt-- The teacher touches the cup and says, "Touch cup."

In this next example, let's assume the teacher wants the student to hand a green block when the teacher says, "Give me green." A green block and a red block are placed in front of the student. The teacher says, "Give me green." If the student hands the green block to the teacher (within 5 seconds and before touching the red block), the teacher praises enthusiastically and delivers a reinforcer. If the student touches the red block or does not touch either block within 5 seconds, the teacher models placing the green block into the teacher's hand, places the green block in front of the student and again says, "Give me green." If the student hands the green block to the teacher (within 5 seconds and before touching the red block), the teacher praises enthusiastically and delivers a reinforcer. If the student touches the red block or does not touch either block within 5 seconds, the teacher takes the student's hand and physically guides the student to place the green block in the teacher's hand.

If the student demonstrates the correct response following the verbal or the model prompts, the response is praised and a reinforcer is delivered. If the student demonstrates an incorrect (or no) response following the verbal or the model prompts, the next prompt is delivered. The 3-step prompting sequence for motor responses always ends with the student demonstrating the correct response even if the teacher needs to help the student make the correct response with physical assistance.

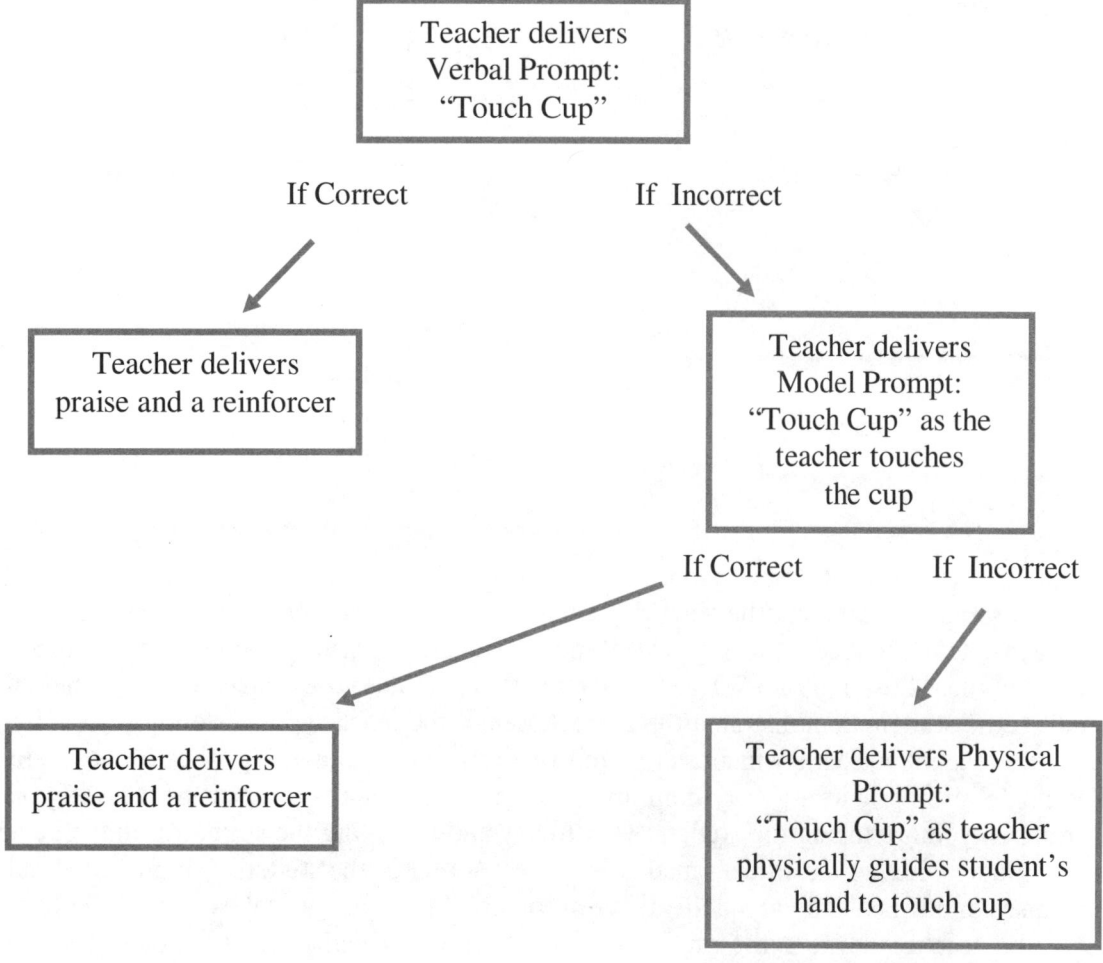

The 3-Step Prompt with a Verbal Response

As mentioned in the previous section on prompting a motor response, any motor response can be physically guided to completion. When the response you are targeting for change is a verbal or vocal response, the same is not true. You cannot physically guide a student to emit a verbal response in the same way you can guide a student to touch. However, you can still use a graduated prompting sequence in order to teach a verbal response. For the sake of consistency and ease of use, we decided to keep the same terminology in the types of prompts so that the same language and system is used throughout The BIG Book of ABA Programs.

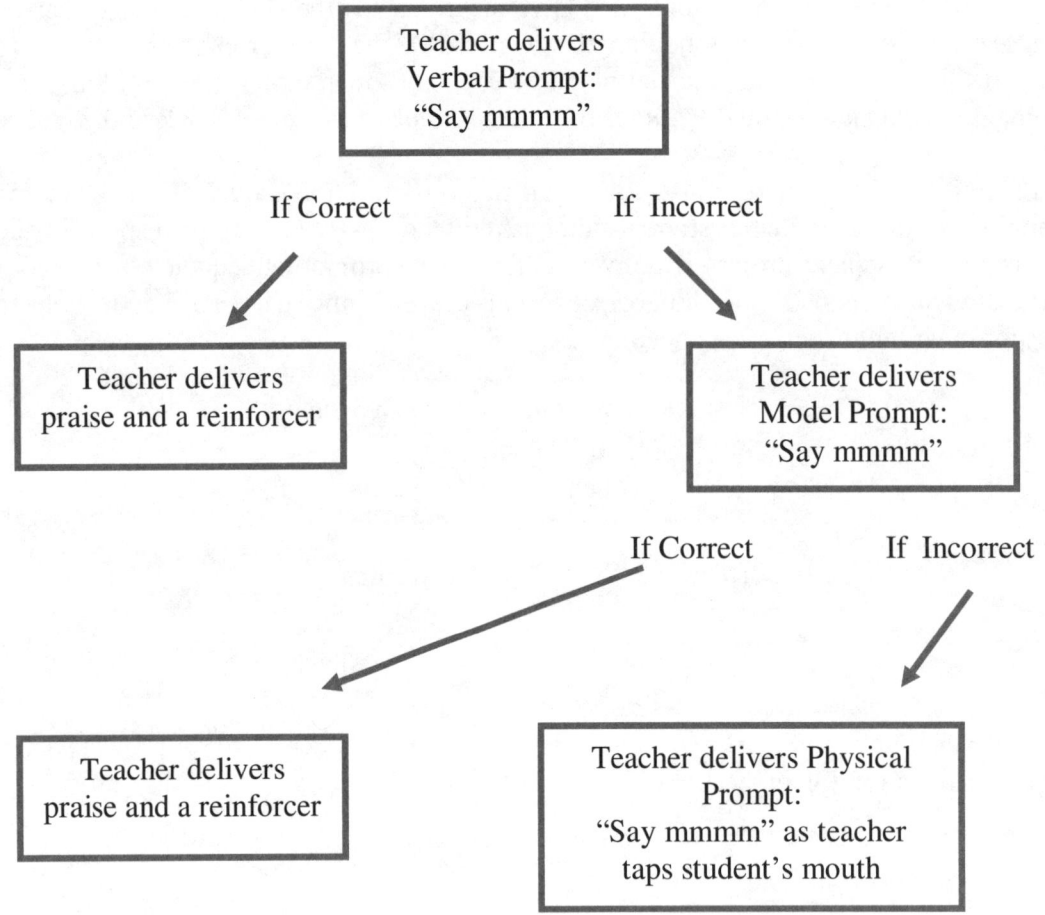

When a verbal response is targeted, the teacher presents the verbal prompt in the manner previously described. That is, the teacher tells the student to say something. For example, when teaching vocal imitation, the teacher might deliver the cue, "Say, mmmm." The teacher waits 5 seconds to evaluate whether the student made the correct sound. If the student demonstrated the correct sound, the teacher praises enthusiastically and delivers a reinforcer. If the student makes an incorrect sound or does not say anything, the teacher delivers the model prompt. The model prompt here is, "Say mmmm." The model prompt is a repeat of the verbal prompt because with both prompts, you are telling the student what to say and modeling the sound to imitate. The teacher waits 5 seconds to evaluate whether the student made the correct sound. If the student demonstrated the correct sound, the teacher praises enthusiastically and delivers a reinforcer. If the student makes an incorrect sound or does not say anything, the teacher delivers the physical prompt. The physical prompt repeats the verbal and model prompt as the teacher touches the student's mouth next to the lips in an attempt to communicate to the student that it is the student's turn to say the requested vocal response. Lightly touching the side of the student's mouth while repeating the cue is very effective to this end. When delivering the model and physical prompts, the teacher is advised to exaggerate the lip, mouth, tongue, and verbalizations so the student has the best model available from which to make his or her own response.

The 3-step is an easy-to-implement prompting sequence in which the student is told to do something, given a chance to do it, told and shown, given a chance to do it, and then given assistance to complete the task. It is applicable for all behaviors and has been widely effective across a vast array of students, behaviors, and settings. For every program in The BIG Book of ABA Programs, the actual words to say and the prompting actions to perform are described.

Consistency

Be absolutely consistent when using the 3-step prompts. Be consistent in the words you deliver as cues. If you use the phrase "Hand me the..." then use that exact phrase each time you deliver that teaching program. Be consistent when delivering the prompts so that you do not say anything other than the prompts. Too often teachers will attempt to coax or use excessive verbal prompts in addition to those in the 3-step system. Avoid these added words and requests. Say only the cues and verbiage described in the protocols. Here is an example of what _NOT_ to say. "Give me the cup. Come on, you can do it. Give me the cup. Give me the cup. You know this one. Come on now, the cup. Give me the cup." This excessive over-prompting should never be used. Stick only to the exact wording in the protocol.

Deliver praise very enthusiastically each and every time the student makes a correct response. Great teachers are those that themselves become reinforcers for correct student responding. This cannot be stated strongly enough. To be an effective teacher you need to act silly, act crazy, be high-pitched when delivering praise. Be enthusiastic and funny. Get into the student's world and make yourself fun and motivating so the student will work for your attention. Finally, be consistent in your variation of the placement of the materials used in the sessions. It is possible for students to make correct motor responses because of unintended reasons. For instance, if a student always chooses the left choice, the square item, something slightly closer than something else, or any number of additional undesirable sources of stimulus control can affect performance, learning, and successful outcomes. To help prevent these issues from affecting performance, be very cautious about material placement. Use semi-random rotation rather than trial-to-trial alternation. Never present the same choices in the same location more than three trials in a row.

Data Collection

When collecting data on ABA teaching programs, you will record data on every learning opportunity (trial) you present to the student. For baseline trials, because there is no prompting used, simply record "+" for correct and "-" for incorrect responding. The scoring system for teaching trials is also quite simple, very easy to implement, and provides very useful information regarding student progress, mastery of skills, and to determine if changes need to be made to existing programs. The 3-step sequence uses verbal, model, and physical prompts. For motor responses, the student will do the desired response on every trial. Data collection is simply a matter of recording what level of prompting was required to obtain the response. Did the student respond correctly after the verbal prompt? If so, then a "V" is recorded. Did the student respond appropriately after the model prompt? If so, an

"M" is recorded. If the student required physical guidance to complete the desired behavior, a "P" is scored for that trial. V, M, or P. Use one letter per trial. It is fast, easy to use, easy to remember, and conveys a lot of meaning beyond whether or not the student responded "correctly" or "incorrectly." During programs that teach verbal responses, the data collection system follows the same pattern. If the student responses correctly following the verbal prompt, a "V" is recorded. If the student responds correctly after the model prompt, an "M" is recorded. If "physical guidance" was used, a "P" is recorded.

Understanding the Protocol

For each teachable step of the ABLLS®-R, a protocol describing how to teach with ABA is provided. Even though the skills vary widely throughout the book, the structure of each protocol is the same. Below is a sample protocol used to teach a skill compatible with ABLLS®-R skill M7. As can be seen, certain critical information on the protocol is provided for you and other, student-specific, information is left open for customization.

Hand Raising In Group
Compatible with ABLLS®-R Code M7

Student's Name:		Start Date:
Objective:	When teacher poses a question to a group of students, student will raise hand and wait to be called on prior to answering.	
Person Implementing Objective:		
Setting/Environment:		
Materials:		
Reinforcers:		
Baseline:	Ask a question to a group of students the answer to which is known to the student. Wait 5 seconds for a response. A correct response is scored (+) if student raises hand before answering- <u>do not reinforce</u>. Move to next trial. An incorrect response is scored (-) if student does not raise hand before answering- <u>do not prompt</u>. Move to next trial.	
Teaching Procedures:	Ask a question to a group of students the answer to which is known to the student. Wait 5 seconds for a response. If student raises hand before answering, praise and provide reinforcer. If student does not raise hand before answering, say, "Raise your hand like this before you answer" as you model hand raising. Wait 5 seconds for a response. If student raises hand, praise and provide reinforcer. If student does not raise hand, physically guide student to raise hand. Score V for correct response that followed verbal prompt. Score M if the correct response followed the model prompt. Score P if physical guidance was used.	
Additional Targets:		

Student's Name: Write the name of the student you are teaching with this program.

Start Date: Write the date the program is first implemented.

Person Implementing the Objective: Write the names of the teachers of this program.

Materials: This space is to list the names of the materials used. Cards, pictures, objects, people, clocks, timers, and any other materials required to implement the program should be listed. Because it is important to use exact consistency of these materials from session to session, the more specific you can be, the better.

Reinforcers: Write the names of the reinforcers to be used when teaching this program. Food items, praise, tickles, tokens, and anything else used as a reinforcer should be listed.

Baseline Procedures: This is the exact wording and set up to be used in the baseline sessions.

Teaching Procedures: This is the exact wording and set up to be used when teaching the student the skill in the program.

Additional Targets: This is the location designed to record the current and future teaching targets. In ABA programs, dozens of different steps can be used to teach a particular skill. These different steps, or targets, can be developmentally sequential so that each skill is increasingly more difficult leading to a terminal goal. For example, in a hand washing program, the first step (the behavior that would be scored correct for "hand washing") might be turning on water. Once turning on water is mastered, the second step might be to turn on water and wet hands. The third step might be to turn on water, wet hands, apply soap, etc. Here, the actual behaviors that would be scored as correct responses change in a developmentally progressive manner so more and more progress is made towards the terminal goal of independent hand washing. All the smaller sub-steps are included in the "Hand Washing" program even though each by themselves does not constitute washing hands. Shoe tying, dressing, handwriting, math, and reading are all programs that follow such developmentally progressive steps. You have to learn to walk before you can learn to run.

Other programs are those in which the terminal behavior is the same from step to step but the materials change so that a wider variety of stimuli are used within a teaching program. For example, to teach a child to choose colors, there is no developmental sequence to follow. That is, it is not necessary to teach a child to choose red before blue, yellow before green, or any one color before any other color. Choosing colors is taught in whichever color order the teacher decides. So in this example, the first step might be red. When red is learned, Step 2 might be purple, Step 3 yellow, Step 4 green, etc. Choosing pictures, letters, numbers, and objects are all examples of these non-developmentally progressive programs. Even though teaching a child to choose a picture or an item does not follow a developmentally progressive series of steps, such learning can be made easier or more difficult and therefore variations in the steps can help facilitate learning. For example, additional steps might involve increasing complexity. For a program in which a student is required to touch a cup, Step 1 might be the cup presented by itself, with no distracter choice available. Step 2 might be a cup with one other item available in the choice array. Step 3 might be cup when 2 other choices are available. For programs in which the student is required to make increasingly longer responses, the additional steps might contain the specific durations needed for correct responding. For example, in a program that teaches eye contact, Step 1 might be for the student to look at the teacher for 1 second. Step 2 might require 3 seconds; Step 3 might require 5 seconds, etc. Each student is different. You might teach 10 different students to touch named objects and for each student the list of what objects are to be taught might be different. The BIG Book of ABA Programs allows for this individualization and customization so that each protocol can be used with student-specific information. Regardless of what the additional steps might be, you should decide those steps in advance and write those steps into the protocol in this location. If you progress through more steps than the protocol has space, simply photocopy a new protocol and continue. For example, if 5 spaces are provided (Steps 1 – Step 5) and the student is about to begin Step 6, photocopy a new protocol of the same teaching program and complete the new protocol with Step 6, 7, 8, 9, and 10.

Learning, Comfort, and Confidence Curve

Even though ABA is simple teaching, when teachers first begin the process, the teaching can feel a bit overwhelming. Maintaining the materials used for each program, maintaining the reinforcers, delivering the reinforcers, recording data, and doing all of these things quickly can take a little time to master. This is normal! This is expected and this is a natural part of the process that all successful teachers go through on the road to effective teaching. Please know that these feelings quickly go away with repeated practice. The process will be second-nature in short order. You will make mistakes. You will go slow to start with and the process will be a little awkward and cumbersome when you first begin. Relax! Trust the method. Trust the decades of research supporting this approach. Trust yourself. You can do it.

The Autism Skill Acquisition Program™

The BIG Book of ABA Programs is one of several important components of the Autism Skill Acquisition Program™ (The *ASAP*™) designed to provide parents, school teachers, and behavior analysts with everything necessary to teach new skills to children with special needs using methods derived from Applied Behavior Analysis. The *ASAP*™ contains the ASAP Guide, The BIG Book of ABA Programs, the ABA Graphing CD, and the ASAP Kit that contains all the teaching accessories, materials, and toys needed for teaching. We highly recommend using the *ASAP*™. In addition to the *ASAP*™ containing all the materials required for implementation, all other vital components are included. The *ASAP*™ contains a program guide filled with additional information on ABA, prompting strategies, preference assessments, program maintenance, organizational strategies, detailed instructions on data collection and the use of the data forms, preformatted computerized graphs to chart progress on 30 customizable programs, a "how-to" CD describing how to use the graphs and how to make additional graphs, and everything else required to begin, implement, and maintain a compete ABA program for your student. The *ASAP*™ is the only all-in-one instructional program that contains everything necessary to understand, implement, and maintain a successful early intervention program—How to teach, what to teach, what materials to use while teaching, how to record data, and how to graph and understand results. The *ASAP*™ is self contained, all-inclusive, and designed to save the user hundreds of thousands of dollars and hundreds of hours of time. For years teachers have struggled with taking the best skills assessment results and turning those results into well-written, behaviorally defined, empirical, defendable goals and teaching programs. ABA has been an unreachable area for many teachers who do not have the time or training to develop the necessary goals, prompting strategies, teaching methods, spreadsheets, data collection sheets, graphs, and materials needed to take the results of the ABLLS®-R and transform those into an entire learning program. The *ASAP*™ provides everything needed to implement the highest quality ABA program for any child.

The *ASAP*™ is available online at the Stimulus Publications website:

www.stimuluspublications.com

ABLLS®-R Reference:

Partington, J. W. (2006). *ABLLS®-R Protocol*. Behavior Analysts, inc.: Pleasant Hills, CA.

CHAPTER 2

ABA Programs Compatible with

ABLLS®-R Domain A

"Cooperation and Reinforcer Effectiveness"

Take A Preferred Item When Offered As Only Choice
Compatible with ABLLS®-R Code A1

Student's Name:		Start Date:	
Objective:		When teacher holds a preferred item in hand and extends hand toward student, student will take the preferred item.	
Person Implementing Objective:			
Setting/Environment:			
Materials:			
Reinforcers:			
Baseline:		Present the preferred item in open hand. Wait 5 seconds for a response. A correct response is scored (+) if student takes item from hand - <u>do not reinforce</u>. Move to next trial. An incorrect response is scored (-) if student does not take item from hand - <u>do not prompt</u>. Move to next trial.	
Teaching Procedures:		Present preferred item in open hand. Wait 5 seconds for a response. If student takes the item, praise and provide access to the item. If student does not take item, say, "Take this" and model the correct response (remove the item from your open hand with your other hand). Wait 5 seconds for a response. If student takes the item, praise and provide access to the item. If student does not take item, say, "Take this" and physically guide student to take item. Score V for correct response that followed verbal prompt. Score M if correct response followed model prompt. Score P if physical guidance was used.	
Additional Targets:			

Take A Preferred Item When Offered With A Nonpreferred Item
Compatible with ABLLS®-R Code A2

Student's Name:		Start Date:	
Objective:	When teacher offers a preferred and a nonpreferred item, student will take the preferred item.		
Person Implementing Objective:			
Setting/Environment:			
Materials:			
Reinforcers:			
Baseline:	At the same time, present a preferred and a nonpreferred item in your hands. Wait 5 seconds for a response. A correct response is scored (+) if student takes the preferred item - <u>do not reinforce</u>. Move to next trial. An incorrect response is scored (-) if student does not take the preferred item - <u>do not prompt</u>. Move to next trial.		
Teaching Procedures:	At the same time, present a preferred and a nonpreferred item in your hands. Wait 5 seconds for a response. If student takes the preferred item, praise and provide access to the item. If student does not take the preferred item, say "Take this" and model taking the preferred item from your open hand with your other hand. Wait 5 seconds for a response. If student takes the preferred item, praise and provide access to the item. If student does not take preferred item, physically guide student to take preferred item. Score V for correct response that followed verbal prompt. Score M if correct response followed model prompt. Score P if physical guidance was used.		
Additional Targets:			

The BIG Book of ABA Programs

Look At A Nonpreferred Item
Compatible with ABLLS®-R Code A3

Student's Name:	Start Date:	
Objective:	When teacher presents a nonpreferred item to student, student will look at the item.	
Person Implementing Objective:		
Setting/Environment:		
Materials:		
Reinforcers:		
Baseline:	Present a nonpreferred item in your open hand. Wait 5 seconds for a response. A correct response is scored (+) if student directs eye contact towards the item - do not reinforce. Move to next trial. An incorrect response is scored (-) if student does not direct eye contact towards the item - do not prompt. Move to next trial.	
Teaching Procedures:	Present a nonpreferred item in your open hand. Wait 5 seconds for a response. If student directs eye contact towards the item, praise and provide reinforcer. If student does not direct eye contact towards the item, say "Look" and hold item in front of student. Wait 5 seconds for a response. If student directs eye contact towards the item, praise and provide access to the reinforcer. If student does not direct eye contact towards the item, physically guide student to look at item. Score V for correct response that followed verbal prompt. Score M if correct response followed model prompt. Score P if physical guidance was used.	
Additional Targets:		

Take A Nonpreferred Item When Offered As Only Choice
Compatible with ABLLS®-R Code A4

Student's Name:		Start Date:
Objective:	When teacher presents a nonpreferred item to student, student will take the item.	

Person Implementing Objective:	
Setting/Environment:	
Materials:	
Reinforcers:	
Baseline:	Present the nonpreferred item in your open hand. Wait 5 seconds for a response. A correct response is scored (+) if student takes item from hand - <u>do not reinforce</u>. Move to next trial. An incorrect response is scored (-) if student does not take item from hand - <u>do not prompt</u>. Move to next trial.
Teaching Procedures:	Present the nonpreferred item in your open hand. Wait 5 seconds for a response. If student takes the item, praise and provide access to the item and reinforcer. If student does not take item, say, "Take this" and model taking the item. Wait 5 seconds for a response. If student takes the item, praise and provide access to the item and reinforcer. If student does not take item, say, "Take this" and physically guide student to take item. Score V for correct response that followed verbal prompt. Score M if correct response followed model prompt. Score P if physical guidance was used.
Additional Targets:	

Come To Teacher And Perform A Simple Task To Access A Preferred Item
Compatible with ABLLS®-R Code A5

Student's Name:		Start Date:
Objective:	When student is at least 5 feet away from teacher and shown a preferred item, student will come to teacher and comply with simple task demand to access preferred item.	
Person Implementing Objective:		
Setting/Environment:		
Materials:		
Reinforcers:		
Baseline:	When student is at least 5 feet away, show student the preferred item. Wait 5 seconds for a response. If student approaches, deliver a simple task demand. A correct response is scored (+) if student comes to you and complies with demand - <u>do not reinforce</u>. Move to next trial. An incorrect response is scored (-) if student does not come to you or does not comply with demand- <u>do not prompt</u>. Move to next trial.	
Teaching Procedures:	When student is at least 5 feet away, show student the preferred item. Wait 5 seconds for a response. If student comes to you, deliver a simple task demand. If student does not come to you, say, "Come here" and gesture to your location. Wait 5 seconds for a response. If student comes to you, praise and deliver a simple task demand. If student does not come to you, physically guide the student to come to you and deliver a simple task demand. When task demand is delivered (regardless of what level of prompting was required to get student to come to you), praise and provide access to the preferred item for compliance. If student does not comply within 5 seconds, model the correct response. If student complies within 5 seconds, praise and allow access to the preferred item. If student does not comply, physically guide student to comply with simple task demand. Score V for compliance with simple task demand that followed the student coming to you unprompted. Score M if a Model prompt was required with the student's approach or with compliance. Score P if the student's approach or compliance was physically guided.	
Additional Targets:		

Wait Appropriately For Instructions
Compatible with ABLLS®-R Code A8

Student's Name:		Start Date:	
Objective:	Prior to the delivery of a task demand, student will wait appropriately for instructions.		

Person Implementing Objective:	
Setting/Environment:	
Materials:	
Reinforcers:	
Baseline:	Place materials and reinforcers within reach of student. Wait 5 seconds for a response. A correct response is scored (+) if student does not touch materials or reinforcers - <u>do not reinforce</u>. Move to next trial. An incorrect response is scored (-) if student does touch materials or reinforcers- <u>do not prompt.</u> Move to next trial.
Teaching Procedures:	Place materials and reinforcers within reach of student, wait 5 seconds for a response. If student waits without touching, praise and provide a reinforcer. If student does not wait without touching, say, "You need to wait" as you gesture to the materials and reinforcers. Wait 5 seconds for a response. If student waits without touching, praise and provide a reinforcer. If student does not wait without touching, physically guide student to wait without touching. Score V if student waited without touching with no prompts. Score M if correct waiting followed model prompt. Score P if physical guidance was used.
Additional Targets:	

Look At Teacher For Instructions
Compatible with ABLLS®-R Code A9

Student's Name:		Start Date:	
Objective:		Prior to the delivery of a task demand, student will look at the teacher.	

Person Implementing Objective:	
Setting/Environment:	
Materials:	
Reinforcers:	
Baseline:	Prior to delivering a task demand, wait 5 seconds for a response. A correct response is scored (+) if student looks at you - <u>do not reinforce</u>. Move to next trial. An incorrect response is scored (-) if student does not look at you- <u>do not prompt.</u> Move to next trial.
Teaching Procedures:	Prior to delivering a demand, wait 5 seconds. If student looks at you, praise and provide a reinforcer. If student does not look at you, say, "Look at me" as you gesture to your face. Wait 5 seconds for a response. If student looks at you, praise and provide a reinforcer. If student does not look at you, say, "Look at me" and physically guide student to look at you. Score V if correct response followed verbal prompt. Score M if correct response followed model prompt. Score P if physical guidance was used.
Additional Targets:	

Look At All Choices Before Responding
Compatible with ABLLS®-R Code A10

Student's Name:		Start Date:
Objective:	When a variety of cards or objects are presented in front of student, student will look at all available choices before responding.	
Person Implementing Objective:		
Setting/Environment:		
Materials:		
Reinforcers:		
Baseline:	Present an array of items in front of the student. Wait 5 seconds for a response. A correct response is scored (+) if student looks at all the items - <u>do not reinforce</u>. Move to next trial. An incorrect response is scored (-) if student does not does not look at all the items - <u>do not prompt</u>. Move to next trial.	
Teaching Procedures:	Present an array of items in front of the student. Wait 5 seconds for a response. If student looks at all items, praise and provide a reinforcer. If student does not look at all the items, say "Look" as you move your hand above all items in array. Wait 5 seconds for a response. If student looks at all items, praise and provide a reinforcer. If student does not look at array, physically guide student to look at the items. Score V for correct response that required no prompts. Score M if correct response followed model prompt. Score P if physical guidance was used.	
Additional Targets:		

Look To Teacher For Facial And Voice Cues
Compatible with ABLLS®-R Code A15

Student's Name:		Start Date:	
Objective:	When student completes a task, student will look to teacher for facial and voice cues.		
Person Implementing Objective:			
Setting/Environment:			
Materials:			
Reinforcers:			
Baseline:	Immediately following student's response within a trial in which praise is used as a reinforcer, observe student for 5 seconds. A correct response is scored (+) if student looks at your face - <u>do not reinforce</u>. Move to next trial. An incorrect response is scored (-) if student does not look at your face - <u>do not prompt</u>. Move to next trial.		
Teaching Procedures:	Immediately following student's response within a trial in which praise is used as a reinforcer, observe student for 5 seconds. If student looks at your face, praise and provide reinforcer. If student does not look at your face, say "Look up here" as you gesture to your face. Wait 5 seconds for a response. If student looks at your face, praise and provide reinforcer. If student does not look to your face, physically guide student to look at your face. Score V for correct response that followed verbal prompt. Score M if correct response followed model prompt. Score P if physical guidance was used.		
Additional Targets:			

Wait For Preferred Item Delivery
Compatible With ABLLS®-R Code A17

Student's Name:	Start Date:
Objective:	After student responds accurately to a mastered task demand, student will wait for the delivery of a preferred item.
Person Implementing Objective:	
Setting/Environment:	
Materials:	
Reinforcers:	
Baseline:	Following task completion of a mastered task in which reinforcement is typically delivered, say, "You can have your _____, (name preferred item) but wait" as you place the preferred item in plain site of the student. Wait 5 seconds (or see target). A correct response is scored (+) if student waits for preferred item without problem behavior and does not reach for the item. Move to next trial. An incorrect response is scored (-) if student demonstrates problem behavior during wait period or reaches for the item - <u>do not prompt</u>. Move to next trial.
Teaching Procedures:	Following task completion of a mastered task in which reinforcement is typically delivered, say, "You can have your _____, (name preferred item) but wait" as you place the preferred item in plain site of the student. Wait 5 seconds (or see target). If student waits for preferred item without demonstrating problem behavior and does not reach for the item, deliver the item. If student demonstrates problem behavior or reaches for the item, block the attempt to reach and briefly remove the item from view. While placing the item in view of the student, say, "You can have your _____, (name preferred item) but wait." If student waits for item without demonstrating problem behavior and does not reach for the item, deliver the item and praise. If student demonstrates problem behavior or reaches for the item, block the attempt to reach and briefly remove the item from view. While placing the item in view of student, tell student, "You can have your ___, (name preferred item) but wait" as you hold student's hands away from the item for the desired period of time. Deliver the preferred item after the time has elapsed. Score V for correct response that followed verbal prompt. Score M if correct response followed model prompt. Score P if physical guidance was used.
Additional Targets:	

Seek Praise For Finishing Work
ABLLS®-R Code A18

Student's Name:		Start Date:	
Objective:	When student finishes a work assignment, student will look to teacher for praise.		

Person Implementing Objective:	
Setting/Environment:	
Materials:	
Reinforcers:	
Baseline:	When student finishes an assigned work task, wait 5 seconds. A correct response is scored (+) if student looks to you or seeks your attention - <u>do not reinforce</u>. Move to next trial. An incorrect response is scored (-) if student does not look to you or seek your attention - <u>do not prompt</u>. Move to next trial.
Teaching Procedures:	When student finishes an assigned work task, wait 5 seconds. If student looks to you or seeks your attention, praise and provide reinforcer. If student does not look to you or seeks your attention, say, "After you finish working you should look at me." Wait 5 seconds for a response. If student looks at you, praise and provide reinforcer. If student does not look at you, repeat the cue, "After you finish working you should look at me" as you physically guide student's head towards yours. Score V if student looked at you following verbal prompt. Score M if student looked at you following model prompt. Score P if physical guidance was used.
Additional Targets:	

CHAPTER 3

ABA Programs Compatible with

ABLLS®-R Domain B

"Visual Performance"

Puzzle- Single Piece Inset
Compatible With ABLLS®-R Code B1

Student's Name:		Start Date:
Objective:	When given a single piece inset-type puzzle and teacher says, "Do puzzle" student will place pieces into correct locations.	
Person Implementing Objective:		
Setting/Environment:		
Materials:		
Reinforcers:		
Baseline:	Place puzzle frame in front of student. Place puzzle(s) piece in front of student and say, "Do puzzle." Wait 5 seconds for a response. A correct response is scored (+) if student places piece(s) into puzzle location - do not reinforce. An incorrect response is scored (-) if student does not place piece(s) into correct location-do not prompt. Move to next trial.	
Teaching Procedures:	Place puzzle frame in front of student. Place one piece(s) in front of student and say, "Do puzzle." Wait 5 seconds for a response. If student places piece(s) into correct location, praise and provide reinforcer. If student does not place piece(s) into correct location, say, "Do puzzle" while pointing to correct location. Wait 5 seconds for a response. If student places piece into correct location, praise and provide reinforcer. If student does not place piece(s) into correct location, say, "Do puzzle" and use physical guidance to ensure piece goes into correct location. Score V for correct response that followed verbal prompt. Score M if correct response followed model prompt. Score P if physical guidance was used.	
Additional Targets:		

Shape Sorter
Compatible With ABLLS®-R Code B2

Student's Name:		Start Date:	
Objective:	Given shape sorter, shape blocks, and teacher says, "Put in" student will place blocks into their corresponding holes.		
Person Implementing Objective:			
Setting/Environment:			
Materials:			
Reinforcers:			
Baseline:	Place shape sorter and shape blocks in front of student and say, "Put in." Wait 5 seconds for a response. A correct response is scored (+) if student places shape into correct hole - <u>do not reinforce</u>. An incorrect response is scored (-) if student does not place shape into correct hole- <u>do not prompt</u>. Move to next trial.		
Teaching Procedures:	Place shape sorter and shape blocks in front of student and say, "Put in." Wait 5 seconds for a response. If student places shape into correct hole, praise and provide reinforcer. If student does not place shape into correct hole, say, "Put in" while gesturing to correct hole. Wait 5 seconds for a response. If student places shape into correct hole, praise and provide reinforcer. If student does not place shape into correct hole, say, "Put in" and use physical guidance to ensure shape goes into hole. Score V for correct response that followed verbal prompt. Score M if correct response followed model prompt. Score P if physical guidance was used.		
Additional Targets:			

Matching Identical Objects
Compatible With ABLLS®-R Code B3

Student's Name:	Start Date:
Objective:	When given an object, an identical object, and teacher says, "Match" student will match object to an identical object.
Person Implementing Objective:	
Setting/Environment:	
Materials:	
Reinforcers:	
Baseline:	Place an object directly in front of student and an identical object approximately 12-24 inches from student as you say, "Match." A correct response is scored (+) if student moves object directly in front of student so that it makes contact with the object further from student - <u>do not reinforce</u>. An incorrect response is scored (-) if student does not match objects-<u>do not prompt</u>. Move to next trial.
Teaching Procedures:	Place an object directly in front of student and an identical object approximately 12-24 inches from student as you say, "Match." Wait 5 seconds for a response. If student moves object directly in front so that it makes contact with the object further away, praise and provide reinforcer. If student does not move object directly in front so that it makes contact with the object further away, say, "Match" and model the matching movement. Wait 5 seconds for a response. If student moves object directly in front so that it makes contact with the object further away, praise and provide reinforcer. If student does not move object directly in front so that it makes contact with the object further away, say, "Match" and use physical guidance to help student move the object to the other object. Score V for correct response that followed verbal prompt. Score M if correct response followed model prompt. Score P if physical guidance was used.
Additional Targets:	

Matching Objects To Pictures
Compatible With ABLLS®-R Code B4

Student's Name:		Start Date:	
Objective:	When given an object, an array of pictures, and teacher says, "Match" student will match picture to corresponding picture.		
Person Implementing Objective:			
Setting/Environment:			
Materials:			
Reinforcers:			
Baseline:	Place an object directly in front of student and a corresponding picture card approximately 12-24 inches from student as you say, "Match." Wait 5 seconds for a response. A correct response is scored (+) if student moves object so that it makes contact with the corresponding picture - <u>do not reinforce</u>. An incorrect response is scored (-) if student does not move object so that it makes contact with the corresponding picture - <u>do not prompt</u>. Move to next trial.		
Teaching Procedures:	Place an object directly in front of the student and a corresponding picture approximately 12-24 inches from student as you say, "Match." Wait 5 seconds for a response. If student moves object so that it makes contact with the corresponding picture, praise and provide reinforcer. If student does not move object so that it makes contact with the corresponding picture, say, "Match" and model the matching movement. Wait 5 seconds for a response. If student moves object so that it makes contact with the corresponding picture, praise and provide reinforcer. If student does not move object so that it makes contact with the corresponding picture, say, "Match" and use physical guidance to help student move the object to the corresponding picture. Score V for correct response that followed verbal prompt. Score M if correct response followed model prompt. Score P if physical guidance was used.		
Additional Targets:			

Matching Identical Pictures
Compatible With ABLLS®-R Code B5

Student's Name:	Start Date:
Objective:	When given a picture, an array of pictures as choices, and teacher says, "Match" student will match picture to an identical picture.
Person Implementing Objective:	
Setting/Environment:	
Materials:	
Reinforcers:	
Baseline:	Place a picture directly in front of student and an array containing an identical picture approximately 12-24 inches from student as you say, "Match." Wait 5 seconds for a response. A correct response is scored (+) if student matches identical pictures - <u>do not reinforce</u>. An incorrect response is scored (-) if student does not match identical pictures-<u>do not prompt</u>. Move to next trial.
Teaching Procedures:	Place a picture directly in front of student and an array containing an identical picture approximately 12-24 inches from student as you say, "Match." Wait 5 seconds for a response. If student matches identical pictures, praise and provide reinforcer. If student does not match identical pictures, say, Match" and model the matching movement. Wait 5 seconds for a response. If student matches identical pictures, praise and provide reinforcer. If student does not match identical pictures, say, "Match" and use physical guidance to help student match identical pictures. Score V for correct response that followed verbal prompt. Score M if correct response followed model prompt. Score P if physical guidance was used.
Additional Targets:	

Matching Pictures To Objects
Compatible With ABLLS®-R Code B6

Student's Name:		Start Date:	
Objective:		When given a picture, an array of objects as choices, and teacher says, "Match" student will match picture to its corresponding object.	
Person Implementing Objective:			
Setting/Environment:			
Materials:			
Reinforcers:			
Baseline:		Place a picture directly in front of the student and an array with a corresponding object approximately 12-24 inches from student as you say, "Match." Wait 5 seconds for a response. A correct response is scored (+) if student moves picture so that it makes contact with the corresponding object - do not reinforce. An incorrect response is scored (-) if student does not match picture to object-do not prompt. Move to next trial.	
Teaching Procedures:		Place a picture directly in front of the student and an array with a corresponding object approximately 12-24 inches from student as you say, "Match." Wait 5 seconds for a response. If student moves picture so that it makes contact with the corresponding object, praise and provide reinforcer. If student does not move picture so that it makes contact with the corresponding object, say, "Match" while modeling the matching movement. Wait 5 seconds for a response. If student moves picture so that it makes contact with the corresponding object, praise and provide reinforcer. If student does not move picture so that it makes contact with the corresponding object, say, "Match" and use physical guidance to help student move the picture to the corresponding object. Score V for correct response that followed verbal prompt. Score M if correct response followed model prompt. Score P if physical guidance was used.	
Additional Targets:			

Quickly Matching Many Pictures
Compatible With ABLLS®-R Code B7

Student's Name:		Start Date:
Objective:	When given several identical pictures and teacher says "Match" student will match pairs of pictures rapidly to their identical matching pictures.	
Person Implementing Objective:		
Setting/Environment:		
Materials:		
Reinforcers:		
Baseline:	Place a pile of identical pictures in front of student as you say, "Match." Wait 5 seconds for a response. A correct response is scored (+) if student matches all picture sets - <u>do not reinforce</u>. An incorrect response is scored (-) if student does not match all pictures sets-<u>do not prompt</u>. Move to next trial.	
Teaching Procedures:	Place a pile of identical pictures in front of student as you say, "Match." Wait 5 seconds for a response. If student matches all pictures, praise and provide reinforcer. If does not match all picture sets, say, "Match" and model the matching movements. Wait 5 seconds for a response. If student matches all pictures, praise and provide reinforcer. If does not match all pictures, say, "Match" and use physical guidance to help student match all remaining pictures. Score V for correct response that followed verbal prompt. Score M if correct response followed model prompt. Score P if physical guidance was used.	
Additional Targets:		

Sorting Into Categories
Compatible With ABLLS®-R Code B8

Student's Name:		Start Date:	
Objective:	When given an assortment of picture cards/objects and teacher says, "Sort" student will place all items from same categories into separate piles.		
Person Implementing Objective:			
Setting/Environment:			
Materials:			
Reinforcers:			
Baseline:	Place assortment of picture cards/objects in front of student and say, "Sort." Wait 5 seconds for a response. A correct response is scored (+) if student separates all cards/objects into correct piles - <u>do not reinforce</u>. An incorrect response is scored (-) if student does not separate all cards/objects into correct piles-<u>do not prompt</u>. Move to next trial.		
Teaching Procedures:	Place assortment of picture cards/objects in front of student and say, "Sort." Wait 5 seconds for a response. If student correctly sorts all cards/objects, praise and provide reinforcer. If student does not sort all cards/objects, say, "Sort" and model correct sorting. Wait 5 seconds for a response. If student correctly sorts all cards/objects, praise and provide reinforcer. If student does not sort all cards/objects, say, "Sort" and physically guide student's hand to sort all picture cards/objects. Score V for correct response that followed verbal prompt. Score M if correct response followed model prompt. Score P if physical guidance was used.		
Additional Targets:			

Block Design Imitation
Compatible With ABLLS®-R Code B9

Student's Name:	Start Date:
Objective:	When teacher makes a block design, gives student a pattern card, identical blocks, and says "Make this" student will create the identical design.
Person Implementing Objective:	
Setting/Environment:	
Materials:	
Reinforcers:	
Baseline:	Make a block design. Present pattern card and blocks to student and say "Make this." Wait 5 seconds for a response. A correct response is scored (+) if student creates design on card - do not reinforce. An incorrect response is scored (-) if student does not create design on card - do not prompt. Move to next trial.
Teaching Procedures:	Make a block design. Present pattern card and blocks to student and say "Make this." Wait 5 seconds for a response. If student makes the identical design, praise and provide reinforcer. If student does not make the identical design, say, "Make this" while pointing to the design card. Wait 5 seconds for a response. If student makes the identical design, praise and provide reinforcer. If student does not make the identical design, say, "Make this" and use physical guidance to complete the design. Score V for correct response that followed verbal prompt. Score M if correct response followed model prompt. Score P if physical guidance was used.
Additional Targets:	

Complete Puzzles
Compatible With ABLLS®-R Code B10

Student's Name:	Start Date:
Objective:	When given an incomplete inset-type puzzle, puzzle pieces, and teacher says "Do puzzle" student will place puzzle pieces into correct locations.
Person Implementing Objective:	
Setting/Environment:	
Materials:	
Reinforcers:	
Baseline:	Place the inset-type puzzle frame in front of student. Place puzzle piece(s) in front of student and say, "Do puzzle." Wait 5 seconds for a response. A correct response is scored (+) if student places piece(s) into correct location - do not reinforce. An incorrect response is scored (-) if student does not place piece(s) into correct location-do not prompt. Move to next trial.
Teaching Procedures:	Place the inset-type puzzle frame in front of student. Place puzzle piece(s) in front of student and say, "Do puzzle." Wait 5 seconds for a response. If student places piece(s) into correct location, praise and provide reinforcer. If student does not place piece(s) into correct location, say, "Do puzzle" while gesturing to correct location. Wait 5 seconds for a response. If student places piece(s) into correct location, praise and provide reinforcer. If student does not place piece(s) into correct location, say, "Do puzzle" and use physical guidance to ensure piece(s) goes into correct location. Score V for correct response that followed verbal prompt. Score M if correct response followed model prompt. Score P if physical guidance was used.
Additional Targets:	

Complete Puzzles
Compatible With ABLLS®-R Code B11

Student's Name:	Start Date:
Objective:	When given an incomplete border frame puzzle, puzzle pieces, and teacher says "Do puzzle" student will place puzzle pieces into correct locations.
Person Implementing Objective:	
Setting/Environment:	
Materials:	
Reinforcers:	
Baseline:	Place the border frame puzzle frame in front of student. Place puzzle piece(s) in front of student and say, "Do puzzle." Wait 5 seconds for a response. A correct response is scored (+) if student places piece(s) into correct location - <u>do not reinforce</u>. An incorrect response is scored (-) if student does not place piece(s) into correct location-<u>do not prompt</u>. Move to next trial.
Teaching Procedures:	Place the border frame puzzle frame in front of student. Place puzzle piece(s) in front of student and say, "Do puzzle." Wait 5 seconds for a response. If student places piece(s) into correct location, praise and provide reinforcer. If student does not place piece(s) into correct location, say, "Do puzzle" while gesturing to correct location. Wait 5 seconds for a response. If student places piece(s) into correct location, praise and provide reinforcer. If student does not place piece(s) into correct location, say, "Do puzzle" and use physical guidance to ensure piece(s) goes into correct location. Score V for correct response that followed verbal prompt. Score M if correct response followed model prompt. Score P if physical guidance was used.
Additional Targets:	

Block Design Imitation
Compatible With ABLLS®-R Code B12

Student's Name:	Start Date:
Objective:	When teacher presents pattern card and gives student blocks and says "Make this" student will place blocks on the pattern card to form the pattern on the card.
Person Implementing Objective:	
Setting/Environment:	
Materials:	
Reinforcers:	
Baseline:	Present pattern card and blocks to student and say "Make this." Wait 5 seconds for a response. A correct response is scored (+) if student creates design on pattern card - do not reinforce. An incorrect response is scored (-) if student does not create design on pattern card -do not prompt. Move to next trial.
Teaching Procedures:	Present pattern card and blocks to student and say "Make this." Wait 5 seconds for a response. If student places blocks on the pattern card to form design on card, praise and provide reinforcer. If student does not place blocks on pattern card to make design on the card, say, "Make this" and gesture to the pattern card. Wait 5 seconds for a response. If student places blocks on the pattern card to form design on card, praise and provide reinforcer. If student does not place blocks on pattern card to make design on the card, say, "Make this" and use physical guidance to complete the design. Score V for correct response that followed verbal prompt. Score M if correct response followed model prompt. Score P if physical guidance was used.
Additional Targets:	

Matching A Sequence Of Objects
ABLLS®-R Code B13

Student's Name:	Start Date:
Objective:	When teacher places objects in specific array, gives student identical object set and says, "Put in order" student will match the order of the model array.
Person Implementing Objective:	
Setting/Environment:	
Materials:	
Reinforcers:	
Baseline:	Place objects in specific array in front of student. Present an identical set of objects in jumbled order in front of student and say, "Put in order." Wait 5 seconds for a response. A correct response is scored (+) if student places all objects in matching order- do not reinforce. An incorrect response is scored (-) if student does not place all objects in matching order-do not prompt. Move to next trial.
Teaching Procedures:	Place objects in specific array in front of student. Present an identical set of objects in jumbled order in front of student and say, "Put in order." Wait 5 seconds for a response. If student places all objects in matching order, praise and provide reinforcer. If student does not place all objects in matching order, say, "Put in order" and gesture to the correct array. If student places all objects in matching order, praise and provide reinforcer. If student does not place all objects in matching order, say, "Put in order" and physically guide student to place objects in matching order. Score V for correct response that followed verbal prompt. Score M if correct response followed model prompt. Score P if physical guidance was used.
Additional Targets:	

Complete Puzzles
Compatible With ABLLS®-R Code B14

Student's Name:		Start Date:	
Objective:		Given an incomplete irregular shape puzzle, puzzle pieces, and teacher says "Do puzzle" student will place puzzle pieces into correct locations.	
Person Implementing Objective:			
Setting/Environment:			
Materials:			
Reinforcers:			
Baseline:		Place the irregular shape puzzle and piece(s) in front of student and say, "Do puzzle." Wait 5 seconds for a response. A correct response is scored (+) if student places piece(s) into correct location - do not reinforce. An incorrect response is scored (-) if student does not place piece(s) into correct location- do not prompt. Move to next trial.	
Teaching Procedures:		Place the irregular shape puzzle and piece(s) in front of student and say, "Do puzzle." Wait 5 seconds for a response. If student places piece(s) into correct location, praise and provide reinforcer. If student does not place piece(s) into correct location, say, "Do puzzle" while gesturing to correct location. Wait 5 seconds for a response. If student places piece(s) into correct location, praise and provide reinforcer. If student does not place piece(s) into correct location, say, "Do puzzle" and use physical guidance to ensure piece(s) goes into correct location. Score V for correct response that followed verbal prompt. Score M if correct response followed model prompt. Score P if physical guidance was used.	
Additional Targets:			

Complete Puzzles
Compatible With ABLLS®-R Code B15

Student's Name:		Start Date:	
Objective:	Given an incomplete jigsaw puzzle, puzzle pieces, and teacher says "Do puzzle" student will place puzzle pieces into correct locations.		
Person Implementing Objective:			
Setting/Environment:			
Materials:			
Reinforcers:			
Baseline:	Place the jigsaw puzzle in front of student. Place puzzle piece(s) in front of student and say, "Do puzzle." Wait 5 seconds for a response. A correct response is scored (+) if student places piece(s) into correct location - <u>do not reinforce</u>. An incorrect response is scored (-) if student does not place piece(s) into correct location-<u>do not prompt</u>. Move to next trial.		
Teaching Procedures:	Place the jigsaw puzzle frame in front of student. Place puzzle piece(s) in front of student and say, "Do puzzle." Wait 5 seconds for a response. If student places piece(s) into correct location, praise and provide reinforcer. If student does not place piece(s) into correct location, say, "Do puzzle" while gesturing to correct location. Wait 5 seconds for a response. If student places piece(s) into correct location, praise and provide reinforcer. If student does not place piece(s) into correct location, say, "Do puzzle" and use physical guidance to ensure piece(s) goes into correct location. Score V for correct response that followed verbal prompt. Score M if correct response followed model prompt. Score P if physical guidance was used.		
Additional Targets:			

Related Picture Matching
Compatible With ABLLS®-R Code B16

Student's Name:		Start Date:	
Objective:	\multicolumn{3}{l	}{When given a picture, an array of picture choices, and teacher says, "Match" student will match picture to a related picture presented in an array.}
Person Implementing Objective:			
Setting/Environment:			
Materials:			
Reinforcers:			
Baseline:	\multicolumn{3}{l	}{Place a picture directly in front of student and a related picture in an array approximately 12-24 inches from student as you say, "Match." Wait 5 seconds for a response. A correct response is scored (+) if student matches related pictures - do not reinforce. An incorrect response is scored (-) if student does not match related pictures-do not prompt. Move to next trial.}
Teaching Procedures:	\multicolumn{3}{l	}{Place a picture directly in front of student and a related picture in an array approximately 12-24 inches from student. Say, "Match." Wait 5 seconds for a response. If student matches related pictures, praise and provide reinforcer. If student does not match related pictures, say, "Match" and model the matching movement. Wait 5 seconds for a response. If student matches related pictures, praise and provide reinforcer. If student does not match related pictures, say, "Match" and use physical guidance to help student match related pictures. Score V for correct response that followed verbal prompt. Score M if correct response followed model prompt. Score P if physical guidance was used.}
Additional Targets:			

Sort Pictures By Function
Compatible With ABLLS®-R Code B17

Student's Name:	Start Date:	
Objective:	\multicolumn{2}{l	}{When given pictures that vary by function and teacher says "Sort" student will place pictures into appropriate piles based on the function of the pictures.}

Person Implementing Objective:	
Setting/Environment:	
Materials:	
Reinforcers:	
Baseline:	Place two picture models approximately 12 inches apart in front of student. Place several pictures directly in front of student. Place a picture with same function as the model from the pile on each model. Say, "Sort." Wait 5 seconds for a response. A correct response is scored (+) if student sorts pictures into correct piles- <u>do not reinforce</u>. An incorrect response is scored (-) if student does not sort pictures into correct piles- <u>do not prompt</u>. Move to next trial.
Teaching Procedures:	Place two picture models approximately 12 inches apart in front of student. Place several pictures directly in front of student. Place a picture with same function as the model from the pile on each model. Say, "Sort." Wait 5 seconds for a response. If student sorts pictures into correct piles, praise and provide reinforcer. If student does not sort pictures into correct piles, say, "Sort" and model sorting. Wait 5 seconds for a response. If student sorts pictures into correct piles, praise and provide reinforcer. If student does not sort pictures into correct piles, say, "Sort" and use physical guidance to help student sort pictures into correct piles. Score V for correct response that followed verbal prompt. Score M if correct response followed model prompt. Score P if physical guidance was used.
Additional Targets:	

Sort Pictures By Feature
Compatible With ABLLS®-R Code B18

Student's Name:	Start Date:	
Objective:	When given pictures that vary by a feature of the picture and teacher says, "Sort" student will place pictures into appropriate piles based on the feature of the pictures.	
Person Implementing Objective:		
Setting/Environment:		
Materials:		
Reinforcers:		
Baseline:	Place two picture models approximately 12 inches apart in front of student. Place several pictures in front of student. Place one picture with same feature as the model from the pile on each model. Say, "Sort." Wait 5 seconds for a response. A correct response is scored (+) if student sorts pictures into correct piles- <u>do not reinforce</u>. An incorrect response is scored (-) if student does not sort pictures into correct piles- <u>do not prompt</u>. Move to next trial.	
Teaching Procedures:	Place two picture models approximately 12 inches apart in front of student. Place several pictures in front of student. Place one picture with same feature as the model from the pile on each model. Say, "Sort." Wait 5 seconds for a response. If student sorts pictures into correct piles, praise and provide reinforcer. If student does not sort pictures into correct piles, say, "Sort" and model sorting. Wait 5 seconds for a response. If student sorts pictures into correct piles, praise and provide reinforcer. If student does not sort pictures into correct piles, say, "Sort" and use physical guidance to help student sort pictures into correct piles. Score V for correct response that followed verbal prompt. Score M if correct response followed model prompt. Score P if physical guidance was used.	
Additional Targets:		

Sort Pictures By Class
Compatible With ABLLS®-R Code B19

Student's Name:		Start Date:	
Objective:	When given pictures that vary by the class membership of the picture and teacher says "Sort" student will place pictures into appropriate piles based on the class of the pictures.		
Person Implementing Objective:			
Setting/Environment:			
Materials:			
Reinforcers:			
Baseline:	Place two picture models approximately 12 inches apart and in front of student. Place several pictures in front of student. Place one picture in same class as the model from the pile on each model. Say, "Sort." Wait 5 seconds for a response. A correct response is scored (+) if student sorts pictures into correct piles- <u>do not reinforce</u>. An incorrect response is scored (-) if student does not sort pictures into correct piles- <u>do not prompt</u>. Move to next trial.		
Teaching Procedures:	Place two picture models approximately 12 inches apart and in front of student. Place several pictures in front of student. Place one picture in same class as the model from the pile on each model. Say, "Sort." Wait 5 seconds for a response. If student sorts pictures into correct piles, praise and provide reinforcer. If student does not sort pictures into correct piles, say, "Sort" and model sorting. Wait 5 seconds for a response. If student sorts pictures into correct piles, praise and provide reinforcer. If student does not sort pictures into correct piles, say, "Sort" and use physical guidance to help student sort pictures into correct piles. Score V for correct response that followed verbal prompt. Score M if correct response followed model prompt. Score P if physical guidance was used.		
Additional Targets:			

Replicating A Sequence Of Objects Following A Delay
Compatible With ABLLS®-R Code B20

Student's Name:		Start Date:	
Objective:	When an array of objects presented in front of student is removed and returned when teacher says, "Put in order" student will be able to replicate the order of the array.		
Person Implementing Objective:			
Setting/Environment:			
Materials:			
Reinforcers:			
Baseline:	Place objects in front of student for 5 seconds. Remove objects. Re-present the objects in jumbled order and say, "Put in order." Wait 5 seconds for a response. A correct response is scored (+) if student places all objects in original order- do not reinforce. An incorrect response is scored (-) if student does not place all objects in original order-do not prompt. Move to next trial.		
Teaching Procedures:	Place objects in front of student for 5 seconds. Remove objects. Re-present the objects in jumbled order and say, "Put in order." Wait 5 seconds for a response. If student places all objects in original order, praise and provide reinforcer. If student does not place all objects in original order, say, "Put in order" and arrange objects into original order for 2 seconds. Jumble order, present objects in front of student and wait 5 seconds. If student places all objects in original order, praise and provide reinforcer. If student does not place all objects in original order, say, "Put in order" and physically guide student to place objects in original order. Score V for correct response that followed verbal prompt. Score M if correct response followed model prompt. Score P if physical guidance was used.		
Additional Targets:			

Finding A Sample Object In An Array
ABLLS®-R Code B21

Student's Name:	Start Date:
Objective:	When student is given an object, then the object is removed and re-presented in an array and teacher says, "Show me same" student will choose the original object.
Person Implementing Objective:	
Setting/Environment:	
Materials:	
Reinforcers:	
Baseline:	Place object in front of student for 5 seconds. Remove object. Present that object with other objects and say, "Show me same." Wait 5 seconds for a response. A correct response is scored (+) if student identifies original object- <u>do not reinforce</u>. An incorrect response is scored (-) if student does not identify original object-<u>do not prompt</u>. Move to next trial.
Teaching Procedures:	Place object in front of student for 5 seconds. Remove object. Present that object with other objects and say, "Show me same." Wait 5 seconds for a response. If student identifies original object, praise and provide reinforcer. If student does not identify original object, say, "Show me same" and point to original object. Wait 5 seconds for a response. If student identifies original object, praise and provide reinforcer. If student does not identify original object, say, "Show me same" and physically guide student to identify original object. Score V for correct response that followed verbal prompt. Score M if correct response followed model prompt. Score P if physical guidance was used.
Additional Targets:	

Adding To A Sequence Of Objects
ABLLS®-R Code B22

Student's Name:	Start Date:
Objective:	When student is presented with a small assortment of objects, shown an array of objects in a specific sequence, and teacher says, "Add next" student will add to and appropriately extend that sequence.
Person Implementing Objective:	
Setting/Environment:	
Materials:	
Reinforcers:	
Baseline:	Place sequence of objects in front of student. Present student with a small assortment objects and say, "Add next." Wait 5 seconds for a response. A correct response is scored (+) if student adds the appropriate object to end of sequence- do not reinforce. An incorrect response is scored (-) if student does not add correct object to end of sequence-do not prompt. Move to next trial.
Teaching Procedures:	Place sequence of objects in front of student. Present student with a small assortment objects and say, "Add next." Wait 5 seconds for a response. If student adds correct object to end of sequence, praise and provide reinforcer. If student does not add correct object to end of sequence say, "Add next" and point to correct object. Wait 5 seconds for a response. If student adds correct object to end of sequence, praise and provide reinforcer. If student does not add correct object to end of sequence, say, "Add next" and physically guide student to place correct object at end of sequence. Score V for correct response that followed verbal prompt. Score M if correct response followed model prompt. Score P if physical guidance was used.
Additional Targets:	

Block Design Imitation
Compatible With ABLLS®-R Code B23

Student's Name:	Start Date:
Objective:	When teacher makes a design with blocks, gives student identical blocks, and says "Make this" student will create the identical design.
Person Implementing Objective:	
Setting/Environment:	
Materials:	
Reinforcers:	
Baseline:	Make a block design, present identical blocks to the student, and say "Make this." Wait 5 seconds for a response. A correct response is scored (+) if student creates identical design - <u>do not reinforce</u>. An incorrect response is scored (-) if student does not create an identical design -<u>do not prompt</u>. Move to next trial.
Teaching Procedures:	Make a block design, present identical blocks to the student, and say "Make this." Wait 5 seconds for a response. If student creates identical design, praise and provide reinforcer. If student does not create identical design say, "Make this" while pointing to the sample design. Wait 5 seconds for a response. If student creates identical design, praise and provide reinforcer. If student does not create identical design say, "Make this" and use physical guidance to complete the design. Score V for correct response that followed verbal prompt. Score M if correct response followed model prompt. Score P if physical guidance was used.
Additional Targets:	

The BIG Book of ABA Programs

Matching Related Object Sequence
Compatible With ABLLS®-R Code B24

Student's Name:		Start Date:	
Objective:	When student is presented with a set of identical objects, and teacher says, "Match" student will place a related item next to each of the identical items.		
Person Implementing Objective:			
Setting/Environment:			
Materials:			
Reinforcers:			
Baseline:	Place a set of identical objects in front of student and give several related objects to student as you say, "Match." Wait 5 seconds for a response. A correct response is scored (+) if student places a related item next to each object in the set of identical objects - do not reinforce. An incorrect response is scored (-) if student does not match related objects to the identical objects-do not prompt. Move to next trial.		
Teaching Procedures:	Place a set of identical objects in front of student and give several related objects to student as you say, "Match." Wait 5 seconds for a response. If student places a related item next to each object in the set of identical objects, praise and provide reinforcer. If student does not place a related item next to each object in the set of identical objects, say, "Match" and model the matching movement. Wait 5 seconds for a response. If student places a related item next to each object in the set of identical objects, praise and provide reinforcer. If student does not place a related item next to each object in the set of identical objects, say, "Match" and use physical guidance to help student move the item to the set of identical items. Score V for correct response that followed verbal prompt. Score M if correct response followed model prompt. Score P if physical guidance was used.		
Additional Targets:			

Arrange Cards Or Pictures By Serial Order
Compatible With ABLLS®-R Code B25

Student's Name:		Start Date:	
Objective:		When student is given an array of items (or pictures) in mixed up order and teacher says, "Put in order" student will arrange in appropriate serial order.	
Person Implementing Objective:			
Setting/Environment:			
Materials:			
Reinforcers:			
Baseline:		Place an array of cards/pictures in mixed up order in front of student and say, "Put in order." Wait 5 seconds for a response. A correct response is scored (+) if student arranges cards/pictures in correct order - <u>do not reinforce</u>. An incorrect response is scored (-) if student does not place cards/pictures in correct order-<u>do not prompt</u>. Move to next trial.	
Teaching Procedures:		Place an array of cards/pictures in mixed up order in front of student and say, "Put in order." Wait 5 seconds for a response. If student arranges cards/pictures in correct order, praise and provide reinforcer. If student does not arrange cards/pictures in correct order, say, "Put in order" and model the correct order. Wait 5 seconds for a response. If student arranges cards/pictures in correct order, praise and provide reinforcer. If student does not arrange cards/pictures in correct order, say, "Put in order" and use physical guidance to help student move cards/pictures into the correct order. Score V for correct response that followed verbal prompt. Score M if correct response followed model prompt. Score P if physical guidance was used.	
Additional Targets:			

Sequences Of Pictures
Compatible With ABLLS®-R Code B26

Student's Name:	Start Date:
Objective:	When student is given sequencing cards and teacher says, "Put in order" student will put cards in order so that they make a logical or chronological sequence of events.
Person Implementing Objective:	
Setting/Environment:	
Materials:	
Reinforcers:	
Baseline:	Place a set of sequencing pictures in front of student and say "Put in order." Wait 5 seconds for a response. A correct response is scored (+) if student arranges cards in correct sequence - <u>do not reinforce</u>. An incorrect response is scored (-) if student does not place cards in correct sequence-<u>do not prompt</u>. Move to next trial.
Teaching Procedures:	Place a set of sequencing pictures in front of student and say "Put in order." Wait 5 seconds for a response. If student arranges cards in correct order, praise and provide reinforcer. If student does not arrange cards in correct order, say, "Put in order" and model the correct order. Wait 5 seconds for a response. If student arranges cards in correct order, praise and provide reinforcer. If student does not arrange cards in correct order, say, "Put in order" and use physical guidance to help student move cards into correct order. Score V for correct response that followed verbal prompt. Score M if correct response followed model prompt. Score P if physical guidance was used.
Additional Targets:	

Completing Mazes
Compatible With ABLLS®-R Code B27

Student's Name:	Start Date:
Objective:	When student is given a writing utensil, a maze, and teacher says, "Do maze" student will draw line from the beginning to the end of the maze without drawing over lines.
Person Implementing Objective:	
Setting/Environment:	
Materials:	
Reinforcers:	
Baseline:	Place a maze and writing utensil in front of student and say, "Do Maze." Wait 5 seconds for a response. A correct response is scored (+) if student draws line from beginning to the end of the maze without crossing lines - <u>do not reinforce</u>. An incorrect response is scored (-) if student does not draw line from beginning to the end of the maze-<u>do not prompt</u>. Move to next trial.
Teaching Procedures:	Place a maze and writing utensil in front of student and say, "Do Maze." Wait 5 seconds for a response. If student draws line from beginning to the end of the maze without crossing lines, praise and provide reinforcer. If student does not draw line from beginning to the end of the maze without crossing lines, say, "Do maze" and model the path. Wait 5 seconds for a response. If student draws line from beginning to the end of the maze without crossing lines, praise and provide reinforcer. If student does not draw line from beginning to the end of the maze without crossing lines, say, "Do maze" and use physical guidance to help student draw line from beginning to the end. Score V for correct response that followed verbal prompt. Score M if correct response followed model prompt. Score P if physical guidance was used.
Additional Targets:	

CHAPTER 4

ABA Programs Compatible with ABLLS®-R Domain C "Receptive Language"

Look At Teacher When Name Is Called
Compatible with ABLLS®-R Code C1

Student's Name:	Start Date:	
Objective:	Student will look in direction of teacher when student's name is called.	
Person Implementing Objective:		
Setting/Environment:		
Materials:		
Reinforcers:		
Baseline:	Say student's name when student is not looking at you. Wait 5 seconds for a response. A correct response is scored (+) if student looks at you - do not reinforce. Move to next trial. An incorrect response is scored (-) if student does not look at you - do not prompt. Move to next trial.	
Teaching Procedures:	Say student's name when student is not looking at you. Wait 5 seconds for a response. If student looks at you, praise and provide reinforcer. If student does not look at you, say student's name while moving one of your hands from student's eyes to your own eyes. Wait 5 seconds for a response. If student looks at you, praise and provide reinforcer. If student does not look at you, physically guide student's face so that it is oriented towards your face. Score V if correct response followed verbal prompt. Score M if correct response followed model prompt. Score P if physical guidance was used.	
Additional Targets:		

Receptive Instruction Following With Preferred Activity
Compatible with ABLLS®-R Code C2

Student's Name:		Start Date:
Objective:		When teacher says, "Go to ____ (name activity)" student will comply with request to perform a preferred activity in context.

Person Implementing Objective:	
Setting/Environment:	
Materials:	
Reinforcers:	
Baseline:	Say, "Go to ____ (name activity)." Wait 5 seconds for a response. A correct response is scored (+) if student complies with the request to engage in the preferred activity - <u>do not reinforce</u>. Move to next trial. An incorrect response is scored (-) if student does not engage in requested activity – <u>do not prompt</u>. Move to next trial.
Teaching Procedures:	Say, "Go to ____ (name activity)." Wait 5 seconds for a response. If student complies with request, praise and provide reinforcer. If student does not comply, say, "Go to ____ (name activity)" and point to the activity. Wait 5 seconds for a response. If student complies with request, praise and provide reinforcer. If student does not comply, say, "Go to ____ (name activity)" and physically guide student to the activity. Score V if correct response followed verbal prompt. Score M if correct response followed model prompt. Score P if physical guidance was used.
Additional Targets:	

Receptive Instruction Following To Look At Preferred Item
Compatible with ABLLS®-R Code C3

Student's Name:		Start Date:
Objective:	When teacher presents a preferred item to student and says, "Look at the ____ (name item)" student will look at a preferred item.	
Person Implementing Objective:		
Setting/Environment:		
Materials:		
Reinforcers:		
Baseline:	Hold a preferred item in hand and say, "Look at the ____ (name the item)." Wait 5 seconds for a response. A correct response is scored (+) if student looks at the item - <u>do not reinforce</u>. Move to next trial. An incorrect response is scored (-) if student does not look at the item- <u>do not prompt</u>. Move to next trial.	
Teaching Procedures:	Hold a preferred item in hand and say, "Look at the ____ (name the item)." Wait 5 seconds for a response. If student looks at item, praise and provide access to the item. If student does not look at item, say, "Look at the ____(name the item)" and point to the item. Wait 5 seconds for a response. If student looks at item, praise and provide access to the item. If student does not look at item, say, "Look at the ____(name the item)" and physically guide student to look at the item. Score V if correct response followed verbal prompt. Score M if correct response followed model prompt. Score P if physical guidance was used.	
Additional Targets:		

Receptive Instruction Following To Touch Preferred Item
Compatible with ABLLS®-R Code C4

Student's Name:	Start Date:
Objective:	When teacher presents a preferred item to student and says, "Touch the ____ (name item)" student will touch the preferred item.
Person Implementing Objective:	
Setting/Environment:	
Materials:	
Reinforcers:	
Baseline:	Hold a preferred item in hand and say, "Touch the ____ (name the item)." Wait 5 seconds for a response. A correct response is scored (+) if student touches the item - <u>do not reinforce</u>. Move to next trial. An incorrect response is scored (-) if student does not touch the item- <u>do not prompt</u>. Move to next trial.
Teaching Procedures:	Hold a preferred item in hand and say, "Touch the ____ (name the item)." Wait 5 seconds for a response. If student touches the item, praise and provide access to the item. If student does not touch the item, "Touch the ____ (name the item)" and point to the item. Wait 5 seconds for a response. If student touches the item, praise and provide access to the item. If student does not touch the item, say "Touch the ____ (name the item)" and physically guide student to touch the item. Score V if correct response followed verbal prompt. Score M if correct response followed model prompt. Score P if physical guidance was used.
Additional Targets:	

Receptive Instruction Following To Touch Nonpreferred Item
Compatible with ABLLS®-R Code C5

Student's Name:	Start Date:
Objective:	When teacher presents a nonpreferred item to student and says, "Touch the ____ (name item)" student will touch the preferred item.
Person Implementing Objective:	
Setting/Environment:	
Materials:	
Reinforcers:	
Baseline:	Hold a nonpreferred item in hand and say, "Touch the ____ (name the item)." Wait 5 seconds for a response. A correct response is scored (+) if student touches the item - <u>do not reinforce</u>. Move to next trial. An incorrect response is scored (-) if student does not touch the item- <u>do not prompt</u>. Move to next trial.
Teaching Procedures:	Hold a nonpreferred item in hand and say, "Touch the ____ (name the item)." Wait 5 seconds for a response. If student touches the item, praise and provide reinforcer. If student does not touch the item, say, "Touch the ____ (name the item)" and point to the item. Wait 5 seconds for a response. If student touches the item, praise and provide reinforcer. If student does not touch the item, say, "Touch the ____ (name the item)" and physically guide student to touch the item. Score V if correct response followed verbal prompt. Score M if correct response followed model prompt. Score P if physical guidance was used.
Additional Targets:	

Receptive Instruction Following With Preferred Activity
Compatible with ABLLS®-R Code C6

Student's Name:		Start Date:
Objective:		When teacher says, "Go to ____ (name activity)" student will comply with request to perform a preferred activity out of context.
Person Implementing Objective:		
Setting/Environment:		
Materials:		
Reinforcers:		
Baseline:		Say, "Go to ____ (name activity)." Wait 5 seconds for a response. A correct response is scored (+) if student complies with the request to engage in the preferred activity - <u>do not reinforce</u>. Move to next trial. An incorrect response is scored (-) if student does not engage in requested activity – <u>do not prompt</u>. Move to next trial.
Teaching Procedures:		Say, "Go to ____ (name activity)." Wait 5 seconds for a response. If student complies with request, praise and provide reinforcer. If student does not comply, say, "Go to ____ (name activity)" and point to the activity. Wait 5 seconds for a response. If student complies with request, praise and provide reinforcer. If student does not comply, say, "Go to ____ (name activity)" and physically guide student to the activity. Score V if correct response followed verbal prompt. Score M if correct response followed model prompt. Score P if physical guidance was used.
Additional Targets:		

Receptive Instruction Following To Nonpreferred Activities
Compatible with ABLLS®-R Code C7

Student's Name:		Start Date:	
Objective:		When teacher instructs student to engage in a nonpreferred activity, for example, "Clean up, or Wash your hands," student will comply with request when it is typically time to perform such an activity.	
Person Implementing Objective:			
Setting/Environment:			
Materials:			
Reinforcers:			
Baseline:		Deliver the cue to engage in the nonpreferred activity. Wait 5 seconds for a response. A correct response is scored (+) if student complies with the request - do not reinforce. Move to next trial. An incorrect response is scored (-) if student does not comply- do not prompt. Move to next trial.	
Teaching Procedures:		Deliver the cue to engage in the nonpreferred activity. Wait 5 seconds for a response. If student complies, praise and provide reinforcer. If student does not comply, repeat the cue and point to the activity. Wait 5 seconds for a response. If student complies, praise and provide reinforcer. If student does not comply, repeat cue and physically guide student to complete the activity. Score V if correct response followed verbal prompt. Score M if correct response followed model prompt. Score P if physical guidance was used.	
Additional Targets:			

Receptive Instruction Following To Give Teacher A Nonpreferred Item
Compatible with ABLLS®-R Code C8

Student's Name:	Start Date:
Objective:	When teacher says, "Give me the _____ (name nonpreferred item)" student will hand the item to teacher.
Person Implementing Objective:	
Setting/Environment:	
Materials:	
Reinforcers:	
Baseline:	Hold out your hand and say, "Give me the _____ (name nonpreferred item)." Wait 5 seconds for a response. A correct response is scored (+) if student hands you the item- <u>do not reinforce</u>. Move to next trial. An incorrect response is scored (-) if student does not hand you the item- <u>do not prompt</u>. Move to next trial.
Teaching Procedures:	Hold out your hand and say, "Give me the _____ (name nonpreferred item)." Wait 5 seconds for a response. If student hands you the item, praise and provide reinforcer. If student does not hand you the item, say, "Give me the _____ (name nonpreferred item)" and point to the item. Wait 5 seconds for a response. If student hands you the item, praise and provide reinforcer. If student does not hand you the item, say, "Give me the _____ (name nonpreferred item)" and physically guide student to hand you the item. Score V if correct response followed verbal prompt. Score M if correct response followed model prompt. Score P if physical guidance was used.
Additional Targets:	

Receptive Instruction Following To Simple Instructions
Compatible with ABLLS®-R Code C9

Student's Name:	Start Date:	
Objective:	When teacher delivers a simple directive, for example, "Wave hands," student will comply with the request.	
Person Implementing Objective:		
Setting/Environment:		
Materials:		
Reinforcers:		
Baseline:	Deliver the cue for student to engage in a simple response. Wait 5 seconds for a response. A correct response is scored (+) if student complies with request- <u>do not reinforce</u>. Move to next trial. An incorrect response is scored (-) if student does not comply with request- <u>do not prompt</u>. Move to next trial.	
Teaching Procedures:	Deliver the cue for student to engage in a simple response. Wait 5 seconds for a response. If student complies with request, praise and provide reinforcer. If student does not comply with request, repeat cue and model the action. Wait 5 seconds for a response. If student complies with request, praise and provide reinforcer. If student does not comply with request, repeat cue and physically guide student to comply. Score V if correct response followed verbal prompt. Score M if correct response followed model prompt. Score P if physical guidance was used.	
Additional Targets:		

Receptive Instruction Following To Touch An Object With A Distracter Present
Compatible with ABLLS®-R Code C10

Student's Name:	Start Date:
Objective:	When two objects are presented and teacher says, "Touch _____ (name object)" student will touch named object.
Person Implementing Objective:	
Setting/Environment:	
Materials:	
Reinforcers:	
Baseline:	Present two objects to student and say, "Touch _____ (name object)." Wait 5 seconds for a response. A correct response is scored (+) if student touches the named object - <u>do not reinforce</u>. Move to next trial. An incorrect response is scored (-) if student does not touch the named object - <u>do not prompt</u>. Move to next trial.
Teaching Procedures:	Present two objects to student and say, "Touch _____ (name object)." Wait 5 seconds for a response. If student touches named object, praise and provide reinforcer. If student does not touch named object, say, "Touch _____ (name object)" and point to the named object. If student touches named object, praise and provide reinforcer. If student does not touch named object, say, "Touch _____ (name object)" and physically guide student to touch named object. Score V for correct response that followed verbal prompt. Score M if correct response followed model prompt. Score P if physical guidance was used.
Additional Targets:	

Receptive Instruction Following To Touch A Preferred Object
Compatible with ABLLS®-R Code C11

Student's Name:	Start Date:
Objective:	When teacher presents a nonpreferred and a preferred object to student and says, "Touch ____ (name preferred object)" student will touch named object.
Person Implementing Objective:	
Setting/Environment:	
Materials:	
Reinforcers:	
Baseline:	At the same time, present a preferred and a nonpreferred object in front of student and say, "Touch ____ (name of preferred object)." Wait 5 seconds for a response. A correct response is scored (+) if student touches the named item - <u>do not reinforce</u>. Move to next trial. An incorrect response is scored (-) if student does not touch the named object - <u>do not prompt</u>. Move to next trial.
Teaching Procedures:	At the same time, present a preferred and a nonpreferred object in front of student and say, "Touch ____ (name of preferred object)." Wait 5 seconds for a response. If student touches named object, praise and provide reinforcer. If student does not touch named object say "Touch ____ (name of preferred object)" and point to the named object. Wait 5 seconds for a response. If student touches named object, provide reinforcer. If student does not touch named object, say "Touch ____ (name of preferred object)" and physically guide student to touch named object. Score V for correct response that followed verbal prompt. Score M if correct response followed model prompt. Score P if physical guidance was used.
Additional Targets:	

Receptive Instruction Following To Select Between Multiple Preferred Objects
Compatible with ABLLS®-R Code C12

Student's Name:	Start Date:

Objective:	When teacher presents multiple preferred objects and says, "Touch _____ (name object)" student will touch named preferred object.
Person Implementing Objective:	
Setting/Environment:	
Materials:	
Reinforcers:	
Baseline:	At the same time, present multiple preferred objects to student and say, "Touch _____ (name object)." Wait 5 seconds for a response. A correct response is scored (+) if student touches the named object - <u>do not reinforce</u>. Move to next trial. An incorrect response is scored (-) if student does not touch the named object - <u>do not prompt</u>. Move to next trial.
Teaching Procedures:	At the same time, present multiple preferred objects in front of the student and say, "Touch _____ (name object)." Wait 5 seconds for a response. If student touches the named object, praise and provide access to the object. If student does not touch named object, say, "Touch _____ (name object)" and point to the named object. Wait 5 seconds for a response. If student touches the named object, praise and allow access to the object. If student does not touch named object, say, "Touch _____ (name object)" and physically guide student to touch named object. Score V for correct response that followed verbal prompt. Score M if correct response followed model prompt. Score P if physical guidance was used.
Additional Targets:	

Receptive Instruction Following To Select Between Multiple Common Items Compatible with ABLLS®-R Code C13

Student's Name:	Start Date:
Objective:	When teacher presents multiple items and says, "Touch _____ (name item)" student will touch named item.
Person Implementing Objective:	
Setting/Environment:	
Materials:	
Reinforcers:	
Baseline:	At the same time, present multiple items to student and say, "Touch _____ (name item)." Wait 5 seconds for a response. A correct response is scored (+) if student touches the named item - <u>do not reinforce</u>. Move to next trial. An incorrect response is scored (-) if student does not touch the named item - <u>do not prompt</u>. Move to next trial.
Teaching Procedures:	At the same time, present multiple items in front of the student and say, "Touch _____ (name item)." Wait 5 seconds for a response. If student touches the named item, praise and provide access to the item. If student does not touch named item, say, "Touch _____ (name item)" and point to the named item. Wait 5 seconds for a response. If student touches the named item, praise and allow access to the item. If student does not touch named item, say, "Touch _____ (name item)" and physically guide student to touch named item. Score V for correct response that followed verbal prompt. Score M if correct response followed model prompt. Score P if physical guidance was used.
Additional Targets:	

Receptive Instruction Following To Select Between Pictures Of Common Items
Compatible with ABLLS®-R Code C14

Student's Name:	Start Date:
Objective:	When teacher presents multiple pictures of objects and says, "Touch _____ (name picture of object)" student will touch named picture.
Person Implementing Objective:	
Setting/Environment:	
Materials:	
Reinforcers:	
Baseline:	At the same time, present multiple pictures of objects to student and say, "Touch _____ (name picture)." Wait 5 seconds for a response. A correct response is scored (+) if student touches the named picture - <u>do not reinforce</u>. Move to next trial. An incorrect response is scored (-) if student does not touch the named picture - <u>do not prompt</u>. Move to next trial.
Teaching Procedures:	At the same time, present multiple pictures of objects in front of the student and say, "Touch _____ (name picture)." Wait 5 seconds for a response. If student touches the named picture, praise and provide reinforcer. If student does not touch named picture, say, "Touch _____ (name picture)" and point to the named picture. Wait 5 seconds for a response. If student touches the named picture, praise and provide reinforcer. If student does not touch named picture, say, "Touch _____ (name picture)" and physically guide student to touch named picture. Score V for correct response that followed verbal prompt. Score M if correct response followed model prompt. Score P if physical guidance was used.
Additional Targets:	

Receptive Body Part Identification
Compatible with ABLLS®-R Code C15

Student's Name:	Start Date:
Objective:	When teacher says, "Touch ____ (body part) student will touch named body on the student's body.
Person Implementing Objective:	
Setting/Environment:	
Materials:	
Reinforcers:	
Baseline:	Say, "Touch ____ (body part)." Wait 5 seconds for a response. A correct response is scored (+) if student touches named body part on self- <u>do not reinforce</u>. Move to next trial. An incorrect response is scored (-) if student does not touch named body part on self- <u>do not prompt</u>. Move to next trial.
Teaching Procedures:	Say, "Touch ____ (body part)." Wait 5 seconds for a response. If student touches named body part on self, praise and provide reinforcer. If student does not touch named body part on self, say, "Touch ____ (body part)" and point to correct body part on student. Wait 5 seconds for a response. If student touches named body part on self, praise and provide reinforcer. If student does not touch named body part on self, say, "Touch ____ (body part)" and physically guide student to touch the body part. Score V if correct response followed verbal prompt. Score M if correct response followed model prompt. Score P if physical guidance was used.
Additional Targets:	

Receptive Instruction Following To Select An Item From Array Of Six Items
Compatible with ABLLS®-R Code C16

Student's Name:	Start Date:
Objective:	When presented with an array of six items and teacher says, "Hand me the _____ (name item)" student will hand teacher named item.
Person Implementing Objective:	
Setting/Environment:	
Materials:	
Reinforcers:	
Baseline:	Place an array of six items in front of student. Say, "Hand me the _____ (name item)." Wait 5 seconds for a response. A correct response is scored (+) if student hands the correct item- <u>do not reinforce</u>. Move to next trial. An incorrect response is scored (-) if student does not hand the correct item –<u>do not prompt</u>. Move to next trial.
Teaching Procedures:	Place an array of six items in front of student. Say, "Hand me the _____ (name item)." Wait 5 seconds for a response. If student hands the correct item, praise and provide reinforcer. If student does not hand the correct item say, "Hand me the _____ (name item)" and point to the correct item. Wait 5 seconds for a response. If student hands the correct item, praise and provide reinforcer. If student does not hand the correct item say, "Hand me the _____ (name item)" and physically guide student to hand the correct item. Score V if correct response followed verbal prompt. Score M if correct response followed model prompt. Score P if physical guidance was used.
Additional Targets:	

Receptive Instruction Following To Select A Picture From Array Of Six Pictures Compatible with ABLLS®-R Code C17

Student's Name:	Start Date:	
Objective:	When presented with an array of six pictures and teacher says, "Hand me the _____ (name picture)" student will hand teacher named picture.	
Person Implementing Objective:		
Setting/Environment:		
Materials:		
Reinforcers:		
Baseline:	Place an array of six pictures in front of student. Say, "Hand me the _____ (name picture)." Wait 5 seconds for a response. A correct response is scored (+) if student hands the correct picture- <u>do not reinforce</u>. Move to next trial. An incorrect response is scored (-) if student does not hand the correct picture–<u>do not prompt</u>. Move to next trial.	
Teaching Procedures:	Place an array of six pictures in front of student. Say, "Hand me the _____ (name picture)." Wait 5 seconds for a response. If student hands the correct picture, praise and provide reinforcer. If student does not hand the correct picture say, "Hand me the _____ (name picture)" and point to the correct picture. Wait 5 seconds for a response. If student hands the correct picture, praise and provide reinforcer. If student does not hand the correct picture say, "Hand me the _____ (name picture)" and physically guide student to hand the correct picture. Score V if correct response followed verbal prompt. Score M if correct response followed model prompt. Score P if physical guidance was used.	
Additional Targets:		

Receptive Instruction Following To Select Pictures In Rapid Succession
Compatible with ABLLS®-R Code C19

Student's Name:		Start Date:
Objective:	When an array of pictures is presented and teacher says, "Hand me the _____ (name picture)" at 2 seconds intervals, student will give named pictures to teacher one by one as pictures are named.	
Person Implementing Objective:		
Setting/Environment:		
Materials:		
Reinforcers:		
Baseline:	Place an array of pictures in front of student. Say, "Hand me the _____ (name picture)." Wait 2 seconds. Say, "Hand me the _____ (name new picture)." Repeat sequence for all pictures. One trial is all pictures in an array. A correct response is scored (+) if student hands all named pictures correctly- <u>do not reinforce</u>. Move to next trial. An incorrect response is scored (-) if student does not hand the correct pictures in the trial- <u>do not prompt</u>. Move to next trial.	
Teaching Procedures:	Place an array of pictures in front of student. Say, "Hand me the _____ (name picture)." Wait 2 seconds. Say, "Hand me the _____ (name new picture)." Repeat sequence for all pictures. For all pictures in array: If student hands named picture, praise and say, "Hand me the _____ (name next picture)." If student does not hand named picture, repeat the verbal instruction while pointing to the correct picture. Wait 2 seconds for a reply. If student hands named picture, praise and say, "Hand me the _____ (name next picture)." If student does not hand named picture, present instruction again and physically guide student to hand named picture. Repeat sequence until all pictures are named. Deliver praise and reinforcer at end of array if student handed all pictures with verbal or model prompts. One trial is all pictures in an array. Score V if correct response followed only verbal prompts. Score M if any correct response followed model prompt. Score P if any response followed a physical prompt.	
Additional Targets:		

Receptive Instruction Following To Touch An Item Using A Variety Of Cues
Compatible with ABLLS®-R Code C20

Student's Name:	Start Date:
Objective:	When items are presented to student and teacher says, "Hand me/Touch the/Point to the, etc. _____ (name item)" student will identify named item.
Person Implementing Objective:	
Setting/Environment:	
Materials:	
Reinforcers:	
Baseline:	Present two items in front of student and say, "Touch _____ (name item)." Wait 5 seconds for a response. A correct response is scored (+) if student touches the named item - <u>do not reinforce</u>. Move to next trial. An incorrect response is scored (-) if student does not touch the named item - <u>do not prompt</u>. Move to next trial. Next trial should use a new cue (Hand me/Touch the/Point to the, etc).
Teaching Procedures:	Present two items in front of student and say, "Touch _____ (name item)." Wait 5 seconds for a response. If student touches named item, praise and provide reinforcer. If student does not touch named item, say, "Touch _____ (name item)" and point to named item. Wait 5 seconds for a response. If student touches named item, praise and provide reinforcer. If student does not touch named item, say, "Touch _____ (name item)" and physically guide student to touch named item. Score V for correct response that followed verbal prompt. Score M if correct response followed model prompt. Score P if physical guidance was used. Move to next trial. Next trial should use a new cue (Hand me/Touch the/Point to the, etc.).
Additional Targets:	

Receptive Body Part Identification On Others
Compatible with ABLLS®-R Code C21

Student's Name:	Start Date:
Objective:	When teacher says, "Touch my ____ (body part) student will touch named body part on the teacher's body.
Person Implementing Objective:	
Setting/Environment:	
Materials:	
Reinforcers:	
Baseline:	Say, "Touch my ____ (body part)." Wait 5 seconds for a response. A correct response is scored (+) if student touches named body part on your body- <u>do not reinforce</u>. Move to next trial. An incorrect response is scored (-) if student does not touch named body part on your body- <u>do not prompt</u>. Move to next trial.
Teaching Procedures:	Say, "Touch my ____ (body part)." Wait 5 seconds for a response. If student touches named body part on your body, praise and provide reinforcer. If student does not touch named body part on your body, say, "Touch my ____ (body part)" and point to correct body part on yourself. Wait 5 seconds for a response. If student touches named body part on your body, praise and provide reinforcer. If student does not touch named body part on your body, say, "Touch my ____ (body part)" and physically guide student to touch the body part. Score V if correct response followed verbal prompt. Score M if correct response followed model prompt. Score P if physical guidance was used.
Additional Targets:	

Receptive Clothing Identification
Compatible with ABLLS®-R Code C22

Student's Name:	Start Date:
Objective:	When teacher says, "Touch ____ (clothing item) student will touch named clothing item on the student's body.
Person Implementing Objective:	
Setting/Environment:	
Materials:	
Reinforcers:	
Baseline:	Say, "Touch ____ (clothing item)." Wait 5 seconds for a response. A correct response is scored (+) if student touches named clothing item on self- do not reinforce. Move to next trial. An incorrect response is scored (-) if student does not touch named clothing item on self- do not prompt. Move to next trial.
Teaching Procedures:	Say, "Touch ____ (clothing item)." Wait 5 seconds for a response. If student touches named clothing item on self, praise and provide reinforcer. If student does not touch named clothing item on self, say, "Touch ____ (clothing item)" and point to correct clothing item on student. Wait 5 seconds for a response. If student touches named clothing item on self, praise and provide reinforcer. If student does not touch named body part on self, say, "Touch ____ (clothing item)" and physically guide student to touch the clothing item. Score V if correct response followed verbal prompt. Score M if correct response followed model prompt. Score P if physical guidance was used.
Additional Targets:	

Receptive Instruction Following: Select Aspects Of Larger Objects Or Pictures
Compatible with ABLLS®-R Code C23

Student's Name:	Start Date:

Objective:	When given a picture or object and teacher says, "Touch ____ (name part of picture or object)" student will touch only the aspect of the object or picture named.
Person Implementing Objective:	
Setting/Environment:	
Materials:	
Reinforcers:	
Baseline:	Present a picture or an object in front of student and say, "Touch ____ (part of picture or item)." Wait 5 seconds for a response. A correct response is scored (+) if student touches the correct aspect of the item or picture - <u>do not reinforce</u>. Move to next trial. An incorrect response is scored (-) if student does not select the correct aspect of the picture or item- <u>do not prompt</u>. Move to next trial.
Teaching Procedures:	Present a picture or an object in front of student and say, "Touch ____ (part of picture or item)." Wait 5 seconds for a response. If student touches named part, praise and provide reinforcer. If student does not touch named part, say, "Touch ____ (part of picture or item)" and point to the correct part of the picture or item. Wait 5 seconds for a response. If student touches named part, praise and provide reinforcer. If student does not touch named part, say, "Touch ____ (part of picture or item)" and physically guide student to touch the named part of the picture or item. Score V if correct response followed verbal prompt. Score M if correct response followed model prompt. Score P if physical guidance was used.
Additional Targets:	

Receptive Identification With Adjectives
Compatible with ABLLS®-R Code C24

Student's Name:	Start Date:
Objective:	When student is given a choice of two pictures or items that vary by some physical dimension and teacher says, "Touch ____ (name adjective that differentiates the choices)" student will touch picture or item that matches description. For example, When a red block and a green ball are presented teacher could say, "Touch the round one" or "Touch the square one."
Person Implementing Objective:	
Setting/Environment:	
Materials:	
Reinforcers:	
Baseline:	Present two pictures or items in front of student and say "Touch ____ (name adjective that differentiates the choices)." Wait 5 seconds for a response. A correct response is scored (+) if student touches the correct item or picture - <u>do not reinforce</u>. Move to next trial. An incorrect response is scored (-) if student does not select the correct picture or item- <u>do not prompt</u>. Move to next trial.
Teaching Procedures:	Present two pictures or items in front of student and say "Touch ____ (name adjective that differentiates the choices)." Wait 5 seconds for a response. If student touches the correct item or picture, praise and provide reinforcer. If student does not select the correct picture or item, say "Touch ____ (name adjective that differentiates the choices)" and point to the correct picture or item. Wait 5 seconds for a response. If student touches correct item or picture, praise and provide reinforcer. If student does not touch correct item or picture, say "Touch ____ (name adjective that differentiates the choices)" and physically guide student to touch the picture or item. Score V if correct response followed verbal prompt. Score M if correct response followed model prompt. Score P if physical guidance was used.
Additional Targets:	

Choose Objects By Attending To Teacher's Eyes
Compatible with ABLLS®-R Code C25

Student's Name:		Start Date:	
Objective:	\multicolumn{3}{l	}{When two identical objects are presented in front of student and teacher says, "Give me that one" as teacher looks at one of the objects, student will give the object looked at by the teacher.}
Person Implementing Objective:			
Setting/Environment:			
Materials:			
Reinforcers:			
Baseline:	\multicolumn{3}{l	}{Present two identical objects in front of student and say, "Give me that one" as you look in the direction of one object. Wait 5 seconds for a response. A correct response is scored (+) if student hands the correct object - <u>do not reinforce</u>. Move to next trial. An incorrect response is scored (-) if student does not hand the correct object - <u>do not prompt</u>. Move to next trial.}
Teaching Procedures:	\multicolumn{3}{l	}{Present two identical objects in front of student and say, "Give me that one." as you look in the direction of the correct choice. Wait 5 seconds for a response. If student hands the correct object, praise and provide reinforcer. If student does not hand correct object, say, "Give me that one" as you make a really obvious look to the object. If student hands the correct object, praise and provide reinforcer. If student does not hand correct object, say, "Give me that one" and physically guide student to hand the object. Score V for correct response that followed verbal prompt. Score M if correct response followed model prompt. Score P if physical guidance was used.}
Additional Targets:			

Comply With Nonverbal Requests
Compatible with ABLLS®-R Code C26

Student's Name:	Start Date:
Objective:	When teacher makes a nonverbal request with hand or arm movements, student will comply with request. For example, if teacher presents items in front of student and points to one, student will hand teacher the item.
Person Implementing Objective:	
Setting/Environment:	
Materials:	
Reinforcers:	
Baseline:	Deliver hand or arm command to student. Wait 5 seconds for a response. A correct response is scored (+) if student complies with the command - <u>do not reinforce</u>. Move to next trial. An incorrect response is scored (-) if student does not comply with command - <u>do not prompt</u>. Move to next trial.
Teaching Procedures:	Deliver hand or arm command to student. Wait 5 seconds for a response. If student complies with command, praise and provide reinforcer. If student does not comply with command, present the hand or arm command again and model the correct response. If student complies with command, praise and provide reinforcer. If student does not comply with command, present command again and physically guide student to comply. Score V for correct response that followed initial nonverbal prompt. Score M if correct response followed model prompt. Score P if physical guidance was used.
Additional Targets:	

Comply With Request To Walk To Specified Person
Compatible with ABLLS®-R Code C27

Student's Name:		Start Date:
Objective:	When teacher says, "Walk to ____ (name person)" student will walk to named person.	

Person Implementing Objective:	
Setting/Environment:	
Materials:	
Reinforcers:	
Baseline:	In a room where multiple people are present, say, "Walk to ____ (name person)." Wait 5 seconds for a response. A correct response is scored (+) if student walks to named person - <u>do not reinforce</u>. Move to next trial. An incorrect response is scored (-) if student does not walk to named person- <u>do not prompt</u>. Move to next trial.
Teaching Procedures:	In a room where multiple people are present, say, "Walk to ____ (name person)." Wait 5 seconds for a response. If student walks to named person, praise and provide reinforcer. If student does not walk to named person, say, "Walk to ____ (name person)" and point to named person. Wait 5 seconds for a response. If student walks to named person, praise and provide reinforcer. If student does not walk to named person, say, "Walk to ____ (name person)" and physically guide student to person. Score V for correct response that followed verbal prompt. Score M if correct response followed model prompt. Score P if physical guidance was used.
Additional Targets:	

Comply With Request To Walk To Specified Person And Deliver Object
Compatible with ABLLS®-R Code C28

Student's Name:	Start Date:
Objective:	When teacher says, "Walk to ____ (name person) and give them the ____ (name object)" student will walk to named person and give them the named object.
Person Implementing Objective:	
Setting/Environment:	
Materials:	
Reinforcers:	
Baseline:	In a room where multiple people are present, say, "Walk to ____ (name person) and give them the ____ (name object)." Wait 5 seconds for a response. A correct response is scored (+) if student walks to named person and gives them named object - <u>do not reinforce</u>. Move to next trial. An incorrect response is scored (-) if student does not walk to named person and give them named object - <u>do not prompt</u>. Move to next trial.
Teaching Procedures:	In a room where multiple people are present, say, "Walk to ____ (name person) and give them the ____ (name object)." Wait 5 seconds for a response. If student walks to named person and gives named object, praise and provide reinforcer. If student does not walk to named person and give named object, say, "Walk to ____ (name person) and give them the ____ (name object)" and point to object and the named person. Wait 5 seconds for a response. If student walks to named person and gives named object, praise and provide reinforcer. If student does not walk to named person and give named object, say, "Walk to ____ (name person) and give them the ____ (name object)" and physically guide student to person and to give named object. Score V for correct response that followed verbal prompt. Score M if correct response followed model prompt. Score P if physical guidance was used.
Additional Targets:	

Comply With Request To Retrieve Objects
Compatible with ABLLS®-R Code C29

Student's Name:		Start Date:	
Objective:	When teacher says, "Get the ____ (name of object) from the ____ (name location) and bring it here" student will retrieve named object.		
Person Implementing Objective:			
Setting/Environment:			
Materials:			
Reinforcers:			
Baseline:	Say, "Get the ____ (name of object) from the ____ (name location)" and bring it here." Wait 5 seconds for a response. A correct response is scored (+) if student retrieves named object from named location - <u>do not reinforce</u>. Move to next trial. An incorrect response is scored (-) if student does not retrieve named object from named location- <u>do not prompt</u>. Move to next trial.		
Teaching Procedures:	Say, "Get the ____ (name of object) from the ____ (name location)" and bring it here." Wait 5 seconds for a response. If student retrieves named object from named location, praise and provide reinforcer. If student does not retrieve named object from named location, say, "Get the ____ (name of object) from the ____ (name location)" and gesture in the direction of the object. Wait 5 seconds for a response. If student retrieves named object from named location, praise and provide reinforcer. If student does not retrieve named object from named location, say, "Get the ____ (name of object) from the ____ (name location)" and physically guide student to retrieve object. Score V for correct response that followed verbal prompt. Score M if correct response followed model prompt. Score P if physical guidance was used.		
Additional Targets:			

Comply With Request To Complete A Task With Another Person
Compatible with ABLLS®-R Code C30

Student's Name:	Start Date:	
Objective:	When teacher says, "Go to ____ (name of person) and ____ (name task)" student will go to the person named and comply with the task demand.	
Person Implementing Objective:		
Setting/Environment:		
Materials:		
Reinforcers:		
Baseline:	Say, "Go to ____ (name person) and ____ (name task)." Wait 5 seconds for a response. A correct response is scored (+) if student goes to named person and complies with task demand- <u>do not reinforce</u>. Move to next trial. An incorrect response is scored (-) if student does not go to named person and comply with task demand - <u>do not prompt</u>. Move to next trial.	
Teaching Procedures:	Say, "Go to ____ (name person) and ____ (name task)." Wait 5 seconds for a response. If student goes to named person and complies with task demand, praise and provide reinforcer. If student does not go to named person and comply with task demand, say, "Go to ____ (name person) and ____ (name task)" and gesture in the direction of the person. Wait 5 seconds for a response. If student goes to named person and complies with task demand, praise and provide reinforcer. If student does not go to named person and comply with task demand, say, "Go to ____ (name person) and ____ (name task)" and physically guide student to person and to complete task. Score V for correct response that followed verbal prompt. Score M if correct response followed model prompt. Score P if physical guidance was used.	
Additional Targets:		

Respond To Variable Cues In Receptive Identification Tasks
Compatible with ABLLS®-R Code C31

Student's Name:		Start Date:	
Objective:		When items are presented to student and teacher says, "Hand me/Touch the/Point to the, etc. ____ (name item)" student will identify named item.	
Person Implementing Objective:			
Setting/Environment:			
Materials:			
Reinforcers:			
Baseline:		Present two items in front of student and say, "Touch ____ (name item)." Wait 5 seconds for a response. A correct response is scored (+) if student touches the named item - <u>do not reinforce</u>. Move to next trial. An incorrect response is scored (-) if student does not touch the named item - <u>do not prompt</u>. Move to next trial. Next trial should use a new cue (Hand me/Touch the/Point to the, etc).	
Teaching Procedures:		Present two items in front of student and say, "Touch ____ (name item)." Wait 5 seconds for a response. If student touches named item, praise and provide reinforcer. If student does not touch named item, say, "Touch ____ (name item)" and point to named item. Wait 5 seconds for a response. If student touches named item, praise and provide reinforcer. If student does not touch named item, say, "Touch ____ (name item)" and physically guide student to touch named item. Score V for correct response that followed verbal prompt. Score M if correct response followed model prompt. Score P if physical guidance was used. Move to next trial. Next trial should use a new cue (Hand me/Touch the/Point to the, etc.).	
Additional Targets:			

Choose Correct Item To Comply With Request
Compatible with ABLLS®-R Code C32

Student's Name:	Start Date:

Objective:	When presented with multiple items, one of which can be used to complete a named task, and teacher gives a directive to complete that task, student will choose the item that allows the request to be completed. For example, Glue, scissors, and a marker are presented and the teacher says, "Cut paper." Student would choose the scissors.
Person Implementing Objective:	
Setting/Environment:	
Materials:	
Reinforcers:	
Baseline:	Present multiple items one of which can be used to complete the named task. Give directive to complete a task. Wait 5 seconds for a response. A correct response is scored (+) if student chooses correct item to complete the task - <u>do not reinforce</u>. Move to next trial. An incorrect response is scored (-) if student does not choose correct item to complete the task - <u>do not prompt</u>. Move to next trial.
Teaching Procedures:	Present multiple items one of which can be used to complete the named task. Give directive to complete a task. Wait 5 seconds for a response. If student chooses correct item to compete the task, praise and provide reinforcer. If student does not choose correct item to complete the task, present the demand again and point to the correct item. Wait 5 seconds for a response. If student chooses correct item to compete the task, praise and provide reinforcer. If student does not choose correct item to complete the task, present demand again and physically guide student to perform the action with the correct item. Score V for correct response that followed verbal prompt. Score M if correct response followed model prompt. Score P if physical guidance was used.
Additional Targets:	

Comply With Requests To Perform Multiple Tasks With Same Item
Compatible with ABLLS®-R Code C33

Student's Name:		Start Date:
Objective:	When presented with an item and teacher tells student to do different movements with the item, student will perform requested actions. For example, "Roll the car." Next trial, "Shake the car." Next trial, "Spin the car."	
Person Implementing Objective:		
Setting/Environment:		
Materials:		
Reinforcers:		
Baseline:	Present item to student. Tell student to do something with the item. Wait 5 seconds for a response. A correct response is scored (+) if student complies with the demand - <u>do not reinforce</u>. Move to next trial in which demand differs. An incorrect response is scored (-) if student does not comply with demand - <u>do not prompt</u>. Move to next trial in which demand differs.	
Teaching Procedures:	Present item to student. Tell student to do something with the item. Wait 5 seconds for a response. If student complies with demand, praise and provide reinforcer. If student does not comply with demand, present the demand again and gesture in the direction of the item. If student complies with demand, praise and provide reinforcer. If student does not comply with demand, present demand again and physically guide student to perform the action with the item. Score V for correct response that followed verbal prompt. Score M if correct response followed model prompt. Score P if physical guidance was used.	
Additional Targets:		

Comply With Requests To Perform Pretend Activities
Compatible with ABLLS®-R Code C34

Student's Name:	Start Date:
Objective:	When teacher says, "Pretend to ____ (name action)" student will act out the action in pretend play.
Person Implementing Objective:	
Setting/Environment:	
Materials:	
Reinforcers:	
Baseline:	With no items present, say, "Pretend to_____ (name action)." Wait 5 seconds for a response. A correct response is scored (+) if student acts out action- <u>do not reinforce</u>. Move to next trial. An incorrect response is scored (-) if student does not act out action- <u>do not prompt</u>. Move to next trial.
Teaching Procedures:	With no items present, say, "Pretend to_____ (name action)." Wait 5 seconds for a response. If student acts out action, praise and provide reinforcer. If student does not act out action, say, "Pretend to_____ (name action)" and model the action. Wait 5 seconds for a response. If student acts out action, praise and provide reinforcer. If student does not act out action, say, "Pretend to_____ (name action)" and physically guide student to perform the action. Score V for correct response that followed verbal prompt. Score M if correct response followed model prompt. Score P if physical guidance was used.
Additional Targets:	

Receptive Identification Of Action Pictures
Compatible with ABLLS®-R Code C35

Student's Name:	Start Date:
Objective:	When presented with an array of action pictures and teacher says, "Show me ____ (name action)" student will choose the picture of the action named by the teacher.
Person Implementing Objective:	
Setting/Environment:	
Materials:	
Reinforcers:	
Baseline:	Present array of action cards to student and say, "Show me ____ (name action)." Wait 5 seconds for a response. A correct response is scored (+) if student touches card depicting named action - <u>do not reinforce</u>. Move to next trial. An incorrect response is scored (-) if student does not touch card depicting named action- <u>do not prompt</u>. Move to next trial.
Teaching Procedures:	Present array of action cards to student and say, "Show me ____ (name action)." Wait 5 seconds for a response. If student touches card depicting named action, praise and provide reinforcer. If student does not touch card depicting named action, say, "Show me ____ (name action)" and gesture to the correct card. If student touches card depicting named action, praise and provide reinforcer. If student does not touch card depicting named action, say, "Show me ____ (name action)" and physically guide student to select correct card. Score V for correct response that followed verbal prompt. Score M if correct response followed model prompt. Score P if physical guidance was used.
Additional Targets:	

Picture Associations
Compatible with ABLLS®-R Code C36

Student's Name:	Start Date:
Objective:	When an array of picture cards is in front of student, and teacher says, "Which one goes with this?" as student is given another picture card, student will choose the picture from the array that is associated with the sample picture.
Person Implementing Objective:	
Setting/Environment:	
Materials:	
Reinforcers:	
Baseline:	Present array of picture cards in front of student. Give student one more picture as you say, "Which picture goes with this?" Wait 5 seconds for a response. A correct response is scored (+) if student chooses the associated card from the array - <u>do not reinforce</u>. Move to next trial. An incorrect response is scored (-) if student does not choose the associated card from the array- <u>do not prompt</u>. Move to next trial.
Teaching Procedures:	Present array of picture cards in front of student. Give student one more picture as you say, "Which picture goes with this?" Wait 5 seconds for a response. If student chooses associated picture card from array, praise and provide reinforcer. If student does not choose associated picture card from array, say, "Which picture goes with this?" and gesture to the associated picture in array. If student chooses associated picture card from array, praise and provide reinforcer. If student does not choose associated picture card from array, say, "Which picture goes with this?" and physically guide student to select associated picture card from array. Score V for correct response that followed verbal prompt. Score M if correct response followed model prompt. Score P if physical guidance was used.
Additional Targets:	

Receptive Identification Of Pictures By Function
Compatible with ABLLS®-R Code C37

Student's Name:	Start Date:

Objective:	When presented with array of picture cards and teacher says, "Which one do you ____ (name function) with?" student will select picture based on the function of the item in the picture. For example, "Which one do you eat with?"
Person Implementing Objective:	
Setting/Environment:	
Materials:	
Reinforcers:	
Baseline:	Present array of picture cards in front of student and say, "Which one do you ____ (name function) with?" Wait 5 seconds for a response. A correct response is scored (+) if student chooses the correct picture - <u>do not reinforce</u>. Move to next trial. An incorrect response is scored (-) if student does not choose the correct picture - <u>do not prompt</u>. Move to next trial.
Teaching Procedures:	Present array of picture cards in front of student and say, "Which one do you ____ (name function) with?" Wait 5 seconds for a response. If student chooses correct picture, praise and provide reinforcer. If student does not choose correct picture, say, "Which one do you ____ (name function) with?" and gesture to the correct picture. Wait 5 seconds for a response. If student chooses correct picture, praise and provide reinforcer. If student does not choose correct picture, say, "Which one do you ____ (name function) with?" and physically guide student to select correct picture. Score V for correct response that followed verbal prompt. Score M if correct response followed model prompt. Score P if physical guidance was used.
Additional Targets:	

Receptive Identification Of Pictures By Feature
Compatible with ABLLS®-R Code C38

Student's Name:		Start Date:	
Objective:	When presented with array of picture cards and teacher says, "Which one has a ____ (name feature)?" student will select picture based on the named feature in the picture. For example, "Which one has feathers?"		
Person Implementing Objective:			
Setting/Environment:			
Materials:			
Reinforcers:			
Baseline:	Present array of picture cards in front of student and say, "Which one has a ____ (name feature)?" Wait 5 seconds for a response. A correct response is scored (+) if student chooses the correct picture - <u>do not reinforce</u>. Move to next trial. An incorrect response is scored (-) if student does not choose the correct picture - <u>do not prompt</u>. Move to next trial.		
Teaching Procedures:	Present array of picture cards in front of student and say, "Which one has a ____ (name feature)?" Wait 5 seconds for a response. If student chooses correct picture, praise and provide reinforcer. If student does not choose correct picture, say, "Which one has a ____ (name feature)?" and gesture to the correct picture. Wait 5 seconds for a response. If student chooses correct picture, praise and provide reinforcer. If student does not choose correct picture, say, "Which one has a ____ (name feature)?" and physically guide student to select correct picture. Score V for correct response that followed verbal prompt. Score M if correct response followed model prompt. Score P if physical guidance was used.		
Additional Targets:			

Receptive Identification Of Pictures By Class
Compatible with ABLLS®-R Code C39

Student's Name:		Start Date:	
Objective:		When presented with array of picture cards and teacher says, "Which one is a/an ____ (name class)?" student will select picture based on the named class of the object in the picture. For example, "Which one is a machine?"	
Person Implementing Objective:			
Setting/Environment:			
Materials:			
Reinforcers:			
Baseline:		Present array of picture cards in front of student and say, "Which one is a/an ____ (name class)?" Wait 5 seconds for a response. A correct response is scored (+) if student chooses the correct picture - <u>do not reinforce</u>. Move to next trial. An incorrect response is scored (-) if student does not choose the correct picture - <u>do not prompt</u>. Move to next trial.	
Teaching Procedures:		Present array of picture cards in front of student and say, "Which one is a/an ____ (name class)?" Wait 5 seconds for a response. If student chooses correct picture, praise and provide reinforcer. If student does not choose correct picture, say, "Which one is a/an ____ (name class)?" and gesture to the correct picture. Wait 5 seconds for a response. If student chooses correct picture, praise and provide reinforcer. If student does not choose correct picture, say, "Which one is a/an ____ (name class)?" and physically guide student to select correct picture. Score V for correct response that followed verbal prompt. Score M if correct response followed model prompt. Score P if physical guidance was used.	
Additional Targets:			

The BIG Book of ABA Programs

Comply With Requests To Choose Multiple Items
Compatible with ABLLS®-R Code C40

Student's Name:	Start Date:	
Objective:	When presented with a large set of items in front of student, and teacher says, "Give me the____ (name item) and the ____ (name different item)" student will give both items to teacher.	
Person Implementing Objective:		
Setting/Environment:		
Materials:		
Reinforcers:		
Baseline:	Present array of items in front of student and say, "Give me the____ (name item) and the ____ (name different item)." Wait 5 seconds for a response. A correct response is scored (+) if student chooses both items - <u>do not reinforce</u>. Move to next trial. An incorrect response is scored (-) if student does not choose both items - <u>do not prompt</u>. Move to next trial.	
Teaching Procedures:	Present array of items in front of student and say, "Give me the____ (name item) and the ____ (name different item)." Wait 5 seconds for a response. If student chooses both items, praise and provide reinforcer. If student does not choose both items, say, "Give me the____ (name item) and the ____ (name different item)" and gesture to the correct items. Wait 5 seconds for a response. If student chooses both items, praise and provide reinforcer. If student does not choose both items, say, "Give me the____ (name item) and the ____ (name different item)" and physically guide student to select both items. Score V for correct response that followed verbal prompt. Score M if correct response followed model prompt. Score P if physical guidance was used.	
Additional Targets:		

www.stimuluspublications.com 94 The Autism Skill Acquisition Program™

Comply With Requests To Choose Multiple Items In Given Order
Compatible with ABLLS®-R Code C41

Student's Name:	Start Date:
Objective:	When presented with a large set of items in front of student, and teacher says, "Give me the ____ (name item) and the ____ (name different item)" student will give both items to teacher in the order they were named.
Person Implementing Objective:	
Setting/Environment:	
Materials:	
Reinforcers:	
Baseline:	Present array of items in front of student and say, "Give me the____ (name item) and the ____ (name different item)." Wait 5 seconds for a response. A correct response is scored (+) if student chooses both items in the order they were named - do not reinforce. Move to next trial. An incorrect response is scored (-) if student does not choose both items in the order they were named - do not prompt. Move to next trial.
Teaching Procedures:	Present array of items in front of student and say, "Give me the____ (name item) and the ____ (name different item)." Wait 5 seconds for a response. If student chooses both items in the order they were named, praise and provide reinforcer. If student does not choose both items in the order they were named, say, "Give me the____ (name item) and the ____ (name different item)" and gesture to the correct items. Wait 5 seconds for a response. If student chooses both items in the order they were named, praise and provide reinforcer. If student does not choose both items in the order they were named, say, "Give me the____ (name item) and the ____ (name different item)" and physically guide student to select both items in the order they were named. Score V for correct response that followed verbal prompt. Score M if correct response followed model prompt. Score P if physical guidance was used.
Additional Targets:	

Comply With Requests To Choose Community Helpers
Compatible with ABLLS®-R Code C42

Student's Name:		Start Date:	
Objective:	When presented with an array of community helper cards and teacher says, "Give me the _____ (name community helper)" student will give the teacher named community helper.		
Person Implementing Objective:			
Setting/Environment:			
Materials:			
Reinforcers:			
Baseline:	Present array of community helper cards to student and say, "Give me the _____ (name community helper)." Wait 5 seconds for a response. A correct response is scored (+) if student chooses the correct community helper - <u>do not reinforce</u>. Move to next trial. An incorrect response is scored (-) if student does not select the correct community helper - <u>do not prompt</u>. Move to next trial.		
Teaching Procedures:	Present array of community helper cards to student and say, "Give me the _____ (name community helper)." Wait 5 seconds for a response. If student chooses the correct community helper, praise and provide reinforcer. If student does not choose the correct community helper, say, "Give me the _____ (name community helper)" and gesture to the correct community helper. Wait 5 seconds for a response. If student chooses the correct community helper, praise and provide reinforcer. If student does not choose the correct community helper, say, "Give me the _____ (name community helper)" physically guide student to select the correct community helper. Score V for correct response that followed verbal prompt. Score M if correct response followed model prompt. Score P if physical guidance was used.		
Additional Targets:			

Comply With Requests To Find Specific Parts Of Complex Scenes
Compatible with ABLLS®-R Code C43

Student's Name:	Start Date:	
Objective:	When shown a complex scene and teacher says, "Show me the ____ (name part of scene)" student will be able to point to named part of scene.	
Person Implementing Objective:		
Setting/Environment:		
Materials:		
Reinforcers:		
Baseline:	Present complex scene in front of student and say, "Show me the ____ (name part of scene)." Wait 5 seconds for a response. A correct response is scored (+) if student points to the named part - <u>do not reinforce</u>. Move to next trial. An incorrect response is scored (-) if student does not point to the named part - <u>do not prompt</u>. Move to next trial.	
Teaching Procedures:	Present complex scene in front of student and say, "Show me the ____ (name part of picture)." Wait 5 seconds for a response. If student points to the named part, praise and provide reinforcer. If student does not point to the named part, say, "Show me the ____ (name part of scene)" and gesture to the named part. Wait 5 seconds for a response. If student points to the named part, praise and provide reinforcer. If student does not point to the named part, say, "Show me the ____ (name part of scene)" and physically guide student to point to named part. Score V for correct response that followed verbal prompt. Score M if correct response followed model prompt. Score P if physical guidance was used.	
Additional Targets:		

Comply With Requests To Find An Object In A Complex Scene By A Part Of The Named Object
Compatible with ABLLS®-R Code C44

Student's Name:	Start Date:

Objective:	When shown a complex scene that only contains a part of a named object and teacher says, "Show me the ____(name object in the picture that is only partially shown)" student will point to the partial object in the scene.
Person Implementing Objective:	
Setting/Environment:	
Materials:	
Reinforcers:	
Baseline:	Present complex scene in front of student in which only part of an object in the scene is pictured and say, "Show me the ____(name object in the picture that is only partially shown)." Wait 5 seconds for a response. A correct response is scored (+) if student points to the named object - <u>do not reinforce</u>. Move to next trial. An incorrect response is scored (-) if student does not point to the named object - <u>do not prompt</u>. Move to next trial.
Teaching Procedures:	Present complex scene in front of student in which only part of an object in the scene is pictured and say, "Show me the ____(name object in the picture that is only partially shown)." Wait 5 seconds for a response. If student points to the named object, praise and provide reinforcer. If student does not point to the named object, say, "Show me the ____(name object in the picture that is only partially shown)" and gesture to the named object. Wait 5 seconds for a response. If student points to the named object, praise and provide reinforcer. If student does not point to the named object, say, "Show me the ____(name object in the picture that is only partially shown)" and physically guide student to point to named object. Score V for correct response that followed verbal prompt. Score M if correct response followed model prompt. Score P if physical guidance was used.
Additional Targets:	

Choose Pictures Corresponding To Different Sounds
Compatible with ABLLS®-R Code C45

Student's Name:		Start Date:	
Objective:	When presented with an array of pictures, a common sound, and teacher says, "What is it?" student will choose the picture from the array that corresponds to the sound.		
Person Implementing Objective:			
Setting/Environment:			
Materials:			
Reinforcers:			
Baseline:	Present an array of picture cards in front of student and play 5 seconds of a recorded sound as you say, "What is it?" Wait 5 seconds for a response. A correct response is scored (+) if student points to the correct picture - <u>do not reinforce</u>. Move to next trial. An incorrect response is scored (-) if student does not point to the correct picture - <u>do not prompt</u>. Move to next trial.		
Teaching Procedures:	Present an array of picture cards in front of student and play 5 seconds of a recorded sound as you say, "What is it?" Wait 5 seconds for a response. If student points to the correct picture, praise and provide reinforcer. If student does not point to the correct picture, play sound again and say, "What is it?" as you gesture to the correct picture. Wait 5 seconds for a response. If student points to the correct picture, praise and provide reinforcer. If student does not point to the correct picture, play sound again and say, "What is it?" as you physically guide student to point to correct picture. Score V for correct response that followed verbal prompt. Score M if correct response followed model prompt. Score P if physical guidance was used.		
Additional Targets:			

Receptively Identify All Examples Of An Object
Compatible with ABLLS®-R Code C46

Student's Name:	Start Date:
Objective:	When presented with a large array of various items and teacher says, "Hand me all the ____ (name type of object)" student will choose each object of the named type from the array.
Person Implementing Objective:	
Setting/Environment:	
Materials:	
Reinforcers:	
Baseline:	Present a large array of objects in front of student and say, "Hand me all the ____ (name type of object)." Wait 5 seconds for a response. A correct response is scored (+) if student hands you all the objects of the type named - <u>do not reinforce</u>. Move to next trial. An incorrect response is scored (-) if student does not hand you all the objects of the named type - <u>do not prompt</u>. Move to next trial.
Teaching Procedures:	Present a large array of objects in front of student and say, "Hand me all the ____ (name type of object)." Wait 5 seconds for a response. If student hands you all the objects of the type named, praise and provide reinforcer. If student does not hand you all the objects of the type named say, "Hand me all the ____ (name type of object)" and gesture to all the correct objects. Wait 5 seconds for a response. If student hands you all the objects of the type named, praise and provide reinforcer. If student does not hand you all the objects of the type named, say, "Hand me all the ____ (name type of object)" and physically guide student to hand you each object of the named variety. Score V for correct response that followed verbal prompt. Score M if correct response followed model prompt. Score P if physical guidance was used.
Additional Targets:	

Receptively Identify Object By Two Adjectives
Compatible with ABLLS®-R Code C47

Student's Name:		Start Date:	
Objective:	When presented with an array of objects and teacher says, "Give me the ____ (name two physical properties of an object)" student will select correct object based on the two named adjectives. For example, "Give me the little green bear."		
Person Implementing Objective:			
Setting/Environment:			
Materials:			
Reinforcers:			
Baseline:	Present an array of objects in front of student and say, "Give me the ____ (name two physical properties of an object)." Wait 5 seconds for a response. A correct response is scored (+) if student hands you the correct object - <u>do not reinforce</u>. Move to next trial. An incorrect response is scored (-) if student does not hand you the correct object - <u>do not prompt</u>. Move to next trial.		
Teaching Procedures:	Present an array of objects in front of student and say, "Give me the ____ (name two physical properties of an object)." Wait 5 seconds for a response. If student hands you the correct object, praise and provide reinforcer. If student does not hand you the correct object, say, "Give me the ____ (name two physical properties of an object)" and gesture to the correct object. Wait 5 seconds for a response. If student hands you the correct object, praise and provide reinforcer. If student does not hand you the correct object, say, "Give me the ____ (name two physical properties of an object)" and physically guide student to hand you the correct object. Score V for correct response that followed verbal prompt. Score M if correct response followed model prompt. Score P if physical guidance was used.		
Additional Targets:			

Receptively Identify Group Of Objects By Physical Dimension
Compatible with ABLLS®-R Code C48

Student's Name:		Start Date:	
Objective:	\multicolumn{3}{l	}{When presented with an array of objects that vary only slightly in physical dimensions and teacher says, "Give me all the ____ (name physical dimension)" student will choose all objects that have a named dimension. For example, "Give me all the small ones."}
Person Implementing Objective:			
Setting/Environment:			
Materials:			
Reinforcers:			
Baseline:	\multicolumn{3}{l	}{Present an array of objects in front of student that vary only slightly in physical dimension and say, "Give me all the ____ (name physical dimension)." Wait 5 seconds for a response. A correct response is scored (+) if student hands you all of the correct objects - <u>do not reinforce</u>. Move to next trial. An incorrect response is scored (-) if student does not hand you all the correct objects - <u>do not prompt</u>. Move to next trial.}
Teaching Procedures:	\multicolumn{3}{l	}{Present an array of objects in front of student that vary only slightly in physical dimension and say, "Give me all the ____ (name physical dimension)." Wait 5 seconds for a response. If student hands you all of the correct objects, praise and provide reinforcer. If student does not hand you all of the correct objects, say, "Give me all the ____ (name physical dimension)" and gesture to the correct objects. Wait 5 seconds for a response. If student hands you all of the correct objects, praise and provide reinforcer. If student does not hand you all of the correct objects, say, "Give me all the ____ (name physical dimension)" and physically guide student to give you all the correct objects. Score V for correct response that followed verbal prompt. Score M if correct response followed model prompt. Score P if physical guidance was used.}
Additional Targets:			

Receptively Identify Multiple Objects By Two Physical Dimensions
Compatible with ABLLS®-R Code C49

Student's Name:		Start Date:	
Objective:		When presented with an array of objects and teacher says, "Give me all the ____ (name two physical properties)" student will choose all objects that have the two named dimensions. For example, "Give me the small green ones."	
Person Implementing Objective:			
Setting/Environment:			
Materials:			
Reinforcers:			
Baseline:		Present an array of objects in front of student and say, "Give me all the ____ (name two physical properties)." Wait 5 seconds for a response. A correct response is scored (+) if student hands you all of the correct objects - <u>do not reinforce</u>. Move to next trial. An incorrect response is scored (-) if student does not hand you all the correct objects - <u>do not prompt</u>. Move to next trial.	
Teaching Procedures:		Present an array of objects in front of student and say, "Give me all the ____ (name two physical properties)." Wait 5 seconds for a response. If student hands you all of the correct objects, praise and provide reinforcer. If student does not hand you all of the correct objects, say, "Give me all the ____ (name two physical properties)" and gesture to the correct objects. Wait 5 seconds for a response. If student hands you all of the correct objects, praise and provide reinforcer. If student does not hand you all of the correct objects, say, "Give me all the ____ (name two physical properties)" and physically guide student to give you all the correct objects. Score V for correct response that followed verbal prompt. Score M if correct response followed model prompt. Score P if physical guidance was used.	
Additional Targets:			

The BIG Book of ABA Programs

Receptively Identify Multiple Objects In Order
Compatible with ABLLS®-R Code C50

Student's Name:		Start Date:	
Objective:	When presented with an array of objects and teacher says, "Give me the ____ (name object) and the ____ (name second object) and the ____ (name third object)" student will choose all three objects in the order they were specified.		
Person Implementing Objective:			
Setting/Environment:			
Materials:			
Reinforcers:			
Baseline:	Present an array of objects in front of student and say, "Give me the ____ (name object) and the ____ (name second object) and the ____ (name third object)." Wait 5 seconds for a response. A correct response is scored (+) if student hands you all of the correct objects in the order they were stated - <u>do not reinforce</u>. Move to next trial. An incorrect response is scored (-) if student does not hand you all the correct objects in the order they were specified - <u>do not prompt</u>. Move to next trial.		
Teaching Procedures:	Present an array of objects in front of student and say, "Give me the ____ (name object) and the ____ (name second object) and the ____ (name third object)." Wait 5 seconds for a response. If student hands you all of the correct objects in the order they were specified, praise and provide reinforcer. If student does not hand you all of the correct objects in the order they were stated, say, "Give me the ____ (name object) and the ____ (name second object) and the ____ (name third object)" and gesture to the correct objects in the order they were specified. Wait 5 seconds for a response. If student hands you all of the correct objects in the order they were stated, praise and provide reinforcer. If student does not hand you all of the correct objects in the order they were stated, say, "Give me the ____ (name object) and the ____ (name second object) and the ____ (name third object)" and physically guide student to give you all the correct objects in the correct order. Score V for correct response that followed verbal prompt. Score M if correct response followed model prompt. Score P if physical guidance was used.		
Additional Targets:			

Receptively Identify Objects Using Prepositions
Compatible with ABLLS®-R Code C51

Student's Name:		Start Date:
Objective:		When student is presented with different objects in different locations around a stationary box and teacher says, "Hand me the ____ (name object) that is ____ (name preposition) the box" student will give the object named by preposition.
Person Implementing Objective:		
Setting/Environment:		
Materials:		
Reinforcers:		
Baseline:		Place a small box on the table in front of student. Place objects around the box (on both sides, above, under, etc.). Say, "Hand me the ____ (name object) that is ____ (name preposition) the box." Wait 5 seconds for a response. A correct response is scored (+) if student hands you the object from the correct location - do not reinforce. Move to next trial. An incorrect response is scored (-) if student does not hand you the object from correct location- do not prompt. Move to next trial.
Teaching Procedures:		Place a small box on the table in front of student. Place objects around the box (on both sides, above, under, etc.). Say, "Hand me the ____ (name object) that is ____ (name preposition) the box." Wait 5 seconds for a response. If student hands you the object from the correct location, praise and provide reinforcer. If student does not hand you the object from the correct location, say, "Hand me the ____ (name object) that is ____ (name preposition) the box" and gesture to the correct object. Wait 5 seconds for a response. If student hands you the object from the correct location, praise and provide reinforcer. If student does not hand you the object from the correct location, say, "Hand me the ____ (name object) that is ____ (name preposition) the box" and physically guide student to give you the object from the correct location. Score V for correct response that followed verbal prompt. Score M if correct response followed model prompt. Score P if physical guidance was used.
Additional Targets:		

Comply With Requests Using Pronouns
Compatible with ABLLS®-R Code C52

Student's Name:	Start Date:

Objective:	When teacher gives student directives that contain pronouns, student will comply with requests. For example, "Where is her arm?" "Where is your arm?" "Where is his arm?"
Person Implementing Objective:	
Setting/Environment:	
Materials:	
Reinforcers:	
Baseline:	For "my" and "your," sit across the table from student. For "his," "her," etc. place pictures or dolls of a male and female on table in front of student. For all pronouns say, "Where is ____ (name pronoun) ____ (name body part)?" Wait 5 seconds for a response. A correct response is scored (+) if student points to correct body part on correct doll or person- <u>do not reinforce</u>. Move to next trial. An incorrect response is scored (-) if student does not point to correct body part on correct doll or person- <u>do not prompt</u>. Move to next trial.
Teaching Procedures:	For "my" and "your," sit across the table from student. For "his," "her," etc. place pictures or dolls of a male and female on table in front of student. For all pronouns say, "Where is ____ (name pronoun) ____ (name body part)?" Wait 5 seconds for a response. If student points to correct body part on correct doll or person, praise and provide reinforcer. If student does not point to correct body part on correct doll or person, say, "Where is ____ (name pronoun) ____ (name body part)?" and gesture to the correct body part on the correct doll or person. Wait 5 seconds for a response. If student points to correct body part on correct doll or person, praise and provide reinforcer. If student does not point to correct body part on correct doll or person, say, "Where is ____ (name pronoun) ____ (name body part)?" and physically guide student to touch correct body part on correct doll or person. Score V for correct response that followed verbal prompt. Score M if correct response followed model prompt. Score P if physical guidance was used.
Additional Targets:	

Receptively Identify Correct Scene Cards
Compatible with ABLLS®-R Code C53

Student's Name:	Start Date:
Objective:	When presented with an array of scene or action cards and teacher says, "Give me ____ (name action or scene)" student will choose the card with a named scene or action.
Person Implementing Objective:	
Setting/Environment:	
Materials:	
Reinforcers:	
Baseline:	Present an array of scene or action cards in front of student and say, "Give me ____ (name action or scene)." Wait 5 seconds for a response. A correct response is scored (+) if student gives you the correct card - <u>do not reinforce</u>. Move to next trial. An incorrect response is scored (-) if student does not give you the correct card - <u>do not prompt</u>. Move to next trial.
Teaching Procedures:	Present an array of scene or action cards in front of student and say, "Give me ____ (name action or scene)." Wait 5 seconds for a response. If student gives you the correct card, praise and provide reinforcer. If student does not give you the correct card, say, "Give me ____ (name action or scene)" and gesture to the correct card. Wait 5 seconds for a response. If student gives you the correct card, praise and provide reinforcer. If student does not give you the correct card, say, "Give me ____ (name action or scene)" and physically guide student to give you correct card. Score V for correct response that followed verbal prompt. Score M if correct response followed model prompt. Score P if physical guidance was used.
Additional Targets:	

The BIG Book of ABA Programs

Receptively Identify Correct Emotion Cards
Compatible with ABLLS®-R Code C54

Student's Name:	Start Date:	
Objective:	When presented with an array of emotion cards and teacher says, "Which one is ____ (name emotion)?" student will choose the card with a named emotion.	
Person Implementing Objective:		
Setting/Environment:		
Materials:		
Reinforcers:		
Baseline:	Present an array of emotion cards in front of student and say, "Which one is ____ (name emotion)?" Wait 5 seconds for a response. A correct response is scored (+) if student gives you the correct card - <u>do not reinforce</u>. Move to next trial. An incorrect response is scored (-) if student does not give you the correct card - <u>do not prompt</u>. Move to next trial.	
Teaching Procedures:	Present an array of emotion cards in front of student and say, "Which one is ____ (name emotion)?" Wait 5 seconds for a response. If student gives you the correct card, praise and provide reinforcer. If student does not give you the correct card, say, "Which one is ____ (name emotion)?" and gesture to the correct card. Wait 5 seconds for a response. If student gives you the correct card, praise and provide reinforcer. If student does not give you the correct card, say, "Which one is ____ (name emotion)?" and physically guide student to give you correct card. Score V for correct response that followed verbal prompt. Score M if correct response followed model prompt. Score P if physical guidance was used.	
Additional Targets:		

Receptively Identify Same Or Different
Compatible with ABLLS®-R Code C55

Student's Name:		Start Date:
Objective:		When two different objects are presented to student, a third is given for comparison, and teacher says, "Which one is the same/different?" student will be able to choose the object that is the same or different from the comparison object.
Person Implementing Objective:		
Setting/Environment:		
Materials:		
Reinforcers:		
Baseline:		Present two different objects to student. Present a third object, identical to one just presented, and say, "Which one is the same/different?" Wait 5 seconds for a response. A correct response is scored (+) if student touches the object that was specified (same or different)- do not reinforce. Move to next trial. An incorrect response is scored (-) if student does not touch the object that was specified (same or different)- do not prompt. Move to next trial.
Teaching Procedures:		Present two different objects to student. Present a third object, identical to one just presented, and say, "Which one is the same/different?" Wait 5 seconds for a response. If student touches the object that was specified (same or different), praise and provide reinforcer. If student does not touch the object that was specified (same or different), say, "Which one is the same/different?" and gesture to the correct object. Wait 5 seconds for a response. If student touches the object that was specified (same or different), praise and provide reinforcer. If student does not touch the object that was specified (same or different), say, "Which one is the same/different?" and physically guide student give you correct object. Score V for correct response that followed verbal prompt. Score M if correct response followed model prompt. Score P if physical guidance was used.
Additional Targets:		

Receptively Identify Objects That Do Not Match Sample Categories
Compatible with ABLLS®-R Code C56

Student's Name:		Start Date:	
Objective:	When a small array of objects is presented in front of student and teacher says, "Which one is not ____ (name physical property)" student will touch object based on physical properties the named object does not have. For example, "Which one is not small?"		
Person Implementing Objective:			
Setting/Environment:			
Materials:			
Reinforcers:			
Baseline:	Present an array of objects in front of student and say, "Which one is not ____ (name physical property)." Wait 5 seconds for a response. A correct response is scored (+) if student touches the correct object - <u>do not reinforce</u>. Move to next trial. An incorrect response is scored (-) if student does not touch the correct object - <u>do not prompt</u>. Move to next trial.		
Teaching Procedures:	Present an array of objects in front of student and say, "Which one is not ____ (name physical property)." Wait 5 seconds for a response. If student touches the correct object, praise and provide reinforcer. If student does not touch the correct object, say, "Which one is not ____ (name physical property)" and gesture to the correct object. Wait 5 seconds for a response. If student touches the correct object, praise and provide reinforcer. If student does not touch the correct object, say, "Which one is not ____ (name physical property)" and physically guide student to give you correct object. Score V for correct response that followed verbal prompt. Score M if correct response followed model prompt. Score P if physical guidance was used.		
Additional Targets:			

Receptively Identify Social Scene Cards
Compatible with ABLLS®-R Code C57

Student's Name:		Start Date:	
Objective:	\multicolumn{3}{l	}{When presented with an array of social scene cards and teacher says, "Give me ____ (name social scene)" student will choose the card with a named scene.}
Person Implementing Objective:			
Setting/Environment:			
Materials:			
Reinforcers:			
Baseline:	\multicolumn{3}{l	}{Present an array of social scene cards in front of student and say, "Give me ____ (name social scene)." Wait 5 seconds for a response. A correct response is scored (+) if student gives you the correct card - <u>do not reinforce</u>. Move to next trial. An incorrect response is scored (-) if student does not give you the correct card - <u>do not prompt</u>. Move to next trial.}
Teaching Procedures:	\multicolumn{3}{l	}{Present an array of social scene cards in front of student and say, "Give me ____ (name social scene)." Wait 5 seconds for a response. If student gives you the correct card, praise and provide reinforcer. If student does not give you the correct card, say, "Give me ____ (name social scene)" and gesture to the correct card. Wait 5 seconds for a response. If student gives you the correct card, praise and provide reinforcer. If student does not give you the correct card, say, "Give me ____ (name social scene)" and physically guide student to give you correct card. Score V for correct response that followed verbal prompt. Score M if correct response followed model prompt. Score P if physical guidance was used.}
Additional Targets:			

CHAPTER 5

ABA Programs Compatible with

ABLLS®-R Domain D

"Imitation"

The BIG Book of ABA Programs

Comply With Request To Imitate Motor Activity With Objects
Compatible with ABLLS®-R Code D1

Student's Name:	Start Date:	
Objective:	When teacher says, "Do this" and performs simple motor activity with an object, student will perform modeled action.	
Person Implementing Objective:		
Setting/Environment:		
Materials:		
Reinforcers:		
Baseline:	Say, "Do this" and perform a simple motor activity with an object. Wait 5 seconds for a response. A correct response is scored (+) if student performs the same action as was demonstrated - <u>do not reinforce</u>. Move to next trial. An incorrect response is scored (-) if student does not perform same action as was demonstrated - <u>do not prompt</u>. Move to next trial.	
Teaching Procedures:	Say, "Do this" and perform a simple motor activity with an object. Wait 5 seconds for a response. If student performs the same action as was demonstrated, praise and provide reinforcer. If student does not perform the same action as was demonstrated, say, "Do this" and perform the motor activity again. Wait 5 seconds for a response. If student performs the same action as was demonstrated, praise and provide reinforcer. If student does not perform the same action as was demonstrated, say, "Do this" and physically guide student to perform action. Score V for correct response that followed verbal prompt. Score M if correct response followed model prompt. Score P if physical guidance was used.	
Additional Targets:		

www.stimuluspublications.com   114   The Autism Skill Acquisition Program™

Comply With Request To Imitate Motor Activity With Object When Multiple Objects Are Present
Compatible with ABLLS®-R Code D2

Student's Name:		Start Date:
Objective:		When multiple objects are present, teacher says, "Do this" and performs simple motor activity with one of the objects, student will perform modeled action with correct object.
Person Implementing Objective:		
Setting/Environment:		
Materials:		
Reinforcers:		
Baseline:		When multiple objects are present, say, "Do this" and perform a simple motor activity with one object. Wait 5 seconds for a response. A correct response is scored (+) if student performs the same action with the same object as was demonstrated - do not reinforce. Move to next trial. An incorrect response is scored (-) if student does not perform same action with the same object as was demonstrated - do not prompt. Move to next trial.
Teaching Procedures:		When multiple objects are present, say, "Do this" and perform a simple motor activity with one object. Wait 5 seconds for a response. If student performs the same action with the same object as was demonstrated, praise and provide reinforcer. If student does not perform the same action with the same object as was demonstrated, say, "Do this" and perform the motor activity again. Wait 5 seconds for a response. If student performs the same action with the same object as was demonstrated, praise and provide reinforcer. If student does not perform the same action with the same object as was demonstrated, say, "Do this" and physically guide student to perform action with correct object. Score V for correct response that followed verbal prompt. Score M if correct response followed model prompt. Score P if physical guidance was used.
Additional Targets:		

Comply With Request To Imitate Gross Motor Activity
Compatible with ABLLS®-R Code D3

Student's Name:	Start Date:
Objective:	When teacher says, "Do this" and performs simple motor activity, student will perform modeled motor activity.
Person Implementing Objective:	
Setting/Environment:	
Materials:	
Reinforcers:	
Baseline:	Say, "Do this" and perform a simple motor activity. Wait 5 seconds for a response. A correct response is scored (+) if student performs the same action as was demonstrated - <u>do not reinforce</u>. Move to next trial. An incorrect response is scored (-) if student does not perform same action as was demonstrated - <u>do not prompt</u>. Move to next trial.
Teaching Procedures:	Say, "Do this" and perform a simple motor activity. Wait 5 seconds for a response. If student performs the same action as was demonstrated, praise and provide reinforcer. If student does not perform the same action as was demonstrated, say, "Do this" and perform the motor activity again. Wait 5 seconds for a response. If student performs the same action as was demonstrated, praise and provide reinforcer. If student does not perform the same action as was demonstrated, say, "Do this" and physically guide student to perform action. Score V for correct response that followed verbal prompt. Score M if correct response followed model prompt. Score P if physical guidance was used.
Additional Targets:	

Comply With Request To Imitate Motor Activity With Lower Body
Compatible with ABLLS®-R Code D4

Student's Name:		Start Date:	
Objective:	When teacher says, "Do this" and performs simple motor activity with lower body, student will perform modeled motor activity.		
Person Implementing Objective:			
Setting/Environment:			
Materials:			
Reinforcers:			
Baseline:	Say, "Do this" and perform a simple motor activity with lower body. Wait 5 seconds for a response. A correct response is scored (+) if student performs the same action as was demonstrated - <u>do not reinforce</u>. Move to next trial. An incorrect response is scored (-) if student does not perform same action as was demonstrated - <u>do not prompt</u>. Move to next trial.		
Teaching Procedures:	Say, "Do this" and perform a simple motor activity with lower body. Wait 5 seconds for a response. If student performs the same action as was demonstrated, praise and provide reinforcer. If student does not perform the same action as was demonstrated, say, "Do this" and perform the motor activity again. Wait 5 seconds for a response. If student performs the same action as was demonstrated, praise and provide reinforcer. If student does not perform the same action as was demonstrated, say, "Do this" and physically guide student to perform action. Score V for correct response that followed verbal prompt. Score M if correct response followed model prompt. Score P if physical guidance was used.		
Additional Targets:			

The BIG Book of ABA Programs

Comply With Request To Imitate Motor Activity With Upper Body
Compatible With ABLLS®-R Code D5

Student's Name:		Start Date:
Objective:	When teacher says, "Do this" and performs simple motor activity with upper body, student will perform modeled motor activity.	
Person Implementing Objective:		
Setting/Environment:		
Materials:		
Reinforcers:		
Baseline:	Say, "Do this" and perform a simple motor activity with upper body. Wait 5 seconds for a response. A correct response is scored (+) if student performs the same action as was demonstrated - <u>do not reinforce</u>. Move to next trial. An incorrect response is scored (-) if student does not perform same action as was demonstrated - <u>do not prompt</u>. Move to next trial.	
Teaching Procedures:	Say, "Do this" and perform a simple motor activity with upper body. Wait 5 seconds for a response. If student performs the same action as was demonstrated, praise and provide reinforcer. If student does not perform the same action as was demonstrated, say, "Do this" and perform the motor activity again. Wait 5 seconds for a response. If student performs the same action as was demonstrated, praise and provide reinforcer. If student does not perform the same action as was demonstrated, say, "Do this" and physically guide student to perform action. Score V for correct response that followed verbal prompt. Score M if correct response followed model prompt. Score P if physical guidance was used.	
Additional Targets:		

Comply With Request To Imitate Motor Activity Requiring Movement Or Non-movement Actions
Compatible with ABLLS®-R Code D6

Student's Name:	Start Date:
Objective:	When teacher says, "Do this" and performs simple motor activities that require movement and non-movement actions, student will perform modeled motor activities. For example, alternate trials of "Do this" while standing on one foot and "Do this" while standing on one foot and shaking outstretched leg.
Person Implementing Objective:	
Setting/Environment:	
Materials:	
Reinforcers:	
Baseline:	Say, "Do this" and perform a simple motor activity that requires movement or non-movement actions. Wait 5 seconds for a response. A correct response is scored (+) if student performs the same action as was demonstrated - <u>do not reinforce</u>. Move to next trial. An incorrect response is scored (-) if student does not perform same action as was demonstrated - <u>do not prompt</u>. Move to next trial.
Teaching Procedures:	Say, "Do this" and perform a simple motor activity that requires movement or non-movement actions. Wait 5 seconds for a response. If student performs the same action as was demonstrated, praise and provide reinforcer. If student does not perform the same action as was demonstrated, say, "Do this" and perform the motor activity again. Wait 5 seconds for a response. If student performs the same action as was demonstrated, praise and provide reinforcer. If student does not perform the same action as was demonstrated, say, "Do this" and physically guide student to perform action. Score V for correct response that followed verbal prompt. Score M if correct response followed model prompt. Score P if physical guidance was used.
Additional Targets:	

The BIG Book of ABA Programs

Comply With Request To Imitate Motor Activity Using Varied Cues
Compatible with ABLLS®-R Code D7

Student's Name:		Start Date:	
Objective:	When teacher uses varied cues such as, "Do this," "Your turn," "Do like I do," etc. and then performs a simple motor action, student will perform an identical action modeled by the teacher.		
Person Implementing Objective:			
Setting/Environment:			
Materials:			
Reinforcers:			
Baseline:	Say, "Do this," "Your turn," "Do like I do," etc. and perform a simple motor activity. Vary cues from trial to trial. Wait 5 seconds for a response. A correct response is scored (+) if student performs the same action as was demonstrated - <u>do not reinforce</u>. Move to next trial. An incorrect response is scored (-) if student does not perform same action as was demonstrated - <u>do not prompt</u>. Move to next trial.		
Teaching Procedures:	Say, "Do this," "Your turn," "Do like I do," etc. and perform a simple motor activity. Vary cues from trial to trial. Wait 5 seconds for a response. If student performs the same action as was demonstrated, praise and provide reinforcer. If student does not perform the same action as was demonstrated, present the cue and the motor activity again. Wait 5 seconds for a response. If student performs the same action as was demonstrated, praise and provide reinforcer. If student does not perform the same action as was demonstrated, present the cue again and physically guide student to perform action. Score V for correct response that followed verbal prompt. Score M if correct response followed model prompt. Score P if physical guidance was used.		
Additional Targets:			

www.stimuluspublications.com   The Autism Skill Acquisition Program™

Comply With Request To Imitate Motor Activity Performed In Front Of A Mirror
Compatible with ABLLS®-R Code D8

Student's Name:		Start Date:	
Objective:	When student is in front of a mirror, teacher says, "Do this" and makes motor movement in the mirror, student will imitate motor activity teacher demonstrated in the mirror.		
Person Implementing Objective:			
Setting/Environment:			
Materials:			
Reinforcers:			
Baseline:	With student in front of mirror, say, "Do this" and perform a simple motor activity in the mirror. Wait 5 seconds for a response. A correct response is scored (+) if student performs the same action as was demonstrated - <u>do not reinforce</u>. Move to next trial. An incorrect response is scored (-) if student does not perform same action as was demonstrated - <u>do not prompt</u>. Move to next trial.		
Teaching Procedures:	With student in front of mirror, say, "Do this" and perform a simple motor activity in the mirror. Wait 5 seconds for a response. If student performs the same action as was demonstrated, praise and provide reinforcer. If student does not perform the same action as was demonstrated, say, "Do this" and perform the motor activity in the mirror again. Wait 5 seconds for a response. If student performs the same action as was demonstrated, praise and provide reinforcer. If student does not perform the same action as was demonstrated, say, "Do this" and physically guide student to perform action. Score V for correct response that followed verbal prompt. Score M if correct response followed model prompt. Score P if physical guidance was used.		
Additional Targets:			

Comply With Request To Imitate Motor Activity Of Head Or Neck
Compatible with ABLLS®-R Code D9

Student's Name:	Start Date:
Objective:	When teacher says, "Do this" and demonstrates a head or neck motor activity, student will imitate motor activity demonstrated.
Person Implementing Objective:	
Setting/Environment:	
Materials:	
Reinforcers:	
Baseline:	Say, "Do this" and perform a simple motor activity with head or neck. Wait 5 seconds for a response. A correct response is scored (+) if student performs the same action as was demonstrated - <u>do not reinforce</u>. Move to next trial. An incorrect response is scored (-) if student does not perform same action as was demonstrated - <u>do not prompt</u>. Move to next trial.
Teaching Procedures:	Say, "Do this" and perform a simple motor activity with head or neck. Wait 5 seconds for a response. If student performs the same action as was demonstrated, praise and provide reinforcer. If student does not perform the same action as was demonstrated, say, "Do this" and perform the motor head and neck activity again. Wait 5 seconds for a response. If student performs the same action as was demonstrated, praise and provide reinforcer. If student does not perform the same action as was demonstrated, say, "Do this" and physically guide student to perform the head and neck action. Score V for correct response that followed verbal prompt. Score M if correct response followed model prompt. Score P if physical guidance was used.
Additional Targets:	

Comply With Request To Imitate Motor Activity Of Mouth And Tongue
Compatible with ABLLS®-R Code D10

Student's Name:		Start Date:	
Objective:	When teacher says, "Do this" and demonstrates a mouth or tongue movement, student will imitate motor activity demonstrated.		
Person Implementing Objective:			
Setting/Environment:			
Materials:			
Reinforcers:			
Baseline:	Say, "Do this" and perform a mouth or tongue movement. Wait 5 seconds for a response. A correct response is scored (+) if student performs the same action as was demonstrated - <u>do not reinforce</u>. Move to next trial. An incorrect response is scored (-) if student does not perform same action as was demonstrated - <u>do not prompt</u>. Move to next trial.		
Teaching Procedures:	Say, "Do this" and perform a mouth or tongue movement. Wait 5 seconds for a response. If student performs the same action as was demonstrated, praise and provide reinforcer. If student does not perform the same action as was demonstrated, say, "Do this" and perform the motor activity again. Wait 5 seconds for a response. If student performs the same action as was demonstrated, praise and provide reinforcer. If student does not perform the same action as was demonstrated, say, "Do this" and physically guide student to perform action. Score V for correct response that followed verbal prompt. Score M if correct response followed model prompt. Score P if physical guidance was used.		
Additional Targets:			

Comply With Request To Imitate Motor Activity Of Face
Compatible with ABLLS®-R Code D11

Student's Name:	Start Date:	
Objective:	When teacher says, "Do this" and demonstrates a facial movement, student will imitate facial movement demonstrated.	
Person Implementing Objective:		
Setting/Environment:		
Materials:		
Reinforcers:		
Baseline:	Say, "Do this" and perform a facial movement. Wait 5 seconds for a response. A correct response is scored (+) if student performs the same action as was demonstrated - <u>do not reinforce</u>. Move to next trial. An incorrect response is scored (-) if student does not perform same action as was demonstrated - <u>do not prompt</u>. Move to next trial.	
Teaching Procedures:	Say, "Do this" and perform a facial movement. Wait 5 seconds for a response. If student performs the same action as was demonstrated, praise and provide reinforcer. If student does not perform the same action as was demonstrated, say, "Do this" and perform the motor activity again. Wait 5 seconds for a response. If student performs the same action as was demonstrated, praise and provide reinforcer. If student does not perform the same action as was demonstrated, say, "Do this" and physically guide student to perform the action. Score V for correct response that followed verbal prompt. Score M if correct response followed model prompt. Score P if physical guidance was used.	
Additional Targets:		

The BIG Book of ABA Programs

Comply With Request To Imitate Fine Motor Activity
Compatible with ABLLS®-R Code D12

Student's Name:		Start Date:
Objective:		When teacher says, "Do this" and demonstrates a fine motor activity, student will imitate motor activity demonstrated.
Person Implementing Objective:		
Setting/Environment:		
Materials:		
Reinforcers:		
Baseline:		Say, "Do this" and perform a fine motor activity. Wait 5 seconds for a response. A correct response is scored (+) if student performs the same action as was demonstrated - <u>do not reinforce</u>. Move to next trial. An incorrect response is scored (-) if student does not perform same action as was demonstrated - <u>do not prompt</u>. Move to next trial.
Teaching Procedures:		Say, "Do this" and perform a fine motor activity. Wait 5 seconds for a response. If student performs the same action as was demonstrated, praise and provide reinforcer. If student does not perform the same action as was demonstrated, say, "Do this" and perform the fine motor activity again. Wait 5 seconds for a response. If student performs the same action as was demonstrated, praise and provide reinforcer. If student does not perform the same action as was demonstrated, say, "Do this" and physically guide student to perform fine motor action. Score V for correct response that followed verbal prompt. Score M if correct response followed model prompt. Score P if physical guidance was used.
Additional Targets:		

www.stimuluspublications.com   The Autism Skill Acquisition Program™

Comply With Request To Imitate Touching Items In Specific Order
Compatible with ABLLS®-R Code D13

Student's Name:	Start Date:
Objective:	When teacher and student each have identical arrays of items and teacher says "Do this" and touches the items in the teacher array in a specific order, student will imitate the specific order in which items are touched by touching the items in the student array.
Person Implementing Objective:	
Setting/Environment:	
Materials:	
Reinforcers:	
Baseline:	Ensure you and student have identical arrays of items. Say, "Do this" as you touch all items in your array in a specific order. Wait 5 seconds for a response. A correct response is scored (+) if student touches each item in the student array in the order demonstrated- <u>do not reinforce</u>. Move to next trial. An incorrect response is scored (-) if student does not touch all items in student array in the order demonstrated - <u>do not prompt</u>. Move to next trial.
Teaching Procedures:	Ensure you and student have identical arrays of items. Say, "Do this" as you touch all items in your array in a specific order. Wait 5 seconds for a response. If student touches each item in student array in order demonstrated, praise and provide reinforcer. If student does not touch each item in student array in order demonstrated, say, "Do this" and touch all items in your array in the same order as previously demonstrated. Wait 5 seconds for a response. If student touches each item in student array in order demonstrated, praise and provide reinforcer. If student does not touch each item in student array in order demonstrated, say, "Do this" and physically guide student to touch items in student array in the demonstrated order. Score V for correct response following verbal. Score M if model prompt was used. Score P if physical guidance was used.
Additional Targets:	

Comply With Request To Imitate Blowing Air Out Of Mouth
Compatible with ABLLS®-R Code D14

Student's Name:		Start Date:
Objective:	When teacher says, "Do this" and blows air out of mouth, student will imitate by blowing air out of mouth.	
Person Implementing Objective:		
Setting/Environment:		
Materials:		
Reinforcers:		
Baseline:	Say, "Do this" and blow air out of your mouth. Wait 5 seconds for a response. A correct response is scored (+) if student blows air out of mouth - <u>do not reinforce</u>. Move to next trial. An incorrect response is scored (-) if student does not blow air out of mouth - <u>do not prompt</u>. Move to next trial.	
Teaching Procedures:	Say, "Do this" and blow air out of your mouth. Wait 5 seconds for a response. If student blows air out of mouth, praise and provide reinforcer. If student does not blow air out of mouth, say, "do this" and blow air out of your mouth again. Wait 5 seconds for a response. If student blows air out of mouth, praise and provide reinforcer. If student does not blow air out of mouth, say, "do this" and physically guide student by gently squeezing student's cheeks as you blow air out of your mouth. Score V for correct response that followed verbal prompt. Score M if correct response followed model prompt. Score P if physical guidance was used.	
Additional Targets:		

Comply With Request To Imitate Speed Of Moving Items
Compatible with ABLLS®-R Code D15

Student's Name:		Start Date:
Objective:	When student and teacher each have an item, teacher says, "Do this" and moves teacher's item quickly or slowly, student will imitate the movement with student's item using the same speed that was demonstrated by the teacher.	
Person Implementing Objective:		
Setting/Environment:		
Materials:		
Reinforcers:		
Baseline:	Ensure you and student each have items. Say, "Do this" and move your item at a given speed (vary trials by moving item quickly or slowly). Wait 5 seconds for a response. A correct response is scored (+) if student moves item at same speed as was demonstrated - <u>do not reinforce</u>. Move to next trial. An incorrect response is scored (-) if student does not move item at same speed as was demonstrated - <u>do not prompt</u>. Move to next trial.	
Teaching Procedures:	Ensure you and student each have items. Say, "Do this" and move your item at a given speed (vary trials by moving item quickly or slowly). Wait 5 seconds for a response. If student moves item at same speed as was demonstrated, praise and provide reinforcer. If student does not move item at same speed as was demonstrated, say, "Do this" and move item at speed previously demonstrated. Wait 5 seconds for a response. If student moves item at same speed as was demonstrated, praise and provide reinforcer. If student does not move item at same speed as was demonstrated, say, "Do this" and physically guide student to move item at same speed as was demonstrated. Score V for correct response that followed verbal prompt. Score M if correct response followed model prompt. Score P if physical guidance was used.	
Additional Targets:		

Comply With Request To Imitate Speed Of Moving Items
Compatible with ABLLS®-R Code D16

Student's Name:		Start Date:	
Objective:		When teacher says, "Do this" and moves an item quickly or slowly and gives item to student, student will imitate the movement using the same speed that was demonstrated.	
Person Implementing Objective:			
Setting/Environment:			
Materials:			
Reinforcers:			
Baseline:		Say, "Do this" as you move item at a given speed (vary trials by moving item quickly or slowly). Give item to student. Wait 5 seconds for a response. A correct response is scored (+) if student moves item at same speed as was demonstrated - <u>do not reinforce</u>. Move to next trial. An incorrect response is scored (-) if student does not move item at same speed as was demonstrated - <u>do not prompt</u>. Move to next trial.	
Teaching Procedures:		Say, "Do this" as you move item at a given speed (vary trials by moving item quickly or slowly). Give item to student. Wait 5 seconds for a response. If student moves item at same speed as was demonstrated, praise and provide reinforcer. If student does not move item at same speed as was demonstrated, say, "Do this" and repeat item movement. Wait 5 seconds for a response. If student moves item at same speed as was demonstrated, praise and provide reinforcer. If student does not move item at same speed as was demonstrated, say, "Do this" and physically guide student to move item at same speed as was demonstrated. Score V for correct response that followed verbal prompt. Score M if correct response followed model prompt. Score P if physical guidance was used.	
Additional Targets:			

Comply With Request To Imitate Speed Of Motor Movement
Compatible with ABLLS®-R Code D17

Student's Name:	Start Date:
Objective:	When teacher says, "Do this" and demonstrates a motor movement quickly or slowly, student will imitate the motor movement using the same speed that was demonstrated.
Person Implementing Objective:	
Setting/Environment:	
Materials:	
Reinforcers:	
Baseline:	Say, "Do this" as you make a gross motor movement at a given speed (vary trials by quick or slow movements). Wait 5 seconds for a response. A correct response is scored (+) if student makes same movement at same speed as was demonstrated - <u>do not reinforce</u>. Move to next trial. An incorrect response is scored (-) if student does not make same movement at same speed as was demonstrated - <u>do not prompt</u>. Move to next trial.
Teaching Procedures:	Say, "Do this" as you make a gross motor movement at a given speed (vary trials by quick or slow movements). Wait 5 seconds for a response. If student makes same movement at same speed as was demonstrated, praise and provide reinforcer. If student does not make same movement at same speed as was demonstrated, say, "Do this" and repeat movement. Wait 5 seconds for a response. If student makes same movement at same speed as was demonstrated, praise and provide reinforcer. If student does not make same movement at same speed as was demonstrated, say, "Do this" and physically guide student to make the same movement at same speed as was demonstrated. Score V for correct response that followed verbal prompt. Score M if correct response followed model prompt. Score P if physical guidance was used.
Additional Targets:	

Comply With Request To Imitate Touching Items In Specific Order Following Model Compatible with ABLLS®-R Code D18

Student's Name:		Start Date:	
Objective:		When student is presented with an array of items and teacher says "Do this" and touches the items in a specific order, student will imitate the specific order in which specific items are touched.	
Person Implementing Objective:			
Setting/Environment:			
Materials:			
Reinforcers:			
Baseline:		Present array of items in front of student. Say, "Do this" as you touch all items in array in a specific order. Wait 5 seconds for a response. A correct response is scored (+) if student touches each item in array in order demonstrated- <u>do not reinforce</u>. Move to next trial. An incorrect response is scored (-) if student does not touch all items in array in the order demonstrated- <u>do not prompt</u>. Move to next trial.	
Teaching Procedures:		Present an array of items in front of student. Say, "Do this" as you touch all items in a specific order. Wait 5 seconds for a response. If student touches each item in order demonstrated, praise and provide reinforcer. If student does not touch each item in order demonstrated, say, "Do this" and touch the same items in the same order. Wait 5 seconds for a response. If student touches each item in order demonstrated, praise and provide reinforcer. If student does not touch each item in order demonstrated, say, "Do this" and physically guide student to touch items in order. Score V for correct response following verbal. Score M if model prompt was used. Score P if physical guidance was used.	
Additional Targets:			

Comply With Request To Imitate Multiple Motor Actions In Specific Order
Compatible with ABLLS®-R Code D19

Student's Name:		Start Date:	
Objective:		When teacher says, "Do this" and demonstrates a series of motor movements, student will imitate the motor movements immediately after teacher demonstrates each movement.	
Person Implementing Objective:			
Setting/Environment:			
Materials:			
Reinforcers:			
Baseline:		Say, "Do this" and perform a motor action. Wait 2 seconds for response. Perform the next motor action. Wait 2 seconds for a response, etc. A correct response is scored (+) if student performs each action immediately after it was demonstrated - <u>do not reinforce</u>. Move to next trial. An incorrect response is scored (-) if student does not perform each motor action immediately after it was demonstrated - <u>do not prompt</u>. Move to next trial.	
Teaching Procedures:		Say, "Do this" and perform a motor action. Wait 2 seconds. If correct action is imitated, perform the next action. If an incorrect action is demonstrated, say, "Do this" and perform the action again. If correct action is imitated, perform the next action. If an incorrect action is demonstrated, say, "Do this" and physically guide student to perform correct action. Repeat for all actions that are to be performed. Score V for correct response following verbal prompt if entire sequence only required verbal prompts. Score M if a model prompt was used at all during sequence. Score P if any response was physically guided.	
Additional Targets:			

Comply With Request To Imitate Motor Movements In Specific Order Following Model
Compatible with ABLLS®-R Code D20

Student's Name:		Start Date:	
Objective:		When teacher says "Do this" and performs multiple motor movements in a specific order, student will imitate the specific order in which motor movements were demonstrated.	
Person Implementing Objective:			
Setting/Environment:			
Materials:			
Reinforcers:			
Baseline:		Say, "Do this" as you perform multiple motor movements in a specific order. Wait 5 seconds for a response. A correct response is scored (+) if student imitates all movements in order demonstrated- <u>do not reinforce</u>. Move to next trial. An incorrect response is scored (-) if student does not imitate all movements in the order demonstrated- <u>do not prompt</u>. Move to next trial.	
Teaching Procedures:		Say, "Do this" as you perform multiple motor movements in a specific order. Wait 5 seconds for a response. If student imitates all movements in order demonstrated, praise and provide reinforcer. If student does not imitate all movements in the order demonstrated, say, "Do this" and repeat movements in the same order. Wait 5 seconds for a response. If student imitates all movements in order demonstrated, praise and provide reinforcer. If student does not imitate all movements in the order demonstrated, say, "Do this" and physically guide student to perform all movements in order. Score V for correct response following verbal. Score M if model prompt was used. Score P if physical guidance was used.	
Additional Targets:			

Comply With Request To Imitate Magnitude Of A Motor Action
Compatible with ABLLS®-R Code D21

Student's Name:		Start Date:	
Objective:		When teacher says, "Do this" and performs a simple motor movement with a certain magnitude, student will imitate the magnitude of an action performed by the teacher. For example, "Do this" as teacher slams block on table or "Do this" as teacher softly touches block on table.	
Person Implementing Objective:			
Setting/Environment:			
Materials:			
Reinforcers:			
Baseline:		Say, "Do this" and perform a motor action with a certain magnitude. Wait 5 seconds for a response. A correct response is scored (+) if student performs the action with the same magnitude as was demonstrated - <u>do not reinforce</u>. Move to next trial. An incorrect response is scored (-) if student does not perform action with same magnitude it was demonstrated - <u>do not prompt</u>. Move to next trial.	
Teaching Procedures:		Say, "Do this" and perform a motor action with a certain magnitude. Wait 5 seconds for a response. If the action is imitated with the correct magnitude, praise and provide reinforcer. If the action is not demonstrated with same magnitude, say, "Do this" and perform the action again. Wait 5 seconds for a response. If the action is imitated with the correct magnitude, praise and provide reinforcer. If the action is not demonstrated with same magnitude, say, "Do this" and physically guide student to perform action with the appropriate magnitude. Score V for correct response that followed verbal prompt. Score M if model prompt was used. Score P if any response was physically guided.	
Additional Targets:			

Comply With Request To Imitate Repetitious Motor Actions
Compatible with ABLLS®-R Code D22

Student's Name:		Start Date:	
Objective:	When teacher says, "Do this" and performs a specific number of repetitive actions, student will imitate the number of actions performed by the teacher.		
Person Implementing Objective:			
Setting/Environment:			
Materials:			
Reinforcers:			
Baseline:	Say, "Do this" and perform a repetitious motor action. Wait 5 seconds for a response. A correct response is scored (+) if student performs the action the same number of times it was demonstrated - <u>do not reinforce</u>. Move to next trial. An incorrect response is scored (-) if student does not perform action the same number of times it was demonstrated - <u>do not prompt</u>. Move to next trial.		
Teaching Procedures:	Say, "Do this" and perform a repetitious motor action. Wait 5 seconds for a response. If student performs the action the same number of times it was demonstrated, praise and provide reinforcer. If student does not perform action the same number of times it was demonstrated, say, "Do this" and perform the repetitious action again. Wait 5 seconds for a response. If student performs the action the same number of times it was demonstrated, praise and provide reinforcer. If student does not perform action the same number of times it was demonstrated, say, "Do this" and physically guide student to perform the repetitious action. Score V for correct response that followed verbal prompt. Score M if model prompt was used. Score P if any response was physically guided.		
Additional Targets:			

Comply With Request To Imitate Vocalization And Motor Action At Same Time
Compatible with ABLLS®-R Code D23

Student's Name:	Start Date:
Objective:	When teacher says, "Do this" and demonstrates a vocalization and motor behavior at the same time, student will imitate the vocalization and motor action at the same time.
Person Implementing Objective:	
Setting/Environment:	
Materials:	
Reinforcers:	
Baseline:	Say, "Do this" and demonstrate a vocalization and a motor action at the same time. Wait 5 seconds for a response. A correct response is scored (+) if student performs both behaviors at the same time- <u>do not reinforce</u>. Move to next trial. An incorrect response is scored (-) if student does not perform both behaviors at the same time- <u>do not prompt</u>. Move to next trial.
Teaching Procedures:	Say, "Do this" and demonstrate a vocalization and a motor action at the same time. Wait 5 seconds for a response. If student performs both behaviors at the same time, praise and provide reinforcer. If student does not perform both behaviors at the same time, say, "Do this" and perform both behaviors again. Wait 5 seconds for a response. If student performs both behaviors at the same time, praise and provide reinforcer. If student does not perform both behaviors at the same time, say, "Do this" and physically guide student to perform motor action while touching student's mouth to physically guide vocalization. Score V for correct response that followed verbal prompt. Score M if model prompt was used. Score P if any response was physically guided.
Additional Targets:	

Comply With Request To Imitate Multiple Motor Actions With Multiple Items In Specific Order
Compatible with ABLLS®-R Code D24

Student's Name:		Start Date:	
Objective:	When an array of items is presented in front of student and teacher says, "Do this" as teacher models actions with different items, student will imitate the actions with the items in the correct order.		
Person Implementing Objective:			
Setting/Environment:			
Materials:			
Reinforcers:			
Baseline:	Present an array of items in front of student. Say, "Do this" and perform a motor action with each item in a specific order. Wait 5 seconds for a response. A correct response is scored (+) if student correctly performs all actions in the order they were demonstrated - <u>do not reinforce</u>. Move to next trial. An incorrect response is scored (-) if student does not correctly perform all actions in the order they were demonstrated - <u>do not prompt</u>. Move to next trial.		
Teaching Procedures:	Present an array of items in front of student. Say, "Do this" and perform a motor action with each item in a specific order. Wait 5 seconds for a response. If student correctly performs all actions in the order they were demonstrated, praise and provide reinforcer. If student does not correctly perform all actions in the order they were demonstrated, say, "Do this" and perform all actions in the order they were first demonstrated. Wait 5 seconds for a response. If student correctly performs all actions in the order they were demonstrated, praise and provide reinforcer. If student does not correctly perform all actions in the order they were demonstrated, say, "Do this" and physically guide student to perform all motor actions in order. Score V for correct response that followed verbal prompt. Score M if model prompt was used. Score P if any response was physically guided.		
Additional Targets:			

Comply With Nonverbal Request To Imitate Multiple Motor Actions
Compatible with ABLLS®-R Code D25

Student's Name:	Start Date:	
Objective:	When teacher performs a motor action in front of student, student will imitate the action.	
Person Implementing Objective:		
Setting/Environment:		
Materials:		
Reinforcers:		
Baseline:	Perform a motor action in front of student. Wait 5 seconds for a response. A correct response is scored (+) if student performs the action that was demonstrated - <u>do not reinforce</u>. Move to next trial. An incorrect response is scored (-) if student does not perform the action that was demonstrated - <u>do not prompt</u>. Move to next trial.	
Teaching Procedures:	Perform a motor action in front of student. Wait 5 seconds for a response. If student performs the action that was demonstrated, praise and provide reinforcer. If student does not perform the action that was demonstrated, repeat the action. Wait 5 seconds for a response. If student performs the action that was demonstrated, praise and provide reinforcer. If student does not perform the action that was demonstrated, repeat the action and then immediately physically guide student to perform the action. Score V for correct response that followed initial prompt. Score M if model prompt was used. Score P if response was physically guided.	
Additional Targets:		

Comply With Request To Imitate A Previously Demonstrated Action
Compatible with ABLLS®-R Code D27

Student's Name:		Start Date:	
Objective:	When teacher performs simple motor activity at least 4 hours earlier, student will perform motor activity upon request.		
Person Implementing Objective:			
Setting/Environment:			
Materials:			
Reinforcers:			
Baseline:	Perform a simple motor activity and say, "I'm going to ask you to do this later." At least 4 hours later, say, "Remember when I told you that I was going to ask you to do what I showed you? Do that now." Wait 5 seconds for a response. A correct response is scored (+) if student performs the same action as was demonstrated earlier- <u>do not reinforce</u>. Move to next trial. An incorrect response is scored (-) if student does not perform same action as was demonstrated - <u>do not prompt</u>. Move to next trial.		
Teaching Procedures:	Perform a simple motor activity and say, "I'm going to ask you to do this later." At least 4 hours later, say, "Remember when I told you that I was going to ask you to do what I showed you? Do that now." Wait 5 seconds for a response. If student performs the same action as was demonstrated, praise and provide reinforcer. If student does not perform the same action demonstrated earlier, say, "Do this" and perform the motor activity again. Wait 5 seconds for a response. If student performs the same action as was demonstrated earlier, praise and provide reinforcer. If student does not perform the same action as was demonstrated earlier, say, "Do this" and physically guide student to perform action. Score V for correct response that followed verbal prompt. Score M if correct response followed model prompt. Score P if physical guidance was used.		
Additional Targets:			

CHAPTER 6

ABA Programs Compatible with

ABLLS®-R Domain E

"Vocal Imitation"

Comply With Request To Imitate Sound
Compatible with ABLLS®-R Code E1

Student's Name:	Start Date:
Objective:	When teacher says, "Say ____ (make sound)" student will imitate that sound.
Person Implementing Objective:	
Setting/Environment:	
Materials:	
Reinforcers:	
Baseline:	Deliver the cue, "Say ____ (make sound)." Wait 5 seconds for a response. A correct response is scored (+) if student imitates sound - <u>do not reinforce</u>. Move to next trial. An incorrect response is scored (-) if student does imitate sound - <u>do not prompt</u>. Move to next trial.
Teaching Procedures:	Deliver the cue, "Say ____ (make sound)." Wait 5 seconds for a response. If student imitates sound, praise and provide reinforcer. If student does not imitate sound, repeat the cue, "Say ____ (make sound)." Wait 5 seconds for a response. If student imitates sound, praise and provide reinforcer. If student does not imitate sound, repeat the cue "Say ____ (make sound)" and physically guide student to make the sound (physically touch the student's mouth). Score V for correct response that followed verbal prompt. Score M if model prompt was used. Score P if physical guidance was used.
Additional Targets:	

Comply With Request To Imitate Sounds In Specific Order
Compatible with ABLLS®-R Code E2

Student's Name:	Start Date:
Objective:	When teacher says, "Say ____ ____ ____ (make series of sounds)" student will imitate sounds in the demonstrated order.
Person Implementing Objective:	
Setting/Environment:	
Materials:	
Reinforcers:	
Baseline:	Deliver the cue, "Say ____ ____ ____ (make series of sounds)." Wait 5 seconds for a response. A correct response is scored (+) if student makes the sounds in the order demonstrated - <u>do not reinforce</u>. Move to next trial. An incorrect response is scored (-) if student does not make the sounds in the order in which they were demonstrated - <u>do not prompt</u>. Move to next trial.
Teaching Procedures:	Deliver the cue, "Say ____ ____ ____ (make series of sounds)." Wait 5 seconds for a response. If sounds are imitated correctly and in proper sequence, praise and provide reinforcer. If sounds are demonstrated incorrectly, repeat the cue, "Say ____ ____ ____ (make series of sounds)." Wait 5 seconds for a response. If sounds are imitated correctly and in proper sequence, praise and provide reinforcer. If sounds are demonstrated incorrectly, repeat the cue, "Say ____ ____ ____ (make series of sounds)" and physically guide student to make the series of sounds (physically touch the student's mouth). Score V for correct response that followed verbal prompt. Score M if model prompt was used. Score P if physical guidance was used.
Additional Targets:	

Comply With Request To Imitate Beginning Sound Of A Word
Compatible with ABLLS®-R Code E3

Student's Name:	Start Date:
Objective:	When teacher says, "Say ____ (say a word)" student will imitate the beginning sound of the word.
Person Implementing Objective:	
Setting/Environment:	
Materials:	
Reinforcers:	
Baseline:	Deliver the cue, "Say _____ (say a word)." Wait 5 seconds for a response. A correct response is scored (+) if student makes the beginning sound of the word - <u>do not reinforce</u>. Move to next trial. An incorrect response is scored (-) if student does not make the beginning sound of the word - <u>do not prompt</u>. Move to next trial.
Teaching Procedures:	Deliver the cue, "Say _____ (say a word)." Wait 5 seconds for a response. If student makes the beginning sound of the word, praise and provide reinforcer. If student does not make the beginning sound of the word, repeat the cue, "Say ____ (say a word)." Wait 5 seconds for a response. If student makes the beginning sound of the word, praise and provide reinforcer. If student does not make the beginning sound of the word, repeat the cue, "Say _____ (say a word)" and physically guide student to make the beginning sound of the word (physically touch student's mouth). Score V for correct response that followed verbal prompt. Score M if model prompt was used. Score P if physical guidance was used.
Additional Targets:	

Comply with Request to Imitate Similar Multiple Sound Sequences
Compatible with ABLLS®-R Code E4

Student's Name:	Start Date:
Objective:	When teacher says, "Say ____ ____ (make a two-sound sequence)" student will imitate the sound sequence. For example, "Say Bo-Bo" or "Say Bo-Be."
Person Implementing Objective:	
Setting/Environment:	
Materials:	
Reinforcers:	
Baseline:	Deliver the cue, "Say ____ ____ (make a two-sound sequence)." Wait 5 seconds for a response. A correct response is scored (+) if student imitates the correct sound sequence - <u>do not reinforce</u>. Move to next trial. An incorrect response is scored (-) if student does not make the two-sound sequence - <u>do not prompt</u>. Move to next trial.
Teaching Procedures:	Deliver the cue, "Say ____ ____ (make a two-sound sequence)." Wait 5 seconds for a response. If student imitates the correct sound sequence, praise and provide reinforcer. If student does not imitate the correct sound sequence, repeat the cue, "Say ____ ____ (make a two-sound sequence)." Wait 5 seconds for a response. If student imitates the correct sound sequence, praise and provide reinforcer. If student does not imitate the correct sound sequence, repeat the cue, "Say ____ ____ (make a two-sound sequence)" and physically guide student to make the sound sequence (physically touch student's mouth). Score V for correct response that followed verbal prompt. Score M if model prompt was used. Score P if physical guidance was used.
Additional Targets:	

The BIG Book of ABA Programs

Comply With Request To Imitate A Variation In Sound
Compatible with ABLLS®-R Code E5

Student's Name:		Start Date:	
Objective:	When teacher says, "Say ____ (make sound variation)" student will imitate the sound as demonstrated. For example, "Say Ahhhhhhhhhhhhh" or "Say Ahh."		
Person Implementing Objective:			
Setting/Environment:			
Materials:			
Reinforcers:			
Baseline:	Deliver the cue, "Say ____ (make a sound variation)." Wait 5 seconds for a response. A correct response is scored (+) if student imitates the correct sound variation - <u>do not reinforce</u>. Move to next trial. An incorrect response is scored (-) if student does not make the sound variation - <u>do not prompt</u>. Move to next trial.		
Teaching Procedures:	Deliver the cue, "Say ____ (make a sound variation)." Wait 5 seconds for a response. If student imitates the correct sound variation, praise and provide reinforcer. If student does not make the sound variation, repeat the cue, "Say ____ (make a sound variation)." Wait 5 seconds for a response. If student imitates the correct sound variation, praise and provide reinforcer. If student does not make the sound variation, repeat the cue, "Say ____ (make a sound variation)" and physically guide student to make the sound variation (physically touch student's mouth). Score V for correct response that followed verbal prompt. Score M if model prompt was used. Score P if physical guidance was used.		
Additional Targets:			

Comply With Request To Imitate A Repeating Sound
Compatible with ABLLS®-R Code E6

Student's Name:	Start Date:
Objective:	When teacher says, "Say ____ ____ ____ (repeat a sound multiple times)" student will imitate the sound the number of times it was demonstrated.
Person Implementing Objective:	
Setting/Environment:	
Materials:	
Reinforcers:	
Baseline:	Deliver the cue, "Say ____ ____ ____ (repeat a sound multiple times)." Wait 5 seconds for a response. A correct response is scored (+) if student imitates the sound the same number of times it was demonstrated by the teacher - do not reinforce. Move to next trial. An incorrect response is scored (-) if student does not imitate the sound the same number of times it was demonstrated by the teacher - do not prompt. Move to next trial.
Teaching Procedures:	Deliver the cue, "Say ____ ____ ____ (repeat a sound multiple times)." Wait 5 seconds for a response. If student imitates the sound the same number of times it was demonstrated by the teacher, praise and provide reinforcer. If student does not imitate the sound the same number of times it was demonstrated by the teacher, repeat the cue, "Say ____ ____ ____ (repeat a sound multiple times)." Wait 5 seconds for a response. If student imitates the sound the same number of times it was demonstrated by the teacher, praise and provide reinforcer. If student does not imitate the sound the same number of times it was demonstrated by the teacher, repeat the cue, "Say ____ ____ ____ (repeat a sound multiple times)" and physically guide student to make the sound repetition (physically touch student's mouth). Score V for correct response that followed verbal prompt. Score M if model prompt was used. Score P if physical guidance was used.
Additional Targets:	

Comply With Request To Imitate Connected Sounds
Compatible with ABLLS®-R Code E7

Student's Name:	Start Date:
Objective:	When teacher says, "Say _____ (say two sounds connected without a break)" student will imitate the connected sounds. For example, "Say mmmmmmaaaaaaaaa."
Person Implementing Objective:	
Setting/Environment:	
Materials:	
Reinforcers:	
Baseline:	Deliver the cue, "Say _____ (say two sounds connected without a break)." Wait 5 seconds for a response. A correct response is scored (+) if student imitates the correct sounds in a connected manner- <u>do not reinforce</u>. Move to next trial. An incorrect response is scored (-) if student does not imitate the sounds in a connected manner - <u>do not prompt</u>. Move to next trial.
Teaching Procedures:	Deliver the cue, "Say _____ (say two sounds connected without a break)." Wait 5 seconds for a response. If student imitates the correct sounds in a connected manner, praise and provide reinforcer. If student does not imitate the sounds in a connected manner, repeat the cue, "Say _____ (say two sounds connected without a break)." Wait 5 seconds for a response. If student imitates the correct sounds in a connected manner, praise and provide reinforcer. If student does not imitate the sounds in a connected manner, repeat the cue, "Say _____ (say two sounds connected without a break)" and physically guide student to make the connected sounds (physically touch student's mouth). Score V for correct response that followed verbal prompt. Score M if model prompt was used. Score P if physical guidance was used.
Additional Targets:	

Comply With Request To Imitate Two-Letter Words
Compatible with ABLLS®-R Code E8

Student's Name:		Start Date:
Objective:	When teacher says, "Say ____ (say a two-letter word with one vowel and one consonant)" student will repeat the word.	
Person Implementing Objective:		
Setting/Environment:		
Materials:		
Reinforcers:		
Baseline:	Deliver the cue, "Say ____ (say two-letter word)." Wait 5 seconds for a response. A correct response is scored (+) if student imitates the word- <u>do not reinforce</u>. Move to next trial. An incorrect response is scored (-) if student does not imitate the word - <u>do not prompt</u>. Move to next trial.	
Teaching Procedures:	Deliver the cue, "Say ____ (say two-letter word)." Wait 5 seconds for a response. If student imitates the word, praise and provide reinforcer. If student does not imitate the word, repeat the cue, "Say ____ (say two-letter word)." Wait 5 seconds for a response. If student imitates the word, praise and provide reinforcer. If student does not imitate the word, repeat the cue, "Say ____ (say two-letter word)" and physically guide student to say the word (physically touch student's mouth). Score V for correct response that followed verbal prompt. Score M if model prompt was used. Score P if physical guidance was used.	
Additional Targets:		

The BIG Book of ABA Programs

Comply With Request To Imitate Two-Letter Words Repetitions
Compatible with ABLLS®-R Code E9

Student's Name:	Start Date:
Objective:	When teacher says, "Say ____ ____(repeat a two-letter word)" student will imitate the word repetition. For example, "Say do do."
Person Implementing Objective:	
Setting/Environment:	
Materials:	
Reinforcers:	
Baseline:	Deliver the cue, "Say ____ ____ (repeat a two-letter word)." Wait 5 seconds for a response. A correct response is scored (+) if student imitates the word repetition- <u>do not reinforce</u>. Move to next trial. An incorrect response is scored (-) if student does not imitate the word repetition- <u>do not prompt</u>. Move to next trial.
Teaching Procedures:	Deliver the cue, "Say ____ ____ (Say two-letter word)." Wait 5 seconds for a response. If student imitates the word repetition, praise and provide reinforcer. If student does not imitate the word repetition, repeat the cue, "Say ____ ____ (repeat a two-letter word)." Wait 5 seconds for a response. If student imitates the word repetition, praise and provide reinforcer. If student does not imitate the word repetition, repeat the cue, "Say ____ ____ (repeat a two-letter word)" and physically guide student to make the word repetition (physically touch student's mouth). Score V for correct response that followed verbal prompt. Score M if model prompt was used. Score P if physical guidance was used.
Additional Targets:	

The Autism Skill Acquisition Program™

Comply With Request to Imitate Three-Letter Words
Compatible with ABLLS®-R Code E9

Student's Name:	Start Date:
Objective:	When teacher says, "Say ____ ____(repeat a three-letter word)" student will imitate the word repetition. For example, "Say cow cow."
Person Implementing Objective:	
Setting/Environment:	
Materials:	
Reinforcers:	
Baseline:	Deliver the cue, "Say ____ ____ (repeat a three-letter word)." Wait 5 seconds for a response. A correct response is scored (+) if student imitates the word repetition- <u>do not reinforce</u>. Move to next trial. An incorrect response is scored (-) if student does not imitate the word repetition- <u>do not prompt</u>. Move to next trial.
Teaching Procedures:	Deliver the cue, "Say ____ ____ (Say three-letter word)." Wait 5 seconds for a response. If student imitates the word repetition, praise and provide reinforcer. If student does not imitate the word repetition, repeat the cue, "Say ____ ____ (repeat a three-letter word)." Wait 5 seconds for a response. If student imitates the word repetition, praise and provide reinforcer. If student does not imitate the word repetition, repeat the cue, "Say ____ ____ (repeat a three-letter word)" and physically guide student to make the word repetition (physically touch student's mouth). Score V for correct response that followed verbal prompt. Score M if model prompt was used. Score P if physical guidance was used.
Additional Targets:	

Comply With Request To Imitate Three-Letter Words
Compatible with ABLLS®-R Code E10

Student's Name:	Start Date:
Objective:	When teacher says, "Say ____ (say a three-letter word)" student will imitate the word. For example, "Say cow."
Person Implementing Objective:	
Setting/Environment:	
Materials:	
Reinforcers:	
Baseline:	Deliver the cue, "Say ____ (say a three-letter word)." Wait 5 seconds for a response. A correct response is scored (+) if student imitates the word - <u>do not reinforce</u>. Move to next trial. An incorrect response is scored (-) if student does not imitate the word - <u>do not prompt</u>. Move to next trial.
Teaching Procedures:	Deliver the cue, "Say ____ (say a three-letter word)." Wait 5 seconds for a response. If student imitates the word, praise and provide reinforcer. If student does not imitate the word, repeat the cue, "Say ____ (say a three-letter word)." Wait 5 seconds for a response. If student imitates the word, praise and provide reinforcer. If student does not imitate the word, repeat the cue, "Say ____ (say a three-letter word)" and physically guide student to say the word (physically touch student's mouth). Score V for correct response that followed verbal prompt. Score M if model prompt was used. Score P if physical guidance was used.
Additional Targets:	

Comply With Request To Imitate Words With Blended Consonants
Compatible with ABLLS®-R Code E11

Student's Name:	Start Date:
Objective:	When teacher says, "Say ____ (say a word containing a blended consonant sound)" student will imitate the word. For example, "Say blue" or "Say shoe."
Person Implementing Objective:	
Setting/Environment:	
Materials:	
Reinforcers:	
Baseline:	Deliver the cue, "Say ____ (say a word containing a blended consonant sound)." Wait 5 seconds for a response. A correct response is scored (+) if student imitates the word - <u>do not reinforce</u>. Move to next trial. An incorrect response is scored (-) if student does not imitate the word - <u>do not prompt</u>. Move to next trial.
Teaching Procedures:	Deliver the cue, "Say ____ (say a word containing a blended consonant sound)." Wait 5 seconds for a response. If student imitates the word, praise and provide reinforcer. If student does not imitate the word, repeat the cue, "Say ____ (say a word containing a blended consonant sound)." Wait 5 seconds for a response. If student imitates the word, praise and provide reinforcer. If student does not imitate the word, repeat the cue, "Say ____ (say a word containing a blended consonant sound)" and physically guide student to say word (physically touch student's mouth). Score V for correct response that followed verbal prompt. Score M if model prompt was used. Score P if physical guidance was used.
Additional Targets:	

Comply With Request To Imitate Words
Compatible with ABLLS®-R Code E12

Student's Name:		Start Date:	
Objective:	When teacher says, "Say ____ (say a word)" student will imitate the word.		

Person Implementing Objective:	
Setting/Environment:	
Materials:	
Reinforcers:	
Baseline:	Deliver the cue, "Say ____ (say a word)." Wait 5 seconds for a response. A correct response is scored (+) if student imitates the word - <u>do not reinforce</u>. Move to next trial. An incorrect response is scored (-) if student does not imitate the word - <u>do not prompt</u>. Move to next trial.
Teaching Procedures:	Deliver the cue, "Say ____ (Say a word)." Wait 5 seconds for a response. If student imitates the word, praise and provide reinforcer. If student does not imitate the word, repeat the cue, "Say ____ (say a word)." Wait 5 seconds for a response. If student imitates the word, praise and provide reinforcer. If student does not imitate the word, repeat the cue, "Say ____ (say a word)" and physically guide student to say word (physically touch student's mouth). Score V for correct response that followed verbal prompt. Score M if model prompt was used. Score P if physical guidance was used.
Additional Targets:	

Comply With Request To Imitate A Phrase
Compatible with ABLLS®-R Code E13

Student's Name:		Start Date:
Objective:	When teacher says, "Say ____ (say a phrase)" student will imitate the phrase.	

Person Implementing Objective:	
Setting/Environment:	
Materials:	
Reinforcers:	
Baseline:	Deliver the cue, "Say ____ (say a phrase)." Wait 5 seconds for a response. A correct response is scored (+) if student imitates the phrase - <u>do not reinforce</u>. Move to next trial. An incorrect response is scored (-) if student does not imitate the phrase - <u>do not prompt</u>. Move to next trial.
Teaching Procedures:	Deliver the cue, "Say ____ (Say a phrase)." Wait 5 seconds for a response. If student imitates the phrase, praise and provide reinforcer. If student does not imitate the phrase, repeat the cue, "Say ____ (Say a phrase)." Wait 5 seconds for a response. If student imitates the phrase, praise and provide reinforcer. If student does not imitate the phrase, repeat the cue, "Say ____ (Say a phrase)" and physically guide student to say phrase (physically touch student's mouth). Score V for correct response that followed verbal prompt. Score M if model prompt was used. Score P if physical guidance was used.
Additional Targets:	

The BIG Book of ABA Programs

Comply With Request To Imitate A Series Of Numbers
Compatible with ABLLS®-R Code E14

Student's Name:	Start Date:
Objective:	When teacher says, "Say ____ ____ ____ ____ (say a series of numbers)" student will imitate the series of numbers.
Person Implementing Objective:	
Setting/Environment:	
Materials:	
Reinforcers:	
Baseline:	Deliver the cue, "Say ____ ____ ____ ____ (say a series of numbers)." Wait 5 seconds for a response. A correct response is scored (+) if student imitates the number series - <u>do not reinforce</u>. Move to next trial. An incorrect response is scored (-) if student does not imitate the number series - <u>do not prompt</u>. Move to next trial.
Teaching Procedures:	Deliver the cue, "Say ____ ____ ____ ____ (say a series of numbers)." Wait 5 seconds for a response. If student imitates the number series, praise and provide reinforcer. If student does not imitate the number series, repeat the cue, "Say ____ ____ ____ ____ (say a series of numbers)." Wait 5 seconds for a response. If student imitates the number series, praise and provide reinforcer. If student does not imitate the number series, repeat the cue, "Say ____ ____ ____ ____ (say a series of numbers)" and physically guide student to say the number series (physically touch student's mouth). Score V for correct response that followed verbal prompt. Score M if model prompt was used. Score P if physical guidance was used.
Additional Targets:	

Comply With Request To Imitate Words Delivered In Fast Or Slow Cadence
Compatible with ABLLS®-R Code E15

Student's Name:		Start Date:	
Objective:	When teacher says, "Say ____ (say word in a fast or slow cadence)" student will repeat the word in the demonstrated cadence. For example, "Say Turtle" or "Say Tuuuuuurrrrrrrrrttttlllle."		
Person Implementing Objective:			
Setting/Environment:			
Materials:			
Reinforcers:			
Baseline:	Deliver the cue, "Say ____ (say a word in fast or slow cadence)." Wait 5 seconds for a response. A correct response is scored (+) if student imitates the word in demonstrated cadence- <u>do not reinforce</u>. Move to next trial. An incorrect response is scored (-) if student does not imitate the word in the demonstrated cadence - <u>do not prompt</u>. Move to next trial.		
Teaching Procedures:	Deliver the cue, "Say ____ (say a word in fast or slow cadence)." Wait 5 seconds for a response. If student imitates the word in demonstrated cadence, praise and provide reinforcer. If student does not imitate the word in demonstrated cadence, repeat the cue, "Say ____ (say word in a fast or slow cadence)." Wait 5 seconds for a response. If student imitates the word in demonstrated cadence, praise and provide reinforcer. If student does not imitate the word in demonstrated cadence, repeat the cue, "Say ____ (say word in a fast or slow cadence)" and physically guide student to say the word in correct cadence (physically touch student's mouth). Score V for correct response that followed verbal prompt. Score M if model prompt was used. Score P if physical guidance was used.		
Additional Targets:			

Comply With Request To Imitate Words Delivered With Variation In Volume
Compatible with ABLLS®-R Code E16

Student's Name:	Start Date:
Objective:	When teacher says, "Say ____ (say a word with high or low volume)" student will repeat the word with the demonstrated volume.
Person Implementing Objective:	
Setting/Environment:	
Materials:	
Reinforcers:	
Baseline:	Deliver the cue, "Say ____ (say a word with high or low volume)." Wait 5 seconds for a response. A correct response is scored (+) if student imitates the word in demonstrated volume- <u>do not reinforce</u>. Move to next trial. An incorrect response is scored (-) if student does not imitate the word in the demonstrated volume - <u>do not prompt</u>. Move to next trial.
Teaching Procedures:	Deliver the cue, "Say ____ (say a word with high or low volume)." Wait 5 seconds for a response. If student imitates the word with demonstrated volume, praise and provide reinforcer. If student does not imitate the word with demonstrated volume, repeat the cue, "Say ____ (Say a word with high or low volume)." Wait 5 seconds for a response. If student imitates the word with demonstrated volume, praise and provide reinforcer. If student does not imitate the word with demonstrated volume, repeat the cue, "Say ____ (Say a word with high or low volume)" and physically guide student to say word in correct volume (physically touch student's mouth). Score V for correct response that followed verbal prompt. Score M if model prompt was used. Score P if physical guidance was used.
Additional Targets:	

Comply With Request To Imitate Words Delivered With Variation In Pitch
Compatible with ABLLS®-R Code E17

Student's Name:		Start Date:
Objective:	When teacher says, "Say ____ (say word with high or low pitch)" student will repeat the word in the demonstrated pitch. For example, "Say puppy" in very deep voice or "Say puppy" in squeaky voice.	
Person Implementing Objective:		
Setting/Environment:		
Materials:		
Reinforcers:		
Baseline:	Deliver the cue, "Say ____ (say a word with high or low pitch)." Wait 5 seconds for a response. A correct response is scored (+) if student imitates the word in demonstrated pitch- do not reinforce. Move to next trial. An incorrect response is scored (-) if student does not imitate the word in the demonstrated pitch - do not prompt. Move to next trial.	
Teaching Procedures:	Deliver the cue, "Say ____ (say a word with high or low pitch)." Wait 5 seconds for a response. If student imitates the word in demonstrated pitch, praise and provide reinforcer. If student does not imitate the word in demonstrated pitch, repeat the cue, "Say ____ (say word with high or low pitch)." Wait 5 seconds for a response. If student imitates the word in demonstrated pitch, praise and provide reinforcer. If student does not imitate the word in demonstrated pitch, repeat the cue, "Say ____ (say word with high or low pitch)" and physically guide student to say word in correct pitch (physically touch student's mouth). Score V for correct response that followed verbal prompt. Score M if model prompt was used. Score P if physical guidance was used.	
Additional Targets:		

Comply With Request To Tell Someone A Short Phrase
Compatible with ABLLS®-R Code E18

Student's Name:	Start Date:
Objective:	When teacher says, "Tell ____ (name of person) ____ (say phrase)" student will repeat the phrase to the named person.
Person Implementing Objective:	
Setting/Environment:	
Materials:	
Reinforcers:	
Baseline:	Say, "Tell ____ (name of person) ____ (say phrase)." Wait 5 seconds for a response. A correct response is scored (+) if student states the correct phrase to the correct person- <u>do not reinforce</u>. Move to next trial. An incorrect response is scored (-) if student does not repeat correct phrase to the correct person- <u>do not prompt</u>. Move to next trial.
Teaching Procedures:	Say, "Tell ____ (name of person) ____ (say phrase)." Wait 5 seconds for a response. If student states the correct phrase to the correct person, praise and provide reinforcer. If student does not repeat correct phrase to the correct person, repeat the cue, "Tell ____ (name of person) ____ (say phrase)" and gesture towards named person. Wait 5 seconds for a response. If student states the correct phrase to the correct person, praise and provide reinforcer. If student does not repeat correct phrase to the correct person, repeat the cue, "Tell ____ (name of person) ____ (say phrase)" and physically guide student to named person and touch student's mouth. Score V for correct response that followed verbal prompt. Score M if model prompt was used. Score P if physical guidance was used.
Additional Targets:	

CHAPTER 7

ABA Programs Compatible with ABLLS®-R Domain F

"Requests"

Manding By Pointing Or Gesturing
Compatible with ABLLS®-R Code F1

Student's Name:	Start Date:	
Objective:	When teacher holds a preferred item out of reach, student will gesture or point to item.	
Person Implementing Objective:		
Setting/Environment:		
Materials:		
Reinforcers:		
Baseline:	Hold a preferred item out of reach. Wait 5 seconds for a response. A correct response is scored (+) if student gestures or points to the item- <u>do not reinforce</u>. Move to next trial. An incorrect response is scored (-) if student does not gesture or point to the item- <u>do not prompt</u>. Move to next trial.	
Teaching Procedures:	Hold a preferred item out of reach. Wait 5 seconds for a response. If student gestures or points to the item, praise and allow access to the item. If student does not gesture or point to the item, show the item to student and again hold it out of reach. If student gestures or points to the item, praise and allow access to the item. If student does not gesture or point to the item, show the item again, hold out of reach, and physically guide student to point. Score V for correct response that followed initial prompt. Score M if model prompt was used. Score P if physical guidance was used.	
Additional Targets:		

Manding By Words Or Signs Following Imitative Prompt
Compatible with ABLLS®-R Code F2

Student's Name:	Start Date:
Objective:	When teacher has a preferred item and says, "What do you want? (state name of item)" student will state the name of the item.
Person Implementing Objective:	
Setting/Environment:	
Materials:	
Reinforcers:	
Baseline:	Hold a preferred item out of reach and say, "What do you want (state name of item)?" Wait 5 seconds for a response. A correct response is scored (+) if student says the name of the item- <u>do not reinforce</u>. Move to next trial. An incorrect response is scored (-) if student does not say the name of the item- <u>do not prompt</u>. Move to next trial.
Teaching Procedures:	Hold a preferred item out of reach and say, "What do you want (state name of item)?" Wait 5 seconds for a response. If student says the name of the item, praise and allow access to the item. If student does not say the name of the item, show the item to student and again hold it out of reach as you say, "What do you want (state name of item)?" Wait 5 seconds for a response. If student says the name of the item, praise and allow access to the item. If student does not say the name of the item, show the item again, hold out of reach, say, "What do you want (state name of item)?" and physically guide student to say name of item (physically touch student's mouth). Score V for correct response that followed verbal prompt. Score M if model prompt was used. Score P if physical guidance was used.
Additional Targets:	

Manding By Words Or Signs
Compatible with ABLLS®-R Code F3

Student's Name:		Start Date:
Objective:	When teacher holds a preferred item out of reach and says, "What do you want?" student will state the name of the item.	
Person Implementing Objective:		
Setting/Environment:		
Materials:		
Reinforcers:		
Baseline:	Hold a preferred item out of reach and say, "What do you want?" Wait 5 seconds for a response. A correct response is scored (+) if student says the name of item- <u>do not reinforce</u>. Move to next trial. An incorrect response is scored (-) if student does not say the name of item- <u>do not prompt</u>. Move to next trial.	
Teaching Procedures:	Hold a preferred item out of reach and say, "What do you want?" Wait 5 seconds for a response. If student says the name of the item, praise and allow access to the item. If student does not say the name of the item, show the item to student and again hold it out of reach as you say, "What do you want?" Wait 5 seconds for a response. If student says the name of the item, praise and allow access to the item. If student does not say the name of the item, show the item again, hold out of reach, say, "What do you want?" and physically guide student to say the name of item (physically touch student's mouth). Score V for correct response that followed verbal prompt. Score M if model prompt was used. Score P if physical guidance was used.	
Additional Targets:		

The BIG Book of ABA Programs

Manding With No Items Present
Compatible with ABLLS®-R Code F4

Student's Name:		Start Date:	
Objective:	When no preferred items are present and teacher says, "What do you want?" student will state the name of an item.		
Person Implementing Objective:			
Setting/Environment:			
Materials:			
Reinforcers:			
Baseline:	With no preferred items present, say, "What do you want?" Wait 5 seconds for a response. A correct response is scored (+) if student says the name of an item- <u>do not reinforce</u>. Move to next trial. An incorrect response is scored (-) if student does not say the name of an item- <u>do not prompt</u>. Move to next trial.		
Teaching Procedures:	With no preferred items present, say, "What do you want?" Wait 5 seconds for a response. If student says the name of an item, praise and allow access to the item. If student does not say the name of an item, state some choices of different items (For example, "Do you want the ball or the crackers or the blocks?") and say, "What do you want?" Wait 5 seconds for a response. If student says the name of an item, praise and allow access to the item. If student does not say the name of an item, say, "What do you want?" and physically guide student to say the name of an item (physically touch student's mouth). Score V for correct response that followed verbal prompt. Score M if model prompt was used. Score P if physical guidance was used.		
Additional Targets:			

www.stimuluspublications.com   165   The Autism Skill Acquisition Program™

Manding With Eye Contact
Compatible with ABLLS®-R Code F7

Student's Name:	Start Date:

Objective:	When a preferred item is present but out of reach and the teacher says, "What do you want?" student will state the name of the item while making eye contact with the teacher.
Person Implementing Objective:	
Setting/Environment:	
Materials:	
Reinforcers:	
Baseline:	When a preferred item is present but out of reach, say, "What do you want?" Wait 5 seconds for a response. A correct response is scored (+) if student says the name of the item while making eye contact- <u>do not reinforce</u>. Move to next trial. An incorrect response is scored (-) if student does not say the name of the item while making eye contact- <u>do not prompt</u>. Move to next trial.
Teaching Procedures:	When a preferred item is present but out of reach, say, "What do you want?" Wait 5 seconds for a response. If student says the name of the item while making eye contact, praise and allow access to the item. If student does not say the name of the item while making eye contact, show student the item and say, "What do you want?" Wait 5 seconds for a response. If student says the name of the item while making eye contact, praise and allow access to the item. If student does not say the name of the item while making eye contact, say, "What do you want?" and physically guide student's head so that it is facing yours as you say the name of the item while touching the student's mouth. Score V for correct response that followed verbal prompt. Score M if model prompt was used. Score P if physical guidance was used.
Additional Targets:	

Manding For Others To Do Something
Compatible with ABLLS®-R Code F8

Student's Name:		Start Date:	
Objective:		When student requires the teacher to perform an action, student will mand for the teacher to perform the action. For example, teacher and student are seated on the floor. Teacher says, "OK, let's go play over there" but remains seated. A correct response would be scored if student mands for teacher to stand up or come to new location.	

Person Implementing Objective:	
Setting/Environment:	
Materials:	
Reinforcers:	
Baseline:	Create a situation in which the student needs you to perform an action. Wait 5 seconds for a response. A correct response is scored (+) if student mands for you to perform an action - <u>do not reinforce</u>. Move to next trial. An incorrect response is scored (-) if student does not mand for you to perform an action- <u>do not prompt</u>. Move to next trial.
Teaching Procedures:	Create a situation in which the student needs you to perform an action. Wait 5 seconds for a response. If student mands for you to perform an action, praise and deliver the reinforcer. If student does not mand for you to perform the action, tell student the exact words to say to request the action. Wait 5 seconds for a response. If student mands for you to perform action, praise and provide reinforcer. If student does not mand for you to perform action, physically guide student to mand for you to perform an action (say the mand as you physically touch student's mouth). Score V for correct response that followed verbal prompt. Score M if model prompt was used. Score P if physical guidance was used.
Additional Targets:	

Manding For Needed Item
Compatible with ABLLS®-R Code F9

Student's Name:	Start Date:	
Objective:	When student is asked to comply with a task demand but is not given all the materials to complete the task, student will mand for the needed materials. For example, tell student to "Write his/her name" but do not provide a pencil.	
Person Implementing Objective:		
Setting/Environment:		
Materials:		
Reinforcers:		
Baseline:	Tell student to complete a task but do not provide necessary materials. Wait 5 seconds for a response. A correct response is scored (+) if student mands for the needed materials- <u>do not reinforce</u>. Move to next trial. An incorrect response is scored (-) if student does not mand for the needed materials- <u>do not prompt</u>. Move to next trial.	
Teaching Procedures:	Tell student to complete a task but do not provide necessary materials. Wait 5 seconds for a response. If student mands for the needed materials, praise and provide reinforcer. If student does not mand for the needed materials, say, "If you need something, let me know." Wait 5 seconds for a response. If student mands for the needed materials, praise and provide reinforcer. If student does not mand for the needed materials, physically guide student to mand for materials (say the mand as you physically touch student's mouth). Score V for correct response that followed verbal prompt. Score M if model prompt was used. Score P if physical guidance was used.	
Additional Targets:		

Yes Or No
Compatible with ABLLS®-R Code F10

Student's Name:		Start Date:
Objective:	When student is asked if he/she wants something, student will reply by nodding head "yes" or shaking head "no."	
Person Implementing Objective:		
Setting/Environment:		
Materials:		
Reinforcers:		
Baseline:	For YES response: Present reinforcer to student and say, "Do you want this?" Wait 5 seconds for a response. A correct response is scored (+) if student nods head up and down- <u>do not reinforce</u>. Move to next trial. An incorrect response is scored (-) if student does not nod head up and down- <u>do not prompt</u>. Move to next trial. For NO response: Present an object student does not like and say, "Do you want this?" Wait 5 seconds for a response. A correct response is scored (+) if student shakes head back and forth- <u>do not reinforce</u>. Move to next trial. An incorrect response is scored (-) if student does not shake head back and forth- <u>do not prompt</u>. Move to next trial.	
Teaching Procedures:	Present item to student and say, "Do you want this?" Wait 5 seconds for a response. If student makes correct head movement (nod for YES or shake for NO), praise and provide reinforcer. If student does not make the correct head movement, say, "Do you want this?" and model the correct head movement for the student. Wait 5 seconds for a response. If the student makes the correct head movement, praise and provide reinforcer. If student does not make correct head movement, say, "Do you want this?" and physically guide student's head to make the correct movement. Score V for correct response that followed verbal prompt. Score M if the correct response followed the model prompt. Score P if physical guidance was used.	
Additional Targets:		

Manding In Complete Sentence Format
Compatible with ABLLS®-R Code F11

Student's Name:	Start Date:
Objective:	When a preferred item is restricted and teacher says, "If you want the ____ (name item) back you have to ask for it" student will mand for item by using a complete sentence.
Person Implementing Objective:	
Setting/Environment:	
Materials:	
Reinforcers:	
Baseline:	Provide student with a preferred item. Restrict the item and say, "If you want the item back, you need to ask for it." Wait 5 seconds for a response. A correct response is scored (+) if student mands for item using a complete sentence- <u>do not reinforce</u>. Move to next trial. An incorrect response is scored (-) if student does not mand for item using a complete sentence- <u>do not prompt</u>. Move to next trial.
Teaching Procedures:	Provide student with a preferred item. Restrict the item and say, "If you want the item back, you need to ask for it." Wait 5 seconds for a response. If student mands for item using a complete sentence, praise and provide the restricted item. If student does not mand for item in complete sentence, say, "If you want the item back, you need to ask for it" and model the correct mand (For, example, "I want _____ please"). Wait 5 seconds for a response. If the student mands in a complete sentence, praise and provide the restricted item. If student does not mand for item in complete sentence, say, "If you want the item back, you need to ask for it" and physically guide student to mand for item (say the mand as you physically touch student's mouth). Score V for correct response that followed verbal prompt. Score M if the correct response followed the model prompt. Score P if physical guidance was used.
Additional Targets:	

Manding For Assistance
Compatible with ABLLS®-R Code F12

Student's Name:		Start Date:	
Objective:	When student is asked to comply with a task demand but something about the task requires assistance, student will mand for assistance. For example, if you say, "Open the jar" when the lid of the jar is on too tight for student to open. A correct response could be, "I need help."		
Person Implementing Objective:			
Setting/Environment:			
Materials:			
Reinforcers:			
Baseline:	Tell student to complete a task in which something about the task requires assistance. Wait 5 seconds for a response. A correct response is scored (+) if student mands for assistance- <u>do not reinforce</u>. Move to next trial. An incorrect response is scored (-) if student does not mand for assistance- <u>do not prompt</u>. Move to next trial.		
Teaching Procedures:	Tell student to complete a task in which something about the task requires assistance. Wait 5 seconds for a response. If student mands for assistance, praise, provide the assistance and reinforcer. If student does not mand for assistance, say, "If you need some help, let me know." Wait 5 seconds for a response. If student mands for assistance, praise, provide the assistance and reinforcer. If student does not mand for assistance, physically guide student to mand for assistance (say the mand as you physically touch student's mouth). V for correct response that followed verbal prompt. Score M if the correct response followed the model prompt. Score P if physical guidance was used.		
Additional Targets:			

Manding For Attention
Compatible with ABLLS®-R Code F14

Student's Name:	Start Date:

Objective:	When teacher says, "Let me know if you need something" and then stops delivering attention to the student, student will mand for attention.
Person Implementing Objective:	
Setting/Environment:	
Materials:	
Reinforcers:	
Baseline:	When student has nothing to engage with, say, "I have some work to do, let me know if you need something." Wait 2 minutes. A correct response is scored (+) if student mands for teacher attention- <u>do not reinforce</u>. Move to next trial. An incorrect response is scored (-) if student does not mand for teacher attention- <u>do not prompt</u>. Move to next trial.
Teaching Procedures:	When student has nothing to engage with, say, "I have some work to do, let me know if you need something." Wait 2 minutes. If student mands for attention, praise and provide attention. If student does not mand for attention, say, "If you want something, you need to say (for example), 'Excuse me, can you talk to me please.'" Wait 5 seconds for a response. If student mands for attention, praise and provide attention. If student does not mand for attention, say, "If you want something, you need to say (for example), 'Excuse me, can you talk to me please'" as you physically guide by touching student's mouth. Score V for correct response that followed verbal prompt. Score M if the correct response followed the model prompt. Score P if physical guidance was used.
Additional Targets:	

Manding To Cease Nonpreferred Activity/Situation
Compatible with ABLLS®-R Code F15

Student's Name:		Start Date:	
Objective:	When the student is presented with an aversive or nonpreferred activity (For example, a loud radio or white noise from the television) student will mand to end the activity.		
Person Implementing Objective:			
Setting/Environment:			
Materials:			
Reinforcers:			
Baseline:	Present the student with an aversive or nonpreferred activity/situation. Wait 5 seconds for a response. A correct response is scored (+) if student mands to end the activity- do not reinforce. Move to next trial. An incorrect response is scored (-) if student does not mand to end the activity- do not prompt. Move to next trial.		
Teaching Procedures:	Present the student with an aversive or nonpreferred activity/situation. Wait 5 seconds for a response. If student mands to end the activity/situation, praise and end the activity. If student does not mand to end the activity/situation, say, "If you want this to stop you need to say, (for example) 'Turn this off please.'" Wait 5 seconds for a response. If student mands to end the activity/situation, praise and end the activity/situation. If student does not mand to end the activity/situation, say, "If you want this to stop you need to say, (for example) 'Turn this off please'" as you physically guide by touching student's mouth. Score V for correct response that followed verbal prompt. Score M if the correct response followed the model prompt. Score P if physical guidance was used.		
Additional Targets:			

The BIG Book of ABA Programs

Using Adjectives When Manding
Compatible with ABLLS®-R Code F16

Student's Name:		Start Date:
Objective:		When the teacher restricts items of different dimensions, the student will request access to an item by using appropriate adjectives.
Person Implementing Objective:		
Setting/Environment:		
Materials:		
Reinforcers:		
Baseline:		Allow access to, and then restrict, multiple similar items. Wait 5 seconds for a response. A correct response is scored (+) if student mands for a restricted item by using appropriate adjectives- <u>do not reinforce</u>. Move to next trial. An incorrect response is scored (-) if student does not mand for a restricted item using appropriate adjectives- <u>do not prompt</u>. Move to next trial.
Teaching Procedures:		Allow access to, and then restrict, multiple similar items. Wait 5 seconds for a response. If student mands for a restricted item using appropriate adjectives, praise and provide access to requested item. If student does not mand with appropriate adjectives, say, "Tell me which one you want." Wait 5 seconds for a response. If student mands for a restricted item using an appropriate adjective, praise and deliver the item. If student does not mand with appropriate adjectives, physically guide by touching student's mouth as you say, "I want the ____ (name item with appropriate adjectives)." Score V for correct response that followed verbal prompt. Score M if the correct response followed the model prompt. Score P if physical guidance was used.
Additional Targets:		

www.stimuluspublications.com · The Autism Skill Acquisition Program™

Using Prepositions When Manding
Compatible with ABLLS®-R Code F17

Student's Name:	Start Date:

Objective:	When the teacher restricts two identical items and places them in different locations, student will request access to an item by using appropriate prepositions.
Person Implementing Objective:	
Setting/Environment:	
Materials:	
Reinforcers:	
Baseline:	Allow access to, and then restrict, two identical items and place them in different locations in front of student. Wait 5 seconds for a response. A correct response is scored (+) if student mands for a restricted item by using appropriate preposition- <u>do not reinforce</u>. Move to next trial. An incorrect response is scored (-) if student does not mand for a restricted item using appropriate preposition- <u>do not prompt</u>. Move to next trial.
Teaching Procedures:	Allow access to, and then restrict, two identical items and place them in different locations in front of student. Wait 5 seconds for a response. If student mands for a restricted item using appropriate preposition, praise and provide access to requested item. If student does not mand using appropriate preposition, say, "Tell me which one you want." If the student mands for a restricted item using an appropriate preposition, praise and deliver the item. If student does not mand for item using appropriate preposition, physically guide student by saying, "I want ____ (name item with appropriate preposition)" as you touch student's mouth. Score V for correct response that followed verbal prompt. Score M if the correct response followed the model prompt. Score P if physical guidance was used.
Additional Targets:	

Manding For Future Objects Or Activities
Compatible with ABLLS®-R Code F18

Student's Name:	Start Date:
Objective:	When the teacher asks student what student wants in the future, student will mand for future object or activity. For example, in the morning you could ask, "What do you want for lunch?" "I want pizza."
Person Implementing Objective:	
Setting/Environment:	
Materials:	
Reinforcers:	
Baseline:	Ask student what he/she wants in the future. Wait 5 seconds for a response. A correct response is scored (+) if student mands for future object or activity- <u>do not reinforce</u>. Move to next trial. An incorrect response is scored (-) if student does not mand for information future object or activity- <u>do not prompt</u>. Move to next trial.
Teaching Procedures:	Ask student what he/she wants in the future. Wait 5 seconds for a response. If student mands for future object or activity, praise and provide access to object or activity later when appropriate. If student does not mand for future object or activity, give the student choices about future objects or activities and again ask student what he/she wants in the future. Wait 5 seconds for a response. If student mands for future object or activity, praise and provide access to object or activity later when appropriate. If student does not mand for future object or activity, physically guide student to mand for future activity (physically touch student's mouth). Score V for correct response that followed verbal prompt. Score M if the correct response followed the model prompt. Score P if physical guidance was used.
Additional Targets:	

Using "What" When Manding
Compatible with ABLLS®-R Code F19

Student's Name:		Start Date:	
Objective:	When teacher shows student an unknown item, student will mand for information about the item using the phrase "What was that?"		
Person Implementing Objective:			
Setting/Environment:			
Materials:			
Reinforcers:			
Baseline:	Seat student next to you and tell student you are going to show something really interesting. Very briefly flash an unknown item in front of student and then remove it very quickly. Wait 5 seconds for a response. A correct response is scored (+) if student mands for information by using the phrase, "What was that?"- do not reinforce. Move to next trial. An incorrect response is scored (-) if student does not mand for information by using the phrase, "What was that?"- do not prompt. Move to next trial.		
Teaching Procedures:	Seat student next to you and tell student you are going to show something really interesting. Very briefly flash an unknown item in front of student and then remove it very quickly. Wait 5 seconds for a response. If student mands for information using the phrase, "What was that?" praise and provide access to the item. If student does not mand for information using the phrase, "What was that?" say, "If you want to know what that was, you have to say, 'What was that?'" Wait 5 seconds for a response. If the student mands for information by using the phrase, "What was that?" praise and deliver the item. If student does not mand for information using the phrase, "What was that?" physically guide student to say, "What was that?" (physically touch student's mouth). Score V for correct response that followed verbal prompt. Score M if the correct response followed the model prompt. Score P if physical guidance was used.		
Additional Targets:			

The BIG Book of ABA Programs

Using "Where" When Manding
Compatible with ABLLS®-R Code F20

Student's Name:		Start Date:	
Objective:	When teacher hides a preferred item and says, "Get the ____ (name hidden item)" student will mand for information using the phrase, "Where is it?"		
Person Implementing Objective:			
Setting/Environment:			
Materials:			
Reinforcers:			
Baseline:	Hide a preferred item. Say, "Get the ____ (name hidden item)." Wait 5 seconds for a response. A correct response is scored (+) if student mands for information by using the phrase, "Where is it?"- <u>do not reinforce</u>. Move to next trial. An incorrect response is scored (-) if student does not mand for information by using the phrase, "Where is it?"- <u>do not prompt</u>. Move to next trial.		
Teaching Procedures:	Hide a preferred item. Say, "Get the ____ (name hidden item)." Wait 5 seconds for a response. If student mands for information using the phrase, "Where is it?" praise and tell student the location of the item. If student does not mand for information using the phrase, "Where is it?" say, "If you want to know where the item is, you have to say, 'Where is it?'" Wait 5 seconds for a response. If the student mands for information by using the phrase, "Where is it?" praise and reveal the location of the item. If student does not mand for information using the phrase, "Where is it?" physically guide student to say, "Where is it?" (physically touch student's mouth). Score V for correct response that followed verbal prompt. Score M if the correct response followed the model prompt. Score P if physical guidance was used.		
Additional Targets:			

Using "Whose" When Manding
Compatible with ABLLS®-R Code F21

Student's Name:	Start Date:
Objective:	When teacher gives student an item and says, "Find out who this belongs to" student will mand for information using the phrase "Whose is this?"
Person Implementing Objective:	
Setting/Environment:	
Materials:	
Reinforcers:	
Baseline:	Give student an item that belongs to someone else and say, "Find out who this belongs to." Wait 5 seconds for a response. A correct response is scored (+) if student mands for information by using the phrase, "Whose is this?"- <u>do not reinforce</u>. Move to next trial. An incorrect response is scored (-) if student does not mand for information by using the phrase, "Whose is this?"- <u>do not prompt</u>. Move to next trial.
Teaching Procedures:	Give student an item that belongs to someone else and say, "Find out who this belongs to." Wait 5 seconds for a response. If student mands for information using the phrase, "Whose is this?" praise and provide reinforcer. If student does not mand for information using the phrase, "Whose is this?" say, "If you want to find out who this belongs to say, 'Whose is this?'" Wait 5 seconds for a response. If the student mands for information by using the phrase, "Whose is this?" praise and provide reinforcer. If student does not mand for information using the phrase, "Whose is this?" physically guide student to mand using the phrase, "Whose is this?" (physically touch student's mouth). Score V for correct response that followed verbal prompt. Score M if the correct response followed the model prompt. Score P if physical guidance was used.
Additional Targets:	

Using Adverbs When Manding
Compatible with ABLLS®-R Code F22

Student's Name:	Start Date:	
Objective:	When student is in situation that requires change, he/she will mand using adverbs appropriate for the situation. For example, when the student is on a swing, teacher pushes student very slowly. Student should mand to be pushed *faster*. If teacher asks if the student wants to be picked up, the teacher only picks him/her up slightly off the ground. Student should mand to be picked up *higher*.	
Person Implementing Objective:		
Setting/Environment:		
Materials:		
Reinforcers:		
Baseline:	Create a situation in which the student requires change. Wait 5 seconds for a response. For whichever situation is created, a correct response is scored (+) if student mands using an appropriate adverb- <u>do not reinforce</u>. Move to next trial. An incorrect response is scored (-) if student does not mand using an appropriate adverb- <u>do not prompt</u>. Move to next trial.	
Teaching Procedures:	Create a situation in which the student requires change. Wait 5 seconds for a response. If student mands using appropriate adverb, praise and comply with mand. If student does not mand using appropriate adverb, say, "If you want me to do something differently, you need to ask." Wait 5 seconds for a response. If the student mands using appropriate adverb, deliver praise and comply with mand. If student does not mand using appropriate adverb, physically guide student to mand using appropriate adverb (physically touch student's mouth). Score V for correct response that followed verbal prompt. Score M if the correct response followed the model prompt. Score P if physical guidance was used.	
Additional Targets:		

Using Pronouns When Manding
Compatible with ABLLS®-R Code F23

Student's Name:		Start Date:	
Objective:		When someone other than student has a preferred item, student will request item by using pronoun appropriate for person with preferred item.	
Person Implementing Objective:			
Setting/Environment:			
Materials:			
Reinforcers:			
Baseline:		Give yourself, student, and others different items. Ensure someone other than student has highly preferred item and student has least preferred item. Say, "Whose item do you want?" Wait 5 seconds for a response. A correct response is scored (+) if student mands using appropriate pronoun- <u>do not reinforce</u>. Move to next trial. An incorrect response is scored (-) if student does not mand using appropriate pronoun- <u>do not prompt</u>. Move to next trial.	
Teaching Procedures:		Give yourself, student, and others different items. Ensure someone other than student has highly preferred item and student has least preferred item. Say, "Whose item do you want?" Wait 5 seconds for a response. If student mands using appropriate pronoun, praise and comply with mand. If student does not mand using appropriate pronoun, say, "If you want ___ (use pronoun) item, you need to ask." If student mands using appropriate pronoun, praise and comply with mand. If student does not mand using appropriate pronoun, physically guide student to mand using appropriate pronoun (physically touch student's mouth). Score V for correct response that followed verbal prompt. Score M if the correct response followed the model prompt. Score P if physical guidance was used.	
Additional Targets:			

The BIG Book of ABA Programs

Using "Which" When Manding
Compatible with ABLLS®-R Code F24

Student's Name:		Start Date:
Objective:	When teacher places several identical items in front of student and says, "Hand me the ____ (name item)" student will mand for information by using "Which one?"	
Person Implementing Objective:		
Setting/Environment:		
Materials:		
Reinforcers:		
Baseline:	Place several identical items in front of student. Say, "Hand me the ____ (name item)." Wait 5 seconds for a response. A correct response is scored (+) if student mands for information using "Which one?"- <u>do not reinforce</u>. Move to next trial. An incorrect response is scored (-) if student does not mand using "Which one?"- <u>do not prompt</u>. Move to next trial.	
Teaching Procedures:	Place several identical items in front of the student. Say, "Hand me the ____ (name item)." Wait 5 seconds for a response. If student mands using "Which one?" praise and comply with mand. If student does not mand using "Which one?" or hands you one of the items, say, "If there are more than one that are the same, you need to ask 'Which one?'" If student mands using "Which one?" deliver praise and comply with mand. If student does not mand using "Which one?" physically guide student to mand using, "Which one?" (physically touch student's mouth). Score V for correct response that followed verbal prompt. Score M if the correct response followed the model prompt. Score P if physical guidance was used.	
Additional Targets:		

The BIG Book of ABA Programs

Using "When" When Manding
Compatible with ABLLS®-R Code F25

Student's Name:		Start Date:
Objective:		When student requires clarification related to time, student will mand for assistance using "when?" For example, "We're going to watch a movie!" "When?"
Person Implementing Objective:		
Setting/Environment:		
Materials:		
Reinforcers:		
Baseline:		Tell student in a very excited voice that student is going to do something highly preferred. Wait 5 seconds for a response. A correct response is scored (+) if student mands for information using "When?" - <u>do not reinforce</u>. Move to next trial. An incorrect response is scored (-) if student does not mand using "When?"- <u>do not prompt</u>. Move to next trial.
Teaching Procedures:		Tell student in a very excited voice that student is going to do something highly preferred. Wait 5 seconds for a response. If student mands using "When?" praise and provide answer. If student does not mand using "When?" say, "If you want to know when we are going to _____ (name activity you stated) you need to ask 'When?'" If student mands using "When?" praise and provide answer. If student does not mand using "When?" physically guide student to mand using, "When?" (physically touch student's mouth). Score V for correct response that followed verbal prompt. Score M if the correct response followed the model prompt. Score P if physical guidance was used.
Additional Targets:		

Using "How" When Manding
Compatible with ABLLS®-R Code F26

Student's Name:	Start Date:	
Objective:	When student is shown a unique or novel object (For example, a shoe string tied in a unique knot) and teacher says, "Do you know how I did that?" student will mand for information using "How?"	
Person Implementing Objective:		
Setting/Environment:		
Materials:		
Reinforcers:		
Baseline:	Show the student a unique or novel item and say, "Do you know how I did that?" Wait 5 seconds for a response. A correct response is scored (+) if student mands for information using "How?" - <u>do not reinforce</u>. Move to next trial. An incorrect response is scored (-) if student does not mand using "How?"- <u>do not prompt</u>. Move to next trial.	
Teaching Procedures:	Show the student a unique or novel item and say, "Do you know how I did that?" Wait 5 seconds for a response. If student mands using "How?" praise and provide reinforcer. If student does not mand using "How?" say, "If you want to know how I did that, you need to ask, 'How?'" Wait 5 seconds for a response. If student mands using "How?" praise and provide reinforcer. If student does not mand using "How?" physically guide student to mand using "How?" (physically touch student's mouth). Score V for correct response that followed verbal prompt. Score M if the correct response followed the model prompt. Score P if physical guidance was used.	
Additional Targets:		

The BIG Book of ABA Programs

Using "Can" When Manding
Compatible with ABLLS®-R Code F27

Student's Name:		Start Date:
Objective:		When teacher places several preferred items near student, student will mand using, "Can." For example, when candy is present, student could mand, "Can I have some?"
Person Implementing Objective:		
Setting/Environment:		
Materials:		
Reinforcers:		
Baseline:		Place several preferred items near student. Wait 5 seconds for a response. A correct response is scored (+) if student mands using "Can I have some?"- <u>do not reinforce</u>. Move to next trial. An incorrect response is scored (-) if student does not mand using "Can I have some?"- <u>do not prompt</u>. Move to next trial.
Teaching Procedures:		Place several preferred items near student. Wait 5 seconds for a response. If student mands with, "Can I have some?" praise and allow access to the items. If student does not mand with, "Can I have some?" say, "If you want to have any of these, you have to say, 'Can I have some?'" Wait 5 seconds for a response. If student mands with, "Can I have some?" praise and allow access to the items. If student does not mand with, "Can I have some?" physically guide student to say "Can I have some" (physically touch student's mouth). Score V for correct response that followed verbal prompt. Score M if model prompt was used. Score P if physical guidance was used.
Additional Targets:		

Using "Why" When Manding
Compatible with ABLLS®-R Code F28

Student's Name:	Start Date:
Objective:	When teacher tells student something that requires clarification, student will mand for assistance using "Why?" For example, if teacher says, "I'm having a party tomorrow" student could ask "Why?"
Person Implementing Objective:	
Setting/Environment:	
Materials:	
Reinforcers:	
Baseline:	Tell student something that requires clarification. Wait 5 seconds for a response. A correct response is scored (+) if student mands for information using "Why?" - <u>do not reinforce</u>. Move to next trial. An incorrect response is scored (-) if student does not mand using "Why?" - <u>do not prompt</u>. Move to next trial.
Teaching Procedures:	Tell student something that requires clarification. Wait 5 seconds for a response. If student mands using "Why?" praise and provide reinforcer. If student does not mand using "Why?" say, "If you want to know more information you need to ask, 'Why?'" Wait 5 seconds for a response. If student mands using "Why?" praise and provide reinforcer. If student does not mand using "Why?" physically guide student to say, "Why?" (physically touch student's mouth). Score V for correct response that followed verbal prompt. Score M if the correct response followed the model prompt. Score P if physical guidance was used.
Additional Targets:	

CHAPTER 8

ABA Programs Compatible with

ABLLS®-R Domain G

"Labeling"

Tacting Preferred Items
Compatible with ABLLS®-R Code G1

Student's Name:	Start Date:

Objective:	When the teacher presents a preferred item to the student and says, "What is this?" student will provide the name of the presented item.
Person Implementing Objective:	
Setting/Environment:	
Materials:	
Reinforcers:	
Baseline:	Present a preferred item to the student and say, "What is this?" Wait 5 seconds for a response. A correct response is scored (+) if student states the name of the item - <u>do not reinforce</u>. Move to next trial. An incorrect response is scored (-) if student does not state the name of the item - <u>do not prompt</u>. Move to next trial.
Teaching Procedures:	Present a preferred item to the student and say, "What is this?" Wait 5 seconds for a response. If the student states the name of the item, praise and provide reinforcer. If the student does not state the name of the item, say, "This is a ___." Remove the item briefly, re-present the item, and say, "What is this?" Wait 5 seconds for a response. If the student states the name of the item, praise and provide reinforcer. If the item name is not stated, physically guide by touching student's mouth as you say, "This is a ___." Score V for correct response that followed verbal prompt. Score M if the correct response followed the model prompt. Score P if physical guidance was used.
Additional Targets:	

Tacting Common Items
Compatible with ABLLS®-R Code G2

Student's Name:		Start Date:	
Objective:	When teacher presents a common object to student and says, "What is this?" student will provide the name of the common object.		
Person Implementing Objective:			
Setting/Environment:			
Materials:			
Reinforcers:			
Baseline:	Present a common item to the student and say, "What is this?" Wait 5 seconds for a response. A correct response is scored (+) if student states the name of the item - <u>do not reinforce</u>. Move to next trial. An incorrect response is scored (-) if student does not state the name of the item- <u>do not prompt</u>. Move to next trial.		
Teaching Procedures:	Present a common item to the student and say, "What is this?" Wait 5 seconds for a response. If the student states the name of the item, praise and provide reinforcer. If the student does not state the name of the item, say, "This is a ____." Remove the item briefly, re-present the item, and say, "What is this?" Wait 5 seconds for a response. If the student states the name of the item, praise and provide reinforcer. If the item name is not stated, physically guide by touching student's mouth as you say, "This is a ____." Score V for correct response that followed verbal prompt. Score M if the correct response followed the model prompt. Score P if physical guidance was used.		
Additional Targets:			

Tacting Names Of Familiar People
Compatible with ABLLS®-R Code G3

Student's Name:		Start Date:	
Objective:	When the teacher points to a familiar person in close proximity to student and says, "Who is that?" student will name the person.		
Person Implementing Objective:			
Setting/Environment:			
Materials:			
Reinforcers:			
Baseline:	Bring a familiar person within 5 feet of the student, point to the person, and say, "Who is that?" Wait 5 seconds for a response. A correct response is scored (+) if student states the name of the person - do not reinforce. Move to next trial. An incorrect response is scored (-) if student does not state the name of the person- do not prompt. Move to next trial.		
Teaching Procedures:	Bring a familiar person within 5 feet of the student, point to the person, and say, "Who is that?" Wait 5 seconds for a response. If the student states the name of the person, praise and provide reinforcer. If the student does not state the name of the person, say, "This is ___." Say, "Who is that?" as you point to the person. Wait 5 seconds for a response. If the student states the name of the person, praise and provide reinforcer. If the person is not named, physically guide by touching student's mouth as you say, "This is ___." Score V for correct response that followed verbal prompt. Score M if the correct response followed the model prompt. Score P if physical guidance was used.		
Additional Targets:			

Tacting Pictures Of Common Items
Compatible with ABLLS®-R Code G4

Student's Name:		Start Date:	
Objective:	When the teacher presents a picture of a common item to student and says, "What is this?" student will provide the name of the common item.		
Person Implementing Objective:			
Setting/Environment:			
Materials:			
Reinforcers:			
Baseline:	Present a picture of a common item to the student and say, "What is this?" Wait 5 seconds for a response. A correct response is scored (+) if student states the name of the item - <u>do not reinforce</u>. Move to next trial. An incorrect response is scored (-) if student does not state the name of the item- <u>do not prompt</u>. Move to next trial.		
Teaching Procedures:	Present a picture of a common item to the student and say, "What is this?" Wait 5 seconds for a response. If the student states the name of the item, praise and provide reinforcer. If the student does not state the name of the item, say, "This is a ___." Remove the item briefly and re-present the picture and say, "What is this?" Wait 5 seconds for a response. If the student states the name of the item, praise and provide reinforcer. If the item name is not stated, physically guide by touching student's mouth as you say, "This is a ___." Score V for correct response that followed verbal prompt. Score M if the correct response followed the model prompt. Score P if physical guidance was used.		
Additional Targets:			

Tacting Parts Of Body
Compatible with ABLLS®-R Code G5

Student's Name:	Start Date:	
Objective:	When teacher touches a part of the student's body and says, "What is this?" the student will state name of body part.	
Person Implementing Objective:		
Setting/Environment:		
Materials:		
Reinforcers:		
Baseline:	Touch a part of the student's body and say, "What is this?" Wait 5 seconds for a response. A correct response is scored (+) if student states the name of the body part - <u>do not reinforce</u>. Move to next trial. An incorrect response is scored (-) if student does not state the name of the body part- <u>do not prompt</u>. Move to next trial.	
Teaching Procedures:	Touch a part of the student's body and say, "What is this?" Wait 5 seconds for a response. If the student states the name of the body part, praise and provide reinforcer. If the student does not state the name of the body part, say, "This is your _____ (name body part)." Say, "What is this?" as you again touch the same part of the body. Wait 5 seconds for a response. If student states the name of the body part, praise and provide reinforcer. If the part is not named, physically guide by moving the student's hand to the body part as you say, "This is your ____ (name body part)." Score V for correct response that followed verbal prompt. Score M if the correct response followed the model prompt. Score P if physical guidance was used.	
Additional Targets:		

Tacting Items Of Clothing
Compatible with ABLLS®-R Code G6

Student's Name:		Start Date:	
Objective:	When teacher touches an item of clothing and says, "What is this?" student will state the name of the item of clothing.		
Person Implementing Objective:			
Setting/Environment:			
Materials:			
Reinforcers:			
Baseline:	Touch an item of clothing and say, "What is this?" Wait 5 seconds for a response. A correct response is scored (+) if student states the name of the item of clothing - <u>do not reinforce</u>. Move to next trial. An incorrect response is scored (-) if student does not state the name of the item of clothing- <u>do not prompt</u>. Move to next trial.		
Teaching Procedures:	Touch an item of clothing and say, "What is this?" Wait 5 seconds for a response. If student states the name of the item of clothing, praise and provide reinforcer. If student does not state the name of the item of clothing, say, "This is a ____ (name clothing item)." Say, "What is this?" as you again touch the item of clothing. Wait 5 seconds for a response. If the student states the name of the item of clothing, praise and provide reinforcer. If the item is not named, physically guide by moving the student's hand to the item of clothing as you say, "This is a ____ (name clothing item)." Score V for correct response that followed verbal prompt. Score M if the correct response followed the model prompt. Score P if physical guidance was used.		
Additional Targets:			

Tacting Actions- Person
Compatible with ABLLS®-R Code G7

Student's Name:		Start Date:	
Objective:	When teacher points to someone engaged in some action and says, "What is he/she doing?" student will name the action.		
Person Implementing Objective:			
Setting/Environment:			
Materials:			
Reinforcers:			
Baseline:	Point to someone engaged in some action and say, "What is he/she doing?" Wait 5 seconds for a response. A correct response is scored (+) if student states the name of the action - <u>do not reinforce</u>. Move to next trial. An incorrect response is scored (-) if student does not state the name of the action- <u>do not prompt</u>. Move to next trial.		
Teaching Procedures:	Point to someone engaged in some action and say, "What is he/she doing?" Wait 5 seconds for a response. If the student states the name of the action, praise and provide reinforcer. If the student does not state the name of the action, say, "He/she is ____ (name action)." Say, "What is he/she doing?" as you again point to the person engaged in some action. Wait 5 seconds for a response. If the student states the name of the action, praise and provide reinforcer. If the action is not named, physically guide by pointing and saying, "He/she is ____ (name action)." Score V for correct response that followed verbal prompt. Score M if the correct response followed the model prompt. Score P if physical guidance was used.		
Additional Targets:			

Tacting Actions In Pictures
Compatible with ABLLS®-R Code G8

Student's Name:	Start Date:
Objective:	When the teacher presents a picture containing someone engaged in some action and says, "What is he/she doing?" student will name the action.
Person Implementing Objective:	
Setting/Environment:	
Materials:	
Reinforcers:	
Baseline:	Present a picture of someone engaged in some action and say, "What is he/she doing?" Wait 5 seconds for a response. A correct response is scored (+) if student states the name of the action - <u>do not reinforce</u>. Move to next trial. An incorrect response is scored (-) if student does not state the name of the action- <u>do not prompt</u>. Move to next trial.
Teaching Procedures:	Present a picture of someone engaged in some action and say, "What is he/she doing?" Wait 5 seconds for a response. If the student states the name of the action, praise and provide reinforcer. If the student does not state the name of the action, say, "He/she is _____ (name action)." Say, "What is he/she doing?" as you point to the picture of someone engaged in some action. Wait 5 seconds for a response. If the student states the name of the action, praise and provide reinforcer. If the action is not named, physically guide by pointing and saying, "He/she is _____ (name action)." Score V for correct response that followed verbal prompt. Score M if the correct response followed the model prompt. Score P if physical guidance was used.
Additional Targets:	

Quickly Tacting Multiple Common Objects
Compatible with ABLLS®-R Code G9

Student's Name:	Start Date:	
Objective:	When teacher places several common objects in front of student and very quickly points to one after another saying, "What is this?" each time one is pointed to, student will name each object within 2 seconds. (For example, What is this? What is this? What is this?). Objects must be those that the student has already demonstrated an ability to name independently.	
Person Implementing Objective:		
Setting/Environment:		
Materials:		
Reinforcers:		
Baseline:	Place several common objects in front of student. At 2 second intervals point to an object as you say, "What is this?" A correct response is scored (+) if student names all objects correctly within 2 seconds of the cue - <u>do not reinforce</u>. Move to next trial. An incorrect response is scored (-) if student does not name all objects correctly or takes longer than 2 seconds when responding to any cue- <u>do not prompt</u>. Move to next trial.	
Teaching Procedures:	Place several common objects in front of student. At 2 second intervals point to an object as you say, "What is this?" If the student states the name of each object within 2 seconds, praise and provide reinforcer. If the student does not state the name of each object within 2 seconds, say, "This is a ____. This is a ____. This is a ____. This is a ____." (as you name each object). Say the original series of cues at 2 second intervals. If student does not state the name of each object within the 2 seconds, physically guide by moving student's hand to each object as you say the name of each object. Score V for correct response that followed verbal prompt. Score M if the correct response followed the model prompt. Score P if physical guidance was used.	
Additional Targets:		

Tacting Common Items Using Articles
Compatible with ABLLS®-R Code G11

Student's Name:		Start Date:	
Objective:	When the teacher presents a common object to student and says, "What is this?" student will name the object using the correct article (For example, *A* cup, *A* spoon, *An* elephant).		
Person Implementing Objective:			
Setting/Environment:			
Materials:			
Reinforcers:			
Baseline:	Present a common object to student and say, "What is this?" Wait 5 seconds for a response. A correct response is scored (+) if student states the name of the object and uses the correct article - <u>do not reinforce</u>. Move to next trial. An incorrect response is scored (-) if student does not state the name of the object or uses the incorrect article - <u>do not prompt</u>. Move to next trial.		
Teaching Procedures:	Present a common object to student and say, "What is this?" Wait 5 seconds for a response. If student states the name of the object and article, praise and provide reinforcer. If student does not state the name of the object with correct article, say, "This is (a/an)____ (name object)." Remove the object briefly and re-present the object and say, "What is this?" Wait 5 seconds for a response. If student states the name of the object with correct article, praise and provide reinforcer. If the object name is not stated with correct article, physically guide by touching student's mouth as you say, "This is (a/an) ____ (name object)." Score V for correct response that followed verbal prompt. Score M if the correct response followed the model prompt. Score P if physical guidance was used.		
Additional Targets:			

Tacting Specific Parts Of Larger Items
Compatible with ABLLS®-R Code G12

Student's Name:	Start Date:
Objective:	When the teacher presents an item to student, points to a specific part of the item, and says, "What is this?" student will name the part of the item.
Person Implementing Objective:	
Setting/Environment:	
Materials:	
Reinforcers:	
Baseline:	Present an item to the student. Point to a specific part of the item and say, "What is this?" Wait 5 seconds for a response. A correct response is scored (+) if student states the name of the part - <u>do not reinforce</u>. Move to next trial. An incorrect response is scored (-) if student does not state the name of the part- <u>do not prompt</u>. Move to next trial.
Teaching Procedures:	Present an item to the student. Point to a specific part of the item and say, "What is this?" Wait 5 seconds for a response. If the student states the name of the part, praise and provide reinforcer. If the student does not state the name of the part, say, "This is a ___ (name part)." Remove the object briefly and point to the specific part and say, "What is this?" If student states the name of the part, praise and provide reinforcer. If the name of the part is not stated, physically guide by moving the student's hand to the part as you say, "This is a ___ (name part)." Score V for correct response that followed verbal prompt. Score M if the correct response followed the model prompt. Score P if physical guidance was used.
Additional Targets:	

Tacting With Adjectives
Compatible with ABLLS®-R Code G13

Student's Name:		Start Date:	
Objective:	When teacher presents an item to the student and says, "What kind of a _____ (item name) is this?" student will name item using an appropriate adjective.		
Person Implementing Objective:			
Setting/Environment:			
Materials:			
Reinforcers:			
Baseline:	Present an item in front of student and say, "What kind of a _____ (item name) is this?" Wait 5 seconds for a response. A correct response is scored (+) if student correctly uses an adjective to describe the item - <u>do not reinforce</u>. Move to next trial. An incorrect response is scored (-) if student does not correctly describe the item with an adjective- <u>do not prompt</u>. Move to next trial.		
Teaching Procedures:	Present an item in front of student and say, "What kind of a _____ (item name) is this?" Wait 5 seconds for a response. If student correctly uses an adjective to describe the item, praise and provide reinforcer. If student does not use an adjective correctly to describe the item, say, "What kind of a _____ (item name) is this?" Wait 5 seconds for a response. If student correctly uses an adjective to describe the item, praise and provide reinforcer. If student does not use an adjective correctly to describe the item, physically guide by touching student's mouth as you tell student the correct response using the correct adjective. Score V for correct response that followed verbal prompt. Score M if the correct response followed the model prompt. Score P if physical guidance was used.		
Additional Targets:			

Tacting Related Pictures
Compatible with ABLLS®-R Code G14

Student's Name:	Start Date:	
Objective:	When student has an array of pictures as choices, a picture for comparison, and teacher asks, "Which goes with this?" student will name the picture from the array that is related to the comparison picture.	
Person Implementing Objective:		
Setting/Environment:		
Materials:		
Reinforcers:		
Baseline:	Place an array of pictures in front of the student. Present a comparison picture to student and say, "Which goes with this?" Wait 5 seconds for a response. A correct response is scored (+) if student correctly names the related picture - <u>do not reinforce</u>. Move to next trial. An incorrect response is scored (-) if student does not correctly name the related picture- <u>do not prompt</u>. Move to next trial.	
Teaching Procedures:	Place an array of pictures in front of student. Present a picture to the student and ask, "Which goes with this?" Wait 5 seconds for a response. If student correctly names the related picture, praise and provide reinforcer. If student does not name the related picture, say "Which goes with this" as you point to the correct picture. Wait 5 seconds for a response. If student correctly names the related picture, praise and provide reinforcer. If student does not name the related picture, physically guide the student's hand to the correct picture and say the name of both pictures (e.g., "The ____ goes with the ____"). Score V for correct response that followed verbal prompt. Score M if the correct response followed the model prompt. Score P if physical guidance was used.	
Additional Targets:		

Tacting By Function
Compatible with ABLLS®-R Code G15

Student's Name:	Start Date:
Objective:	When teacher an array of objects to a student and asks about the function of an object (For example, Which one do you write with? Which one do you drive? etc.) student will respond by naming the correct object.
Person Implementing Objective:	
Setting/Environment:	
Materials:	
Reinforcers:	
Baseline:	Place an array of objects in front of student and ask, "Which one do you ____ with?" Wait 5 seconds for a response. A correct response is scored (+) if student names the object with appropriate function - <u>do not reinforce</u>. Move to next trial. An incorrect response is scored (-) if student does not name the object with appropriate function- <u>do not prompt</u>. Move to next trial.
Teaching Procedures:	Place an array of objects in front of student and ask, "Which one do you ____ with?" Wait 5 seconds for a response. If student names the object with appropriate function, praise and provide reinforcer. If student does not name the object with appropriate function, say, "Which one do you ____ with?" as you point to the correct object. Wait 5 seconds for a response. If student names the object with appropriate function, praise and provide reinforcer. If student does not name the object with appropriate function, physically guide student's hand to the correct object and say the name of the object and the function. Score V for correct response that followed verbal prompt. Score M if the correct response followed the model prompt. Score P if physical guidance was used.
Additional Targets:	

Tacting By Feature
Compatible with ABLLS®-R Code G16

Student's Name:	Start Date:	
Objective:	When teacher presents an array objects to a student and asks about a specific feature of an object (For example, Which one has wheels? Which one has legs?) student will respond by naming the correct object.	
Person Implementing Objective:		
Setting/Environment:		
Materials:		
Reinforcers:		
Baseline:	Place an array of objects in front of student and ask, "Which one has a ____ (name feature)?" Wait 5 seconds for a response. A correct response is scored (+) if student names the object with appropriate feature - <u>do not reinforce</u>. Move to next trial. An incorrect response is scored (-) if student does not name the object with appropriate feature- <u>do not prompt</u>. Move to next trial.	
Teaching Procedures:	Place an array of objects in front of student and ask, "Which one has a ____ (name feature)?" Wait 5 seconds for a response. If student names the object with appropriate feature, praise and provide reinforcer. If student does not name the object with appropriate feature, say, "Which one has a ____ (name feature)?" as you point to the correct object. Wait 5 seconds for a response. If student names the object with appropriate feature, praise and provide reinforcer. If student does not name the object with appropriate feature, physically guide the student's hand to the correct object and say the name of the object and the feature. Score V for correct response that followed verbal prompt. Score M if the correct response followed the model prompt. Score P if physical guidance was used.	
Additional Targets:		

Tacting By Class
Compatible with ABLLS®-R Code G17

Student's Name:		Start Date:	
Objective:	When teacher presents an array of objects to student and asks which belongs to a particular class (For example, Which one is an animal? Which one is a vehicle?) student will respond by naming the correct object.		
Person Implementing Objective:			
Setting/Environment:			
Materials:			
Reinforcers:			
Baseline:	Place an array of objects in front of student and ask, "Which one is a/an ____ (name the class of one of the objects)?" Wait 5 seconds for a response. A correct response is scored (+) if student names the object with appropriate class - <u>do not reinforce</u>. Move to next trial. An incorrect response is scored (-) if student does not name the object with appropriate class- <u>do not prompt</u>. Move to next trial.		
Teaching Procedures:	Place an array of objects in front of student and ask, "Which one is a/an ____ (name the class of one of the objects)?" Wait 5 seconds for a response. If student names the object with appropriate class, praise and provide reinforcer. If student does not name the object with appropriate class, say, "Which one is a/an ____ (name the class of one of the objects)?" as you point to the correct object. Wait 5 seconds for a response. If student names the object with appropriate class, praise and provide reinforcer. If student does not name the object with appropriate class, physically guide the student's hand to the correct object and say the name of the object and the class. Score V for correct response that followed verbal prompt. Score M if the correct response followed the model prompt. Score P if physical guidance was used.		
Additional Targets:			

Tacting Multiple Common Items
Compatible with ABLLS®-R Code G18

Student's Name:		Start Date:	
Objective:	When teacher presents multiple common items to student and says, "What are these?" student will provide the names of the common items.		
Person Implementing Objective:			
Setting/Environment:			
Materials:			
Reinforcers:			
Baseline:	Present multiple common items to student and say, "What are these?" Wait 5 seconds for a response. A correct response is scored (+) if student states the names of the items - do not reinforce. Move to next trial. An incorrect response is scored (-) if student does not state the names of the items- do not prompt. Move to next trial.		
Teaching Procedures:	Present multiple common items to student and say, "What are these?" Wait 5 seconds for a response. If student states the names of the items, praise and provide reinforcer. If student does not state the names of the items, say, "This is a____ (name item) and this is a _____ (name item)." Remove the items briefly, re-present and say, "What are these?" Wait 5 seconds for a response. If student states the names of the items, praise and provide reinforcer. If the items are not named, physically guide student's hand to touch each item as you state the names of the items. Score V for correct response that followed verbal prompt. Score M if the correct response followed the model prompt. Score P if physical guidance was used.		
Additional Targets:			

The BIG Book of ABA Programs

Tacting Multiple Pictures Of Common Items
Compatible with ABLLS®-R Code G19

Student's Name:		Start Date:	
Objective:	When teacher presents multiple pictures of common items to student and says, "What are these?" student will provide the names of the common items in the pictures.		
Person Implementing Objective:			
Setting/Environment:			
Materials:			
Reinforcers:			
Baseline:	Present multiple pictures of common items to student and say, "What are these?" Wait 5 seconds for a response. A correct response is scored (+) if student states the names of the items in the pictures- <u>do not reinforce</u>. Move to next trial. An incorrect response is scored (-) if student does not state the names of the items in the pictures- <u>do not prompt</u>. Move to next trial.		
Teaching Procedures:	Present multiple pictures of common items to student and say, "What are these?" Wait 5 seconds for a response. If student states the names of the items in the pictures, praise and provide reinforcer. If student does not state the names of the items in the pictures, say, "This is a___ (name item) and this is a ____ (name item)." Remove the pictures briefly, re-present them and say, "What are these?" Wait 5 seconds for a response. If student states the names of the items in the pictures, praise and provide reinforcer. If the items in the pictures are not named, physically guide the student's hand to each picture as you state the names of the items in the pictures. Score V for correct response that followed verbal prompt. Score M if the correct response followed the model prompt. Score P if physical guidance was used.		
Additional Targets:			

Tacting Multiple Common Items Using Articles
Compatible with ABLLS®-R Code G20

Student's Name:	Start Date:
Objective:	When the teacher presents multiple common items to student and says, "What are these?" student will name the items using the correct articles. For example, *A* cup and *a* spoon.
Person Implementing Objective:	
Setting/Environment:	
Materials:	
Reinforcers:	
Baseline:	Present multiple common items to student and say, "What are these?" Wait 5 seconds for a response. A correct response is scored (+) if student states the names of the items and uses the correct articles - <u>do not reinforce</u>. Move to next trial. An incorrect response is scored (-) if student does not state the names of the items with correct articles- <u>do not prompt</u>. Move to next trial.
Teaching Procedures:	Present multiple common items to student and say, "What are these?" Wait 5 seconds for a response. If student states the names of the items with correct articles, praise and provide reinforcer. If student does not state the names of the items with correct articles, say, "This is (a/an) ____ and this is (a/an) ____." Remove the items briefly, re-present them and say, "What are these?" Wait 5 seconds for a response. If student states the names of the items with correct articles, praise and provide reinforcer. If the item names are not stated with correct articles, physically guide student's hand to touch each one as you say, "This is (a/an) ____ and this is (a/an)____." Score V for correct response that followed verbal prompt. Score M if the correct response followed the model prompt. Score P if physical guidance was used.
Additional Targets:	

Tacting Verb-Noun Combinations
Compatible with ABLLS®-R Code G21

Student's Name:		Start Date:
Objective:		When teacher presents a picture of someone engaged in some action and says, "What is he/she doing?" student will correctly identify the appropriate verb and noun combination. (For example, Fly kite; Throw ball)
Person Implementing Objective:		
Setting/Environment:		
Materials:		
Reinforcers:		
Baseline:		Present student with a picture of someone engaged in some action and say, "What is he/she doing?" Wait 5 seconds for a response. A correct response is scored (+) if student states the appropriate verb and noun combination - <u>do not reinforce</u>. Move to next trial. An incorrect response is scored (-) if student does not state the appropriate verb and noun combination- <u>do not prompt</u>. Move to next trial.
Teaching Procedures:		Present student with a picture of someone engaged in some action and say, "What is he/she doing?" Wait 5 seconds for a response. If the student states the appropriate verb and noun combination, praise and provide reinforcer. If student does not state the appropriate verb and noun combination, say, "He/she is ____ (noun and verb). Say, "What is he/she doing?" Wait 5 seconds for a response. If student states the appropriate verb and noun combination, praise and provide reinforcer. If the appropriate verb and noun combination is not named, physically guide student's hand to the picture and state the appropriate verb noun combination. Score V for correct response that followed verbal prompt. Score M if the correct response followed the model prompt. Score P if physical guidance was used.
Additional Targets:		

The BIG Book of ABA Programs

Tacting With Adjective-Noun Combination
Compatible with ABLLS®-R Code G22

Student's Name:	Start Date:	
Objective:	When teacher presents an item to student and says, "What is this?" student will respond with an appropriate adjective-noun combination. (For example: Blue bird).	
Person Implementing Objective:		
Setting/Environment:		
Materials:		
Reinforcers:		
Baseline:	Present item to student and say, "What is this?" Wait 5 seconds for a response. A correct response is scored (+) if student uses an appropriate adjective-noun combination to describe the item - <u>do not reinforce</u>. Move to next trial. An incorrect response is scored (-) if student does not use an appropriate adjective-noun combination to describe the item- <u>do not prompt</u>. Move to next trial.	
Teaching Procedures:	Present item to student and say, "What is this?" Wait 5 seconds for a response. If student uses an appropriate adjective-noun combination to describe the item, praise and provide reinforcer. If student does not use an appropriate adjective-noun combination, state the appropriate adjective-noun combination and say, "What is this?" Wait 5 seconds for a response. If student uses an appropriate adjective-noun combination to describe the item, praise and provide reinforcer. If student does not use an appropriate adjective-noun combination, physically guide student's hand to touch the item and tell student the appropriate adjective-noun combination. Score V for correct response that followed verbal prompt. Score M if the correct response followed the model prompt. Score P if physical guidance was used.	
Additional Targets:		

Tacting Yes Or No By Moving Head
Compatible with ABLLS®-R Code G23

Student's Name:		Start Date:	
Objective:	When teacher presents an item to student and says, "Is this a ____ (name item)?" student will respond by appropriately nodding head up and down for "yes" or shaking head back and forth for "no."		
Person Implementing Objective:			
Setting/Environment:			
Materials:			
Reinforcers:			
Baseline:	Present an item to student and say, "Is this a ____ (name item)?" Wait 5 seconds for a response. A correct response is scored (+) if student uses appropriate head gesture to communicate YES or NO - <u>do not reinforce</u>. Move to next trial. An incorrect response is scored (-) if student does not use appropriate head gesture to communicate YES or NO- <u>do not prompt</u>. Move to next trial.		
Teaching Procedures:	Present an item to student and say, "Is this a ____ (name item)?" Wait 5 seconds for a response. If student uses appropriate head gesture to communicate YES or NO, praise and provide reinforcer. If student does not use appropriate head gesture to communicate YES or NO, make the correct head gesture with your head as you say either: "YES this is a ____ (name item)." or "NO, this is not a ____ (name item)." Then say, "Is this a (name item)?" Wait 5 seconds for a response. If student uses appropriate head gesture to communicate YES or NO, praise and provide reinforcer. If student does not use appropriate head gesture to communicate YES or NO, physically guide student's head to make the correct movement as you again say either: "YES this is a ____ (name item)." or "NO, this is not a ____ (name item)." Score V for correct response that followed verbal prompt. Score M if the correct response followed the model prompt. Score P if physical guidance was used.		
Additional Targets:			

Tacting Function Of Objects
Compatible with ABLLS®-R Code G24

Student's Name:	Start Date:
Objective:	When teacher presents an object to student and says, "What is this used for?" student will state the function of the object.
Person Implementing Objective:	
Setting/Environment:	
Materials:	
Reinforcers:	
Baseline:	Present an object to student and say, "What is this used for?" Wait 5 seconds for a response. A correct response is scored (+) if student states the correct function of the object - <u>do not reinforce</u>. Move to next trial. An incorrect response is scored (-) if student does not state correct function of the object- <u>do not prompt</u>. Move to next trial.
Teaching Procedures:	Present an object to student and say, "What is this used for?" Wait 5 seconds for a response. If student correctly states the function of the object, praise and provide reinforcer. If student does not correctly state the function of the object, say, "A ____ (name object) is for ____ (name function)." Say, "What is this used for?" Wait 5 seconds for a response. If student correctly states the function of the object, praise and provide reinforcer. If student does not correctly state the function of the object, physically guide student's hand to the object and again say, "A ____ (name object) is for ____ (name function)." Score V for correct response that followed verbal prompt. Score M if the correct response followed the model prompt. Score P if physical guidance was used.
Additional Targets:	

Tacting Class Of Objects
Compatible with ABLLS®-R Code G25

Student's Name:	Start Date:
Objective:	When teacher presents an object to student and says, "What is a/an ____ (name object)?" student will state the class to which the object belongs.
Person Implementing Objective:	
Setting/Environment:	
Materials:	
Reinforcers:	
Baseline:	Present an object to student and say, "What is a/an ____ (name object)?" Wait 5 seconds for a response. A correct response is scored (+) if student states the correct class for the object - do not reinforce. Move to next trial. An incorrect response is scored (-) if student does not state correct class for the object- do not prompt. Move to next trial.
Teaching Procedures:	Present an object to student and say, "What is a/an ____ (name object)?" Wait 5 seconds for a response. If student correctly states the class for the object, praise and provide reinforcer. If student does not correctly state the class for the object, say, "A ____ (name object) is a ____ (name class)." Say, "What is a/an ____ (name object)?" Wait 5 seconds for a response. If student correctly states the class for the object, praise and provide reinforcer. If student does not correctly state the class for the object, physically guide student's hand to the object and again say, "A ____ (name object) is a ____ (name class)." Score V for correct response that followed verbal prompt. Score M if the correct response followed the model prompt. Score P if physical guidance was used.
Additional Targets:	

Tacting Variety Of Item Properties
Compatible with ABLLS®-R Code G26

Student's Name:		Start Date:	
Objective:	When teacher presents an object to student to which the student has demonstrated the ability to tact feature, function, class, and ownership, and asks a variety of different questions about the properties of the object, student will answer the questions correctly. For example, "What is this? Whose is this? What is this used for? What shape is this? etc."		
Person Implementing Objective:			
Setting/Environment:			
Materials:			
Reinforcers:			
Baseline:	Present an object to student to which the student has demonstrated the ability to tact feature, function, class, and ownership and ask any of several different questions. Wait 5 seconds for a response. A correct response is scored (+) if student states the correct answer to the question posed - <u>do not reinforce</u>. Move to next trial. An incorrect response is scored (-) if student does not correctly answer question posed- <u>do not prompt</u>. Move to next trial.		
Teaching Procedures:	Present an object to student to which the student has demonstrated the ability to tact feature, function, class, and ownership and ask any of several different questions. Wait 5 seconds for a response If student correctly answers the question, praise and provide reinforcer. If student does not answer question correctly, say the answer to the question and ask the question again. Wait 5 seconds for a response. If student correctly answers the question, praise and provide reinforcer. If student does not answer question correctly, physically guide student to answer question (physically touch student's mouth). Score V if question was answered following verbal prompt. Score M if correct answer followed model prompt. Score P if physical guidance was used.		
Additional Targets:			

Tacting Class Of A Set of Objects
Compatible with ABLLS®-R Code G27

Student's Name:		Start Date:	
Objective:		When teacher presents a set of objects that belong to the same class of objects and says, "What are these?" student will state the class to which the objects belong.	
Person Implementing Objective:			
Setting/Environment:			
Materials:			
Reinforcers:			
Baseline:		Present to student a set of objects that belong to the same class and say, "What are these?" Wait 5 seconds for a response. A correct response is scored (+) if student states the correct class for the objects - <u>do not reinforce</u>. Move to next trial. An incorrect response is scored (-) if student does not state correct class for the object- <u>do not prompt</u>. Move to next trial.	
Teaching Procedures:		Present to student a set of objects that belong to the same class and say, "What are these?" Wait 5 seconds for a response. If student correctly states the class for the objects, praise and provide reinforcer. If student does not correctly state the class for the objects, say, "These are ___ (name class)." Say, "What are these?" Wait 5 seconds for a response. If student correctly states the class for the objects, praise and provide reinforcer. If student does not correctly state the class for the objects, physically guide student's hand to the objects and again say, "These are ___ (name class)." Score V for correct response that followed verbal prompt. Score M if the correct response followed the model prompt. Score P if physical guidance was used.	
Additional Targets:			

Tacting Missing Parts Of Pictures
Compatible with ABLLS®-R Code G28

Student's Name:	Start Date:
Objective:	When teacher presents an incomplete picture to student and says, "What is missing from this picture?" student will state the missing part of the picture.
Person Implementing Objective:	
Setting/Environment:	
Materials:	
Reinforcers:	
Baseline:	Present an incomplete picture to student and ask, "What is missing from this picture?" Wait 5 seconds for a response. A correct response is scored (+) if student states the missing part - <u>do not reinforce</u>. Move to next trial. An incorrect response is scored (-) if student does not state the missing part- <u>do not prompt</u>. Move to next trial.
Teaching Procedures:	Present an incomplete picture to student and ask, "What is missing from this picture?" Wait 5 seconds for a response. If student correctly states the missing part, praise and provide reinforcer. If student does not correctly state the missing part, point to the missing part and say, "The ____ is missing." Say, "What is missing from this picture?" Wait 5 seconds for a response. If student correctly states the missing part, praise and provide reinforcer. If student does not correctly state the missing part, physically guide student's hand to the missing part and again say, "The ____ is missing." Score V for correct response that followed verbal prompt. Score M if the correct response followed the model prompt. Score P if physical guidance was used.
Additional Targets:	

Tacting Objects That Do Not Belong With A Set Of Objects
Compatible with ABLLS®-R Code G29

Student's Name:	Start Date:
Objective:	When teacher presents a group of objects to student in which one object does not belong and says, "Which one does not go with these?" student will state the name of the object that does not belong with the others.
Person Implementing Objective:	
Setting/Environment:	
Materials:	
Reinforcers:	
Baseline:	Present student with a group of objects to which one object does not belong and say, "Which one does not go with these?" Wait 5 seconds for a response. A correct response is scored (+) if student states the name of the object that does not belong with the others - do not reinforce. Move to next trial. An incorrect response is scored (-) if student does not state the name of the object that does not belong with the others- do not prompt. Move to next trial.
Teaching Procedures:	Present student with a group of objects to which one object does not belong and say, "Which one does not go with these?" Wait 5 seconds for a response. If student correctly states the name of the object that does not belong with the others, praise and provide reinforcer. If student does not correctly state the name of the object that does not belong with the others, point to the object that does not belong with the others and say, "This one is a ____ (name reason it does not fit) and these are ___ (name group)." Say, "Which one does not go with these?" Wait 5 seconds for a response. If student correctly states the name of the object that does not belong with the others, praise and provide reinforcer. If student does not correctly state the name of the object that does not belong with the others, physically guide student's hand to the object that does not belong with the others and again say, "This one is a ____ (name reason it does not fit) and these are ____ (name group)." Score V for correct response that followed verbal prompt. Score M if the correct response followed the model prompt. Score P if physical guidance was used.
Additional Targets:	

Tacting A Problem In A Picture
Compatible with ABLLS®-R Code G30

Student's Name:		Start Date:	
Objective:	When teacher presents a picture containing a problem to student and says, "What is wrong in this picture?" student will name the problem. For example, "The train is off the tracks or, The boat is sinking."		
Person Implementing Objective:			
Setting/Environment:			
Materials:			
Reinforcers:			
Baseline:	Present a picture to student that depicts a problem and say, "What is wrong in this picture?" Wait 5 seconds for a response. A correct response is scored (+) if student states the name of problem - <u>do not reinforce</u>. Move to next trial. An incorrect response is scored (-) if student does not state the name of the problem- <u>do not prompt</u>. Move to next trial.		
Teaching Procedures:	Present a picture to student that depicts a problem and say, "What is wrong in this picture?" Wait 5 seconds for a response. If student correctly states the name of the problem, praise and provide reinforcer. If student does not correctly state the name of the problem, point to the problem in the picture as you describe the problem. Say, "What is wrong in this picture?" Wait 5 seconds for a response. If student correctly states the name of the problem, praise and provide reinforcer. If student does not correctly state the name of the problem, physically guide student's hand to the problem in the picture and again describe the problem. Score V for correct response that followed verbal prompt. Score M if the correct response followed the model prompt. Score P if physical guidance was used.		
Additional Targets:			

The BIG Book of ABA Programs

Tacting Community Helpers
Compatible with ABLLS®-R Code G31

Student's Name:		Start Date:
Objective:	When teacher presents a picture of a community helper to student and says, "What kind of person is this?" student will name the community helper.	
Person Implementing Objective:		
Setting/Environment:		
Materials:		
Reinforcers:		
Baseline:	Present a picture of a community helper to student and say, "What kind of person is this?" Wait 5 seconds for a response. A correct response is scored (+) if student states the name of the community helper - <u>do not reinforce</u>. Move to next trial. An incorrect response is scored (-) if student does not state the name of the community helper - <u>do not prompt</u>. Move to next trial.	
Teaching Procedures:	Present a picture of a community helper to student and say, "What kind of person is this?" Wait 5 seconds for a response. If student correctly states the name of the community helper, praise and provide reinforcer. If student does not correctly state the name of the community helper, point to the picture and say, "This is a/an _____ (name community helper)." Say, "What kind of person is this?" Wait 5 seconds for a response. If student correctly states the name of the community helper, praise and provide reinforcer. If student does not correctly state the name of the community helper, physically guide student's hand to the picture and say, "This is a/an _____ (name community helper)." Score V for correct response that followed verbal prompt. Score M if the correct response followed the model prompt. Score P if physical guidance was used.	
Additional Targets:		

www.stimuluspublications.com   The Autism Skill Acquisition Program™

Tacting Known Objects From Far Away
Compatible with ABLLS®-R Code G32

Student's Name:	Start Date:
Objective:	When teacher points to a known object from far away and says, "What is that?" student will name the object.
Person Implementing Objective:	
Setting/Environment:	
Materials:	
Reinforcers:	
Baseline:	Point to a known object from far away and say, "What is that?" Wait 5 seconds for a response. A correct response is scored (+) if student states the name of the object - <u>do not reinforce</u>. Move to next trial. An incorrect response is scored (-) if student does not state the name of the object-<u>do not prompt</u>. Move to next trial.
Teaching Procedures:	Point to a known object from far away and say, "What is that?" Wait 5 seconds for a response. If student correctly states the name of the object, praise and provide reinforcer. If student does not correctly state the name of the object, point to the object again and say, "That is a/an ____." Say, "What is that?" Wait 5 seconds for a response. If student correctly states the name of the object, praise and provide reinforcer. If student does not correctly state the name of the object, physically guide student's hand so that they are pointing to the object and say, "That is a/an ____." Score V for correct response that followed verbal prompt. Score M if the correct response followed the model prompt. Score P if physical guidance was used.
Additional Targets:	

Tacting Sounds
Compatible with ABLLS®-R Code G33

Student's Name:	Start Date:	
Objective:	When the teacher plays a recorded sound and asks, "What sound is this?" student will name the sound.	
Person Implementing Objective:		
Setting/Environment:		
Materials:		
Reinforcers:		
Baseline:	Play a recorded sound and say, "What sound is this?" Wait 5 seconds for a response. A correct response is scored (+) if student states the name of the sound - <u>do not reinforce</u>. Move to next trial. An incorrect response is scored (-) if student does not state the name of the sound - <u>do not prompt</u>. Move to next trial.	
Teaching Procedures:	Play a recorded sound and say, "What sound is this?" Wait 5 seconds for a response. If student correctly states the name of the sound, praise and provide reinforcer. If student does not correctly state the name of the sound, say, "This is a/an ____ (name sound)." Replay the sound and say, "What sound is this?" Wait 5 seconds for a response. If student correctly states the name of the sound, praise and provide reinforcer. If student does not correctly state the name of the sound, say, "This is a/an ____ (name sound)" and physically guide student to name the sound (physically touch student's mouth). Score V for correct response that followed verbal prompt. Score M if the correct response followed the model prompt. Score P if physical guidance was used.	
Additional Targets:		

Tacting Verb-Noun Combinations With Articles
Compatible with ABLLS®-R Code G34

Student's Name:	Start Date:
Objective:	When teacher presents a picture of someone engaged in some action and says, "What is he/she doing?" student will correctly identify the appropriate verb and noun combination with article. For example, Fly *a* kite; Throw *a* ball.
Person Implementing Objective:	
Setting/Environment:	
Materials:	
Reinforcers:	
Baseline:	Present a picture of someone engaged in some action and say, "What is he/she doing?" Wait 5 seconds for a response. A correct response is scored (+) if student states the appropriate verb and noun combination with article - <u>do not reinforce</u>. Move to next trial. An incorrect response is scored (-) if student does not state the appropriate verb and noun combination with article - <u>do not prompt</u>. Move to next trial.
Teaching Procedures:	Present a picture of someone engaged in some action and say, "What is he/she doing?" Wait 5 seconds for a response. If student states the appropriate verb and noun combination with article, praise and provide reinforcer. If student does not state the appropriate verb and noun combination with article, say, "He/she is ____ (noun, verb, and article). Say, "What is he/she doing?" Wait 5 seconds for a response. If student states the appropriate verb and noun combination with article, praise and provide reinforcer. If student does not state the appropriate verb and noun combination with article, physically guide student's hand to the picture and state the appropriate verb noun combination with article. Score V for correct response that followed verbal prompt. Score M if the correct response followed the model prompt. Score P if physical guidance was used.
Additional Targets:	

Tacting Prepositions
Compatible with ABLLS®-R Code G35

Student's Name:	Start Date:
Itemive:	When teacher places an item in front of student and then places a second item near the first and says, "Where is the ____ (second item)" student will correctly identify the location of the second item by using a preposition.
Person Implementing Itemive:	
Setting/Environment:	
Materials:	
Reinforcers:	
Baseline:	With an item in front of student, place a second item near the first and say, "Where is the ____ (second item)?" Wait 5 seconds for a response. A correct response is scored (+) if student uses the correct preposition to state the location of the second item - <u>do not reinforce</u>. Move to next trial. An incorrect response is scored (-) if student does not use the correct preposition to state the location of the second item-<u>do not prompt</u>. Move to next trial.
Teaching Procedures:	With an item in front of student, place a second item near the first and say, "Where is the ____ (second item)?" Wait 5 seconds for a response. If student uses the correct preposition to state the location of the second item, praise and provide reinforcer. If student does not use the correct preposition to state the location of the second item, say, "The ____ (second item) is ____ (preposition) the ____ (first item)." Say, "Where is the ____ (second item)?" Wait 5 seconds for a response. If student uses the correct preposition to state the location of the second item, praise and provide reinforcer. If student does not use the correct preposition to state the location of the second item, physically guide student's hand to touch the second item as you say, "The ____ (second item) is ____ (preposition) the ____ (first item)." Score V for correct response that followed verbal prompt. Score M if the correct response followed the model prompt. Score P if response followed the physical prompt.
Additional Targets:	

The BIG Book of ABA Programs

Tacting Articles With Prepositions
Compatible with ABLLS®-R Code G36

Student's Name:		Start Date:	
Itemive:		When teacher places an item in front of student and then places a second item near the first and asks student, "Where is the ____ (second item)?" student will correctly identify the location of the second item by using the correct article and preposition. For example, Next to *the* box; On *a* chair; Behind *an* elephant, etc.	
Person Implementing Itemive:			
Setting/Environment:			
Materials:			
Reinforcers:			
Baseline:		With an item in front of student, place a second item near the first and say, "Where is the ____ (second item)?" Wait 5 seconds for a response. A correct response is scored (+) if student uses the correct preposition and article to state the location of the second item - <u>do not reinforce</u>. Move to next trial. An incorrect response is scored (-) if student does not use the correct preposition and article to state the location of the second item-<u>do not prompt</u>. Move to next trial.	
Teaching Procedures:		With an item in front of student, place a second item near the first and say, "Where is the ____ (second item)?" Wait 5 seconds for a response. If student uses the correct preposition and article to state the location of the second item, praise and provide reinforcer. If student does not use the correct preposition and article to state the location of the second item, say, "The ____ (second item) is ____ (preposition and article) ____ (first item)." Say, "Where is the ____ (second item)?" Wait 5 seconds for a response. If student uses the correct preposition and article to state the location of the second item, praise and provide reinforcer. If student does not use the correct preposition and article to state the location of the second item, physically guide student's hand to touch the second item as you say, "The ____ (second item) is (preposition and article) ____ (first item)." Score V for correct response that followed verbal prompt. Score M if the correct response followed the model prompt. Score P if response followed the physical prompt.	
Additional Targets:			

www.stimuluspublications.com   The Autism Skill Acquisition Program™

Tacting Pronouns
Compatible with ABLLS®-R Code G37

Student's Name:	Start Date:
Objective:	When teacher points to someone performing an action and asks the question, "Who is ____ (name action)?" student will use correct pronoun to describe who is performing the action.
Person Implementing Objective:	
Setting/Environment:	
Materials:	
Reinforcers:	
Baseline:	Point to someone performing an action and say, "Who is ____ (name action)?" Wait 5 seconds for a response. A correct response is scored (+) if student uses the correct pronoun to describe who is performing the action - <u>do not reinforce</u>. Move to next trial. An incorrect response is scored (-) if student does not use the correct pronoun to describe who is performing the action- <u>do not prompt</u>. Move to next trial.
Teaching Procedures:	Point to someone performing an action and ask, "Who is ____ (name action)?" Wait 5 seconds for a response. If student uses the correct pronoun to describe who is performing the action, praise and provide reinforcer. If student does not use the correct pronoun to describe who is performing the action, say, "____ (pronoun) is ____ (name action)." Point to someone performing an action and say, "Who is ____ (name action)?" Wait 5 seconds for a response. If student uses the correct pronoun to describe who is performing the action, praise and provide reinforcer. If student does not use the correct pronoun to describe who is performing the action, physically guide the student's hand to point to the person performing the action as you say, "____ (pronoun) is ____ (name action)." Score V for correct response that followed verbal prompt. Score M if the correct response followed the model prompt. Score P if physical guidance was used.
Additional Targets:	

Tacting Helping Verbs To Describe Actions With Pronouns
Compatible with ABLLS®-R Code G38

Student's Name:	Start Date:
Objective:	When teacher points to someone performing an action and says, "Who is ____ (name action)?" student will use the correct helping verb, verb, and pronoun to describe the person performing the action. For, example, He *is* walking; They *are* running.
Person Implementing Objective:	
Setting/Environment:	
Materials:	
Reinforcers:	
Baseline:	Point to someone performing an action and say, "Who is ____ (name action)?" Wait 5 seconds for a response. A correct response is scored (+) if student uses the correct helping verb, verb, and pronoun to describe who is performing the action - <u>do not reinforce</u>. Move to next trial. An incorrect response is scored (-) if student does not use the correct helping verb, verb, and pronoun to describe who is performing the action- <u>do not prompt</u>. Move to next trial.
Teaching Procedures:	Point to someone performing an action and say, "Who is ____ (name action)?" Wait 5 seconds for a response. If student uses the correct helping verb, verb, and pronoun to describe who is performing the action, praise and provide reinforcer. If student does not use the correct helping verb, verb, and pronoun to describe who is performing the action, say, "____ (pronoun) ____ (helping verb) ____ (name action)." Point to someone performing an action and say "Who is ____ (name action)?" Wait 5 seconds for a response. If student uses the correct helping verb, verb, and pronoun to describe who is performing the action, praise and provide reinforcer. If student does not use the correct helping verb, verb, and pronoun to describe who is performing the action, physically guide the student's hand to point to the person performing the action as you say, "____ (pronoun) ____ (helping verb) ____ (name action)." Score V for correct response that followed verbal prompt. Score M if the correct response followed the model prompt. Score P if physical guidance was used.
Additional Targets:	

Tacting Descriptions Of Pictured Activities
Compatible with ABLLS®-R Code G39

Student's Name:	Start Date:
Objective:	When teacher shows student a picture of an ongoing activity and says, "What is going on in this picture?" student will describe the activity in the picture.
Person Implementing Objective:	
Setting/Environment:	
Materials:	
Reinforcers:	
Baseline:	Present student with a picture of an ongoing activity and say, "What is going on in this picture?" Wait 5 seconds for a response. A correct response is scored (+) if student accurately describes the activity in the picture - <u>do not reinforce</u>. Move to next trial. An incorrect response is scored (-) if student does not accurately describe the activity in the picture- <u>do not prompt</u>. Move to next trial.
Teaching Procedures:	Present student with a picture of an ongoing activity and say, "What is going on in this picture?" Wait 5 seconds for a response. If student accurately describes the activity in the picture, praise and provide reinforcer. If student does not accurately describe the activity in the picture, say, "____ (pronoun/noun) ____ is ____ (ongoing activity)." Say "What is going on in this picture?" Wait 5 seconds for a response. If student accurately describes the activity in the picture, praise and provide reinforcer. If student does not accurately describe the activity in the picture, physically guide the student's hand to point to the picture as you say, "____ (pronoun/noun) ____ is ____ (ongoing activity)." Score V for correct response that followed verbal prompt. Score M if the correct response followed the model prompt. Score P if physical guidance was used.
Additional Targets:	

Tacting Descriptions Of Parts Of Pictured Activities
Compatible with ABLLS®-R Code G40

Student's Name:		Start Date:	
Objective:	\multicolumn{3}{l	}{When teacher shows student a picture of an ongoing activity and asks about one aspect of the picture, student will correctly describe the aspect of the picture that was asked about. For example, What is the firefighter doing? Who is the monkey talking to?}
Person Implementing Objective:			
Setting/Environment:			
Materials:			
Reinforcers:			
Baseline:	\multicolumn{3}{l	}{Present student with a picture of an ongoing activity and ask about one aspect of the picture. Wait 5 seconds for a response. A correct response is scored (+) if student accurately describes the aspect of the picture - <u>do not reinforce</u>. Move to next trial. An incorrect response is scored (-) if student does not accurately describe the aspect of the picture- <u>do not prompt</u>. Move to next trial.}
Teaching Procedures:	\multicolumn{3}{l	}{Present student with a picture of an ongoing activity and ask about one aspect of the picture. Wait 5 seconds for a response. If student accurately describes the aspect of the picture, praise and provide reinforcer. If student does not accurately describe the aspect of the picture, point to the aspect of the picture and say, (for example) "The monkey is talking to the bear" Ask student again about the aspect of the picture. Wait 5 seconds for a response. If student accurately describes the aspect of the picture, praise and provide reinforcer. If student does not accurately describe the aspect of the picture, physically guide student's hand to point to the aspect of the picture as you again describe the aspect of the picture. Score V for correct response that followed verbal prompt. Score M if the correct response followed the model prompt. Score P if physical guidance was used.}
Additional Targets:			

Tacting Adverbs
Compatible with ABLLS®-R Code G41

Student's Name:		Start Date:	
Objective:		When teacher shows student a picture of an ongoing activity and asks about the action of the picture, student will respond with an appropriate adverb. For example, teacher says, "How is the rabbit running?" "Quickly"	
Person Implementing Objective:			
Setting/Environment:			
Materials:			
Reinforcers:			
Baseline:		Present a picture of an ongoing activity to student and ask about the activity. Wait 5 seconds for a response. A correct response is scored (+) if student accurately describes the action with an adverb - <u>do not reinforce</u>. Move to next trial. An incorrect response is scored (-) if student does not accurately describe the action with an adverb- <u>do not prompt</u>. Move to next trial.	
Teaching Procedures:		Present a picture of an ongoing activity to student and ask about the activity. Wait 5 seconds for a response. If student accurately describes the action with an adverb, praise and provide reinforcer. If student does not accurately describe the action with an adverb, point to picture and tell student the appropriate adverb. Ask student about picture again. Wait 5 seconds for a response. If student accurately describes the action with an adverb, praise and provide reinforcer. If student does not accurately describe the action with an adverb, physically guide the student's hand to point to the picture as you tell the student the appropriate adverb. Score V for correct response that followed verbal prompt. Score M if the correct response followed the model prompt. Score P if physical guidance was used.	
Additional Targets:			

Tacting Emotions
Compatible with ABLLS®-R Code G42

Student's Name:	Start Date:
Objective:	When teacher shows student an emotion card and says, "What is he/she feeling?" student will identify correct emotion.
Person Implementing Objective:	
Setting/Environment:	
Materials:	
Reinforcers:	
Baseline:	Present an emotion card to student and say, "What is he/she feeling?" Wait 5 seconds for a response. A correct response is scored (+) if student accurately describes the emotion - <u>do not reinforce</u>. Move to next trial. An incorrect response is scored (-) if student does not accurately describe the emotion- <u>do not prompt</u>. Move to next trial.
Teaching Procedures:	Present an emotion card to student and ask, "What is he/she feeling?" Wait 5 seconds for a response. If student accurately describes the emotion, praise and provide reinforcer. If student does not accurately describe the emotion, say, "He/she is ____ (emotion)." Say, "What is he/she feeling?" Wait 5 seconds for a response. If student accurately describes the emotion, praise and provide reinforcer. If student does not accurately describe the emotion, physically guide the student's hand to point to the picture as you say, ""He/she is ____ (emotion)." Score V for correct response that followed verbal prompt. Score M if the correct response followed the model prompt. Score P if physical guidance was used.
Additional Targets:	

Tacting Emotions
Compatible with ABLLS®-R Code G43

Student's Name:	Start Date:
Objective:	When student is demonstrating observable emotional behaviors, (e.g., laughing, frowning, crying, etc.) and teacher says, "Tell me how you feel." Student will tact emotional state (e.g., happy, sad, hurt, etc.).
Person Implementing Objective:	
Setting/Environment:	
Materials:	
Reinforcers:	
Baseline:	When student is demonstrating observable emotional behaviors say, "Tell me how you feel." Wait 5 seconds for a response. A correct response is scored (+) if student states an appropriate emotion - <u>do not reinforce</u>. Move to next trial. An incorrect response is scored (-) if student does not state an appropriate emotion - <u>do not prompt</u>. Move to next trial.
Teaching Procedures:	When student is demonstrating observable emotional behaviors say, "Tell me how you feel." Wait 5 seconds for a response. If student states an appropriate emotion, praise and provide reinforcer. If student does not state an appropriate emotion, tell student an appropriate emotion based on student's behaviors. Say, "Tell me how you feel." Wait 5 seconds for a response. If student states an appropriate emotion, praise and provide reinforcer. If student does not state an appropriate emotion, physically guide student to tell you an appropriate emotion (Physically touch student's mouth). Score V for correct response that followed verbal prompt. Score M if the correct response followed the model prompt. Score P if physical guidance was used.
Additional Targets:	

Tacting With Multiple Descriptors
Compatible with ABLLS®-R Code G44

Student's Name:	Start Date:
Objective:	When teacher presents an item to student and says, "What is this?" student will respond with at least three descriptors. For example, Big (1) blue (2) bird on a tree (3).
Person Implementing Objective:	
Setting/Environment:	
Materials:	
Reinforcers:	
Baseline:	Present an item to student and say, "What is this?" Wait 5 seconds for a response. A correct response is scored (+) if student uses at least 3 appropriate descriptors for the item - <u>do not reinforce</u>. Move to next trial. An incorrect response is scored (-) if student does not use at least 3 appropriate descriptors for the item- <u>do not prompt</u>. Move to next trial.
Teaching Procedures:	Present an item to student and ask, "What is this?" Wait 5 seconds for a response. If student uses at least 3 appropriate descriptors for the item, praise and provide reinforcer. If student does not use at least 3 appropriate descriptors for the item, point to item and state at least 3 appropriate descriptors. Say, "What is this?" Wait 5 seconds for a response. If student uses at least 3 appropriate descriptors for the item, praise and provide reinforcer. If student does not use at least 3 appropriate descriptors for the item, physically guide student's hand to touch the item and tell student the appropriate descriptors. Score V for correct response that followed verbal prompt. Score M if the correct response followed the model prompt. Score P if physical guidance was used.
Additional Targets:	

Tacting With Multiple Descriptors With Article
Compatible with ABLLS®-R Code G45

Student's Name:		Start Date:	
Objective:		When teacher presents an item to student and says, "What is this?" student will respond with appropriate article and at least three descriptors. Example: *A* (article) big (1) blue (2) bird on a tree (3).	
Person Implementing Objective:			
Setting/Environment:			
Materials:			
Reinforcers:			
Baseline:		Present an item to student and ask, "What is this?" Wait 5 seconds for a response. A correct response is scored (+) if student uses appropriate article and at least 3 appropriate descriptors for the item - do not reinforce. Move to next trial. An incorrect response is scored (-) if student does not use appropriate article and at least 3 appropriate descriptors for the item- do not prompt. Move to next trial.	
Teaching Procedures:		Present an item to student and ask, "What is this?" Wait 5 seconds for a response. If student uses appropriate article and at least 3 appropriate descriptors for the item, praise and provide reinforcer. If student does not use appropriate article and at least 3 appropriate descriptors for the item, state the appropriate article and at least 3 appropriate descriptors. Say, "What is this?" Wait 5 seconds for a response. If student uses appropriate article and at least 3 appropriate descriptors for the item, praise and provide reinforcer. If student does not use appropriate article and at least 3 appropriate descriptors for the item, physically guide student's hand to touch the item and tell student the appropriate article and descriptors. Score V for correct response that followed verbal prompt. Score M if the correct response followed the model prompt. Score P if physical guidance was used.	
Additional Targets:			

The BIG Book of ABA Programs

Tacting Social Scenarios
Compatible with ABLLS®-R Code G46

Student's Name:	Start Date:
Objective:	When teacher presents a picture to student that shows a social interaction and asks, "What is going on in this picture?" student will describe the social interaction in the picture.
Person Implementing Objective:	
Setting/Environment:	
Materials:	
Reinforcers:	
Baseline:	Present a picture of a social scene to student and say, "What is going on in this picture?" Wait 5 seconds for a response. A correct response is scored (+) if student describes the social interaction in the picture - <u>do not reinforce</u>. Move to next trial. An incorrect response is scored (-) if student does not describe the social situation in the picture- <u>do not prompt</u>. Move to next trial.
Teaching Procedures:	Present a picture of a social scene to student and say, "What is going on in this picture?" Wait 5 seconds for a response. If student describes the social interaction in the picture, praise and provide reinforcer. If student does not describe the social interaction in the picture, point to the picture and describe the social interaction. Say, "What is going on in this picture?" Wait 5 seconds for a response. If student describes the social interaction in the picture, praise and provide reinforcer. If student does not describe the social interaction in the picture, physically guide student's hand to touch the picture as you again describe the social interaction. Score V for correct response that followed verbal prompt. Score M if the correct response followed the model prompt. Score P if physical guidance was used.
Additional Targets:	

www.stimuluspublications.com   232   The Autism Skill Acquisition Program™

CHAPTER 9

ABA Programs Compatible with

ABLLS®-R Domain H

"Intraverbals"

Adding Missing Words To Songs
Compatible with ABLLS®-R Code H1

Student's Name:		Start Date:	
Objective:		When teacher sings a familiar song and then stops with a word/phrase unsung, student will fill in the word/phrase that comes next. For example, "Mary had a little ____."	
Person Implementing Objective:			
Setting/Environment:			
Materials:			
Reinforcers:			
Baseline:		Sing a verse of a familiar song and stop singing with a word/phrase unsung. Wait 5 seconds for a response. A correct response is scored (+) if student sings the next word or verse - <u>do not reinforce</u>. Move to next trial. An incorrect response is scored (-) if student does not sing the next word or verse- <u>do not prompt</u>. Move to next trial.	
Teaching Procedures:		Sing a verse of a familiar song and stop singing with a word/phrase unsung. Wait 5 seconds for a response. If student sings the next word or verse, praise and provide reinforcer. If student does not sing the next word or verse, tell the student what the next word or verse should be. For example, say, "Mary had a little *lamb*. So you would say *lamb*." Sing the song and again stop singing. Wait 5 seconds for a response. If student sings the next word or verse, praise and provide reinforcer. If student does not sing the next word or verse, physically guide by touching student's mouth as you say, (for example) "You say '*lamb*.' Mary had a little *lamb*." Score V for correct response that followed verbal prompt. Score M if the correct response followed the model prompt. Score P if physical guidance was used.	
Additional Targets:			

Adding Missing Words To Phrases
Compatible with ABLLS®-R Code H2

Student's Name:	Start Date:
Objective:	When teacher says a familiar phrase but leaves out the last word, student will fill in the word that comes next. For example, "Let's ride the roller ____."
Person Implementing Objective:	
Setting/Environment:	
Materials:	
Reinforcers:	
Baseline:	Say a familiar phrase but leave out the last word. Wait 5 seconds for a response. A correct response is scored (+) if student says the next word - <u>do not reinforce</u>. Move to next trial. An incorrect response is scored (-) if student does not say the next word- <u>do not prompt</u>. Move to next trial.
Teaching Procedures:	Say a familiar phrase but leave out the last word. Wait 5 seconds for a response. If student says the next word, praise and provide reinforcer. If student does not say the next word, tell the student what the next word should be. For example, say, "Let's ride the roller *coaster*. So you would say *coaster*." Say the familiar phrase again leaving out the last word. Wait 5 seconds for a response. If student says the next word, praise and provide reinforcer. If student does not say the next word, physically guide by touching student's mouth as you say, (for example) "You say '*coaster*.' Let's ride the roller *coaster*." Score V for correct response that followed verbal prompt. Score M if the correct response followed the model prompt. Score P if you physical guidance was used.
Additional Targets:	

American Sign Language
Compatible with ABLLS®-R Code H3

Student's Name:	Start Date:	
Objective:	When teacher says, "What is the sign for ____ (name a letter, word, or object)?" student will produce the appropriate American Sign Language sign.	
Person Implementing Objective:		
Setting/Environment:		
Materials:		
Reinforcers:		
Baseline:	Say, "What is the sign for ____ (name a letter, word, or object)?" Wait 5 seconds for a response. A correct response is scored (+) if student makes the correct sign - <u>do not reinforce</u>. Move to next trial. An incorrect response is scored (-) if student does not make the correct sign- <u>do not prompt</u>. Move to next trial.	
Teaching Procedures:	Say, "What is the sign for ____ (name a letter, word, or object)?" Wait 5 seconds for a response. If student makes the correct sign, praise and provide reinforcer. If student does not make the correct sign, say, "The sign for ____ (name a letter, word, or object) is like this" as you make the sign with your hand. Say, "What is the sign for ____ (name a letter, word, or object)?" Wait 5 seconds for a response. If student makes the correct sign, praise and provide reinforcer. If student does not make the correct sign, physically guide the correct sign with the student's hand. Score V for correct response that followed verbal prompt. Score M if the correct response followed the model prompt. Score P if physical guidance was used.	
Additional Targets:		

Sounds Made By Animals
Compatible with ABLLS®-R Code H4

Student's Name:	Start Date:
Objective:	When teacher asks the student, "What sound does a/an _____ (animal) make?" student will make the correct animal sound.
Person Implementing Objective:	
Setting/Environment:	
Materials:	
Reinforcers:	
Baseline:	Say, "What sound does a/an _____ (animal) make?" Wait 5 seconds for a response. A correct response is scored (+) if student makes the correct animal sound - <u>do not reinforce</u>. Move to next trial. An incorrect response is scored (-) if student does not make the correct animal sound- <u>do not prompt</u>. Move to next trial.
Teaching Procedures:	Say, "What sound does a/an _____ (animal) make?" Wait 5 seconds for a response. If student makes the correct sound, praise and provide reinforcer. If student does not make the correct sound, you say, "A/an _____ (animal) makes a _____ sound" as you make the sound. Say, "What sound does a/an _____ (animal) make?" Wait 5 seconds for a response. If student makes the correct sound, praise and provide reinforcer. If student does not make the correct sound, physically guide by repeating the prompt, "A/an _____ (animal) makes a _____ sound" as you touch the student's mouth. Score V for correct response that followed verbal prompt. Score M if the correct response followed the model prompt. Score P if physical prompting was used.
Additional Targets:	

Student Information
Compatible with ABLLS®-R Code H5

Student's Name:	Start Date:
Objective:	When teacher says, "What is your ____ (name, street address, birth day, telephone number, etc.)?" student will answer using correct information.
Person Implementing Objective:	
Setting/Environment:	
Materials:	
Reinforcers:	
Baseline:	Say, What is your ____ (name, street address, birth day, telephone number, etc.)?" Wait 5 seconds for a response. A correct response is scored (+) if student provides correct answer - <u>do not reinforce</u>. Move to next trial. An incorrect response is scored (-) if student does not provide correct answer- <u>do not prompt</u>. Move to next trial.
Teaching Procedures:	Say, What is your ____ (name, street address, birth day, telephone number, etc.)?" Wait 5 seconds for a response. If student provides the correct information, praise and provide reinforcer. If student does not provide the correct information, tell student the correct information. Say, What is your ____ (name, street address, birth day, telephone number, etc.)?" Wait 5 seconds for a response. If student provides the correct information, praise and provide reinforcer. If student does not provide the correct information, physically guide by repeating the answer as you touch the student's mouth. Score V for correct response that followed verbal prompt. Score M if the correct response followed the model prompt. Score P if physical guidance was used.
Additional Targets:	

Adding Missing Words To Phrases
Compatible with ABLLS®-R Code H6

Student's Name:		Start Date:	
Objective:	\multicolumn{3}{l	}{When teacher says a familiar phrase but leaves out the last word, student will fill in the word that comes next. For example, "Let's go to the ____."}

Person Implementing Objective:	
Setting/Environment:	
Materials:	
Reinforcers:	
Baseline:	Say a familiar phrase but leave out the last word. Wait 5 seconds for a response. A correct response is scored (+) if student says the next word - <u>do not reinforce</u>. Move to next trial. An incorrect response is scored (-) if student does not say the next word- <u>do not prompt</u>. Move to next trial.
Teaching Procedures:	Say a familiar phrase but leave out the last word. Wait 5 seconds for a response. If student says the next word, praise and provide reinforcer. If student does not say the next word, tell the student what the next word should be. For example, say, "Let's go to the *playground*. So you would say *playground*." Say the familiar phrase again leaving out the last word. Wait 5 seconds for a response. If student says the next word, praise and provide reinforcer. If student does not say the next word, physically guide by touching student's mouth as you say, (for example) "You say '*playground*.' Let's go to the *playground*." Score V for correct response that followed verbal prompt. Score M if the correct response followed the model prompt. Score P if you physical guidance was used.
Additional Targets:	

Word Pairing
Compatible with ABLLS®-R Code H7

Student's Name:		Start Date:	
Objective:	When teacher says, "What is something that goes with a _____ (noun)?" student will respond by stating a related noun. For example, "What is something that goes with a knife?" "Fork"		
Person Implementing Objective:			
Setting/Environment:			
Materials:			
Reinforcers:			
Baseline:	Say, "What is something that goes with a _____ (noun)?" Wait 5 seconds for a response. A correct response is scored (+) if student states an appropriate related item - <u>do not reinforce</u>. Move to next trial. An incorrect response is scored (-) if student does not state an appropriate related item- <u>do not prompt</u>. Move to next trial.		
Teaching Procedures:	Say, "What is something that goes with a _____ (noun)?" Wait 5 seconds for a response. If student states an appropriate related item, praise and provide reinforcer. If student does not state an appropriate related item, tell student a related noun. Say, "What is something that goes with a _____ (noun)?" Wait 5 seconds for a response. If student states an appropriate related item, praise and provide reinforcer. If student does not state an appropriate related item, physically guide by again telling student a related noun as you touch student's mouth. Score V for correct response that followed verbal prompt. Score M if the correct response followed the model prompt. Score P if physical guidance was used.		
Additional Targets:			

Missing Words Related To Function
Compatible with ABLLS®-R Code H8

Student's Name:	Start Date:
Objective:	When teacher makes a statement related to the function of an object but leaves off the last word, student will complete the statement. For example, "You cut grass with a ____." "Lawnmower"
Person Implementing Objective:	
Setting/Environment:	
Materials:	
Reinforcers:	
Baseline:	Make a statement to student related to the function of an object but leave off the last word. Wait 5 seconds for a response. A correct response is scored (+) if student finishes the statement with the appropriate object - <u>do not reinforce</u>. Move to next trial. An incorrect response is scored (-) if student does not finish the statement with an appropriate object- <u>do not prompt</u>. Move to next trial.
Teaching Procedures:	Make a statement to student related to the function of an object but leave off the last word. Wait 5 seconds for a response. If student finishes the statement with the appropriate object, praise and provide reinforcer. If student does not finish the statement with the appropriate object, tell student the object. Repeat the original statement again leaving off the last word. Wait 5 seconds for a response. If student finishes the statement with the appropriate object, praise and provide reinforcer. If student does not finish the statement with the appropriate object, physically guide by telling student the related object as you touch student's mouth. Score V for correct response that followed verbal prompt. Score M if the correct response followed the model prompt. Score P if physical guidance was used.
Additional Targets:	

Missing Function
Compatible with ABLLS®-R Code H9

Student's Name:	Start Date:

Objective:	When teacher says, "You use a ____ (noun) for ____" student will state the function of the object. For example, "You use a lawnmower for ____" "Cutting the grass"
Person Implementing Objective:	
Setting/Environment:	
Materials:	
Reinforcers:	
Baseline:	Say, "You use a ____ (noun) for ____." Wait 5 seconds for a response. A correct response is scored (+) if student states correct function of item named - <u>do not reinforce</u>. Move to next trial. An incorrect response is scored (-) if student does not state correct function of item named- <u>do not prompt</u>. Move to next trial.
Teaching Procedures:	Say, "You use a ____ (noun) for ____." Wait 5 seconds for a response. If student states the correct function of the object named, praise and provide reinforcer. If student does not state correct function of the object named, tell student the function. Say, "You use a ____ (noun) for ____." Wait 5 seconds for a response. If student states the correct function of the object named, praise and provide reinforcer. If student does not state correct function of the object named, physically guide by telling student the function as you touch the student's mouth. Score V for correct response that followed verbal prompt. Score M if the correct response followed the model prompt. Score P if physical guidance was used.
Additional Targets:	

"What" Questions
Compatible with ABLLS®-R Code H10

Student's Name:	Start Date:
Objective:	When teacher asks student about "what" is found in certain locations, student will respond with appropriate items found in that location. For example, "What things are in a classroom?" "Desks, chairs, kids"
Person Implementing Objective:	
Setting/Environment:	
Materials:	
Reinforcers:	
Baseline:	Say, "What things are in a ____ (name location)?" Wait 5 seconds for a response. A correct response is scored (+) if student states appropriate items found in that location - <u>do not reinforce</u>. Move to next trial. An incorrect response is scored (-) if student does not state appropriate objects found in that location- <u>do not prompt</u>. Move to next trial.
Teaching Procedures:	Say, "What things are in a ____ (name location)?" Wait 5 seconds for a response. If student states appropriate items found in that location, praise and provide reinforcer. If student does not state appropriate items found in that location, say "You find ____, (name objects) in ____ (name location)." Say, "What things are in a ____ (name location)?" Wait 5 seconds for a response. If student states appropriate items found in that location, praise and provide reinforcer. If student does not state appropriate items found in that location, physically guide by repeating the prompt "You find ____, (name objects) in ____ (name location)." as you touch the student's mouth. Score V for correct response that followed verbal prompt. Score M if the correct response followed the model prompt. Score P if physical guidance was used.
Additional Targets:	

"What" Questions About Function
Compatible with ABLLS®-R Code H11

Student's Name:	Start Date:
Objective:	When teacher asks student about "What" can be used to serve a certain function, student will respond with appropriate item that serves that function. For example, "What can you use to cut grass?" "Lawnmower"
Person Implementing Objective:	
Setting/Environment:	
Materials:	
Reinforcers:	
Baseline:	Say, "What can be used to _____ (name function)?" Wait 5 seconds for a response. A correct response is scored (+) if student states appropriate item that serves that function- <u>do not reinforce</u>. Move to next trial. An incorrect response is scored (-) if student does not state appropriate item that serves that function- <u>do not prompt</u>. Move to next trial.
Teaching Procedures:	Say, "What can be used to _____ (name function)?" Wait 5 seconds for a response. If student states appropriate item that serves that function, praise and provide reinforcer. If student does not state appropriate item that serves that function, say "A ____ (name item) is used to ____ (name function)." Say, "What can be used to ____ (name function)?" Wait 5 seconds for a response. If student states appropriate item that serves that function, praise and provide reinforcer. If student does not state appropriate item that serves that function, physically guide by repeating the prompt "A ____ (name item) is used to ____ (name function)." as you touch student's mouth. Score V for correct response that followed verbal prompt. Score M if the correct response followed the model prompt. Score P if physical guidance was used.
Additional Targets:	

"Where" Questions
Compatible with ABLLS®-R Code H12

Student's Name:	Start Date:
Objective:	When teacher asks student about "Where" a particular item is found, student will respond with location for that item. For example, "Where do you find chalk?" "Classroom"
Person Implementing Objective:	
Setting/Environment:	
Materials:	
Reinforcers:	
Baseline:	Say, "Where do you find a ____ (name item)?" Wait 5 seconds for a response. A correct response is scored (+) if student states appropriate location for item - <u>do not reinforce</u>. Move to next trial. An incorrect response is scored (-) if student does not state appropriate location for item- <u>do not prompt</u>. Move to next trial.
Teaching Procedures:	Say, "Where do you find a ____ (name item)?" Wait 5 seconds for a response. If student states appropriate location for item, praise and provide reinforcer. If student does not state appropriate location for item, say "You find a ____ (name item) in a ____ (name area)." Say, "Where do you find a ____ (name item)?" Wait 5 seconds for a response. If student states appropriate location for item, praise and provide reinforcer. If student does not state appropriate location for item, physically guide by repeating the prompt "You find a ____ (name item) in a ____ (name area)" as you touch student's mouth. Score V for correct response that followed verbal prompt. Score M if the correct response followed the model prompt. Score P if physical guidance was used.
Additional Targets:	

Answer Questions About "Where" Activities Take Place
Compatible with ABLLS®-R Code H13

Student's Name:	Start Date:
Objective:	When teacher asks student about "Where" a particular activity takes place, student will respond with appropriate location for that activity. For example, "Where do you do your school work?" "Desk"
Person Implementing Objective:	
Setting/Environment:	
Materials:	
Reinforcers:	
Baseline:	Say, "Where do you ____ (name activity)?" Wait 5 seconds for a response. A correct response is scored (+) if student states appropriate location for activity - <u>do not reinforce</u>. Move to next trial. An incorrect response is scored (-) if student does not state appropriate location for activity- <u>do not prompt</u>. Move to next trial.
Teaching Procedures:	Say, "Where do you ____ (name activity)?" Wait 5 seconds for a response. If student states appropriate location for activity, praise and provide reinforcer. If student does not state appropriate location for activity, say "You ____ (name activity) in a ____ (name area)." Say, "Where do you ____ (name activity)?" Wait 5 seconds for a response. If student states appropriate location for activity, praise and provide reinforcer. If student does not state appropriate location for activity, physically guide by repeating the prompt "You ____ (name activity) in a ____ (name area)." as you touch the student's mouth. Score V for correct response that followed verbal prompt. Score M if the correct response followed the model prompt. Score P if physical guidance was used.
Additional Targets:	

Missing Words Related To Class
Compatible with ABLLS®-R Code H14

Student's Name:		Start Date:	
Objective:	When teacher makes a statement related to the class of objects but leaves off the last word, the student will complete the statement. For example, "You draw with ____" "Crayons"		
Person Implementing Objective:			
Setting/Environment:			
Materials:			
Reinforcers:			
Baseline:	Make a statement related to the class of an object but leave off the last word. Wait 5 seconds for a response. A correct response is scored (+) if student finishes the statement with the appropriate object - <u>do not reinforce</u>. Move to next trial. An incorrect response is scored (-) if student does not finish the statement with an appropriate object- <u>do not prompt</u>. Move to next trial.		
Teaching Procedures:	Make a statement related to the class of an object but leave off the last word. Wait 5 seconds for a response. If student finishes the statement with the appropriate object, praise and provide reinforcer. If student does not finish the statement with the appropriate object, tell student the object. Repeat the original statement again leaving off the last word. Wait 5 seconds for a response. If student finishes the statement with the appropriate object, praise and provide reinforcer. If student does not finish the statement with the appropriate object, physically guide by telling student the object as you touch student's mouth. Score V for correct response that followed verbal prompt. Score M if the correct response followed the model prompt. Score P if physical guidance was used.		
Additional Targets:			

Responding With Multiple Answers
Compatible with ABLLS®-R Code H15

Student's Name:	Start Date:
Objective:	When teacher asks student a question, the student will answer with multiple items. For example, "What are some pets?" "Dog, cat, gerbil, bunny, guinea pig"
Person Implementing Objective:	
Setting/Environment:	
Materials:	
Reinforcers:	
Baseline:	Say, "What are some ____ (name category)?" Wait 5 seconds for a response. A correct response is scored (+) if student answers with multiple appropriate items - <u>do not reinforce</u>. Move to next trial. An incorrect response is scored (-) if student does not answer with multiple appropriate items- <u>do not prompt</u>. Move to next trial.
Teaching Procedures:	Say, "What are some ____ (name category)?" Wait 5 seconds for a response. If student answers the question with multiple appropriate items, praise and provide reinforcer. If student does not answer the question with multiple appropriate items, tell student multiple items. Say, "What are some ____ (name category)?" Wait 5 seconds for a response. If student answers the question with multiple appropriate items, praise and provide reinforcer. If student does not answer the question with multiple appropriate items, physically guide by telling student multiple correct items as you touch student's mouth. Score V for correct response that followed verbal prompt. Score M if the correct response followed the model prompt. Score P if physical guidance was used.
Additional Targets:	

Describing The Features Of Objects
Compatible with ABLLS®-R Code H16

Student's Name:		Start Date:	
Objective:	When teacher makes a statement about the feature of an object but leaves off the last word, student will finish the sentence by adding the appropriate feature. For example, "Pencils have ___" "Erasers"		
Person Implementing Objective:			
Setting/Environment:			
Materials:			
Reinforcers:			
Baseline:	Make a statement describing the feature of an object but leave off the last word. Wait 5 seconds for a response. A correct response is scored (+) if student finishes the statement with appropriate feature - <u>do not reinforce</u>. Move to next trial. An incorrect response is scored (-) if student does not finish the statement with an appropriate feature- <u>do not prompt</u>. Move to next trial.		
Teaching Procedures:	Make a statement describing the feature of an object but leave off the last word. Wait 5 seconds for a response. If student finishes the statement with appropriate feature, praise and provide reinforcer. If student does not finish the statement with appropriate feature, tell student the missing feature. Repeat the original statement leaving off last word. Wait 5 seconds for a response. If student finishes the statement with appropriate feature, praise and provide reinforcer. If student does not finish the statement with appropriate feature, physically guide by telling student the missing feature as you touch student's mouth. Score V for correct response that followed verbal prompt. Score M if the correct response followed the model prompt. Score P if physical guidance was used.		
Additional Targets:			

State Name Of Object When Given A Feature Of The Object
Compatible with ABLLS®-R Code H17

Student's Name:		Start Date:	
Objective:		When teacher tells student a prominent feature of an object, student will state the name of the object. For example, "Something with an eraser." "Pencil"	
Person Implementing Objective:			
Setting/Environment:			
Materials:			
Reinforcers:			
Baseline:		Make a statement describing a prominent feature of an object. Wait 5 seconds for a response. A correct response is scored (+) if student states the name of the object - <u>do not reinforce</u>. Move to next trial. An incorrect response is scored (-) if student does not state the name of the object- <u>do not prompt</u>. Move to next trial.	
Teaching Procedures:		Make a statement describing a prominent feature of an object. Wait 5 seconds for a response. If student states the name of the object, praise and provide reinforcer. If student does not state the name of the object, tell student the object. Repeat the original statement. Wait 5 seconds for a response. If student states the name of the object, praise and provide reinforcer. If student does not state the name of the object, physically guide by telling student the object as you touch student's mouth. Score V for correct response that followed verbal prompt. Score M if the correct response followed the model prompt. Score P if physical guidance was used.	
Additional Targets:			

Describing The Class To Which An Object Belongs
Compatible with ABLLS®-R Code H18

Student's Name:		Start Date:	
Objective:	\multicolumn{3}{l	}{When teacher makes a statement about the class to which an object belongs but leaves off the last word, student will finish the sentence by adding the appropriate class for the object. For example, "Pencils are something you ____" "Write with."}
Person Implementing Objective:			
Setting/Environment:			
Materials:			
Reinforcers:			
Baseline:	\multicolumn{3}{l	}{Make a statement describing the class to which an object belongs but leave off the last word. Wait 5 seconds for a response. A correct response is scored (+) if student finishes the statement with appropriate class - <u>do not reinforce</u>. Move to next trial. An incorrect response is scored (-) if student does not finish the statement with appropriate class- <u>do not prompt</u>. Move to next trial.}
Teaching Procedures:	\multicolumn{3}{l	}{Make a statement describing the class to which an object belongs but leave off the last word. Wait 5 seconds for a response. If student finishes the statement with appropriate class, praise and provide reinforcer. If student does not finish statement with the appropriate class, tell student the correct class. Repeat the original statement. Wait 5 seconds for a response. If student finishes the statement with appropriate class, praise and provide reinforcer. If student does not finish the statement with the appropriate class, physically guide by telling student the correct class as you touch student's mouth. Score V for correct response that followed verbal prompt. Score M if the correct response followed the model prompt. Score P if physical guidance was used.}
Additional Targets:			

States Name Of Object Seen Earlier In Day
Compatible with ABLLS®-R Code H19

Student's Name:		Start Date:	
Objective:	When teacher shows student an object and then asks student later what was seen, student will name the object.		
Person Implementing Objective:			
Setting/Environment:			
Materials:			
Reinforcers:			
Baseline:	Show student an object. Wait for some period of time and then ask student what object was seen earlier. Wait 5 seconds for a response. A correct response is scored (+) if student states the name of the object seen earlier- <u>do not reinforce</u>. Move to next trial. An incorrect response is scored (-) if student does not state the name of the object seen earlier- <u>do not prompt</u>. Move to next trial.		
Teaching Procedures:	Show student an object. Wait for some period of time and then ask student what object was seen earlier. Wait 5 seconds for a response. If student states the name of the object seen earlier, praise and provide reinforcer. If student does not state the name of the object seen earlier, say, "I showed you a/an ____ (name object) earlier." Again ask the student what object was seen earlier. Wait 5 seconds for a response. If student states the name of the object seen earlier, praise and provide reinforcer. If student does not state the name of the object seen earlier, physically guide by saying, "I showed you the ____ (name object) earlier" as you show student the object again. Score V for correct response that followed verbal prompt. Score M if the correct response followed the model prompt. Score P if physical guidance was used.		
Additional Targets:			

States Name Of Activity Seen Earlier In Day
Compatible with ABLLS®-R Code H20

Student's Name:	Start Date:
Objective:	When teacher shows student an ongoing activity and then asks student later what was seen, student will name the activity.
Person Implementing Objective:	
Setting/Environment:	
Materials:	
Reinforcers:	
Baseline:	Show student an ongoing activity. Wait for some period of time and then ask student what activity was seen earlier. Wait 5 seconds for a response. A correct response is scored (+) if student states the name of the activity seen earlier- <u>do not reinforce</u>. Move to next trial. An incorrect response is scored (-) if student does not state the name of the activity seen earlier- <u>do not prompt</u>. Move to next trial.
Teaching Procedures:	Show student an ongoing activity. Wait for some period of time and then ask student what activity was seen earlier. Wait 5 seconds for a response. If student states the name of the activity seen earlier, praise and provide reinforcer. If student does not state the name of the activity seen earlier, say, "I showed you a/an ____ (name activity) earlier." Again ask the student what activity was seen earlier. Wait 5 seconds for a response. If student states the name of the activity seen earlier, praise and provide reinforcer. If student does not state the name of the activity seen earlier, physically guide by saying, "I showed you the ____ (name activity) earlier" as you show student the activity again. Score V for correct response that followed verbal prompt. Score M if the correct response followed the model prompt. Score P if physical guidance was used.
Additional Targets:	

States Name Of Person Seen Earlier In Day
Compatible with ABLLS®-R Code H21

Student's Name:	Start Date:
Objective:	When teacher shows student a person and then asks the student later who was seen, student will name the person.
Person Implementing Objective:	
Setting/Environment:	
Materials:	
Reinforcers:	
Baseline:	Show student a person. Wait for some period of time and then ask student who was seen earlier. Wait 5 seconds for a response. A correct response is scored (+) if student states the name of the person seen earlier- <u>do not reinforce</u>. Move to next trial. An incorrect response is scored (-) if student does not state the name of the person seen earlier- <u>do not prompt</u>. Move to next trial.
Teaching Procedures:	Show student a person. Wait for some period of time and then ask student who was seen earlier. Wait 5 seconds for a response. If student states the name of the person seen earlier, praise and provide reinforcer. If student does not state the name of the person seen earlier, say, "I showed you ____ (name person) earlier." Again ask student who was seen earlier. Wait 5 seconds for a response. If student states the name of the person seen earlier, praise and provide reinforcer. If student does not state the name of the person seen earlier, physically guide by saying, "I showed you ____ (name person) earlier" as you show student the person again. Score V for correct response that followed verbal prompt. Score M if the correct response followed the model prompt. Score P if physical guidance was used.
Additional Targets:	

Adds Comments To Teacher Comments
Compatible with ABLLS®-R Code H22

Student's Name:		Start Date:	
Objective:	When teacher shows student a scene or picture and makes a comment about it, student will make a related comment about the picture or scene.		
Person Implementing Objective:			
Setting/Environment:			
Materials:			
Reinforcers:			
Baseline:	Show a scene or picture and make a comment about the scene or picture. Wait 5 seconds for a response. A correct response is scored (+) if student makes a related comment about the picture- <u>do not reinforce</u>. Move to next trial. An incorrect response is scored (-) if student does not make a related comment about the picture- <u>do not prompt</u>. Move to next trial.		
Teaching Procedures:	Show a scene or picture and make a comment about the scene or picture. Wait 5 seconds for a response. If student makes a related comment about the picture, praise and provide reinforcer. If student does not make a related comment about the picture, repeat the comment you made and then say, "You should say something about the picture too." Wait 5 seconds for a response. If student makes related comment about the picture, praise and provide reinforcer. If related comment is not made, physically guide by repeating the comment you made again saying, "You should say something about the picture too" as you take the student's hand and move it to the picture. Score V for correct response that followed verbal prompt. Score M if the correct response followed the model prompt. Score P if physical guidance was used.		
Additional Targets:			

The BIG Book of ABA Programs

"What" Questions About Things In The Community
Compatible with ABLLS®-R Code H23

Student's Name:		Start Date:	
Objective:		When teacher asks student about "What" is found in certain locations in the community, student will respond with appropriate items found in that location. For example, "What things are downtown?" "Buildings"	
Person Implementing Objective:			
Setting/Environment:			
Materials:			
Reinforcers:			
Baseline:		Say, "What things are (in the) ____ (name community area)?" Wait 5 seconds for a response. A correct response is scored (+) if student states an appropriate item found in that area - <u>do not reinforce</u>. Move to next trial. An incorrect response is scored (-) if student does not state an appropriate item found in that area- <u>do not prompt</u>. Move to next trial.	
Teaching Procedures:		Say, "What things are (in the) ____ (name community area)?" Wait 5 seconds for a response. If student states an appropriate item found in that area, praise and provide reinforcer. If student does not state an appropriate item found in that area, say, "You find ____, (name an item) in ____ (name community area)." Say, "What things are (in the) ____ (name community area)?" Wait 5 seconds for a response. If student states an appropriate item found in that area, praise and provide reinforcer. If student does not state an appropriate item found in that area, physically guide by repeating the prompt "You find ____ (name an item) in ____ (name community area)" as you touch student's mouth. Score V for correct response that followed verbal prompt. Score M if the correct response followed the model prompt. Score P if physical guidance was used.	
Additional Targets:			

www.stimuluspublications.com   The Autism Skill Acquisition Program™

"What" Questions About Activities In The Community
Compatible with ABLLS®-R Code H24

Student's Name:		Start Date:	
Objective:		When teacher asks student about "What" student can do in certain locations in the community, student will respond with appropriate activities common to that location. For example, "What things can you do downtown?" "Ride in a taxi"	
Person Implementing Objective:			
Setting/Environment:			
Materials:			
Reinforcers:			
Baseline:		Say, "What things can you do ____ (name community area)?" Wait 5 seconds for a response. A correct response is scored (+) if student states an appropriate activity common in that area - <u>do not reinforce</u>. Move to next trial. An incorrect response is scored (-) if student does not state an activity common in that area- <u>do not prompt</u>. Move to next trial.	
Teaching Procedures:		Say, "What things can you do ____ (name community area)?" Wait 5 seconds for a response. If student states an appropriate activity common in that area, praise and provide reinforcer. If student does not state an appropriate activity common in that area, say, "You can____, (name an activity) in ____ (name community area)." Say, "What things can you do ____ (name community area)?" Wait 5 seconds for a response. If student states an appropriate activity common in that area, praise and provide reinforcer. If student does not state an appropriate activity common in that area, physically guide by repeating the prompt "You can ____, (name activity) ____ (name community area)." as you touch student's mouth. Score V for correct response that followed verbal prompt. Score M if the correct response followed the model prompt. Score P if physical guidance was used.	
Additional Targets:			

"Where" Questions About The Location of Things In The Community
Compatible with ABLLS®-R Code H25

Student's Name:	Start Date:
Objective:	When teacher asks student about "Where" some item or activity is located in the community, student will respond with appropriate location for that item. For example, "Where can you feed the ducks?" "Park"
Person Implementing Objective:	
Setting/Environment:	
Materials:	
Reinforcers:	
Baseline:	Say, "Where can you find a ____ (name item)?" or "Where can you ____ (name activity)?" Wait 5 seconds for a response. A correct response is scored (+) if student states an appropriate location for that item or activity - <u>do not reinforce</u>. Move to next trial. An incorrect response is scored (-) if student does not state an appropriate location for that item or activity - <u>do not prompt</u>. Move to next trial.
Teaching Procedures:	Say, "Where can you find a ____ (name item)?" or "Where can you ____ (name activity)?" Wait 5 seconds for a response. If student states an appropriate location for that item or activity, praise and provide reinforcer. If student does not state an appropriate location for that item or activity, say, "You find ____ (name item) in a ____ (name community area)." Say, "Where can you find a ____ (name item)?" or "Where can you ____ (name activity)?" Wait 5 seconds for a response. If student states an appropriate location for that item or activity, praise and provide reinforcer. If student does not state an appropriate location for that item or activity, physically guide by repeating the prompt "You find ____ (name item) in a ____ (name community area)." as you touch student's mouth. Score V for correct response that followed verbal prompt. Score M if the correct response followed the model prompt. Score P if physical guidance was used.
Additional Targets:	

Responding With Multiple Answers About The Community
Compatible with ABLLS®-R Code H26

Student's Name:	Start Date:

Objective:	When teacher asks student a question about the community, student will answer with multiple items. For example, "What can you buy at the mall?" "Shirts, ice cream, jewelry, candy, shoes"
Person Implementing Objective:	
Setting/Environment:	
Materials:	
Reinforcers:	
Baseline:	Say, "What are some things you ____ (see, buy, find) when you are in the/at the ____ (name community location)?" Wait 5 seconds for a response. A correct response is scored (+) if student answers with appropriate items - <u>do not reinforce</u>. Move to next trial. An incorrect response is scored (-) if student does not answer with appropriate items- <u>do not prompt</u>. Move to next trial.
Teaching Procedures:	Say, "What are some things you ____ (see, buy, find) when you are in the/at the ____ (name community location)?" Wait 5 seconds for a response. If student answers with appropriate items, praise and provide reinforcer. If student does not answer with appropriate items, say, "You ____ (see, find, buy)____ (name objects) in the/at the ____ (name community location)." Wait 5 seconds for a response. If student answers with appropriate items, praise and provide reinforcer. If student does not answer with appropriate items, physically guide by again telling student the appropriate items as you touch student's mouth. Score V for correct response that followed verbal prompt. Score M if the correct response followed the model prompt. Score P if physical guidance was used.
Additional Targets:	

Naming The Class To Which Objects Belong
Compatible with ABLLS®-R Code H27

Student's Name:	Start Date:

Objective:	When teacher asks "What are ____, ____, and ____?" and provides multiple examples of items belonging to a class, student will state the name of the class to which the items belong. For example, "What are shirts, pants, and socks?" "Clothes"
Person Implementing Objective:	
Setting/Environment:	
Materials:	
Reinforcers:	
Baseline:	Say, "What are ____, ____, and ____ (name several items in a class)?" Wait 5 seconds for a response. A correct response is scored (+) if student answers with appropriate class - <u>do not reinforce</u>. Move to next trial. An incorrect response is scored (-) if student does not answer with appropriate class- <u>do not prompt</u>. Move to next trial.
Teaching Procedures:	Say, "What are ____, ____, and ____ (name several items in a class)?" Wait 5 seconds for a response. If student names appropriate class, praise and provide reinforcer. If student does not name appropriate class, tell student the class to which the items belong. Say, "What are ____, ____, and ____ (name several items in a class)?" Wait 5 seconds for a response. If student names appropriate class, praise and provide reinforcer. If student does not name appropriate class, physically guide by again telling student the appropriate class as you touch student's mouth. Score V for correct response that followed verbal prompt. Score M if the correct response followed the model prompt. Score P if physical guidance was used.
Additional Targets:	

"Who" Questions
Compatible with ABLLS®-R Code H28

Student's Name:		Start Date:	
Objective:	\multicolumn{3}{l	}{When teacher asks student "Who" an item belongs to or "Who" does something, student will respond with appropriate name or occupation of person. For, example, "Who helps sick people?" "Doctor" "Whose backpack is that?" "Kassidy's"}

Person Implementing Objective:	
Setting/Environment:	
Materials:	
Reinforcers:	
Baseline:	Say, "Who ____ (name activity)?" or "Whose ____(name object) is that?" Wait 5 seconds for a response. A correct response is scored (+) if student states appropriate name or profession of person - <u>do not reinforce</u>. Move to next trial. An incorrect response is scored (-) if student does not state appropriate name or profession of person- <u>do not prompt</u>. Move to next trial.
Teaching Procedures:	Say, "Who ____ (name activity)?" or "Whose ____ (name object) is that?" Wait 5 seconds for a response. If student states appropriate name or profession of person, praise and provide reinforcer. If student does not state appropriate name or profession, say, "A ____ (name profession and activity), or "That's ____ (name person and that person's item)." Say, "Who ____ (name activity)?" or "Whose ____ (name object) is that?" Wait 5 seconds for a response. If student states appropriate name or profession of person, praise and provide reinforcer. If student does not state appropriate name or profession, physically guide by repeating the prompt "A ____ (name profession and activity), or "That's ____ (name person and that person's item)" as you touch student's mouth. Score V for correct response that followed verbal prompt. Score M if the correct response followed the model prompt. Score P if physical guidance was used.
Additional Targets:	

"When" Questions
Compatible with ABLLS®-R Code H29

Student's Name:		Start Date:	
Objective:	When teacher asks student about "When" an activity occurs, student will respond with appropriate time for that activity. For example, "When do you wake up?" "Morning"		
Person Implementing Objective:			
Setting/Environment:			
Materials:			
Reinforcers:			
Baseline:	Say, "When do you _____ (name activity)?" Wait 5 seconds for a response. A correct response is scored (+) if student states appropriate time for that activity - do not reinforce. Move to next trial. An incorrect response is scored (-) if student does not state time for that activity- do not prompt. Move to next trial.		
Teaching Procedures:	Say, "When do you _____ (name activity)?" Wait 5 seconds for a response. If student states appropriate time for that activity, praise and provide reinforcer. If student does not state appropriate time for that activity, say "You _____ (name activity) at/in the _____ (name time)." Say, "When do you _____ (name activity)?" Wait 5 seconds for a response. If student states appropriate time for that activity, praise and provide reinforcer. If student does not state appropriate time for that activity, physically guide by repeating the prompt "You _____ (name activity) at _____(name time)" as you touch student's mouth. Score V for correct response that followed verbal prompt. Score M if the correct response followed the model prompt. Score P if physical guidance was used.		
Additional Targets:			

"When, Who, Where, And What" Questions In Varied Order
Compatible with ABLLS®-R Code H30

Student's Name:		Start Date:	
Objective:		When teacher asks student "When, Who, Where and What" questions, student will respond with correct answer for the type of question posed. For example, "When do you wake up?" "Morning"; "Where do you sleep?" "Bed"; "Whose bed do you sleep in?" "Mine"	
Person Implementing Objective:			
Setting/Environment:			
Materials:			
Reinforcers:			
Baseline:		Ask student a question from any of several different types (When, Who, Where and What). Wait 5 seconds for a response. A correct response is scored (+) if student answers question correctly - <u>do not reinforce</u>. Move to next trial. An incorrect response is scored (-) if student does not answer question correctly- <u>do not prompt</u>. Move to next trial. Subsequent trials should include questions of a different type.	
Teaching Procedures:		Ask student a question from any of several different types (When, Who, Where and What). Wait 5 seconds for a response. If student answers question correctly, praise and provide reinforcer. If student does not answer question correctly, provide answer to the question and ask the question again. Wait 5 seconds for a response. If student answers question correctly, praise and provide reinforcer. If student does not answer the question correctly, physically guide by again telling student the answer to the question as you touch student's mouth. Score V for correct response that followed verbal prompt. Score M if the correct response followed the model prompt. Score P if physical guidance was used.	
Additional Targets:			

The BIG Book of ABA Programs

"Which" Questions
Compatible with ABLLS®-R Code H31

Student's Name:		Start Date:	
Objective:	When teacher asks student "Which" of two choices meets the given criteria, student will respond with correct choice. For example, "Which animal lives on a farm, a tiger or a cow?" "Cow"		
Person Implementing Objective:			
Setting/Environment:			
Materials:			
Reinforcers:			
Baseline:	Ask student a "Which" question requiring a choice. Wait 5 seconds for a response. A correct response is scored (+) if student states correct choice- <u>do not reinforce</u>. Move to next trial. An incorrect response is scored (-) if student does not state correct choice- <u>do not prompt</u>. Move to next trial.		
Teaching Procedures:	Ask student a "Which" question requiring a choice. Wait 5 seconds for a response. If student states correct choice, praise and provide reinforcer. If student does not state correct choice, tell student the correct choice and ask student the question again. Wait 5 seconds for a response. If student states correct choice, praise and provide reinforcer. If student does not state correct choice, physically guide by telling student the correct choice as you touch student's mouth. Score V for correct response that followed verbal prompt. Score M if the correct response followed the model prompt. Score P if physical guidance was used.		
Additional Targets:			

"How" Questions
Compatible with ABLLS®-R Code H32

Student's Name:		Start Date:	
Objective:	When teacher asks student about "How" an activity occurs, student will respond with correct description. For example, "How do you wash your hands?" "Rub them together with soap and water"		
Person Implementing Objective:			
Setting/Environment:			
Materials:			
Reinforcers:			
Baseline:	Say, "How do you ____ (name activity)?" Wait 5 seconds for a response. A correct response is scored (+) if student states correct description- <u>do not reinforce</u>. Move to next trial. An incorrect response is scored (-) if student does not state correct description- <u>do not prompt</u>. Move to next trial.		
Teaching Procedures:	Say, "How do you ____ (name activity)?" Wait 5 seconds for a response. If student states correct description, praise and provide reinforcer. If student does not state correct description, say, "You ____ (name activity) by ____ (name correct description)." Say, "How do you ____ (name activity)?" Wait 5 seconds for a response. If student states correct description, praise and provide reinforcer. If student does not state correct description, physically guide by again telling student the correct description as you touch student's mouth. Score V for correct response that followed verbal prompt. Score M if the correct response followed the model prompt. Score P if physical guidance was used.		
Additional Targets:			

"Why" Questions
Compatible with ABLLS®-R Code H33

Student's Name:	Start Date:

Objective:	When teacher asks student about "Why" an activity occurs, student will respond with correct description. For example, "Why do you brush your teeth?" "To clean them"
Person Implementing Objective:	
Setting/Environment:	
Materials:	
Reinforcers:	
Baseline:	Say, "Why do you ____ (name activity)?" Wait 5 seconds for a response. A correct response is scored (+) if student states correct description- <u>do not reinforce</u>. Move to next trial. An incorrect response is scored (-) if student does not state correct description- <u>do not prompt</u>. Move to next trial.
Teaching Procedures:	Say, "Why do you ____ (name activity)?" Wait 5 seconds for a response. If student states correct description, praise and provide reinforcer. If student does not state correct description, say, "You ____ (name activity) to ____ (name correct description)." Say, "Why do you ____ (name activity)?" Wait 5 seconds for a response. If student states correct description, praise and provide reinforcer. If student does not state correct description, physically guide by again telling student the correct description as you touch student's mouth. Score V for correct response that followed verbal prompt. Score M if the correct response followed the model prompt. Score P if physical guidance was used.
Additional Targets:	

Answer Questions About Sequencing
Compatible with ABLLS®-R Code H34

Student's Name:		Start Date:	
Objective:	When teacher asks student "How" an activity occurs, student will respond with appropriate steps required to complete the task. For example, "How do you brush your teeth?" "Pick up tooth brush, put on toothpaste, rinse my mouth, rinse my toothbrush"		
Person Implementing Objective:			
Setting/Environment:			
Materials:			
Reinforcers:			
Baseline:	Say, "How do you ____ (name activity)?" Wait 5 seconds for a response. A correct response is scored (+) if student states correct sequence of steps to complete the task- <u>do not reinforce</u>. Move to next trial. An incorrect response is scored (-) if student does not state correct sequence of steps to complete the task- <u>do not prompt</u>. Move to next trial.		
Teaching Procedures:	Say, "How do you ____ (name activity)?" Wait 5 seconds for a response. If student states correct sequence of steps to complete the task, praise and provide reinforcer. If student does not state correct sequence of steps to complete the task, say, "You ____ (name activity) by ____ (name appropriate sequence)." Say, "How do you ____ (name activity)?" Wait 5 seconds for a response. If student states correct sequence of steps to complete the task, praise and provide reinforcer. If student does not state correct sequence of steps to complete the task, physically guide by again telling student the correct sequence of steps required to complete the task as you touch student's mouth. Score V for correct response that followed verbal prompt. Score M if the correct response followed the model prompt. Score P if physical guidance was used.		
Additional Targets:			

Name Activity When Given Sequence Of Steps
Compatible with ABLLS®-R Code H35

Student's Name:		Start Date:	
Objective:		When teacher provides student with the steps required to complete an activity, student will name the activity. For example, "What are you doing when you pick up tooth brush, put on toothpaste, rinse your mouth, and rinse your toothbrush?" "Brushing teeth"	

Person Implementing Objective:	
Setting/Environment:	
Materials:	
Reinforcers:	
Baseline:	Say, "What are you doing when you ____ (state sequence of steps)?" Wait 5 seconds for a response. A correct response is scored (+) if student states correct activity- <u>do not reinforce</u>. Move to next trial. An incorrect response is scored (-) if student does not state correct activity. Move to next trial.
Teaching Procedures:	Say, "What are you doing when you ____ (state sequence of steps)?" Wait 5 seconds for a response. If student states correct activity, praise and provide reinforcer. If student does not state correct activity, say, "When you ____ (name sequence) you are ____ (name activity)." Say, "What are you doing when you ____ (state sequence of steps)?" Wait 5 seconds for a response. If student states correct activity, praise and provide reinforcer. If student does not state correct activity, physically guide by again telling student the correct activity as you touch student's mouth. Score V for correct response that followed verbal prompt. Score M if the correct response followed the model prompt. Score P if physical guidance was used.
Additional Targets:	

Name Item When Given Description
Compatible with ABLLS®-R Code H36

Student's Name:	Start Date:
Objective:	When teacher gives student a description of an item, student will name the item. For example, "What is round, has white and black spots, and is kicked around?" "Soccer ball"
Person Implementing Objective:	
Setting/Environment:	
Materials:	
Reinforcers:	
Baseline:	Say, "What is ____ (state multiple descriptors of an item)?" Wait 5 seconds for a response. A correct response is scored (+) if student states correct item- <u>do not reinforce</u>. Move to next trial. An incorrect response is scored (-) if student does not state correct item- <u>do not prompt</u>. Move to next trial.
Teaching Procedures:	Say, "What is ____ (state multiple descriptors of an item)?" Wait 5 seconds for a response. If student states correct item, praise and provide reinforcer. If student does not state correct item, say, "A ____ (name item) has ____ (name descriptors)." Say, "What is ____ (state multiple descriptors of an item)?" Wait 5 seconds for a response. If student states correct item, praise and provide reinforcer. If student does not state correct item, physically guide by again telling student the correct item as you touch student's mouth. Score V for correct response that followed verbal prompt. Score M if the correct response followed the model prompt. Score P if physical guidance was used.
Additional Targets:	

Answering Yes/No Questions About Objects That Are Not Present
Compatible with ABLLS®-R Code H37

Student's Name:	Start Date:
Objective:	When teacher asks student questions requiring a "Yes" or a "No" response about an object that is not present, student will answer the question by correctly indicating yes or no. For example say, "Are apples purple?" "No"
Person Implementing Objective:	
Setting/Environment:	
Materials:	
Reinforcers:	
Baseline:	Ask student a question requiring a yes or a no response about an object that is not present. Wait 5 seconds for a response. A correct response is scored (+) if student correctly indicates yes or no- <u>do not reinforce</u>. Move to next trial. An incorrect response is scored (-) if student does not correctly indicate yes or no. Move to next trial.
Teaching Procedures:	Ask student a question requiring a yes or a no response about an object that is not present. Wait 5 seconds for a response. If student correctly indicates yes or no, praise and provide reinforcer. If student does not correctly indicate yes or no, tell student the correct response. Repeat the original question. Wait 5 seconds for a response. If student correctly indicates yes or no, praise and provide reinforcer. If student does not correctly indicate yes or no, physically guide by again telling student the correct answer as you touch student's mouth. Score V for correct response that followed verbal prompt. Score M if the correct response followed the model prompt. Score P if physical guidance was used.
Additional Targets:	

Answering Two-Variable Questions About Items
Compatible with ABLLS®-R Code H38

Student's Name:		Start Date:	
Objective:	When teacher asks student two-variable questions, student will answer the question with correct information. For example, "What are some furry pets?" (variables are furry and pets) "Cat and dog"		
Person Implementing Objective:			
Setting/Environment:			
Materials:			
Reinforcers:			
Baseline:	Ask student a two-variable question. Wait 5 seconds for a response. A correct response is scored (+) if student states correct items- <u>do not reinforce</u>. Move to next trial. An incorrect response is scored (-) if student does not state correct items- <u>do not prompt</u>. Move to next trial.		
Teaching Procedures:	Ask the student a two-variable question. Wait 5 seconds for a response. If student states correct items, praise and provide reinforcer. If student does not state correct items, tell the student the correct items. Repeat the original question. Wait 5 seconds for a response. If student states correct items, praise and provide reinforcer. If student does not state correct items, physically guide by again telling student the correct answer as you touch student's mouth. Score V for correct response that followed verbal prompt. Score M if the correct response followed the model prompt. Score P if physical guidance was used.		
Additional Targets:			

Answering Three-Variable Questions About Items
Compatible with ABLLS®-R Code H39

Student's Name:		Start Date:	
Objective:	When teacher asks student three-variable questions, student will answer the question with appropriate information. For example, "What are some small, furry, pets?" (variables are small, furry, and pets) "Hamster and rabbit"		
Person Implementing Objective:			
Setting/Environment:			
Materials:			
Reinforcers:			
Baseline:	Ask student a three-variable question. Wait 5 seconds for a response. A correct response is scored (+) if student states correct items- <u>do not reinforce</u>. Move to next trial. An incorrect response is scored (-) if student does not state correct items- <u>do not prompt</u>. Move to next trial.		
Teaching Procedures:	Ask student a three-variable question. Wait 5 seconds for a response. If student states appropriate items, praise and provide reinforcer. If student does not state appropriate items, tell the student the appropriate items. Repeat the original question. Wait 5 seconds for a response. If student states appropriate items, praise and provide reinforcer. If student does not state appropriate items physically guide by again telling student the correct answer as you touch student's mouth. Score V for correct response that followed verbal prompt. Score M if the correct response followed the model prompt. Score P if physical guidance was used.		
Additional Targets:			

Provide Descriptions For Items
Compatible with ABLLS®-R Code H40

Student's Name:	Start Date:
Objective:	When teacher asks student to describe an item, student will provide at least three relevant details about the item.
Person Implementing Objective:	
Setting/Environment:	
Materials:	
Reinforcers:	
Baseline:	Say, "Describe a/an ____ (name item)." Wait 5 seconds for a response. A correct response is scored (+) if student provides at least three relevant details about the item- <u>do not reinforce</u>. Move to next trial. An incorrect response is scored (-) if student does not provide at least three relevant details about the item- <u>do not prompt</u>. Move to next trial.
Teaching Procedures:	Say, "Describe a/an ____ (name item)." Wait 5 seconds for a response. If student provides at least three relevant details about the item, praise and provide reinforcer. If student does not provide at least three relevant details about the item, say, "A ____ (name item) has ____ and ____ and ____ (naming three details)." Say, "Describe a/an ____ (name item)." Wait 5 seconds for a response. If student provides at least three relevant details about the item, praise and provide reinforcer. If student does not provide at least three relevant details about the item, physically guide by again telling student the appropriate details as you touch student's mouth. Score V for correct response that followed verbal prompt. Score M if the correct response followed the model prompt. Score P if physical guidance was used.
Additional Targets:	

Name Activities Before And After Other Activities
Compatible with ABLLS®-R Code H41

Student's Name:		Start Date:	
Objective:	When teacher asks student to describe what happens before or after a named activity, student will name those activities. For example: "What do you do *before* you go to the playground?" or "What do you do *after* you go to the playground?"		
Person Implementing Objective:			
Setting/Environment:			
Materials:			
Reinforcers:			
Baseline:	Say, "What do you do before/after you ____ (name activity)?" Wait 5 seconds for a response. A correct response is scored (+) if student states correct activity- <u>do not reinforce</u>. Move to next trial. An incorrect response is scored (-) if student does not state correct activity- <u>do not prompt</u>. Move to next trial.		
Teaching Procedures:	Say, "What do you do before/after you ____ (name activity)?" Wait 5 seconds for a response. If student states correct activity, praise and provide reinforcer. If student does not state correct activity, say, "You ____ (name activity) before/after you ____ (name activity)." Say, "What do you do before/after ____ (name activity)?" Wait 5 seconds for a response. If student states correct activity, praise and provide reinforcer. If student does not state correct activity, physically guide by again telling student what is done before or after activity as you touch student's mouth. Score V for correct response that followed verbal prompt. Score M if the correct response followed the model prompt. Score P if physical guidance was used.		
Additional Targets:			

Describe Previous And Future Events
Compatible with ABLLS®-R Code H42

Student's Name:	Start Date:
Objective:	When teacher asks student about previous or future events, student will accurately report what has happened or what is to happen. For example, "What did you have for lunch?" or "What are you going to have for dinner?"
Person Implementing Objective:	
Setting/Environment:	
Materials:	
Reinforcers:	
Baseline:	Say, "What did you ____ (name previous event)?" or "What are you going to ____ (name future event)?" Wait 5 seconds for a response. A correct response is scored (+) if student states correct past or future event- <u>do not reinforce</u>. Move to next trial. An incorrect response is scored (-) if student does not state correct past or future event- do not prompt. Move to next trial.
Teaching Procedures:	Say, "What did you ____ (name previous event)?" or "What are you going to ____ (name future event)?" Wait 5 seconds for a response. If student states correct past or future event, praise and provide reinforcer. If student does not state correct past or future event, tell student the correct past or future event. Say, "What did you ____ (name previous event)?" or "What are you going to ____ (name future event)?" Wait 5 seconds for a response. If student states correct past or future event, praise and provide reinforcer. If student does not state correct past or future event, physically guide by again telling student the correct past or future event as you touch student's mouth. Score V for correct response that followed verbal prompt. Score M if the correct response followed the model prompt. Score P if physical guidance was used.
Additional Targets:	

Conversation Skills
Compatible with ABLLS®-R Code H43

Student's Name:	Start Date:

Objective:	When teacher begins a conversation with student, student will maintain the conversation. For example "Tell me about your dog."
Person Implementing Objective:	
Setting/Environment:	
Materials:	
Reinforcers:	
Baseline:	Say, "Tell me about ____ (name event or item)." Wait 5 seconds for a response. If a correct response is made, make comment on same topic. Continue until multiple exchanges are made. A correct response is scored (+) if student provides correct number of exchanges- <u>do not reinforce</u>. Move to next trial. An incorrect response is scored (-) if student does not provide correct number of exchanges- <u>do not prompt</u>. Move to next trial.
Teaching Procedures:	Say, "Tell me about ____ (name event or item)." Wait 5 seconds for a response. If a correct response is made, make comment on same topic. Continue until multiple exchanges have been made. If at any point student does not answer a question or make a relevant topical remark, tell student, "We are talking about ____ (name event or item)" and repeat the question or comment made. Wait 5 seconds for a response. Continue until all exchanges are made. Score V if student provided correct number of exchanges without model or physical prompts. Score M if model prompts were used. Score P if physical guidance was used.
Additional Targets:	

Answer Unique Questions
Compatible with ABLLS®-R Code H44

Student's Name:		Start Date:	
Objective:	When teacher asks student a question previously taught using different wording, student will answer the newly phrased question.		
Person Implementing Objective:			
Setting/Environment:			
Materials:			
Reinforcers:			
Baseline:	Ask student a question previously taught but ask the question using different wording. Wait 5 seconds for a response. A correct response is scored (+) if student states correct answers to question- <u>do not reinforce</u>. Move to next trial. An incorrect response is scored (-) if student does not answer question correctly- <u>do not prompt</u>. Move to next trial.		
Teaching Procedures:	Ask student a question previously taught but ask the question using different wording. Wait 5 seconds for a response. If a correct answer is given, praise and provide reinforcer. If a correct answer is not given, tell student the answer and repeat the question posed. Wait 5 seconds for a response. If a correct answer is given, praise and provide reinforcer. If a correct answer is not given, tell student the answer as you touch student's mouth. Score V for correct response that followed verbal prompt. Score M if the correct response followed the model prompt. Score P if physical guidance was used.		
Additional Targets:			

Answer Questions About Current/Recent Events
Compatible with ABLLS®-R Code H45

Student's Name:		Start Date:	
Objective:	When teacher asks student about a current or recent event, student will respond with correct answer. For example, "What did you do this weekend?"		
Person Implementing Objective:			
Setting/Environment:			
Materials:			
Reinforcers:			
Baseline:	Ask student a question about a current/recent event. Wait 5 seconds for a response. A correct response is scored (+) if student states correct answer - <u>do not reinforce</u>. Move to next trial. An incorrect response is scored (-) if student does not state correct answer- <u>do not prompt</u>. Move to next trial.		
Teaching Procedures:	Ask student a question about a current/recent event. Wait 5 seconds for a response. If student states correct answer, praise and provide reinforcer. If student does not state correct answer, give student the correct answer. Repeat the original question. Wait 5 seconds for a response. If student states correct answer, praise and provide reinforcer. If student does not state correct answer, physically guide by again telling student the correct answer as you touch student's mouth. Score V for correct response that followed verbal prompt. Score M if the correct response followed the model prompt. Score P if physical guidance was used.		
Additional Targets:			

Answer Questions About Current/Recent Events Using Several Answers
Compatible with ABLLS®-R Code H46

Student's Name:		Start Date:	
Objective:	When teacher asks student about a current/recent event, student will respond with several appropriate answers. For example, "What all did you do this weekend?"		
Person Implementing Objective:			
Setting/Environment:			
Materials:			
Reinforcers:			
Baseline:	Ask student a question about a current/recent event. Wait 5 seconds for a response. A correct response is scored (+) if student states several correct answers - <u>do not reinforce</u>. Move to next trial. An incorrect response is scored (-) if student does not state several correct answers- <u>do not prompt</u>. Move to next trial.		
Teaching Procedures:	Ask student a question about a current/recent event. Wait 5 seconds for a response. If student states several correct answers, praise and provide reinforcer. If student does not state several correct answers, give student the answers. Repeat the original question. Wait 5 seconds for a response. If student states several correct answers, praise and provide reinforcer. If student does not state several correct answers, physically guide by again telling student the correct answers as you touch student's mouth. Score V for correct response that followed verbal prompt. Score M if the correct response followed the model prompt. Score P if physical guidance was used.		
Additional Targets:			

Answering Questions Requiring Several Responses In A Small Group
Compatible with ABLLS®-R Code H47

Student's Name:		Start Date:
Objective:	When student is in a small group of students and teacher asks the student about a recent event, student will respond with several appropriate answers. For example, "What did you do at lunch today?"	
Person Implementing Objective:		
Setting/Environment:		
Materials:		
Reinforcers:		
Baseline:	While in a small group of students, ask student a question about a recent event. Wait 5 seconds for a response. A correct response is scored (+) if student states several correct answers - do not reinforce. Move to next trial. An incorrect response is scored (-) if student does not state several correct answers- do not prompt. Move to next trial.	
Teaching Procedures:	While in a small group of students, ask student a question about a recent event. Wait 5 seconds for a response. If student states several correct answers, praise and provide reinforcer. If student does not state several correct answers, give student the correct answers. Repeat the original question. Wait 5 seconds for a response. If student states several correct answers, praise and provide reinforcer. If student does not state several correct answers, physically guide by again telling student the correct answers as you touch student's mouth. Score V for correct response that followed verbal prompt. Score M if the correct response followed the model prompt. Score P if physical guidance was used.	
Additional Targets:		

Story Telling About Recent Events
Compatible with ABLLS®-R Code H48

Student's Name:		Start Date:	
Objective:		When teacher asks student to tell about a recent event, student will respond with several correct answers. For example, "Tell me a story about going to the doctor yesterday?"	
Person Implementing Objective:			
Setting/Environment:			
Materials:			
Reinforcers:			
Baseline:		Ask student to tell you a story about a recent event. Wait 5 seconds for a response. A correct response is scored (+) if student states several correct details in chronological order - <u>do not reinforce</u>. Move to next trial. An incorrect response is scored (-) if student does not state several correct details in chronological order- <u>do not prompt</u>. Move to next trial.	
Teaching Procedures:		Ask student to tell you a story about a recent event. Wait 5 seconds for a response. If student states several correct details in chronological order, praise and provide reinforcer. If student does not state several correct details in chronological order, give student several correct details in chronological order. Repeat the original question. Wait 5 seconds for a response. If student states several correct details in chronological order, praise and provide reinforcer. If student does not state several correct details in chronological order, physically guide by telling student several correct details in chronological order as you touch the student's mouth. Score V for correct response that followed verbal prompt. Score M if the correct response followed the model prompt. Score P if physical guidance was used.	
Additional Targets:			

CHAPTER 10

ABA Programs Compatible with

ABLLS®-R Domain J

"Syntax and Grammar"

Speaking In Sentences
Compatible with ABLLS®-R Code J1

Student's Name:	Start Date:
Objective:	When teacher presents a card depicting a scene to student and asks student to describe the scene, student will respond with a complete sentence.
Person Implementing Objective:	
Setting/Environment:	
Materials:	
Reinforcers:	
Baseline:	Show student a picture of a scene and say, "Tell me what you see." Wait 5 seconds for a response. A correct response is scored (+) if student states an appropriate complete sentence - <u>do not reinforce</u>. Move to next trial. An incorrect response is scored (-) if student does not state an appropriate complete sentence- <u>do not prompt</u>. Move to next trial.
Teaching Procedures:	Show student a picture of a scene and say, "Tell me what you see." Wait 5 seconds for a response. If student states an appropriate complete sentence, praise and provide reinforcer. If student does not state an appropriate complete sentence, add the words required to turn the response given into the correct form. For example, if student says, "Blue sky" you say (for example) "I see a light blue sky." Show the card again and say, "Tell me what you see." Wait 5 seconds for a response. If student states an appropriate complete sentence, praise and provide reinforcer. If student does not state an appropriate complete sentence, physically guide by again turning the response into the complete sentence as you touch student's mouth. Score V for correct response that followed verbal prompt. Score M if the correct response followed the model prompt. Score P if physical guidance was used.
Additional Targets:	

Proper Syntax
Compatible with ABLLS®-R Code J2

Student's Name:	Start Date:
Objective:	When teacher presents a card depicting a scene to student, points to one aspect of the scene and asks student, "What is this?" student will respond using correct syntax. Proper syntax requires an adjective or verb to precede a noun, etc.
Person Implementing Objective:	
Setting/Environment:	
Materials:	
Reinforcers:	
Baseline:	Show student a picture of a scene, point to one aspect of the scene and say, "What is this?" Wait 5 seconds for a response. A correct response is scored (+) if student states an appropriate answer using correct syntax- <u>do not reinforce</u>. Move to next trial. An incorrect response is scored (-) if student does not state an appropriate answer using correct syntax- <u>do not prompt</u>. Move to next trial.
Teaching Procedures:	Show student a picture of a scene, point to one aspect of the scene and say, "What is this?" Wait 5 seconds for a response. If student states an appropriate answer using correct syntax, praise and provide reinforcer. If student does not state an appropriate answer using correct syntax, repeat the given response using correct syntax. For example, if the student says, "Sky Blue" you say, "Blue sky." Show student a picture of a scene, point to one aspect of the scene and say, "What is this?" Wait 5 seconds for a response. If student states an appropriate answer using correct syntax, praise and provide reinforcer. If student does not state an appropriate answer using correct syntax, physically guide by again repeating the response with correct syntax as you touch student's mouth. Score V for correct response that followed verbal prompt. Score M if the correct response followed the model prompt. Score P if physical guidance was used.
Additional Targets:	

The BIG Book of ABA Programs

Using Articles In Sentences
Compatible with ABLLS®-R Code J3

Student's Name:	Start Date:	
Objective:	When teacher presents a common object to student and says, "What is this?" student will name the object in a complete sentence using the correct article (For example, That is *a* cup; This is *the* spoon, This is *an* elephant).	
Person Implementing Objective:		
Setting/Environment:		
Materials:		
Reinforcers:		
Baseline:	Present a common object to student and say, "What is this?" Wait 5 seconds for a response. A correct response is scored (+) if student states the name of the object in a complete sentence and uses the correct article - <u>do not reinforce</u>. Move to next trial. An incorrect response is scored (-) if student does not state the name of the object in a complete sentence or uses the incorrect article- <u>do not prompt</u>. Move to next trial.	
Teaching Procedures:	Present a common object to student and say, "What is this?" Wait 5 seconds for a response. If student states the name of the object in a complete sentence and with the correct article, praise and provide reinforcer. If student does not state the name of the object in a complete sentence with correct article, say, "This is (a/an)____ (name object)." Remove the object briefly and re-present the object and say, "What is this?" Wait 5 seconds for a response. If student states the name of the object in a complete sentence with correct article, praise and provide reinforcer. If the object name is not stated in a complete sentence with correct article, physically guide by touching student's mouth as you say, "This is (a/an) ____ (name object)." Score V for correct response that followed verbal prompt. Score M if the correct response followed the model prompt. Score P if physical guidance was used.	
Additional Targets:		

Adding "ing" To Present Tense Verbs
Compatible with ABLLS®-R Code J4

Student's Name:		Start Date:	
Objective:		When teacher presents a card depicting an action to student and says, "What is he/she doing?" student will respond using correct present tense verb ending in "ing."	
Person Implementing Objective:			
Setting/Environment:			
Materials:			
Reinforcers:			
Baseline:		Show student a picture of an action and say, "What is he/she doing?" Wait 5 seconds for a response. A correct response is scored (+) if student states an appropriate present tense verb ending in "ing"- <u>do not reinforce</u>. Move to next trial. An incorrect response is scored (-) if student does not state an appropriate present tense verb ending in "ing."- <u>do not prompt</u>. Move to next trial.	
Teaching Procedures:		Show student a picture of an action and say, "What is he/she doing?" Wait 5 seconds for a response. If student states an appropriate present tense verb ending in "ing," praise and provide reinforcer. If student does not state an appropriate present tense verb ending in "ing," provide present tense verb ending in "ing." Say, "What is he/she doing?" Wait 5 seconds for a response. If student states an appropriate present tense verb ending in "ing," praise and provide reinforcer. If student does not state an appropriate present tense verb ending in "ing," physically guide by again providing correct present tense verb ending in "ing" as you touch student's mouth. Score V for correct response that followed verbal prompt. Score M if the correct response followed the model prompt. Score P if physical guidance was used.	
Additional Targets:			

The BIG Book of ABA Programs

Plural Nouns With Regular Form
Compatible with ABLLS®-R Code J5

Student's Name:		Start Date:
Objective:	\multicolumn{2}{l}{When teacher presents multiple similar or identical objects to student and asks, "What are these?" student will respond using correct plural ending in "s" or "es"}
Person Implementing Objective:		
Setting/Environment:		
Materials:		
Reinforcers:		
Baseline:		Present the student with multiple similar or identical objects. Say, "What are these?" Wait 5 seconds for a response. A correct response is scored (+) if student names objects using appropriate plural ending in "s" or "es"- <u>do not reinforce</u>. Move to next trial. An incorrect response is scored (-) if student does not name objects using appropriate plural ending in "s" or "es." – <u>do not prompt</u>. Move to next trial.
Teaching Procedures:		Present the student with multiple similar or identical items. Say, "What are these?" Wait 5 seconds for a response. If student names objects using appropriate plural ending in "s" or "es," praise and provide reinforcer. If student does not names objects using appropriate plural ending in "s" or "es," provide appropriate plural ending in "s" or "es." Say, "What are these?" Wait 5 seconds for a response. If student names objects using appropriate plural ending in "s" or "es," praise and provide reinforcer. If student does not name objects using appropriate plural ending in "s" or "es," physically guide by again giving the appropriate plural ending in "s" or "es" as you touch student's mouth. Score V for correct response that followed verbal prompt. Score M if the correct response followed the model prompt. Score P if physical guidance was used.
Additional Targets:		

The BIG Book of ABA Programs

Past Tense Verbs With Irregular Form
Compatible with ABLLS®-R Code J6

Student's Name:	Start Date:
Objective:	When teacher asks student about the past tense of a verb, student will respond using correct past tense verb. For example, "What is the past tense of eat?" "Ate"
Person Implementing Objective:	
Setting/Environment:	
Materials:	
Reinforcers:	
Baseline:	Say, "What is the past tense of ____ (name verb)?" Wait 5 seconds for a response. A correct response is scored (+) if student says appropriate past tense- do not reinforce. Move to next trial. An incorrect response is scored (-) if student does not say appropriate past tense- do not prompt. Move to next trial.
Teaching Procedures:	Say, "What is the past tense of ____ (name verb)?" Wait 5 seconds for a response. If student says appropriate past tense, praise and provide reinforcer. If student does not say appropriate past tense, provide the correct past tense. Say, "What is the past tense of ____ (name verb)?" Wait 5 seconds for a response. If student says appropriate past tense, praise and provide reinforcer. If student does not say appropriate past tense, physically guide by again giving the correct past tense as you touch student's mouth. Score V for correct response that followed verbal prompt. Score M if the correct response followed the model prompt. Score P if physical guidance was used.
Additional Targets:	

Using Contractions
Compatible with ABLLS®-R Code J7

Student's Name:	Start Date:
Objective:	When teacher asks student to make two words into one, student will respond using correct contraction. For example, "How do you make the words "can" and "not" into one word?" "Can't"
Person Implementing Objective:	
Setting/Environment:	
Materials:	
Reinforcers:	
Baseline:	Say, "How do you make the words ____ and ____ (name two words that make a common contraction) into one word?" Wait 5 seconds for a response. A correct response is scored (+) if student says appropriate contraction- <u>do not reinforce</u>. Move to next trial. An incorrect response is scored (-) if student does not say appropriate contraction- <u>do not prompt</u>. Move to next trial.
Teaching Procedures:	Say, "How do you make the words ____ and ____ (name two words that make a common contraction) into one word?" Wait 5 seconds for a response. If student says appropriate contraction, praise and provide reinforcer. If student does not say appropriate contraction, provide the contraction. For example, "You can make the words 'can' and 'not' in to 'can't.'" Say, "How do you make the words ____ and ____ (name two words that make a common contraction) into one word?" Wait 5 seconds for a response. If student says appropriate contraction, praise and provide reinforcer. If student does not say appropriate contraction, physically guide by again giving the correct contraction as you touch student's mouth. Score V for correct response that followed verbal prompt. Score M if the correct response followed the model prompt. Score P if physical guidance was used.
Additional Targets:	

Present Tense
Compatible with ABLLS®-R Code J8

Student's Name:		Start Date:	
Objective:		When student is engaged in an activity and teacher asks "What are you doing right now?" student will respond using "am" and appropriate form of verb re-presenting the current activity. For example, "I am reading"	
Person Implementing Objective:			
Setting/Environment:			
Materials:			
Reinforcers:			
Baseline:		When student is engaged in an activity, say, "What are you doing right now?" Wait 5 seconds for a response. A correct response is scored (+) if student uses "am" and appropriate verb- <u>do not reinforce</u>. Move to next trial. An incorrect response is scored (-) if student does not use "am" and appropriate verb- <u>do not prompt</u>. Move to next trial.	
Teaching Procedures:		When student is engaged in an activity, say, "What are you doing right now?" Wait 5 seconds for a response. If student uses "am" and appropriate verb, praise and provide reinforcer. If student does not use "am" and appropriate verb, provide "am" and appropriate verb. For example, "You are reading, so you should say, 'I am reading.'" Say, "What are you doing right now?" Wait 5 seconds for a response. If student uses "am" and appropriate verb, praise and provide reinforcer. If student does not use "am" and appropriate verb, physically guide by again giving "am" and the correct verb as you touch student's mouth. Score V for correct response that followed verbal prompt. Score M if the correct response followed the model prompt. Score P if physical guidance was used.	
Additional Targets:			

Past Tense Verbs With Regular Form
Compatible with ABLLS®-R Code J9

Student's Name:	Start Date:
Objective:	When teacher asks student about the past tense of a verb, student will respond using correct past tense verb. For example, "What is the past tense of dance?" "Danced"
Person Implementing Objective:	
Setting/Environment:	
Materials:	
Reinforcers:	
Baseline:	Say, "What is the past tense of ____ (name verb)?" Wait 5 seconds for a response. A correct response is scored (+) if student says appropriate past tense- do not reinforce. Move to next trial. An incorrect response is scored (-) if student does not say appropriate past tense-do not prompt. Move to next trial.
Teaching Procedures:	Say, "What is the past tense of ____ (name verb)?" Wait 5 seconds for a response. If student says appropriate past tense, praise and provide reinforcer. If student does not say appropriate past tense, say, "The past tense of ____ (verb) is ____ (past tense of verb)." Say, "What is the past tense of ____ (name verb)?" Wait 5 seconds for a response. If student says appropriate past tense, praise and provide reinforcer. If student does not say appropriate past tense, physically guide by again giving the correct past tense as you touch student's mouth. Score V for correct response that followed verbal prompt. Score M if the correct response followed the model prompt. Score P if physical guidance was used.
Additional Targets:	

Answering In The Possessive
Compatible with ABLLS®-R Code J10

Student's Name:	Start Date:	
Objective:	When teacher asks student to whom an object belongs, student will respond using correct possessive form. For example, "Whose backpack is that?" "Nikkie's" or "That is Nikkie's backpack?"	
Person Implementing Objective:		
Setting/Environment:		
Materials:		
Reinforcers:		
Baseline:	Point to an object and say, "Whose ____ (name object) is that?" Wait 5 seconds for a response. A correct response is scored (+) if student says appropriate form of possessive- <u>do not reinforce</u>. Move to next trial. An incorrect response is scored (-) if student does not say appropriate form of possessive- <u>do not prompt</u>. Move to next trial.	
Teaching Procedures:	Point to an object and say, "Whose ____ (name object) is that?" Wait 5 seconds for a response. If student says appropriate form of possessive, praise and provide reinforcer. If student does not say appropriate form of possessive, provide the possessive. For example, "That is Nikkie's backpack." Say, "Whose ____ (name object) is that?" Wait 5 seconds for a response. If student says appropriate form of possessive, praise and provide reinforcer. If student does not say appropriate form of possessive, physically guide by again giving the correct possessive as you touch student's mouth. Score V for correct response that followed verbal prompt. Score M if the correct response followed the model prompt. Score P if physical guidance was used.	
Additional Targets:		

Answering In The Negative
Compatible with ABLLS®-R Code J11

Student's Name:		Start Date:	
Objective:		When teacher asks student a question the answer to which is negative, student will respond in a complete sentence using correct negative form. For example, "Is that your backpack?" "That is not my backpack"	
Person Implementing Objective:			
Setting/Environment:			
Materials:			
Reinforcers:			
Baseline:		Ask student a question to which the answer is negative. Wait 5 seconds for a response. A correct response is scored (+) if student responds in a complete sentence using appropriate form of negative- <u>do not reinforce</u>. Move to next trial. An incorrect response is scored (-) if student does not respond in a complete sentence using appropriate form of negative- <u>do not prompt</u>. Move to next trial.	
Teaching Procedures:		Ask student a question to which the answer is negative. Wait 5 seconds for a response. If student responds in a complete sentence using appropriate form of negative, praise and provide reinforcer. If student does not respond in a complete sentence using appropriate form of negative, provide the appropriate form of the negative. Ask the question again. Wait 5 seconds for a response. If student responds in a complete sentence using appropriate form of negative, praise and provide reinforcer. If student does not respond in a complete sentence using appropriate form of negative, physically guide by again giving the correct form of the negative as you touch student's mouth. Score V for correct response that followed verbal prompt. Score M if the correct response followed the model prompt. Score P if physical guidance was used.	
Additional Targets:			

The BIG Book of ABA Programs

Answering With Words Indicating Location
Compatible with ABLLS®-R Code J12

Student's Name:	Start Date:
Objective:	When teacher asks student where an item is located, student will respond in a complete sentence using correct word indicating location. For example, "Where is you your backpack?" "It's over there"
Person Implementing Objective:	
Setting/Environment:	
Materials:	
Reinforcers:	
Baseline:	Say, "Where is the/your ____ (name item)?" Wait 5 seconds for a response. A correct response is scored (+) if student responds in a complete sentence using appropriate words expressing location- <u>do not reinforce</u>. Move to next trial. An incorrect response is scored (-) if student does not respond in a complete sentence using appropriate words expressing location- <u>do not prompt</u>. Move to next trial.
Teaching Procedures:	Say, "Where is the/your ____ (name item)?" Wait 5 seconds for a response. If student responds in a complete sentence using appropriate words expressing location, praise and provide reinforcer. If student does not respond in a complete sentence using appropriate words expressing location, say, "The ____ (name item) is ____ (provide word or phrase expressing location)." Say, "Where is the/your ____ (name item)?" Wait 5 seconds for a response. If student responds in a complete sentence using appropriate words expressing location, praise and provide reinforcer. If student does not respond in a complete sentence using appropriate words expressing location, physically guide by again giving the correct appropriate words expressing location as you touch student's mouth. Score V for correct response that followed verbal prompt. Score M if the correct response followed the model prompt. Score P if physical guidance was used.
Additional Targets:	

The BIG Book of ABA Programs

Answering In The Future Tense
Compatible with ABLLS®-R Code J13

Student's Name:		Start Date:	
Objective:	When teacher asks about an upcoming activity, student will respond using appropriate form of verb representing the future activity. For example, "What will you do at lunch this afternoon?" "I will eat my lunch"		
Person Implementing Objective:			
Setting/Environment:			
Materials:			
Reinforcers:			
Baseline:	Ask student a question about what they *will* do. Wait 5 seconds for a response. A correct response is scored (+) if student uses appropriate future tense- do not reinforce. Move to next trial. An incorrect response is scored (-) if student does use appropriate future tense- do not prompt. Move to next trial.		
Teaching Procedures:	Ask student a question about what they *will* do. Wait 5 seconds for a response. If student uses appropriate future tense, praise and provide reinforcer. If student does not use appropriate future tense, say, "You will ____ (name future event), so you should say, 'I will ____ (name future event).'" Repeat original question. Wait 5 seconds for a response. If student uses appropriate future tense, praise and provide reinforcer. If student does not use appropriate future tense, physically guide by again giving the correct future tense as you touch student's mouth. Score V for correct response that followed verbal prompt. Score M if the correct response followed the model prompt. Score P if physical guidance was used.		
Additional Targets:			

Answering With Conjunctions
Compatible with ABLLS®-R Code J14

Student's Name:	Start Date:
Objective:	When teacher asks a question to which the answer requires a conjunction, student will respond using appropriate conjunction. For example, "Who lives at home with you?" "My mom *and* dad" (Conjunction examples: and, or, but, etc.)
Person Implementing Objective:	
Setting/Environment:	
Materials:	
Reinforcers:	
Baseline:	Ask student a question to which the answer requires the use of a conjunction. Wait 5 seconds for a response. A correct response is scored (+) if student uses appropriate conjunction- do not reinforce. Move to next trial. An incorrect response is scored (-) if student does use appropriate conjunction- do not prompt. Move to next trial.
Teaching Procedures:	Ask student a question to which the answer requires the use of a conjunction. Wait 5 seconds for a response. If student uses appropriate conjunction, praise and provide reinforcer. If student does not use appropriate conjunction, provide the appropriate conjunction. Ask the original question again. Wait 5 seconds for a response. If student uses appropriate conjunction, praise and provide reinforcer. If student does not use appropriate conjunction, physically guide by again giving the correct conjunction as you touch student's mouth. Score V for correct response that followed verbal prompt. Score M if the correct response followed the model prompt. Score P if physical guidance was used.
Additional Targets:	

The BIG Book of ABA Programs

Plural Nouns With Irregular Form
Compatible with ABLLS®-R Code J15

Student's Name:	Start Date:
Objective:	When teacher presents multiple similar or identical objects to student and asks, "What are these?" student will respond using correct irregular plural. For example, "What are these?" "Mice"
Person Implementing Objective:	
Setting/Environment:	
Materials:	
Reinforcers:	
Baseline:	Present student with multiple similar or identical items and ask, "What are these?" Wait 5 seconds for a response. A correct response is scored (+) if student names objects using appropriate irregular plural - <u>do not reinforce</u>. Move to next trial. An incorrect response is scored (-) if student does not name objects using appropriate irregular plural- <u>do not prompt</u>. Move to next trial.
Teaching Procedures:	Present student with multiple similar or identical items and ask, "What are these?" Wait 5 seconds for a response. If student names objects using appropriate irregular plural, praise and provide reinforcer. If student does not name objects using appropriate irregular plural, say "These are ____ (name irregular plural)." Show student the objects again and say, "What are these?" Wait 5 seconds for a response. If student names objects using appropriate irregular plural, praise and provide reinforcer. If student does not name objects using appropriate irregular plural, physically guide by again giving the correct plural as you touch student's mouth. Score V for correct response that followed verbal prompt. Score M if the correct response followed the model prompt. Score P if physical guidance was used.
Additional Targets:	

Answer Questions Using Comparatives
Compatible with ABLLS®-R Code J16

Student's Name:	Start Date:
Objective:	When teacher presents multiple objects to student that vary on some physical dimension and asks which item meets some comparative criterion, student will respond using correct comparative. For example, "Which of these is the shortest?" "This is the shortest"
Person Implementing Objective:	
Setting/Environment:	
Materials:	
Reinforcers:	
Baseline:	Present student with multiple items that vary along some physical dimension and ask which item meets some comparative criterion. Wait 5 seconds for a response. A correct response is scored (+) if student answers question correctly using appropriate comparative- <u>do not reinforce</u>. Move to next trial. An incorrect response is scored (-) if student does not answer question correctly using appropriate comparative- <u>do not prompt</u>. Move to next trial.
Teaching Procedures:	Present student with multiple items that vary along some physical dimension and ask which item meets some comparative criterion. Wait 5 seconds for a response. If student answers question correctly using appropriate comparative, praise and provide reinforcer. If student does not answer question correctly using appropriate comparative, gesture to the correct item and say, "This is the ____ (name comparative)." Show student the items again and ask original question. Wait 5 seconds for a response. If student answers question correctly using appropriate comparative, praise and provide reinforcer. If student does not answer question correctly using appropriate comparative, physically guide by again giving the appropriate comparative as you touch student's mouth. Score V for correct response that followed verbal prompt. Score M if the correct response followed the model prompt. Score P if physical guidance was used.
Additional Targets:	

Answer Questions Using Demonstratives
Compatible with ABLLS®-R Code J17

Student's Name:	Start Date:

Objective:	When teacher presents objects to student that vary on some physical dimension and asks which objects meet some criterion, student will respond using correct demonstratives. For example, "Which of these are blue?" "*These* are blue." (Demonstrative examples: these, that, this, those, etc.)
Person Implementing Objective:	
Setting/Environment:	
Materials:	
Reinforcers:	
Baseline:	Present student with multiple objects that vary along some physical dimension. Say, "Which ones are ____ (name some physical dimension)?" Wait 5 seconds for a response. A correct response is scored (+) if student answers question correctly using appropriate demonstratives- <u>do not reinforce</u>. Move to next trial. An incorrect response is scored (-) if student does not answer question correctly using appropriate demonstratives- <u>do not prompt</u>. Move to next trial.
Teaching Procedures:	Present student with multiple objects that vary along some physical dimension. Say, "Which ones are ____ (name some physical dimension)?" Wait 5 seconds for a response. If student answers question correctly using appropriate demonstrative, praise and provide reinforcer. If student does not answer question correctly using appropriate demonstrative, gesture to the correct objects and say, "____ (name demonstrative) is/are ____ (name physical dimension)." Show student the items again and ask original question. Wait 5 seconds for a response. If student answers question correctly using appropriate demonstrative, praise and provide reinforcer. If student does not answer question correctly using appropriate demonstrative, physically guide by again saying, "____ (name demonstrative) is/are ____ (name physical dimension)" as you touch student's mouth. Score V for correct response that followed verbal prompt. Score M if the correct response followed the model prompt. Score P if physical guidance was used.
Additional Targets:	

Answer Questions Using Words Expressing Uncertainty
Compatible with ABLLS®-R Code J18

Student's Name:	Start Date:
Objective:	When teacher asks student a question to which the answer is unknowable, student will guess with language that expresses uncertainty. For example, "How many fingers am I holding up behind my back?" "*I think* you are holding up four fingers."
Person Implementing Objective:	
Setting/Environment:	
Materials:	
Reinforcers:	
Baseline:	Ask student a question to which the answer is unknowable. Wait 5 seconds for a response. A correct response is scored (+) if student guesses using language that expresses uncertainty- <u>do not reinforce</u>. Move to next trial. An incorrect response is scored (-) if student does not guess using language that expresses uncertainty- <u>do not prompt</u>. Move to next trial.
Teaching Procedures:	Ask student a question to which the answer is unknowable. Wait 5 seconds for a response. If student guesses using language that expresses uncertainty, praise and provide reinforcer. If student does not guess using language that expresses uncertainty, tell the student answer using language that expresses uncertainty. For example, "If you are unsure of the answer, you should say, 'I *think* you are holding up 4 fingers.'" Ask the original question again. Wait 5 seconds for a response. If student guesses using language that expresses uncertainty, praise and provide reinforcer. If student does not guess using language that expresses uncertainty, physically guide by again giving the correct language as you touch the student's mouth. Score V for correct response that followed verbal prompt. Score M if the correct response followed the model prompt. Score P if physical guidance was used.
Additional Targets:	

Answer Questions Using Words Expressing Quantification
Compatible with ABLLS®-R Code J19

Student's Name:	Start Date:
Objective:	When teacher asks student a question to which the answer requires quantification, student will use appropriate expression of quantification. For example, "How often do you eat everyday?" "I eat 3 times a day."
Person Implementing Objective:	
Setting/Environment:	
Materials:	
Reinforcers:	
Baseline:	Ask student a question the answer to which requires quantification. Wait 5 seconds for a response. A correct response is scored (+) if student responds using language that expresses quantification- <u>do not reinforce</u>. Move to next trial. An incorrect response is scored (-) if student does not respond using language that expresses quantification- <u>do not prompt</u>. Move to next trial.
Teaching Procedures:	Ask student a question the answer to which requires quantification. Wait 5 seconds for a response. If student responds using language that expresses quantification, praise and provide reinforcer. If student does not respond using language that expresses quantification, provide student with choices that use quantification. For example, say, "You ____ (name activity from original question) ____ (name quantification) each day." Ask the original question again. Wait 5 seconds for a response. If student responds using language that expresses quantification, praise and provide reinforcer. If student does not respond using language that expresses quantification, physically guide by telling student language that expresses quantification as you touch student's mouth. Score V for correct response that followed verbal prompt. Score M if the correct response followed the model prompt. Score P if physical guidance was used.
Additional Targets:	

The BIG Book of ABA Programs

Answer Questions Using Words Expressing Emotion
Compatible with ABLLS®-R Code J20

Student's Name:	Start Date:
Objective:	When teacher asks student how student should respond to a question when feeling a certain emotion, student will use appropriate expression of the stated emotion. For example, "If you are *happy* when answering the question, 'Do you want to go to the circus?' how might you answer the question?" "I would be happy to go to the circus."
Person Implementing Objective:	
Setting/Environment:	
Materials:	
Reinforcers:	
Baseline:	Ask student how he/she would answer a question when feeling a certain emotion. Wait 5 seconds for a response. A correct response is scored (+) if student responds using language that expresses the stated emotion- <u>do not reinforce</u>. Move to next trial. An incorrect response is scored (-) if student does not respond using language that expresses stated emotion- <u>do not prompt</u>. Move to next trial.
Teaching Procedures:	Ask student how he/she would answer a question when feeling a certain emotion. Wait 5 seconds for a response. If student responds using language that expresses the stated emotion, praise and provide reinforcer. If student does not respond using language that expresses stated emotion, provide the student with language that expresses the stated emotion. Ask the original question again. Wait 5 seconds for a response. If student responds using language that expresses the stated emotion, praise and provide reinforcer. If student does not respond using language that expresses stated emotion, physically guide by again giving the student the language that expresses stated emotion as you touch student's mouth. Score V for correct response that followed verbal prompt. Score M if the correct response followed the model prompt. Score P if physical guidance was used.
Additional Targets:	

CHAPTER 11

ABA Programs Compatible with

ABLLS®-R Domain K

"Play and Leisure"

Makes Contact With Toys
Compatible with ABLLS®-R Code K1

Student's Name:	Start Date:	
Objective:	When teacher presents student with a toy, student will make physical contact with the toy.	
Person Implementing Objective:		
Setting/Environment:		
Materials:		
Reinforcers:		
Baseline:	Place a toy in front of student. Say, "Play with toy." Wait 5 seconds for a response. A correct response is scored (+) if student makes physical contact with toy- <u>do not reinforce</u>. Move to next trial. An incorrect response is scored (-) if student does not make physical contact with toy- <u>do not prompt</u>. Move to next trial.	
Teaching Procedures:	Place a toy in front of student. Say, "Play with toy." Wait 5 seconds for a response. If student makes physical contact with toy, praise and provide reinforcer. If student does not make physical contact with toy, briefly place student's hands on toy as you say, "Play with toy." Wait 5 seconds for a response. If student makes physical contact with toy praise and provide reinforcer. If student does not make physical contact with toy, physically guide student's hand to make contact with toy. Score V for correct response that followed verbal prompt. Score M if the correct response followed the model prompt. Score P if physical guidance was used.	
Additional Targets:		

Share Toys
Compatible with ABLLS®-R Code K2

Student's Name:		Start Date:	
Objective:	When student is playing with a toy, student allows teacher to touch and share toy.		
Person Implementing Objective:			
Setting/Environment:			
Materials:			
Reinforcers:			
Baseline:	While student is engaged in toy play, hold out your hand and say, "My turn." Wait 5 seconds for a response. A correct response is scored (+) if student gives you the toy- <u>do not reinforce</u>. Move to next trial. An incorrect response is scored (-) if student does not give you the toy- <u>do not prompt</u>. Move to next trial.		
Teaching Procedures:	While student is engaged in toy play, hold out your hand and say, "My turn." Wait 5 seconds for a response. If student gives you the toy, praise and provide reinforcer. If student does not give you the toy, hold out your hand again and say, "My turn." Wait 5 seconds for a response. If student gives you the toy, praise and provide reinforcer. If student does not give you the toy, physically guide student's hand to give you the toy. Score V for correct response that followed verbal prompt. Score M if the correct response followed the model prompt. Score P if physical guidance was used.		
Additional Targets:			

Plays With Toys In Appropriate Manner
Compatible with ABLLS®-R Code K5

Student's Name:	Start Date:	
Objective:	When teacher presents a toy to student and says, "Play with toy" student will engage/play with toy in the appropriate manner.	
Person Implementing Objective:		
Setting/Environment:		
Materials:		
Reinforcers:		
Baseline:	Present a toy to student and say, "Play with toy." Wait 5 seconds for a response. A correct response is scored (+) if student engages/plays with toy in appropriate manner- <u>do not reinforce</u>. Move to next trial. An incorrect response is scored (-) if student does not engage/play with toy in appropriate manner- <u>do not prompt</u>. Move to next trial.	
Teaching Procedures:	Present a toy to student and say, "Play with toy." Wait 5 seconds for a response. If student engages/plays with toy in appropriate manner, praise and provide reinforcer. If student does not engage/play with toy in appropriate manner, model appropriate toy play and say, "Play with toy." Wait 5 seconds for a response. If student engages/plays with toy in appropriate manner, praise and provide reinforcer. If student does not engage/play with toy in appropriate manner, physically guide student to engage/play with toy in an appropriate manner. Score V for correct response that followed verbal prompt. Score M if the correct response followed the model prompt. Score P if physical guidance was used.	
Additional Targets:		

Talks To Teacher While Playing With Toys
Compatible with ABLLS®-R Code K6

Student's Name:		Start Date:	
Objective:	\multicolumn{3}{l	}{When student is playing with a toy and teacher asks a question with a known answer, student will answer question while continuing to play with toy.}
Person Implementing Objective:			
Setting/Environment:			
Materials:			
Reinforcers:			
Baseline:	\multicolumn{3}{l	}{While student is playing with a toy, ask student a question with a known answer. Wait 5 seconds for a response. A correct response is scored (+) if student engages/plays with toy and provides correct answer to the question- do not reinforce. Move to next trial. An incorrect response is scored (-) if student does not engage/play with toy when answering question or answers question incorrectly- do not prompt. Move to next trial.}
Teaching Procedures:	\multicolumn{3}{l	}{While student is playing with a toy, ask student a question with a known answer. Wait 5 seconds for a response. If student engages/plays with toy in appropriate manner and provides correct answer to the question, praise and provide reinforcer. If student does not engage/play with toy when answering question or answers question incorrectly, provide the answer to the question and if the student stopped playing, gesture back to the toy. Ask the question again. Wait 5 seconds for a response. If student engages/plays with toy in appropriate manner and provides correct answer to the question, praise and provide reinforcer. If student does not engage/play with toy when answering question or answers question incorrectly, physically guide student to play with the toy as you provide the answer to the question. Score V for correct response that followed verbal prompt. Score M if the correct response followed the model prompt. Score P if physical guidance was used.}
Additional Targets:			

The BIG Book of ABA Programs

Plays With A Toy In Varied Appropriate Ways
Compatible with ABLLS®-R Code K7

Student's Name:	Start Date:
Objective:	When teacher presents a toy to student and says, "Play with toy" student will engage/play with toy with several different appropriate variations.
Person Implementing Objective:	
Setting/Environment:	
Materials:	
Reinforcers:	
Baseline:	Present a toy to student and say, "Play with toy." Wait 5 seconds for a response. A correct response is scored (+) if student engages/plays with toy in appropriate manner- <u>do not reinforce</u>. Move to next trial. An incorrect response is scored (-) if student does not engage/play with toy in appropriate manner- <u>do not prompt</u>. Move to next trial. On the first trial, student can play in any appropriate manner. Subsequent trials require appropriate responses not demonstrated on the previous trial.
Teaching Procedures:	Present a toy to student and say, "Play with toy." Wait 5 seconds for a response. If student engages/plays with toy in appropriate manner different from previous trial, praise and provide reinforcer. If student does not engage/play with toy in appropriate manner different from previous trial, say, "How else can you play with this toy?" Wait 5 seconds for a response. If student engages/plays with toy in appropriate manner different than previous trial, praise and provide reinforcer. If toy play was not different previous trial, physically guide student to engage/play with the toy in an appropriate manner different from previous trial. Score V for correct response that followed verbal prompt. Score M if the correct response followed the model prompt. Score P if physical guidance was used.
Additional Targets:	

Share Toys With Peers
Compatible with ABLLS®-R Code K8

Student's Name:		Start Date:
Objective:	When student is playing with a toy and peer asks, "Can I play?" student allows peer to have toy or take a turn.	
Person Implementing Objective:		
Setting/Environment:		
Materials:		
Reinforcers:		
Baseline:	While student is engaged in toy play, have peer approach student and say, "Can I play?" Wait 5 seconds for a response. A correct response is scored (+) if student gives peer toy or lets peer take a turn- <u>do not reinforce</u>. Move to next trial. An incorrect response is scored (-) if student does not give peer toy or take a turn- <u>do not prompt</u>. Move to next trial.	
Teaching Procedures:	While student is engaged in toy play, have peer approach student and say, "Can I play?" Wait 5 seconds for a response. If student gives peer toy or allows peer to take a turn, praise and provide reinforcer. If student does not give peer toy or allow peer to take a turn, point to the toy and then to the peer as you say, "Share your toys." Wait 5 seconds for a response. If student gives peer toy or allows peer to take a turn, praise and provide reinforcer. student does not give peer toy or allow peer to take a turn, physically guide student to give peer the toy. Score V for correct response that followed verbal prompt. Score M if the correct response followed the model prompt. Score P if physical guidance was used.	
Additional Targets:		

Pretending To Be Others
Compatible with ABLLS®-R Code K10

Student's Name:		Start Date:	
Objective:	When teacher tells student to act like a certain person or character, student will act out that role.		
Person Implementing Objective:			
Setting/Environment:			
Materials:			
Reinforcers:			
Baseline:	Say, "Let's play make believe. Pretend you're a ____ (name person or character)." Wait 5 seconds for a response. A correct response is scored (+) if student demonstrates behavior consistent with named person or character- <u>do not reinforce</u>. Move to next trial. An incorrect response is scored (-) if student does not demonstrate behavior consistent with named person or character- <u>do not prompt</u>. Move to next trial.		
Teaching Procedures:	Say, "Let's play make believe. Pretend you're a ____ (name person or character)." Wait 5 seconds for a response. If student demonstrates behavior consistent with named person or character, praise and provide reinforcer. If student does not demonstrate behavior consistent with named person or character, say, "____ (name person or character) does things like ____ (name behaviors) so you should act like that too." Say, "Pretend you're a ____ (name person or character)." Wait 5 seconds for a response. If student demonstrates behavior consistent with named person or character, praise and provide reinforcer. If student does not demonstrate behavior consistent with named person or character, physically guide student to demonstrate behaviors consistent with the person or character. If behaviors are all verbal, tell the student again what to say. Score V for correct response that followed verbal prompt. Score M if the correct response followed the model prompt. Score P if physical guidance was used.		
Additional Targets:			

Talks To Peers While Playing With Toys
Compatible with ABLLS®-R Code K11

Student's Name:		Start Date:	
Objective:	When student is playing with a toy and peer asks a question with a known answer, student will answer question while continuing to play with toy.		
Person Implementing Objective:			
Setting/Environment:			
Materials:			
Reinforcers:			
Baseline:	While student is playing with a toy, have peer ask student a question with a known answer. Wait 5 seconds for a response. A correct response is scored (+) if student engages/plays with toy and provides correct answer to the question- <u>do not reinforce</u>. Move to next trial. An incorrect response is scored (-) if student does not engage/play with toy when answering question or answers question incorrectly- <u>do not prompt</u>. Move to next trial.		
Teaching Procedures:	While student is playing with a toy, have peer ask student a question with a known answer. Wait 5 seconds for a response. If student engages/plays with toy in appropriate manner and provides correct answer to the question, praise and provide reinforcer. If student does not engage/play with toy when answering question or answers question incorrectly, provide the answer to the question and if student stopped playing, gesture back to the toy. Have the peer ask the question again. Wait 5 seconds for a response. If student engages/plays with toy in appropriate manner and provides correct answer to the question, praise and provide reinforcer. If student does not engage/play with toy when answering question or answers question incorrectly, physically guide student to play with the toy as you provide the answer to the question. Score V for correct response that followed verbal prompt. Score M if the correct response followed the model prompt. Score P if physical guidance was used.		
Additional Targets:			

Plays With Ball
Compatible with ABLLS®-R Code K12

Student's Name:	Start Date:
Objective:	When teacher tells student to roll/kick/throw ball, student will roll/kick/throw ball to teacher.
Person Implementing Objective:	
Setting/Environment:	
Materials:	
Reinforcers:	
Baseline:	Give student a ball and say, "____ (roll/kick/throw) the ball." Wait 5 seconds for a response. A correct response is scored (+) if student rolls/kicks/throws ball to teacher- <u>do not reinforce</u>. Move to next trial. An incorrect response is scored (-) if student does not roll/kick/throw ball to teacher- <u>do not prompt</u>. Move to next trial.
Teaching Procedures:	Give student a ball and say, "____ (roll/kick/throw) the ball." Wait 5 seconds for a response. If student rolls/kicks/throws ball to teacher, praise and provide reinforcer. If student does not roll/kick/throw ball to teacher, demonstrate the roll/kick/throw by rolling, kicking, or throwing ball back to student as you say, "____ (roll/kick/throw) ball like this." Say "____ (roll/kick/throw) the ball." Wait 5 seconds for a response. If student rolls/kicks/throws ball to teacher, praise and provide reinforcer. If student does not roll/kick/throw ball to teacher, physically guide student to roll/kick/throw the ball. Score V for correct response that followed verbal prompt. Score M if the correct response followed the model prompt. Score P if physical guidance was used.
Additional Targets:	

CHAPTER 12

ABA Programs Compatible with

ABLLS®-R Domain L

"Social Interaction"

The BIG Book of ABA Programs

Tolerates Peer Proximity
Compatible with ABLLS®-R Code L1

Student's Name:		Start Date:	
Objective:	When student is near peers, student will refrain from inappropriate behaviors.		

Person Implementing Objective:	
Setting/Environment:	
Materials:	
Reinforcers:	
Baseline:	Seat student by peers and say, "Sit quietly." Wait ____ seconds (see target for duration). A correct response is scored (+) if student remains close to peers without demonstrating inappropriate behavior- <u>do not reinforce</u>. Move to next trial. An incorrect response is scored (-) if student does not remain close to peers without demonstrating inappropriate behavior- <u>do not prompt</u>. Move to next trial.
Teaching Procedures:	Seat student by peers and say, "Sit quietly." Wait ____ seconds (see target for duration). If student remains close to peers without demonstrating inappropriate behavior, praise and provide reinforcer. If student does not remain close to peers without demonstrating inappropriate behavior, say, "You need to sit here and remain quiet." Say, "Sit quietly." Wait ____ seconds (see target for duration). If student remains close to peers without demonstrating inappropriate behavior, praise and provide reinforcer. If student does not remain close to peers without demonstrating inappropriate behavior, physically guide student to wait in area for duration indicated by step. Score V for correct response that followed verbal prompt. Score M if the correct response followed the model prompt. Score P if physical guidance was used.
Additional Targets:	

Take A Reinforcer When Offered By Peer
Compatible with ABLLS®-R Code L2

Student's Name:		Start Date:	
Objective:	When a reinforcer is offered to student by a peer, student will take the reinforcer.		
Person Implementing Objective:			
Setting/Environment:			
Materials:			
Reinforcers:			
Baseline:	Have peer present a reinforcer to student. Wait 5 seconds for a response. A correct response is scored (+) if student takes reinforcer from peer - <u>do not reinforce</u>. Move to next trial. An incorrect response is scored (-) if student does not take reinforcer from peer - <u>do not prompt</u>. Move to next trial.		
Teaching Procedures:	Have peer present a reinforcer to student. Wait 5 seconds for a response. If student takes the reinforcer within 5 seconds, praise and provide access to the item. If student does not take reinforcer, say "Take the ____ (name item) like this" as you model taking the item from peer. Wait 5 seconds for a response. If student takes the reinforcer, praise and provide access to the item. If student does not take reinforcer, say "Take the ____ (name item) like this" as you physically guide student to take item. Score V for correct response that followed verbal prompt. Score M if correct response followed model prompt. Score P if physical guidance was used.		
Additional Targets:			

Gives High Fives
Compatible with ABLLS®-R Code L3

Student's Name:	Start Date:
Objective:	When teacher reaches hand in air and says, "High five" student will slap teachers hand.
Person Implementing Objective:	
Setting/Environment:	
Materials:	
Reinforcers:	
Baseline:	Extend arm and hand towards student. Say, "High five." Wait 5 seconds for response. A correct response is scored (+) if student slaps your hand- <u>do not reinforce</u>. Move to next trial. An incorrect response is scored (-) if student does not slap your hand- <u>do not prompt</u>. Move to next trial.
Teaching Procedures:	Extend arm and hand towards student. Say, "High five." Wait 5 seconds for response. If student slaps your hand, praise and provide reinforcer. If student does not slap your hand, say, "Slap my hand when I say High Five." Say, "High Five" as you again extend your arm and hand to student. Wait 5 seconds for a response. If student slaps your hand, praise and provide reinforcer. If student does not slap your hand, physically guide student to slap your hand. Score V for correct response that followed verbal prompt. Score M if the correct response followed the model prompt. Score P if physical guidance was used.
Additional Targets:	

Observes What Others Are Doing
Compatible with ABLLS®-R Code L4

Student's Name:	Start Date:

Objective:	When peers are engaged in activity close to student and teacher says, "Look what they are doing" student will look at peers engaged in activity.
Person Implementing Objective:	
Setting/Environment:	
Materials:	
Reinforcers:	
Baseline:	When peers are engaged in activity close to student, say, "Look what they are doing." Wait 5 seconds for response. A correct response is scored (+) if student looks at peers- <u>do not reinforce</u>. Move to next trial. An incorrect response is scored (-) if student does not look at peers- <u>do not prompt</u>. Move to next trial.
Teaching Procedures:	When peers are engaged in activity close to student, say, "Look what they are doing." Wait 5 seconds for response. If student looks at peers, praise and provide reinforcer. If student does not look at peers, say, "Look at what they are doing" as you gesture towards the peers. Wait 5 seconds for a response. If student looks at peers, praise and provide reinforcer. If student does not look at peers, physically guide student to look at peers. Score V for correct response that followed verbal prompt. Score M if the correct response followed the model prompt. Score P if physical guidance was used.
Additional Targets:	

Looks At Peers To Gain Attention
Compatible with ABLLS®-R Code L5

Student's Name:	Start Date:	
Objective:	When peer is several feet away, and teacher instructs student to obtain peer's attention, student will approach and make eye contact with peer.	
Person Implementing Objective:		
Setting/Environment:		
Materials:		
Reinforcers:		
Baseline:	When peer is several feet away from student say, "Go get ____'s (name peer) attention." Wait 5 seconds for response. A correct response is scored (+) if student approaches and makes eye contact with peer - <u>do not reinforce</u>. Move to next trial. An incorrect response is scored (-) if student does not approach peer and make eye contact with peer- <u>do not prompt</u>. Move to next trial.	
Teaching Procedures:	When peer is several feet away from student say, "Go get ____'s (name peer) attention." Wait 5 seconds for response. If student approaches and makes eye contact with peer, praise and provide reinforcer. If student does not approach and make eye contact with peer, say, "Go get ____'s (name peer) attention" as you gesture towards the peer. Wait 5 seconds for a response. If student approaches and makes eye contact with peer, praise and provide reinforcer. If student does not approach and make eye contact with peer, physically guide student to approach and make eye contact with peer. Score V for correct response that followed verbal prompt. Score M if the correct response followed the model prompt. Score P if physical guidance was used.	
Additional Targets:		

The BIG Book of ABA Programs

Ask Peer To Play
Compatible with ABLLS®-R Code L6

Student's Name:	Start Date:
Objective:	When peer is several feet away and teacher instructs student to ask peer to play, student will approach and ask peer to play.
Person Implementing Objective:	
Setting/Environment:	
Materials:	
Reinforcers:	
Baseline:	When peer is several feet away from student say, "Go see if ____ (name peer) wants to play." Wait 5 seconds for response. A correct response is scored (+) if student approaches peer and says "Do you want to play?"- <u>do not reinforce</u>. Move to next trial. An incorrect response is scored (-) if student does not approach peer and say "Do you want to play?" - <u>do not prompt</u>. Move to next trial.
Teaching Procedures:	When peer is several feet away from student say, "Go see if ____ (name peer) wants to play." Wait 5 seconds for response. If student approaches peer and says "Do you want to play?" praise and provide reinforcer. If student does not approach peer and say "Do you want to play?" say, "Go ask ____ (name peer) if they want to play" as you gesture towards peer. Wait 5 seconds for a response. If student approaches peer and says "Do you want to play?" praise and provide reinforcer. If student does not approach peer and say "Do you want to play?" physically guide student to approach peer as you ask peer if he/she wants to play. Score V for correct response that followed verbal prompt. Score M if the correct response followed the model prompt. Score P if physical guidance was used.
Additional Targets:	

www.stimuluspublications.com   The Autism Skill Acquisition Program™

Looks At Teacher When Teacher Delivers Reinforcer
Compatible with ABLLS®-R Code L7

Student's Name:	Start Date:
Objective:	When teacher is about to deliver a known reinforcer, student will look in direction of teacher.
Person Implementing Objective:	
Setting/Environment:	
Materials:	
Reinforcers:	
Baseline:	After student completes a task and you are about to deliver a reinforcer, wait 5 seconds for response. A correct response is scored (+) if student looks at you- <u>do not reinforce</u>. Move to next trial. An incorrect response is scored (-) if student does not look at you- <u>do not prompt</u>. Move to next trial.
Teaching Procedures:	After student completes a task and you are about to deliver a reinforcer, wait 5 seconds for response. If student looks at you, praise and provide reinforcer. If student does not look at you, say, "When you finish what you're doing, look at me" as you gesture towards your face. Wait 5 seconds for a response. If student looks at you, praise and provide reinforcer. If student does not look at you, physically guide student to look at you. Score V for correct response that followed verbal prompt. Score M if the correct response followed the model prompt. Score P if physical guidance was used.
Additional Targets:	

Compliance With One-Step Directions
Compatible with ABLLS®-R Code L8

Student's Name:	Start Date:
Objective:	When teacher delivers a one-step task demand, student will respond within 5 seconds and complete the task.
Person Implementing Objective:	
Setting/Environment:	
Materials:	
Reinforcers:	
Baseline:	Tell student to do a one-step task. Wait 5 seconds for response. A correct response is scored (+) if student initiates compliance within 5 seconds and completes task- <u>do not reinforce</u>. Move to next trial. An incorrect response is scored (-) if student does not initiate compliance within 5 seconds and complete task- <u>do not prompt</u>. Move to next trial.
Teaching Procedures:	Tell student to do a one-step task. Wait 5 seconds for response. If student initiates compliance within 5 seconds and completes task, praise and provide reinforcer. If student does not initiate compliance within 5 seconds or does not complete task, redeliver the demand as you gesture in the direction of the task objective. Wait 5 seconds for a response. If student initiates compliance within 5 seconds and completes task, praise and provide reinforcer. If student does not initiate compliance within 5 seconds or does not complete task, physically guide student to complete the task. Score V for correct response that followed verbal prompt. Score M if the correct response followed the model prompt. Score P if physical guidance was used.
Additional Targets:	

Imitates Behavior Of Peers
Compatible with ABLLS®-R Code L9

Student's Name:	Start Date:
Objective:	When teacher tells student to do what a peer is doing, student will imitate peer's behavior.
Person Implementing Objective:	
Setting/Environment:	
Materials:	
Reinforcers:	
Baseline:	When peer is engaged in an activity that can be imitated, say, "Do what he/she is doing." Wait 5 seconds for response. A correct response is scored (+) if student imitates behavior of peer- <u>do not reinforce</u>. Move to next trial. An incorrect response is scored (-) if student does not imitate behavior of peer- <u>do not prompt</u>. Move to next trial.
Teaching Procedures:	When peer is engaged in an activity that can be imitated, say, "Do what he/she is doing." Wait 5 seconds for response. If student imitates behavior of peer, praise and provide reinforcer. If student does not imitate behavior of peer, say, "Do what he/she is doing" as you gesture in the direction of the peer. Wait 5 seconds for a response. If student imitates behavior of peer, praise and provide reinforcer. If student does not imitate behavior of peer, physically guide student to complete the behavior being demonstrated by the peer. Score V for correct response that followed verbal prompt. Score M if the correct response followed the model prompt. Score P if physical guidance was used.
Additional Targets:	

Say Hello And Goodbye To Others
Compatible with ABLLS®-R Code L10

Student's Name:	Start Date:
Objective:	When teacher says "Hello" or "Goodbye" to student, student will say "Hello" or Goodbye" back to teacher.
Person Implementing Objective:	
Setting/Environment:	
Materials:	
Reinforcers:	
Baseline:	Say "Hello" or "Goodbye" to student. Wait 5 seconds for response. A correct response is scored (+) if student says "Hello" or "Goodbye"- <u>do not reinforce</u>. Move to next trial. An incorrect response is scored (-) if student does not say "Hello" or "Goodbye"- <u>do not prompt</u>. Move to next trial.
Teaching Procedures:	Say "Hello" or "Goodbye" to student. Wait 5 seconds for response. If student says "Hello" or "Goodbye," praise and provide reinforcer. If student does not say "Hello" or "Goodbye," say, "When someone says 'Hello' or 'Goodbye' to you, you need to say it back." Redeliver "Hello" or "Goodbye." Wait 5 seconds for a response. If student says "Hello" or "Goodbye," praise and provide reinforcer. If student does not say "Hello" or "Goodbye," physically guide student to say "Hello" or "Goodbye" as you touch student's mouth. Score V for correct response that followed verbal prompt. Score M if the correct response followed the model prompt. Score P if physical guidance was used.
Additional Targets:	

Plays With Peers When Peer Initiates
Compatible with ABLLS®-R Code L12

Student's Name:	Start Date:	
Objective:	When peer approaches and asks student to play a game, student goes with peer to play.	
Person Implementing Objective:		
Setting/Environment:		
Materials:		
Reinforcers:		
Baseline:	Have peer approach and ask student, "Do you want to play over here?" Wait 5 seconds for response. A correct response is scored (+) if student says "Yes" and goes with peer- <u>do not reinforce</u>. Move to next trial. An incorrect response is scored (-) if student does not say "Yes" and go with peer- <u>do not prompt</u>. Move to next trial.	
Teaching Procedures:	Have peer approach and ask student, "Do you want to play over here?" Wait 5 seconds for response. If student says "Yes" and goes with peer, praise and provide reinforcer. If student does not say "Yes" and go with peer, say, "When someone asks you to go play, you need to go play with them." Have peer ask student again. Wait 5 seconds for a response. If student says "Yes" and goes with peer, praise and provide reinforcer. If student does not say "Yes" and go with peer, physically guide student to go with peer. Score V for correct response that followed verbal prompt. Score M if the correct response followed the model prompt. Score P if physical guidance was used.	
Additional Targets:		

Share Toys With Peers
Compatible with ABLLS®-R Code L13

Student's Name:		Start Date:	
Objective:	When student is playing with a toy and peer asks, "Can I play?" student allows peer to have toy or take a turn.		
Person Implementing Objective:			
Setting/Environment:			
Materials:			
Reinforcers:			
Baseline:	While student is engaged in toy play, have peer approach student and say, "Can I play?" Wait 5 seconds for a response. A correct response is scored (+) if student gives peer toy or allows peer to take a turn- <u>do not reinforce</u>. Move to next trial. An incorrect response is scored (-) if student does not give peer toy or allow peer to take a turn- <u>do not prompt</u>. Move to next trial.		
Teaching Procedures:	While student is engaged in toy play, have peer approach student and say, "Can I play?" Wait 5 seconds for a response. If student gives peer toy or allows peer to take a turn, praise and provide reinforcer. If student does not give peer toy or allows peer to take a turn, point to the toy and then to the peer as you say, "Share your toys." Wait 5 seconds for a response. If student gives peer toy or allows peer to take a turn, praise and provide reinforcer. If student does not give peer toy or allow peer to take a turn, physically guide student to give peer the toy. Score V for correct response that followed verbal prompt. Score M if the correct response followed the model prompt. Score P if physical guidance was used.		
Additional Targets:			

Finding A Person Who Leaves Them
Compatible with ABLLS®-R Code L14

Student's Name:	Start Date:

Objective:	When teacher and student are engaged in a play activity and teacher leaves area, student will look and try to find teacher.
Person Implementing Objective:	
Setting/Environment:	
Materials:	
Reinforcers:	
Baseline:	While you are engaged in a play activity with student, without saying anything, get up and leave the immediate area so that student cannot see you. Wait 5 seconds for a response. A correct response is scored (+) if student leaves play area to try to find you- <u>do not reinforce</u>. Move to next trial. An incorrect response is scored (-) if student does not leave play are to find you- <u>do not prompt</u>. Move to next trial.
Teaching Procedures:	While you are engaged in a play activity with student, without saying anything, get up and leave the immediate area so that student cannot see you. Wait 5 seconds for a response. If student leaves play area to find you, praise and provide reinforcer. If student does not leave play area to find you, stay out of sight and say, "I'm over here." Wait 5 seconds for a response. If student leaves area to find you, praise and provide reinforcer. If student does not leave play area to find you, physically guide student to move to your location. Score V for correct response that followed verbal prompt. Score M if the correct response followed the model prompt. Score P if physical guidance was used.
Additional Targets:	

The BIG Book of ABA Programs

Recruit Adult Attention Before Engaging In Activities
Compatible with ABLLS®-R Code L15

Student's Name:		Start Date:
Objective:	When student is told to do a physical activity, student looks to adult before completing the activity. For example, student will look to adult before swinging on the monkey bars.	
Person Implementing Objective:		
Setting/Environment:		
Materials:		
Reinforcers:		
Baseline:	Tell student to engage in some physical activity. Wait 5 seconds for a response. A correct response is scored (+) if student looks at you prior to beginning the activity- <u>do not reinforce</u>. Move to next trial. An incorrect response is scored (-) if student does not look at you prior to beginning the activity- <u>do not prompt</u>. Move to next trial.	
Teaching Procedures:	Tell student to engage in some physical activity. Wait 5 seconds for a response. If student looks at you prior to beginning activity, praise and provide reinforcer. If student does not look at you prior to beginning the activity, say, "You need to look over at me before you begin." If student already completed the activity without looking, redeliver the initial demand. Wait 5 seconds for a response. If student looks at you prior to beginning the activity, praise and provide reinforcer. If student does not look at you prior to beginning the activity, approach student where the activity should and say, "You need to look over at me before you start" as you physically guide student to look at you. Score V for correct response that followed verbal prompt. Score M if the correct response followed the model prompt. Score P if physical guidance was used.	
Additional Targets:		

Maintaining Eye Contact
Compatible with ABLLS®-R Code L17

Student's Name:	Start Date:	
Objective:	When student and teacher are in close proximity and teacher calls student's name, student will make eye contact with teacher.	
Person Implementing Objective:		
Setting/Environment:		
Materials:		
Reinforcers:		
Baseline:	When student is close, call student's name. Wait 5 seconds for a response. A correct response is scored (+) if student makes eye contact - <u>do not reinforce</u>. Move to next trial. An incorrect response is scored (-) if student does not make eye contact- <u>do not prompt</u>. Move to next trial.	
Teaching Procedures:	When student is close, call student's name. Wait 5 seconds for a response. If student makes eye contact, praise and provide reinforcer. If student does not make eye contact, gesture to your eyes as you say, "You need to look at my eyes when I call your name." Call student's name again. Wait 5 seconds for a response. If student makes eye contact, praise and provide reinforcer. If student does not make eye contact, say, "You need to look at my eyes when I call your name" as you physically guide student to look at your face. Score V for correct response that followed verbal prompt. Score M if the correct response followed the model prompt. Score P if physical guidance was used.	
Additional Targets:		

Asks Peer To Share A Toy
Compatible with ABLLS®-R Code L18

Student's Name:		Start Date:	
Objective:		When peer has a toy and teacher instructs student to ask peer for toy, student will ask peer to share the toy.	
Person Implementing Objective:			
Setting/Environment:			
Materials:			
Reinforcers:			
Baseline:		When peer has a toy, say, "Ask ____ (name peer) if you can use the toy." Wait 5 seconds for a response. A correct response is scored (+) if student asks peer for the toy- <u>do not reinforce</u>. Move to next trial. An incorrect response is scored (-) if student does not ask peer for the toy- <u>do not prompt</u>. Move to next trial.	
Teaching Procedures:		When peer has a toy, say, "Ask ____ (name peer) if you can use the toy." Wait 5 seconds for a response. If student asks peer for the toy, praise and provide reinforcer. If student does not ask peer for the toy, gesture to the peer as you say, "Say to ____ (name peer), 'Can I have the toy please?'" Wait 5 seconds for a response. If student asks peer for the toy, praise and provide reinforcer. If student does not ask peer for the toy, say, "Say to ____ (name peer), 'Can I have the toy please?'" as you physically guide by touching student's mouth. Score V for correct response that followed verbal prompt. Score M if the correct response followed the model prompt. Score P if physical guidance was used.	
Additional Targets:			

Asks Peer To Share A Portion Of Peer's Toys
Compatible with ABLLS®-R Code L19

Student's Name:	Start Date:
Objective:	When peer has a toy that has many parts of pieces and teacher instructs student to ask peer to share, student will ask peer to share some of the parts or pieces.
Person Implementing Objective:	
Setting/Environment:	
Materials:	
Reinforcers:	
Baseline:	When peer has a toy that contains many parts of pieces, say, "Ask ____ (name peer) if you can play with some of his/her toys." Wait 5 seconds for a response. A correct response is scored (+) if student asks peer for the some of the pieces- <u>do not reinforce</u>. Move to next trial. An incorrect response is scored (-) if student does not ask peer for some of the pieces- <u>do not prompt</u>. Move to next trial.
Teaching Procedures:	When peer has a toy that contains many parts of pieces, say, "Ask ____ (name peer) if you can play with some of his/her toys." Wait 5 seconds for a response. If student asks peer for some of the pieces, praise and provide reinforcer. If student does not ask peer for some of the pieces, gesture to the peer as you say, "Say to ____ (name peer), 'Can I play with some of those please?'" Wait 5 seconds for a response. If student asks peer for some of the pieces, praise and provide reinforcer. If student does not ask peer for some of the pieces, say, "Say to ____ (name peer), 'Can I have some of those please?'" as you physically guide student to peer. Score V for correct response that followed verbal prompt. Score M if the correct response followed the model prompt. Score P if physical guidance was used.
Additional Targets:	

Offers To Share Toy With Peer
Compatible with ABLLS®-R Code L20

Student's Name:		Start Date:	
Objective:	When student has a toy and peer is close and teacher instructs student to share toys with peer, student will offer to share toy with peer.		

Person Implementing Objective:	
Setting/Environment:	
Materials:	
Reinforcers:	
Baseline:	When student has a toy and peer is in close proximity, say, "Ask ____ (name peer) if he/she would like to share your toy." Wait 5 seconds for a response. A correct response is scored (+) if student asks peer if peer wants to share student's toy- <u>do not reinforce</u>. Move to next trial. An incorrect response is scored (-) if student does not ask peer if peer wants to share student's toy- <u>do not prompt</u>. Move to next trial.
Teaching Procedures:	When student has a toy and peer is in close proximity, say, "Ask ____ (name peer) if he/she would like to share your toy." Wait 5 seconds for a response. If student asks peer to share student's toy, praise and provide reinforcer. If student does not ask peer to share student's toy, gesture to the peer as you say, "Say to ____ (name peer), 'Do you want to play with this?'" Wait 5 seconds for a response. If student asks peer to share student's toy, praise and provide reinforcer. If student does not ask peer to share student's toy, say, "Say to ____ (name peer), 'Do you want to play with this?'" as you physically guide student to peer. Score V for correct response that followed verbal prompt. Score M if the correct response followed the model prompt. Score P if physical guidance was used.
Additional Targets:	

Greets Others
Compatible with ABLLS®-R Code L21

Student's Name:		Start Date:	
Objective:		Student will initiate greetings/farewell to others when entering or leaving classroom.	

Person Implementing Objective:	
Setting/Environment:	
Materials:	
Reinforcers:	
Baseline:	When student enters or leaves classroom, wait 5 seconds for a response. A correct response is scored (+) if student says "Hello" (upon entering) or "Goodbye" (upon leaving)- <u>do not reinforce</u>. Move to next trial. An incorrect response is scored (-) if student does not say "Hello" (upon entering) or "Goodbye" (upon leaving)- <u>do not prompt</u>. Move to next trial.
Teaching Procedures:	When student enters or leaves classroom, wait 5 seconds for a response. If student says "Hello" (upon entering) or "Goodbye" (upon leaving), praise and provide reinforcer. If student does not say "Hello" (upon entering) or "Goodbye" (upon leaving), say, "You need to say 'Hello' when you come in the classroom" or "You need to say, 'Goodbye' before you leave the classroom." Instruct student to reenter or re-exit the room. Wait 5 seconds for a response. If student says "Hello" (upon entering) or "Goodbye" (upon leaving), praise and provide reinforcer. If student does not say "Hello" (upon entering) or "Goodbye" (upon leaving) say, "You need to say 'Hello' when you come in the classroom" or "You need to say 'Goodbye' before you leave the classroom" as you physically guide by touching student's mouth. Score V for correct response that followed verbal prompt. Score M if the correct response followed the model prompt. Score P if physical guidance was used.
Additional Targets:	

Join Ongoing Activity
Compatible with ABLLS®-R Code L22

Student's Name:	Start Date:
Objective:	When peers are engaged in an activity, student will approach peers and ask to join peers in play.
Person Implementing Objective:	
Setting/Environment:	
Materials:	
Reinforcers:	
Baseline:	When peers are engaged in a group play activity, say, "Go over there and see if you can play with them." Wait 5 seconds for a response. A correct response is scored (+) if student approaches group and asks to join- <u>do not reinforce</u>. Move to next trial. An incorrect response is scored (-) if student does not approach group and ask to join- <u>do not prompt</u>. Move to next trial.
Teaching Procedures:	When peers are engaged in a group play activity, say, "Go over there and see if you can play with them." Wait 5 seconds for a response. If student approaches group and asks to join, praise and provide reinforcer. If student does not approach group and ask to join, point to the peers and say, "You need to go over there and say, 'Can I play with you?'" Wait 5 seconds for a response. If student approaches peers and asks to play, praise and provide reinforcer. If student does not approach group and ask to play, physically guide student to group and ask peers if student can play. Score V for correct response that followed verbal prompt. Score M if the correct response followed the model prompt. Score P if physical guidance was used.
Additional Targets:	

The BIG Book of ABA Programs

Follow Peers When Peers Go Somewhere
Compatible with ABLLS®-R Code L23

Student's Name:		Start Date:
Objective:	When peers in close proximity to student suddenly get up and leave, student will follow peers.	
Person Implementing Objective:		
Setting/Environment:		
Materials:		
Reinforcers:		
Baseline:	When peers are in close proximity to student and suddenly leave the area as a group, wait 5 seconds for a response. A correct response is scored (+) if student follows peers- <u>do not reinforce</u>. Move to next trial. An incorrect response is scored (-) if student does not follow peers- <u>do not prompt</u>. Move to next trial.	
Teaching Procedures:	When peers are in close proximity to student and suddenly leave the area as a group, wait 5 seconds for a response. If student follows peers, praise and provide reinforcer. If student does not follow peers, point to peers and say, "You need to go with them to see where they are going." Wait 5 seconds for a response. If the student follows peers, praise and provide reinforcer. If student does not follow peers, physically guide student to peers. Score V for correct response that followed verbal prompt. Score M if the correct response followed the model prompt. Score P if physical guidance was used.	
Additional Targets:		

www.stimuluspublications.com   336   The Autism Skill Acquisition Program™

Follow Peer's Directives
Compatible with ABLLS®-R Code L24

Student's Name:		Start Date:	
Objective:	When a peer gives student a directive, student will comply with peer's demand.		

Person Implementing Objective:	
Setting/Environment:	
Materials:	
Reinforcers:	
Baseline:	After peer delivers a directive to student, wait 5 seconds for a response. A correct response is scored (+) if student complies with peer's request- <u>do not reinforce</u>. Move to next trial. An incorrect response is scored (-) if student does not comply with peer's request- <u>do not prompt</u>. Move to next trial.
Teaching Procedures:	After peer delivers a directive to student, wait 5 seconds for a response. If student complies with peer's request, praise and provide reinforcer. If student does not comply with peer's request, have peer redeliver the request. Wait 5 seconds for a response. If student complies with peer's request, praise and provide reinforcer. If student does not comply with peer's request, physically guide student to comply with peer's request. Score V for correct response that followed verbal prompt. Score M if the correct response followed the model prompt. Score P if physical guidance was used.
Additional Targets:	

Change Behavior From Peer Model
Compatible with ABLLS®-R Code L25

Student's Name:		Start Date:	
Objective:	When student and peers are engaged in an activity and all peers change their behavior, student will make the same change in student's behavior.		
Person Implementing Objective:			
Setting/Environment:			
Materials:			
Reinforcers:			
Baseline:	When student and peers are in engaged in identical activity and peers change their behavior, wait 5 seconds for a response. A correct response is scored (+) if student makes the same change in student's behavior- <u>do not reinforce</u>. Move to next trial. An incorrect response is scored (-) if student does not make the same change in student's behavior- <u>do not prompt</u>. Move to next trial.		
Teaching Procedures:	When student and peers are in engaged in identical activity and peers change their behavior, wait 5 seconds for a response. If student makes the same change in student's behavior, praise and provide reinforcer. If student does not make the same change in student's behavior, point to peers and say, "Everyone just ____ (name change in behavior), so you should too." Wait 5 seconds for a response. If student makes the same change in student's behavior, praise and provide reinforcer. If student does not make the same change in student's behavior, physically guide student to make same behavior change. Score V for correct response that followed verbal prompt. Score M if the correct response followed the model prompt. Score P if physical guidance was used.		
Additional Targets:			

Helping Peers Who Need Assistance
Compatible with ABLLS®-R Code L26

Student's Name:		Start Date:
Objective:	When a peer expresses the need for help, student will provide help.	

Person Implementing Objective:	
Setting/Environment:	
Materials:	
Reinforcers:	
Baseline:	Have peer approach student and make a statement requesting help. When peer makes request, wait 5 seconds for a response. A correct response is scored (+) if student offers help or helps peer- <u>do not reinforce</u>. Move to next trial. An incorrect response is scored (-) if student does not offer to help or help peer- <u>do not prompt</u>. Move to next trial.
Teaching Procedures:	Have peer approach student and make a statement requesting help. When peer makes request, wait 5 seconds for a response. If student offers help or helps peer, praise and provide reinforcer. If student does not offer help or help peer, gesture in some way to what the peer requires help with and say, "Your friend needs your help, you should offer to help him/her." Have peer re-deliver the request for help. Wait 5 seconds for a response. If student offers help or helps peer, praise and provide reinforcer. If student does not offer help or help peer, physically guide student help peer. Score V for correct response that followed verbal prompt. Score M if the correct response followed the model prompt. Score P if physical guidance was used.
Additional Targets:	

Reports What Is Liked By Peers
Compatible with ABLLS®-R Code L27

Student's Name:	Start Date:
Objective:	When teacher asks student what a peer likes, student will answer with correct information about peer preferences.
Person Implementing Objective:	
Setting/Environment:	
Materials:	
Reinforcers:	
Baseline:	Say, "Which one of your friends likes ____ (name item, activity, movie, TV show, etc.)?" Wait 5 seconds for a response. A correct response is scored (+) if student correctly identifies peer- <u>do not reinforce</u>. Move to next trial. An incorrect response is scored (-) if student does not correctly identify peer- <u>do not prompt</u>. Move to next trial.
Teaching Procedures:	Say, "Which one of your friends likes ____ (name item, activity, movie, TV show, etc.)?" Wait 5 seconds for a response. If student correctly identifies peer, praise and provide reinforcer. If student does not correctly identify peer, point to peer and provide correct answer. For example, "Melanie likes Sesame Street." Say, "Which one of your friends likes ____ (name item, activity, movie, TV show, etc.)?" Wait 5 seconds for a response. If student correctly identifies peer, praise and provide reinforcer. If student does not correctly identify peer, physically guide student to point to peer as you again say, (for example) "Melanie likes Sesame Street." Score V for correct response that followed verbal prompt. Score M if the correct response followed the model prompt. Score P if physical guidance was used.
Additional Targets:	

Student Tells Peers Of Things That Might Be Of Interest To Them
Compatible with ABLLS®-R Code L28

Student's Name:	Start Date:
Objective:	When teacher shows student an item that might be of interest to a peer, student tells peer about item.
Person Implementing Objective:	
Setting/Environment:	
Materials:	
Reinforcers:	
Baseline:	Show student an item that is highly preferred by a peer. Wait 5 seconds for a response. A correct response is scored (+) if student tells peer about item - <u>do not reinforce</u>. Move to next trial. An incorrect response is scored (-) if student does not tell peer about item - <u>do not prompt</u>. Move to next trial.
Teaching Procedures:	Show student an item that is highly preferred by a peer. Wait 5 seconds for a response. If student tells peer about item, praise and provide reinforcer. If student does not tell peer about item, point to peer and say, (for example) "Amadi likes Dora, you should tell her I have Dora over here." Wait 5 seconds for a response. If student tells peer about item, praise and provide reinforcer. If student does not tell peer about item, physically guide student to peer as you say, (for example) "Amadi, look what we have." Score V for correct response that followed verbal prompt. Score M if the correct response followed the model prompt. Score P if physical guidance was used.
Additional Targets:	

Looks to Peers For Response
Compatible with ABLLS®-R Code L29

Student's Name:		Start Date:	
Objective:	When student is engaged in an activity, student will look to peers in for reaction or response.		
Person Implementing Objective:			
Setting/Environment:			
Materials:			
Reinforcers:			
Baseline:	When student is engaged in a preferred activity, wait 5 seconds for a response. A correct response is scored (+) if student looks to peers - do not reinforce. Move to next trial. An incorrect response is scored (-) if student does not look to peers- do not prompt. Move to next trial.		
Teaching Procedures:	When student is engaged in a preferred activity, wait 5 seconds for a response. If student looks to peers, praise and provide reinforcer. If student does not look to peers, say, "When peers are around, you should look over to see if they are paying attention to you." Wait 5 seconds for a response. If student looks to peers, praise and provide reinforcer. If student does not look to peers, say, "When peers are around, you should look over to see if they are paying attention to you" as you physically guide student's head to face peers. Score V for correct response that followed verbal prompt. Score M if the correct response followed the model prompt. Score P if physical guidance was used.		
Additional Targets:			

Relay Information To A Peer
Compatible with ABLLS®-R Code L30

Student's Name:	Start Date:
Objective:	When teacher instructs student to pass-on information to a peer, student will repeat to peer what was told to them.
Person Implementing Objective:	
Setting/Environment:	
Materials:	
Reinforcers:	
Baseline:	Tell student a brief statement. Point to peer and say, "Go tell him/her what I just told you." Wait 5 seconds for a response. A correct response is scored (+) if student tells peer the exact message - <u>do not reinforce</u>. Move to next trial. An incorrect response is scored (-) if student does not tell peer the exact message- <u>do not prompt</u>. Move to next trial.
Teaching Procedures:	Tell student a brief statement. Point to peer and say, "Go tell him/her what I just told you." Wait 5 seconds for a response. If student tells peer the exact message, praise and provide reinforcer. If student does not tell peer the exact message, point to peer, repeat the message to student and again say, "Go tell him/her what I just told you." Wait 5 seconds for a response. If student tells peer the exact message, praise and provide reinforcer. If student does not tell peer the exact message, physically guide student to peer and repeat message as you touch student's mouth. Score V for correct response that followed verbal prompt. Score M if the correct response followed the model prompt. Score P if physical guidance was used.
Additional Targets:	

Appropriate Interruption
Compatible with ABLLS®-R Code L31

Student's Name:	Start Date:
Objective:	When two adults are talking and student needs to tell one of the adults something, student will wait for the conversation to stop before telling the adult.
Person Implementing Objective:	
Setting/Environment:	
Materials:	
Reinforcers:	
Baseline:	While two adults are talking, have student ask one adult a question. Wait 5 seconds for a response. A correct response is scored (+) if student waits until adults stop talking to ask question- <u>do not reinforce</u>. Move to next trial. An incorrect response is scored (-) if student does not wait until adults stop talking to ask question- <u>do not prompt</u>. Move to next trial.
Teaching Procedures:	While two adults are talking, tell student to go ask one adult a question. Wait 5 seconds for a response. If student waits until adults stop talking to ask question, praise and provide reinforcer. If student does not wait until adults stop talking to ask question, say, "You need to wait until they finish talking and then you can ask." Repeat initial demand. Wait 5 seconds for a response. If student waits until adults stop talking to ask question, praise and provide reinforcer. If student does not waits until adults stop talking to ask question, physically guide student to adults, wait for them to stop talking and then tell student to ask the question. Score V for correct response that followed verbal prompt. Score M if the correct response followed the model prompt. Score P if physical guidance was used.
Additional Targets:	

Reciprocal Communication
Compatible with ABLLS®-R Code L32

Student's Name:	Start Date:
Objective:	When a peer asks student a question, student will respond with appropriate topic related content.
Person Implementing Objective:	
Setting/Environment:	
Materials:	
Reinforcers:	
Baseline:	Have peer ask student a question about something of interest to student. Wait 5 seconds for a response. A correct response is scored (+) if student responds with appropriate topic related content- <u>do not reinforce</u>. Move to next trial. An incorrect response is scored (-) if student does not respond with appropriate topic related content- <u>do not prompt</u>. Move to next trial.
Teaching Procedures:	Have peer ask student a question about something of interest to student. Wait 5 seconds for a response. If student responds to peer with appropriate topic related content, praise and provide reinforcer. If student does not respond to peer with appropriate topic related content, say, "If someone asks you something, you should say something back to them." Have peer repeat question. Wait 5 seconds for a response. If student responds to peer with appropriate topic related content, praise and provide reinforcer. If student does not responds to peer with appropriate topic related content, physically guide by touching student's mouth as you make a related comment. Score V for correct response that followed verbal prompt. Score M if the correct response followed the model prompt. Score P if physical guidance was used.
Additional Targets:	

Gain Other's Attention
Compatible with ABLLS®-R Code L34

Student's Name:		Start Date:	
Objective:	When student seeks adult attention, student will demonstrate a range of appropriate behaviors to gain attention.		
Person Implementing Objective:			
Setting/Environment:			
Materials:			
Reinforcers:			
Baseline:	When student asks you a question and you do not answer, wait 5 seconds for a response. A correct response is scored (+) if student uses appropriate attention seeking strategy- <u>do not reinforce</u>. Move to next trial. An incorrect response is scored (-) if student does not use appropriate attention seeking strategy- <u>do not prompt</u>. Move to next trial.		
Teaching Procedures:	When student asks you a question and you do not answer, wait 5 seconds for a response. If student uses appropriate attention seeking strategy, praise and provide reinforcer. If student does not use appropriate attention seeking strategy, say, "If you ask someone a question and they do not answer, you should try to make eye contact with them, tap them gently, or say their name. Try it again, ask me the question again." Have student repeat question and do not answer it. Wait 5 seconds for a response. If student uses appropriate attention seeking strategy, praise and provide reinforcer. If student does not use appropriate attention seeking strategy, physically guide student to make eye contact with you, tap you gently, etc. Score V for correct response that followed verbal prompt. Score M if the correct response followed the model prompt. Score P if physical guidance was used.		
Additional Targets:			

CHAPTER 13

ABA Programs Compatible with

ABLLS®-R Domain M

"Group Instruction"

Sits With Small Group
Compatible with ABLLS®-R Code M1

Student's Name:		Start Date:	
Objective:	When teacher says, "Sit with group" student will sit appropriately with a small group of peers.		
Person Implementing Objective:			
Setting/Environment:			
Materials:			
Reinforcers:			
Baseline:	Say, "Sit with group." Wait 5 seconds for a response. A correct response is scored (+) if student sits appropriately in small group - <u>do not reinforce</u>. Move to next trial. An incorrect response is scored (-) if student does sit appropriately in small group- <u>do not prompt</u>. Move to next trial.		
Teaching Procedures:	Say "Sit with group." Wait 5 seconds for a response. If student sits appropriately in small group, praise and provide reinforcer. If student does not sit appropriately in small group, say, "You need to sit quietly with the group" as you gesture to the small group. Wait 5 seconds for a response. If student sits appropriately in small group, praise and provide reinforcer. If student does not sit appropriately in small group, physically guide student to remain in group for desired duration. Score V for correct response that followed verbal prompt. Score M if the correct response followed the model prompt. Score P if physical guidance was used.		
Additional Targets:			

Sits With Large Group
Compatible with ABLLS®-R Code M2

Student's Name:		Start Date:	
Objective:	When teacher says, "Sit with group" student will sit appropriately with a large group of peers.		
Person Implementing Objective:			
Setting/Environment:			
Materials:			
Reinforcers:			
Baseline:	Say, "Sit with group." Wait 5 seconds for a response. A correct response is scored (+) if student sits appropriately in large group- <u>do not reinforce</u>. Move to next trial. An incorrect response is scored (-) if student does not sit appropriately in large group- <u>do not prompt</u>. Move to next trial.		
Teaching Procedures:	Say, "Sit with group." Wait 5 seconds for a response. If student sits appropriately in large group, praise and provide reinforcer. If student does not sit appropriately in large group, say, "You need to sit quietly with the group." as you gesture to the large group. Wait 5 seconds for a response. If student sits appropriately in large group, praise and provide reinforcer. If student does not sit appropriately in large group, physically guide student to remain in large group for desired duration. Score V for correct response that followed verbal prompt. Score M if the correct response followed the model prompt. Score P if physical guidance was used.		
Additional Targets:			

The BIG Book of ABA Programs

Looks At Teacher When Teacher Is Speaking To A Group
Compatible with ABLLS®-R Code M3

Student's Name:		Start Date:	
Objective:	When student is sitting with peers but not attending to teacher and teacher says, "Pay attention to the teacher" student will direct head towards teacher.		
Person Implementing Objective:			
Setting/Environment:			
Materials:			
Reinforcers:			
Baseline:	When in a group setting and teacher is presenting instructions to group, say, "Pay attention to teacher." Wait 5 seconds for a response. A correct response is scored (+) if student has head directed towards teacher- <u>do not reinforce</u>. Move to next trial. An incorrect response is scored (-) if student does not have head directed towards teacher- <u>do not prompt</u>. Move to next trial.		
Teaching Procedures:	When in a group setting and teacher is presenting instructions to group say, "Pay attention to teacher." Wait 5 seconds for a response. If student has head directed towards teacher, praise and provide reinforcer. If student does not have head directed towards teacher, say, "Look at teacher when he/she is talking" as you gesture towards teacher. Wait 5 seconds for a response. If student has head directed towards teacher, praise and provide reinforcer. If student does not have head directed towards teacher, physically guide student to look at teacher. Score V for correct response that followed verbal prompt. Score M if the correct response followed the model prompt. Score P if physical guidance was used.		
Additional Targets:			

Looks At Peers When Peers Respond In A Group
Compatible with ABLLS®-R Code M4

Student's Name:	Start Date:
Objective:	When a peer is responding in a group setting and teacher says to student, "Pay attention to the person talking" student will direct head towards peer.
Person Implementing Objective:	
Setting/Environment:	
Materials:	
Reinforcers:	
Baseline:	When in a group setting and peer is responding in the group, say, "Pay attention to the person talking." Wait 5 seconds for a response. A correct response is scored (+) if student has head directed towards the peer talking- <u>do not reinforce</u>. Move to next trial. An incorrect response is scored (-) if student does not have head directed towards the peer talking- <u>do not prompt</u>. Move to next trial.
Teaching Procedures:	When in a group setting and peer is responding in the group, say, "Pay attention to the person talking." Wait 5 seconds for a response. If student has head directed towards the peer talking, praise and provide reinforcer. If student does not have head directed towards the peer talking, say, "Look at the person talking" as you gesture towards the peer talking. Wait 5 seconds for a response. If student has head directed towards the peer talking, praise and provide reinforcer. If student does not have head directed towards the peer talking, physically guide student to look at peer talking. Score V for correct response that followed verbal prompt. Score M if the correct response followed the model prompt. Score P if physical guidance was used.
Additional Targets:	

Complies With Instructions Delivered To A Group
Compatible with ABLLS®-R Code M5

Student's Name:		Start Date:	
Objective:	When teacher delivers a task demand to students in a group, student will comply with demand.		
Person Implementing Objective:			
Setting/Environment:			
Materials:			
Reinforcers:			
Baseline:	Deliver a demand to a group of students. Wait 5 seconds for a response. A correct response is scored (+) if student complies with demand- <u>do not reinforce</u>. Move to next trial. An incorrect response is scored (-) if student does not comply with demand- <u>do not prompt</u>. Move to next trial.		
Teaching Procedures:	Deliver a demand to a group of students. Wait 5 seconds for a response. If student complies with demand, praise and provide reinforcer. If student does not comply with demand, deliver the demand again to the entire group as you gesture towards the focus of the demand. Wait 5 seconds for a response. If student complies with demand, praise and provide reinforcer. If student does not comply with demand, physically guide student to comply as you redeliver demand to student. Score V for correct response that followed verbal prompt. Score M if the correct response followed the model prompt. Score P if physical guidance was used.		
Additional Targets:			

Makes Correct Choice When Choice Is Given To The Group
Compatible with ABLLS®-R Code M6

Student's Name:		Start Date:	
Objective:		When teacher delivers a demand to a group in which the demand requires student to make a choice, student will make correct choice. For example, "Raise your hand if you are a boy."	
Person Implementing Objective:			
Setting/Environment:			
Materials:			
Reinforcers:			
Baseline:		Deliver a demand to a group of students in which the demand requires student to make a choice. Wait 5 seconds for a response. A correct response is scored (+) if student complies with demand by making correct choice- <u>do not reinforce</u>. Move to next trial. An incorrect response is scored (-) if student does not comply with demand or makes incorrect choice- <u>do not prompt</u>. Move to next trial.	
Teaching Procedures:		Deliver a demand to a group of students in which the demand requires student to make a choice. Wait 5 seconds for a response. If student complies with demand by making correct choice, praise and provide reinforcer. If student does not comply with demand by making correct choice, deliver the demand again as you gesture or emphasize the correct choice to student. For example, say, "Raise your hand if you are *a boy*." Wait 5 seconds for a response. If student complies with demand by making correct choice, praise and provide reinforcer. If student does not comply with demand by making correct choice, physically guide student to make correct choice. Score V for correct response that followed verbal prompt. Score M if the correct response followed the model prompt. Score P if physical guidance was used.	
Additional Targets:			

Hand Raising In Group
Compatible with ABLLS®-R Code M7

Student's Name:	Start Date:
Objective:	When teacher poses a question to a group of students, student will raise hand and wait to be called on prior to answering.
Person Implementing Objective:	
Setting/Environment:	
Materials:	
Reinforcers:	
Baseline:	Ask a question to a group of students the answer to which is known to the student. Wait 5 seconds for a response. A correct response is scored (+) if student raises hand before answering- <u>do not reinforce</u>. Move to next trial. An incorrect response is scored (-) if student does not raise hand before answering- <u>do not prompt</u>. Move to next trial.
Teaching Procedures:	Ask a question to a group of students the answer to which is known to the student. Wait 5 seconds for a response. If student raises hand before answering, praise and provide reinforcer. If student does not raise hand before answering, say, "Raise your hand like this before you answer" as you model hand raising. Wait 5 seconds for a response. If student raises hand, praise and provide reinforcer. If student does not raise hand, physically guide student to raise hand. Score V for correct response that followed verbal prompt. Score M if the correct response followed the model prompt. Score P if physical guidance was used.
Additional Targets:	

Hand Raising In Group To Answer A Question
Compatible with ABLLS®-R Code M8

Student's Name:		Start Date:
Objective:	When teacher poses a question to a group of students, student will raise hand and wait to be called on by teacher.	
Person Implementing Objective:		
Setting/Environment:		
Materials:		
Reinforcers:		
Baseline:	When teacher asks a question to a group of students, wait 5 seconds for a response. A correct response is scored (+) if student raises hand and waits to be called on by teacher- <u>do not reinforce</u>. Move to next trial. An incorrect response is scored (-) if student does not raise hand and wait to be called on by teacher- <u>do not prompt</u>. Move to next trial.	
Teaching Procedures:	When teacher asks a question to a group of students, wait 5 seconds for a response. If student raises hand and waits to be called on by teacher, praise and provide reinforcer. If student does not raise hand and wait to be called on by teacher, say, "Raise your hand and wait for the teacher to call on you" as you model raising your hand. Wait 5 seconds for a response. If student raises hand and waits to be called on by teacher, praise and provide reinforcer. If student does not raise hand and wait to be called on, physically guide student to raise hand. Score V for correct response that followed verbal prompt. Score M if the correct response followed the model prompt. Score P if physical guidance was used.	
Additional Targets:		

Tact Object After Hand Raising In Group
Compatible with ABLLS®-R Code M9

Student's Name:	Start Date:	
Objective:	When teacher poses a question to a group of students asking about the name of an object, student will raise hand and when called on, correctly identify object.	
Person Implementing Objective:		
Setting/Environment:		
Materials:		
Reinforcers:		
Baseline:	When teacher says to a group of students, "What is this?" as teacher holds up an object. Wait 5 seconds for a response. A correct response is scored (+) if student raises hand and correctly identifies object when called on- <u>do not reinforce</u>. Move to next trial. An incorrect response is scored (-) if student does not raise hand or does not correctly name object when called on- <u>do not prompt</u>. Move to next trial.	
Teaching Procedures:	When teacher says to a group of students, "What is this?" as teacher holds up an object. Wait 5 seconds for a response. If student raises hand and when called on correctly identifies the object, praise and provide reinforcer. If student does not raise hand before answering or does not correctly name the object, say, "That's a ____ (name object). Raise your hand and wait for the teacher to call on you" as you model raising your hand. When teacher again says, "What is this?" Wait 5 seconds for a response. If student raises hand and when called on correctly identifies object, praise and provide reinforcer. If student does not raise hand or does not correctly identify the object, physically guide student to raise hand and tell student the name of the object. Score V for correct response that followed verbal prompt. Score M if the correct response followed the model prompt. Score P if physical guidance was used.	
Additional Targets:		

Answering Question After Hand Raising In Group
Compatible with ABLLS®-R Code M10

Student's Name:	Start Date:
Objective:	When teacher poses a question to a group of students, student will raise hand and when called on, correctly answer question.
Person Implementing Objective:	
Setting/Environment:	
Materials:	
Reinforcers:	
Baseline:	When teacher asks a question to a group of students. Wait 5 seconds for a response. A correct response is scored (+) if student raises hand and answers question correctly when called on- <u>do not reinforce</u>. Move to next trial. An incorrect response is scored (-) if student does not raise hand before answering or answers question incorrectly when called on- <u>do not prompt</u>. Move to next trial.
Teaching Procedures:	When teacher asks a question to a group of students. Wait 5 seconds for a response. If student raises hand and when called on by teacher answers the question correctly, praise and provide reinforcer. If student does not raise hand before answering or answers question incorrectly, say, "Raise your hand and wait for teacher to call on you" as you model raising your hand. Wait 5 seconds for a response. If student raises hand and when called on answers question correctly, praise and provide reinforcer. If student does not raise hand or answers question incorrectly, physically guide student to raise hand and tell student the answer to the question. Score V for correct response that followed verbal prompt. Score M if the correct response followed the model prompt. Score P if physical guidance was used.
Additional Targets:	

The BIG Book of ABA Programs

Alternate Responding In Group
Compatible with ABLLS®-R Code M11

Student's Name:		Start Date:	
Objective:	When teacher poses a question to a group of students in which all students are required to answer, student will wait for student's turn to answer.		
Person Implementing Objective:			
Setting/Environment:			
Materials:			
Reinforcers:			
Baseline:	When teacher asks a question to a group of students in which all students are required to answer. Wait 5 seconds for a response. A correct response is scored (+) if student waits turn before answering- <u>do not reinforce</u>. Move to next trial. An incorrect response is scored (-) if student does not wait turn to answer- <u>do not prompt</u>. Move to next trial.		
Teaching Procedures:	When teacher asks a question to a group of students in which all students are required to answer. Wait 5 seconds for a response. If student waits turn to answer, praise and provide reinforcer. If student does not wait turn to answer, say, "Wait until it is your turn." Wait 5 seconds for a response. If student waits turn to answer, praise and provide reinforcer. If student does not wait turn to answer, physically guide by putting your hand in front of student in a way that communicates waiting, as you again say, "You need to wait your turn." Score V for correct response that followed verbal prompt. Score M if the correct response followed the model prompt. Score P if physical guidance was used.		
Additional Targets:			

www.stimuluspublications.com   The Autism Skill Acquisition Program™

CHAPTER 14

ABA Programs Compatible with

ABLLS®-R Domain N

"Follow Classroom Routines"

Performs Consistent Routine In Classroom
Compatible with ABLLS®-R Code N1

Student's Name:		Start Date:
Objective:	When student enters classroom for the first time in the morning, student will perform several tasks in the same way each day. (For example, student hangs up jacket, puts backpack in cubby, brings daily journal to teacher, etc.)	
Person Implementing Objective:		
Setting/Environment:		
Materials:		
Reinforcers:		
Baseline:	When student enters classroom for the first time for the day, say, "Put your stuff away." Wait 5 seconds for a response. A correct response is scored (+) if student performs the classroom routine- <u>do not reinforce</u>. Move to next trial. An incorrect response is scored (-) if student does not perform classroom routine- <u>do not prompt</u>. Move to next trial.	
Teaching Procedures:	When student enters classroom for the first time for the day, say, "Put your stuff away." Wait 5 seconds for a response. If student performs the classroom routine, praise and provide reinforcer. If student does not perform the classroom routine, tell student what he/she is to do as you gesture towards the locations for the tasks. Wait 5 seconds for a response. If student performs the classroom routine, praise and provide reinforcer. If student does not perform the classroom routine, physically guide student to perform the classroom routine. Score V for correct response that followed verbal prompt. Score M if the correct response followed the model prompt. Score P if physical guidance was used.	
Additional Targets:		

Engage in Play Activities By Self
Compatible with ABLLS®-R Code N2

Student's Name:	Start Date:
Objective:	When teacher instructs student to engage in play activities by self, student will engage in play activity without interacting with anyone else.
Person Implementing Objective:	
Setting/Environment:	
Materials:	
Reinforcers:	
Baseline:	Say, "Play with the ____ (name activity) by yourself." Wait 5 seconds for a response. A correct response is scored (+) if student engages in activity without interacting with anyone else- <u>do not reinforce</u>. Move to next trial. An incorrect response is scored (-) if student does not engage in activity without engaging with anyone else- <u>do not prompt</u>. Move to next trial.
Teaching Procedures:	Say, "Play with the ____ (name activity) by yourself." Wait 5 seconds for a response. If student engages in activity without interacting with anyone else, praise and provide reinforcer. If student does not engage with activity without engaging with anyone else, say, "Work by yourself" as you gesture to the activity. Wait 5 seconds for a response. If student engages in activity without interacting with anyone else, praise and provide reinforcer. If student does not engage with activity without engaging with anyone else, physically guide student to work by self. Score V for correct response that followed verbal prompt. Score M if the correct response followed the model prompt. Score P if physical guidance was used.
Additional Targets:	

Waits During Transitions
Compatible with ABLLS®-R Code N3

Student's Name:	Start Date:
Objective:	When teacher indicates a change of activity and tells student to "Wait," student will wait appropriately during transition from activity to activity.
Person Implementing Objective:	
Setting/Environment:	
Materials:	
Reinforcers:	
Baseline:	Say, "We are going to change activities, wait a minute please." Wait 5 seconds for a response. A correct response is scored (+) if student waits quietly in place- <u>do not reinforce</u>. Move to next trial. An incorrect response is scored (-) if student does not wait quietly in place- <u>do not prompt</u>. Move to next trial.
Teaching Procedures:	Say, "We are going to change activities, wait a minute please." Wait 5 seconds for a response. If student waits quietly in place, praise and provide reinforcer. If student does not wait quietly in place, say, "Wait" as you gesture to the place in which student is to wait. Wait 5 seconds for a response. If student waits quietly in place, praise and provide reinforcer. If student does not wait quietly in place, physically guide student to wait in place. Score V for correct response that followed verbal prompt. Score M if the correct response followed the model prompt. Score P if physical guidance was used.
Additional Targets:	

The BIG Book of ABA Programs

Transitions
Compatible with ABLLS®-R Code N4

Student's Name:		Start Date:
Objective:	When told to change activities, student will transition from one activity to another.	

Person Implementing Objective:	
Setting/Environment:	
Materials:	
Reinforcers:	
Baseline:	When student is engaged in one activity, say, "Stop what you are doing and go to ____ (name new activity)." Wait 5 seconds for a response. A correct response is scored (+) if student moves to new activity without disruptive behavior- <u>do not reinforce</u>. Move to next trial. An incorrect response is scored (-) if student does not move to new activity without disruptive behavior- <u>do not prompt</u>. Move to next trial.
Teaching Procedures:	When student is engaged in one activity, say, "Stop what you are doing and go to ____ (name new activity)." Wait 5 seconds for a response. If student moves to new activity without disruptive behavior, praise and provide reinforcer. If student does not move to new activity without disruptive behavior, say, "Stop what you are doing and go to ____ (name new activity)" as you gesture to the place in which student is to transition. Wait 5 seconds for a response. If student moves to new activity without disruptive behavior, praise and provide reinforcer. If student does not move to new activity without disruptive behavior, physically guide student to new activity. Score V for correct response that followed verbal prompt. Score M if the correct response followed the model prompt. Score P if physical guidance was used.
Additional Targets:	

www.stimuluspublications.com   363   The Autism Skill Acquisition Program™

Takes Turns In Classroom
Compatible with ABLLS®-R Code N5

Student's Name:		Start Date:	
Objective:	When several students are told to do an activity, student will wait turn to complete the activity.		
Person Implementing Objective:			
Setting/Environment:			
Materials:			
Reinforcers:			
Baseline:	Tell several students to complete an activity. Wait 5 seconds for a response. A correct response is scored (+) if student waits turn to complete activity- <u>do not reinforce</u>. Move to next trial. An incorrect response is scored (-) if student does not wait turn to complete activity- <u>do not prompt</u>. Move to next trial.		
Teaching Procedures:	Tell several students to complete an activity. Wait 5 seconds for a response. If student waits turn to complete activity, praise and provide reinforcer. If student does not wait turn to complete activity, say, "You need to wait your turn" as you gesture to location of activity. Wait 5 seconds for a response. If student waits turn to complete activity, praise and provide reinforcer. If student does not wait turn to complete activity, physically guide student to wait. Score V for correct response that followed verbal prompt. Score M if the correct response followed the model prompt. Score P if physical guidance was used.		
Additional Targets:			

Complies With Demand To Line Up
Compatible with ABLLS®-R Code N6

Student's Name:	Start Date:

Objective:	When teacher tells student to "Line up", student will get in line.
Person Implementing Objective:	
Setting/Environment:	
Materials:	
Reinforcers:	
Baseline:	Say, "Line up." Wait 5 seconds for a response. A correct response is scored (+) if student gets in line- <u>do not reinforce</u>. Move to next trial. An incorrect response is scored (-) if student does not get in line- <u>do not prompt</u>. Move to next trial.
Teaching Procedures:	Say, "Line up." Wait 5 seconds for a response. If student gets in line, praise and provide reinforcer. If student does not get in line, say, "Line up" as you gesture to the location of the line. Wait 5 seconds for a response. If student gets in line, praise and provide reinforcer. If student does not get in line, physically guide student get in line. Score V for correct response that followed verbal prompt. Score M if the correct response followed the model prompt. Score P if physical guidance was used.
Additional Targets:	

The BIG Book of ABA Programs

Engage in Educational Activities By Self
Compatible with ABLLS®-R Code N7

Student's Name:	Start Date:
Objective:	When teacher instructs student to engage in educational activities by self, student will engage in educational activity without interacting with anyone else.
Person Implementing Objective:	
Setting/Environment:	
Materials:	
Reinforcers:	
Baseline:	Say, "Do the ____ (name activity) by yourself." Wait 5 seconds for a response. A correct response is scored (+) if student engages in activity without interacting with anyone else- <u>do not reinforce</u>. Move to next trial. An incorrect response is scored (-) if student does not engage in activity without engaging with anyone else- <u>do not prompt</u>. Move to next trial.
Teaching Procedures:	Say, "Do the ____ (name activity) by yourself." Wait 5 seconds for a response. If student engages in activity without interacting with anyone else, praise and provide reinforcer. If student does not engage with activity without engaging with anyone else, say, "Work by yourself" as you gesture to the activity. Wait 5 seconds for a response. If student engages in activity without interacting with anyone else, praise and provide reinforcer. If student does not engage with activity without engaging with anyone else, physically guide student to work by self. Score V for correct response that followed verbal prompt. Score M if the correct response followed the model prompt. Score P if physical guidance was used.
Additional Targets:	

Retrieve Materials
Compatible with ABLLS®-R Code N8

Student's Name:		Start Date:	
Objective:	When teacher tells student to retrieve academic supplies, student will retrieve supplies.		

Person Implementing Objective:	
Setting/Environment:	
Materials:	
Reinforcers:	
Baseline:	Say, "Get your ____ (name academic supplies)." Wait 5 seconds for a response. A correct response is scored (+) if student retrieves supplies- <u>do not reinforce</u>. Move to next trial. An incorrect response is scored (-) if student does not retrieve supplies- <u>do not prompt</u>. Move to next trial.
Teaching Procedures:	Say, "Get your ____ (name academic supplies)." Wait 5 seconds for a response. If student retrieves supplies, praise and provide reinforcer. If student does not retrieve supplies, say, "Get your ____ (name academic supplies)" as you gesture to the location of the supplies. Wait 5 seconds for a response. If student retrieves supplies, praise and provide reinforcer. If student does not retrieve supplies, physically guide student retrieve supplies. Score V for correct response that followed verbal prompt. Score M if the correct response followed the model prompt. Score P if physical guidance was used.
Additional Targets:	

The BIG Book of ABA Programs

Takes Completed Academic Work To Teacher
Compatible with ABLLS®-R Code N9

Student's Name:		Start Date:
Objective:	When student completes academic tasks, student will bring competed work to teacher.	
Person Implementing Objective:		
Setting/Environment:		
Materials:		
Reinforcers:		
Baseline:	When student completes an academic task, wait 5 seconds for a response. A correct response is scored (+) if student takes completed work to teacher- <u>do not reinforce</u>. Move to next trial. An incorrect response is scored (-) if student does not take completed work to teacher- <u>do not prompt</u>. Move to next trial.	
Teaching Procedures:	When student completes an academic task, wait 5 seconds for a response. If student takes completed work to teacher, praise and provide reinforcer. If student does not take completed work to teacher, say, "When you finish your work, you need to take it to the teacher" as you gesture to the location of teacher. Wait 5 seconds for a response. If student takes completed work to teacher, praise and provide reinforcer. If student does not take completed work to teacher, physically guide student to take completed work to teacher. Score V for correct response that followed verbal prompt. Score M if the correct response followed the model prompt. Score P if physical guidance was used.	
Additional Targets:		

www.stimuluspublications.com   The Autism Skill Acquisition Program™

Waits In A Standing Position During Transitions
Compatible with ABLLS®-R Code N10

Student's Name:		Start Date:	
Objective:	When teacher tells student to change activities, student will wait in a standing position during transition.		
Person Implementing Objective:			
Setting/Environment:			
Materials:			
Reinforcers:			
Baseline:	Say, "We are going to change activities, wait a minute please." Wait 5 seconds for a response. A correct response is scored (+) if student waits quietly in a standing position- <u>do not reinforce</u>. Move to next trial. An incorrect response is scored (-) if student does not wait quietly in a standing position in - <u>do not prompt</u>. Move to next trial.		
Teaching Procedures:	Say, "We are going to change activities, wait a minute please." Wait 5 seconds for a response. If student waits quietly in a standing, praise and provide reinforcer. If student does not wait quietly in a standing position, say, "Wait" as you gesture to the place in which student is to wait. Wait 5 seconds for a response. If student waits quietly in a standing position, praise and provide reinforcer. If student does not wait quietly in a standing position, physically guide student to wait in standing position. Score V for correct response that followed verbal prompt. Score M if the correct response followed the model prompt. Score P if physical guidance was used.		
Additional Targets:			

CHAPTER 15

ABA Programs Compatible with ABLLS®-R Domain P "Generalized Responding"

Stimulus Generalization
Compatible with ABLLS®-R Code P1

Student's Name:	Start Date:

Objective:	When teacher presents a previously mastered task to student with new materials, student will respond to new stimuli in same accurate manner as with the stimuli used in teaching that task.
Person Implementing Objective:	
Setting/Environment:	
Materials:	
Reinforcers:	
Baseline:	Using new items not previously taught in a previously mastered task, deliver cue for the task. Wait 5 seconds for a response. A correct response is scored (+) if student responds correctly- <u>do not reinforce</u>. Move to next trial. An incorrect response is scored (-) if student does not respond correctly- <u>do not prompt</u>. Move to next trial.
Teaching Procedures:	Using new items not previously taught in a previously mastered task, deliver cue for the task. Wait 5 seconds for a response. If student responds correctly, praise and provide reinforcer. If student does not respond correctly, re-deliver cue for the task and gesture towards or model the correct response. Wait 5 seconds for a response. If student responds correctly, praise and provide reinforcer. If student does not respond correctly, physically guide student to respond correctly. Score V for correct response that followed verbal prompt. Score M if the correct response followed the model prompt. Score P if physical guidance was used.
Additional Targets:	

Teacher Generalization
Compatible with ABLLS®-R Code P2

Student's Name:	Start Date:

Objective:	When a new teacher presents a mastered task to student, student will respond to demand with new teacher in same accurate manner as teacher who provided the instruction of the task when it was mastered.
Person Implementing Objective:	
Setting/Environment:	
Materials:	
Reinforcers:	
Baseline:	Using a new teacher, deliver cue for a mastered task. Wait 5 seconds for a response. A correct response is scored (+) if student responds correctly- <u>do not reinforce</u>. Move to next trial. An incorrect response is scored (-) if student does not respond correctly- <u>do not prompt</u>. Move to next trial.
Teaching Procedures:	Using a new teacher, deliver cue for a mastered task. Wait 5 seconds for a response. If student responds correctly, praise and provide reinforcer. If student does not respond correctly, re-deliver cue for the task and gesture towards or model the correct response. Wait 5 seconds for a response. If student responds correctly, praise and provide reinforcer. If student does not respond correctly, physically guide student to respond correctly. Score V for correct response that followed verbal prompt. Score M if the correct response followed the model prompt. Score P if physical guidance was used.
Additional Targets:	

Setting Generalization
Compatible with ABLLS®-R Code P3

Student's Name:		Start Date:
Objective:		When teacher presents a mastered task in a new location, student will respond to demand in new setting in same accurate manner as the setting used in teaching the mastered skill.
Person Implementing Objective:		
Setting/Environment:		
Materials:		
Reinforcers:		
Baseline:		In a new location, deliver cue for a mastered task. Wait 5 seconds for a response. A correct response is scored (+) if student responds correctly- <u>do not reinforce</u>. Move to next trial. An incorrect response is scored (-) if student does not respond correctly- <u>do not prompt</u>. Move to next trial.
Teaching Procedures:		In a new location, deliver cue for a mastered task. Wait 5 seconds for a response. If student responds correctly, praise and provide reinforcer. If student does not respond correctly, re-deliver cue for the task and gesture towards the correct response. Wait 5 seconds for a response. If student responds correctly, praise and provide reinforcer. If student does not respond correctly, physically guide student to respond correctly. Score V for correct response that followed verbal prompt. Score M if the correct response followed the model prompt. Score P if physical guidance was used.
Additional Targets:		

Generalization Of Skills From Individualized To Group Settings
Compatible with ABLLS®-R Code P4

Student's Name:	Start Date:
Objective:	When teacher presents a task in a group setting that was mastered in an individual setting, student will respond to demand in group settings in same accurate manner as the individualized setting used in teaching.
Person Implementing Objective:	
Setting/Environment:	
Materials:	
Reinforcers:	
Baseline:	In a group setting, deliver cue for a mastered task. Wait 5 seconds for a response. A correct response is scored (+) if student responds correctly- <u>do not reinforce</u>. Move to next trial. An incorrect response is scored (-) if student does not respond correctly- <u>do not prompt</u>. Move to next trial.
Teaching Procedures:	In a group setting, deliver cue for a mastered task. Wait 5 seconds for a response. If student responds correctly, praise and provide reinforcer. If student does not respond correctly, re-deliver cue for the task and gesture towards or model the correct response. Wait 5 seconds for a response. If student responds correctly, praise and provide reinforcer. If student does not respond correctly, physically guide student to respond correctly. Score V for correct response that followed verbal prompt. Score M if the correct response followed the model prompt. Score P if physical guidance was used.
Additional Targets:	

Generalization Of Response Topography
Compatible with ABLLS®-R Code P5

Student's Name:	Start Date:	
Objective:	When teacher presents a mastered task, student will respond to previously mastered demand with new response topography.	
Person Implementing Objective:		
Setting/Environment:		
Materials:		
Reinforcers:		
Baseline:	Deliver cue for a mastered task. Wait 5 seconds for a response. A correct response is scored (+) if student responds with a new response topography- <u>do not reinforce</u>. Move to next trial. An incorrect response is scored (-) if student does not respond with a new response topography- <u>do not prompt</u>. Move to next trial.	
Teaching Procedures:	Deliver cue for a mastered task. Wait 5 seconds for a response. If student responds with new response topography, praise and provide reinforcer. If student does not respond with new response topography, re-deliver cue for the task and gesture towards or model correct response. Wait 5 seconds for a response. If student responds with new response topography, praise and provide reinforcer. If student does not respond with new response topography, physically guide student to respond correctly. Score V for correct response that followed verbal prompt. Score M if the correct response followed the model prompt. Score P if physical guidance was used.	
Additional Targets:		

Words Taught In Tact Training Used In Other Language Skills
Compatible with ABLLS®-R Code P6

Student's Name:	Start Date:
Objective:	Student will use the words taught in tact training as responses to other language skill questions. For example, if "Car" was taught in tact training, ask student, "What is something you drive?"
Person Implementing Objective:	
Setting/Environment:	
Materials:	
Reinforcers:	
Baseline:	Ask student a question the answer to which is the name of an object taught in tact training. Wait 5 seconds for a response. A correct response is scored (+) if student answers question correctly- <u>do not reinforce</u>. Move to next trial. An incorrect response is scored (-) if student does not answer question correctly- <u>do not prompt</u>. Move to next trial.
Teaching Procedures:	Ask student a question the answer to which is the name of an object taught in tact training. Wait 5 seconds for a response. If student answers question correctly, praise and provide reinforcer. If student does not answer question correctly, tell student the correct answer. Repeat the initial cue. Wait 5 seconds for a response. If student answers question correctly, praise and provide reinforcer. If student does not answer question correctly, physically guide by touching student's mouth as you repeat the correct response. Score V for correct response that followed verbal prompt. Score M if the correct response followed the model prompt. Score P if physical guidance was used.
Additional Targets:	

CHAPTER 16

ABA Programs Compatible with

ABLLS®-R Domain Q

"Reading Skills"

Receptive Identification Of Letter
Compatible with ABLLS®-R Code Q1

Student's Name:		Start Date:	
Objective:	\multicolumn{3}{l	}{When several letters are presented to student, student will choose the letter named by the teacher.}
Person Implementing Objective:			
Setting/Environment:			
Materials:			
Reinforcers:			
Baseline:	\multicolumn{3}{l	}{Present letter cards in front of student and say, "Give me ____ (name letter)." Wait 5 seconds for a response. A correct response is scored (+) if student selects the named letter - <u>do not reinforce</u>. Move to next trial. An incorrect response is scored (-) if student does not select the named letter- <u>do not prompt</u>. Move to next trial.}
Teaching Procedures:	\multicolumn{3}{l	}{Present letter cards in front of student and say, "Give me ____ (name letter)." Wait 5 seconds for a response. If student selects named letter, praise and provide reinforcer. If student does not select the named letter, say, "Give me ____ (name letter)" as you point to the correct letter. Wait 5 seconds for a response. If student selects named letter, praise and provide reinforcer. If student does not select the named letter, physically guide student to select the named letter. Score V if correct response followed verbal prompt. Score M if correct response followed model prompt. Score P if physical guidance was used.}
Additional Targets:			

Expressive Identification Of Letters
Compatible with ABLLS®-R Code Q2

Student's Name:	Start Date:
Objective:	When teacher presents a letter to student and says, "What letter?" student will correctly name the letter.
Person Implementing Objective:	
Setting/Environment:	
Materials:	
Reinforcers:	
Baseline:	Present a letter to student and say, "What letter?" Wait 5 seconds for a response. A correct response is scored (+) if student names letter - <u>do not reinforce</u>. Move to next trial. An incorrect response is scored (-) if student does not name letter- <u>do not prompt</u>. Move to next trial.
Teaching Procedures:	Present a letter to student and say, "What letter?" Wait 5 seconds for a response. If student names letter, praise and provide reinforcer. If student does not name the letter, say, "What letter?" as you point to the letter. Wait 5 seconds for a response. If student names letter, praise and provide reinforcer. If student does not name the letter, physically guide student to touch the letter as you say, "This is a/an ____ (name letter). Score V if correct response followed verbal prompt. Score M if correct response followed model prompt. Score P if physical guidance was used.
Additional Targets:	

The BIG Book of ABA Programs

Receptive Identification Of Letters By Their Sound
Compatible with ABLLS®-R Code Q3

Student's Name:		Start Date:	
Objective:	When teacher presents an array of letters to student and asks, "Which letter says ____ (make letter sound)?" student will select correct letter.		
Person Implementing Objective:			
Setting/Environment:			
Materials:			
Reinforcers:			
Baseline:	Present an array of letters to student and say, "Which letter says ____ (make letter sound)?" Wait 5 seconds for a response. A correct response is scored (+) if student selects correct letter - <u>do not reinforce</u>. Move to next trial. An incorrect response is scored (-) if student does not select correct letter- <u>do not prompt</u>. Move to next trial.		
Teaching Procedures:	Present an array of letters to student and say, "Which letter says ____ (make letter sound)?" Wait 5 seconds for a response. If student selects correct letter, praise and provide reinforcer. If student does not select correct letter, say, "Which letter says ____ (make letter sound)?" as you point to the correct letter. Wait 5 seconds for a response. If student selects correct letter, praise and provide reinforcer. If student does not select correct letter, physically guide student to touch the letter as you say, "The ____ (name letter) makes the ____ sound (make letter sound)." Score V if correct response followed verbal prompt. Score M if correct response followed model prompt. Score P if physical guidance was used.		
Additional Targets:			

The BIG Book of ABA Programs

Expressive Identification Of Letters Sounds
Compatible with ABLLS®-R Code Q4

Student's Name:	Start Date:
Objective:	When teacher presents a letter to the student and asks, "What sound does this make?" student will make correct letter sound.
Person Implementing Objective:	
Setting/Environment:	
Materials:	
Reinforcers:	
Baseline:	Present a letter to student and say, "What sound does this make?" Wait 5 seconds for a response. A correct response is scored (+) if student makes correct letter sound- <u>do not reinforce</u>. Move to next trial. An incorrect response is scored (-) if student does not make correct letter sound- <u>do not prompt</u>. Move to next trial.
Teaching Procedures:	Present a letter to student and say, "What sound does this make?" Wait 5 seconds for a response. If student makes correct letter sound, praise and provide reinforcer. If student does not make correct letter sound, say, "What sound does this make?" as you point to the letter. Wait 5 seconds for a response. If student makes correct letter sound, praise and provide reinforcer. If student does not make correct letter sound, physically guide student to touch the letter as you say, "The ____ (name letter) makes the ____ sound (make letter sound)." Score V if correct response followed verbal prompt. Score M if correct response followed model prompt. Score P if physical guidance was used.
Additional Targets:	

Word To Picture Matching
Compatible with ABLLS®-R Code Q5

Student's Name:	Start Date:

Objective:	When teacher presents pictures and a card containing a printed word of one of the pictures to student and says, "Match" student will move the word card to the picture of the word. For example, the card containing the word "DOG" is moved to the picture of the dog.
Person Implementing Objective:	
Setting/Environment:	
Materials:	
Reinforcers:	
Baseline:	Present and array of pictures to student. Present card with a printed word to student and say, "Match." Wait 5 seconds for a response. A correct response is scored (+) if student moves word card to correct picture- <u>do not reinforce</u>. Move to next trial. An incorrect response is scored (-) if student does not move word card to correct picture- <u>do not prompt</u>. Move to next trial.
Teaching Procedures:	Present and array of pictures to student. Present card with a printed word to student and say, "Match." Wait 5 seconds for a response. If student moves word card to correct picture, praise and provide reinforcer. If student does not move word card to correct picture, say, "Match" as you point to the correct picture. Wait 5 seconds for a response. If student moves word card to correct picture, praise and provide reinforcer. If student does not move word card to correct picture, physically guide student to move the word card to the correct picture. Score V if correct response followed verbal prompt. Score M if correct response followed model prompt. Score P if physical guidance was used.
Additional Targets:	

Matching Words Of Different Fonts
Compatible with ABLLS®-R Code Q6

Student's Name:		Start Date:
Objective:		When word cards of one font are in front of student and the teacher presents one of those words on a card in a different font and says, "Match" student will move the word card in one font to the word card of the other font.
Person Implementing Objective:		
Setting/Environment:		
Materials:		
Reinforcers:		
Baseline:		Present array of word cards of one font to student. Present a word card in a different font to student and say, "Match." Wait 5 seconds for a response. A correct response is scored (+) if student moves word card in one font to same word card in the other font- <u>do not reinforce</u>. Move to next trial. An incorrect response is scored (-) if student does not move word card in one font to same word card in the other font- <u>do not prompt</u>. Move to next trial.
Teaching Procedures:		Present array of word cards of one font to student. Present a word card in a different font to student and say, "Match." Wait 5 seconds for a response. If student moves word card in one font to same word card in the other font, praise and provide reinforcer. If student does not move word card in one font to same word card in the other font, say, "Match" as you point to the correct word card. Wait 5 seconds for a response. If student moves word card in one font to same word card in the other font, praise and provide reinforcer. If student does not move word card in one font to same word card in the other font, physically guide student to move the word card in one font to the same word card in the other font. Score V if correct response followed verbal prompt. Score M if correct response followed model prompt. Score P if physical guidance was used.
Additional Targets:		

Naming Letters Within Words
Compatible with ABLLS®-R Code Q7

Student's Name:		Start Date:	
Objective:	When teacher presents a printed word to student and says, "Name the letters" student will say the names of the letters in the word from left to right.		
Person Implementing Objective:			
Setting/Environment:			
Materials:			
Reinforcers:			
Baseline:	Present word card to student and say, "Name the letters." Wait 5 seconds for a response. A correct response is scored (+) if student names the letters from left to right- <u>do not reinforce</u>. Move to next trial. An incorrect response is scored (-) if student does not name the letters from left to right- <u>do not prompt</u>. Move to next trial.		
Teaching Procedures:	Present word card to student and say, "Name the letters." Wait 5 seconds for a response. If student names the letters from left to right, praise and provide reinforcer. If student does not name the letters from left to right, say, "Name the letters" as you point to each letter from left to right. Wait 5 seconds for a response. If student names the letters from left to right, praise and provide reinforcer. If student does not name the letters from left to right, physically guide student to touch each letter from left to right as you say each letter name. Score V if correct response followed verbal prompt. Score M if correct response followed model prompt. Score P if physical guidance was used.		
Additional Targets:			

Match Letters To Letters In A Word
Compatible with ABLLS®-R Code Q8

Student's Name:	Start Date:
Objective:	When teacher presents a word card to student and then presents all the individual letters in the word to student and says, "Match" student will place the individual letters on their identical letters in the word card.
Person Implementing Objective:	
Setting/Environment:	
Materials:	
Reinforcers:	
Baseline:	Present word card to student. Present all the individual letters in the word to student and say, "Match." Wait 5 seconds for a response. A correct response is scored (+) if student places all the individual letters on their identical letters in the word card- <u>do not reinforce</u>. Move to next trial. An incorrect response is scored (-) if student does not place all the individual letters on their identical letters in the word card- <u>do not prompt</u>. Move to next trial.
Teaching Procedures:	Present word card to student. Present all the individual letters in the word to student and say, "Match." Wait 5 seconds for a response. If student places all the individual letters on their identical letters in the word card, praise and provide reinforcer. If student does not place all the individual letters on their identical letters in the word card, say, "Match" as you model placing one letter on its identical letter in the word card. Wait 5 seconds for a response. If student places all the individual letters on their identical letters in the word card, praise and provide reinforcer. If student does not place all the individual letters on their identical letters in the word card, physically guide student to place all the individual letters on their identical letters in the word card. Score V if correct response followed verbal prompt. Score M if correct response followed model prompt. Score P if physical guidance was used.
Additional Targets:	

Word Completion
Compatible with ABLLS®-R Code Q9

Student's Name:		Start Date:	
Objective:	When teacher presents a picture of a three letter word (for example, dog, mop, can, cat, bat) and a word card containing the printed word of the picture with one letter missing from the word to student (for example D _ G), and then presents individual letters, one of which is the missing letter from the word card and says, "Complete the word" student will move the correct individual letter to the missing space in the word card completing the word.		
Person Implementing Objective:			
Setting/Environment:			
Materials:			
Reinforcers:			
Baseline:	Present a picture of a three letter word to student. Present a word card containing the printed word of the picture with one letter missing from the word. Present individual letters, one of which is the missing letter from the word card, and say, "Complete the word." Wait 5 seconds for a response. A correct response is scored (+) if student places correct letter into the missing space on the word card- <u>do not reinforce</u>. Move to next trial. An incorrect response is scored (-) if student does not place correct letter into the missing space on the word card- <u>do not prompt</u>. Move to next trial.		
Teaching Procedures:	Present a picture of a three letter word to student. Present a word card containing the printed word of the picture with one letter missing from the word. Present individual letters, one of which is the missing letter from the word card, and say, "Complete the word." Wait 5 seconds for a response. If student places correct letter into the missing space on the word card, praise and provide reinforcer. If student does not place correct letter into the missing space on the word card, say, "Complete the word" as you point to the correct letter and the missing space in the word card. Wait 5 seconds for a response. If student places correct letter into the missing space on the word card, praise and provide reinforcer. If student does not place correct letter into the missing space on the word card, physically guide student to place the correct letter into the space on the word card. Score V if correct response followed verbal prompt. Score M if correct response followed model prompt. Score P if physical guidance was used.		
Additional Targets:			

The BIG Book of ABA Programs

Word Reading
Compatible with ABLLS®-R Code Q10

Student's Name:	Start Date:	
Objective:	When teacher presents a word to student and asks, "What word is this?" student will read the word.	
Person Implementing Objective:		
Setting/Environment:		
Materials:		
Reinforcers:		
Baseline:	Present a word to student and say, "What word is this?" Wait 5 seconds for a response. A correct response is scored (+) if student reads the word - <u>do not reinforce</u>. Move to next trial. An incorrect response is scored (-) if student does not read the word- <u>do not prompt</u>. Move to next trial.	
Teaching Procedures:	Present a word to student and say, "What word is this?" Wait 5 seconds for a response. If student reads the word, praise and provide reinforcer. If student does not read the word, say, "What word is this?" as you point to the word. Wait 5 seconds for a response. If student reads the word, praise and provide reinforcer. If student does not read the word, physically guide student to touch the word as you say, "This is ____ (name word)." Score V if correct response followed verbal prompt. Score M if correct response followed model prompt. Score P if physical guidance was used.	
Additional Targets:		

www.stimuluspublications.com   389   The Autism Skill Acquisition Program™

Sound Out Words
Compatible with ABLLS®-R Code Q11

Student's Name:		Start Date:	
Objective:	When teacher presents an unknown word to student and asks, "What word is this?" student will attempt to read the word by sounding out the letters of the word.		
Person Implementing Objective:			
Setting/Environment:			
Materials:			
Reinforcers:			
Baseline:	Present an unknown word to student and say, "What word is this?" Wait 5 seconds for a response. A correct response is scored (+) if student attempts to read the word by sounding out the letters - <u>do not reinforce</u>. Move to next trial. An incorrect response is scored (-) if student does not attempt to read the word by sounding out the letters- <u>do not prompt</u>. Move to next trial.		
Teaching Procedures:	Present an unknown word to student and say, "What word is this?" Wait 5 seconds for a response. If student attempts to read the word by sounding out the letters, praise and provide reinforcer. If student does not attempt to read the word by sounding out the letters, say, "What word is this?" as you point to the word and make the letter sound of the first letter in the word. Wait 5 seconds for a response. If student attempts to read the word by sounding out the letters, praise and provide reinforcer. If student does not attempt to read the word by sounding out the letters, physically guide student to touch the word as you sound out the letters and say the word. Score V if correct response followed verbal prompt. Score M if correct response followed model prompt. Score P if physical guidance was used.		
Additional Targets:			

Read Multiple Words
Compatible with ABLLS®-R Code Q12

Student's Name:	Start Date:
Objective:	When teacher presents multiple words to student and says, "Read the words" student will read the words.
Person Implementing Objective:	
Setting/Environment:	
Materials:	
Reinforcers:	
Baseline:	Present multiple words to student and say, "Read the words." Wait 5 seconds for a response. A correct response is scored (+) if student reads the words - <u>do not reinforce</u>. Move to next trial. An incorrect response is scored (-) if student does not read the words- <u>do not prompt</u>. Move to next trial.
Teaching Procedures:	Present multiple words to student and say, "Read the words." Wait 5 seconds for a response. If student reads the words, praise and provide reinforcer. If student does not read the words, say, "Read the words" as you point to the words. Wait 5 seconds for a response. If student reads the words, praise and provide reinforcer. If student does not read the words, physically guide student to touch the words as you read the words. Score V if correct response followed verbal prompt. Score M if correct response followed model prompt. Score P if physical guidance was used.
Additional Targets:	

Read Sentences
Compatible with ABLLS®-R Code Q13

Student's Name:		Start Date:	
Objective:	When teacher presents a sentence to student and says, "Read the sentence" student will read the sentence.		
Person Implementing Objective:			
Setting/Environment:			
Materials:			
Reinforcers:			
Baseline:	Present a sentence to student and say, "Read the sentence." Wait 5 seconds for a response. A correct response is scored (+) if student reads the sentence - <u>do not reinforce</u>. Move to next trial. An incorrect response is scored (-) if student does not read the sentence- <u>do not prompt</u>. Move to next trial.		
Teaching Procedures:	Present a sentence to student and say, "Read the sentence." Wait 5 seconds for a response. If student reads the sentence, praise and provide reinforcer. If student does not read the sentence, say, "Read the sentence" as you point to the words. Wait 5 seconds for a response. If student reads the sentence, praise and provide reinforcer. If student does not read the sentence, physically guide student to touch the words as you read the sentence. Score V if correct response followed verbal prompt. Score M if correct response followed model prompt. Score P if physical guidance was used.		
Additional Targets:			

Complete A Sentence
Compatible with ABLLS®-R Code Q14

Student's Name:	Start Date:

Objective:	When teacher presents a sentence to student that is missing a word and then presents several words to student and says, "Complete the sentence" student will move the correct word into the incomplete sentence.
Person Implementing Objective:	
Setting/Environment:	
Materials:	
Reinforcers:	
Baseline:	Present a sentence with a word missing to student. Present individual words to student and say, "Complete the sentence." Wait 5 seconds for a response. A correct response is scored (+) if student moves the correct individual word into the incomplete sentence - <u>do not reinforce</u>. Move to next trial. An incorrect response is scored (-) if student does not move the correct individual word into the incomplete sentence- <u>do not prompt</u>. Move to next trial.
Teaching Procedures:	Present a sentence with a word missing to student. Present individual words to student and say, "Complete the sentence." Wait 5 seconds for a response. If student moves the correct individual word into the incomplete sentence, praise and provide reinforcer. If student does not move the correct individual word into the incomplete sentence, say, "Complete the sentence" as you point to the word and then to the incomplete sentence. Wait 5 seconds for a response. If student moves the correct individual word into the incomplete sentence, praise and provide reinforcer. If student does not move the correct individual word into the incomplete sentence, physically guide student to move the correct individual word into the incomplete sentence. Score V if correct response followed verbal prompt. Score M if correct response followed model prompt. Score P if physical guidance was used.
Additional Targets:	

Follow Written Directions
Compatible with ABLLS®-R Code Q15

Student's Name:	Start Date:

Objective:	When teacher presents a written task demand to student and says, "Read this and do what it says" student will comply with written task demand.
Person Implementing Objective:	
Setting/Environment:	
Materials:	
Reinforcers:	
Baseline:	Present a written task demand to student and say, "Read this and do what it says." Wait 5 seconds for a response. A correct response is scored (+) if student complies with written demand- <u>do not reinforce</u>. Move to next trial. An incorrect response is scored (-) if student does not comply with written demand- <u>do not prompt</u>. Move to next trial.
Teaching Procedures:	Present a written task demand to student and say, "Read this and do what it says." Wait 5 seconds for a response. If student complies with written demand, praise and provide reinforcer. If student does not comply with written demand, say, "Read this and do what it says" as you point to the written demand. Wait 5 seconds for a response. If student complies with the written demand, praise and provide reinforcer. If student does not comply with the written demand, read the demand aloud and physically guide student to comply with the written demand. Score V if correct response followed verbal prompt. Score M if correct response followed model prompt. Score P if physical guidance was used.
Additional Targets:	

The BIG Book of ABA Programs

Follow Written Instructions On A Worksheet
Compatible with ABLLS®-R Code Q16

Student's Name:		Start Date:	
Objective:	When teacher presents a worksheet to student that contains written directions for how to complete the worksheet, student will read the directions and begin the worksheet.		
Person Implementing Objective:			
Setting/Environment:			
Materials:			
Reinforcers:			
Baseline:	Present student with worksheet containing written directions and say, "Read what to do and get started." Wait 5 seconds for a response. A correct response is scored (+) if student correctly begins worksheet- <u>do not reinforce</u>. Move to next trial. An incorrect response is scored (-) if student does not correctly begin worksheet- <u>do not prompt</u>. Move to next trial.		
Teaching Procedures:	Present student with worksheet containing written directions and say, "Read what to do and get started." Wait 5 seconds for a response. If student correctly begins worksheet, praise and provide reinforcer. If student does not correctly begin worksheet, say, "Read what to do and get started" as you point to the written directions on the worksheet. Wait 5 seconds for a response. If student correctly begins worksheet, praise and provide a reinforcer. If student does not correctly begin worksheet, read the directions aloud and physically guide student to begin worksheet. Score V if correct response followed verbal prompt. Score M if correct response followed model prompt. Score P if physical guidance was used.		
Additional Targets:			

www.stimuluspublications.com — The Autism Skill Acquisition Program™

Answer Questions About What Was Read
Compatible with ABLLS®-R Code Q17

Student's Name:		Start Date:
Objective:	\multicolumn{2}{l	}{After student reads a sentence and teacher asks a question about the sentence, student will provide correct answer. For example, student reads the sentence: Mike has a dog named Baxter. The teacher could ask the question, "What was the dog's name?" "Baxter" or "Who had a dog named Baxter?" "Mike"}
Person Implementing Objective:		
Setting/Environment:		
Materials:		
Reinforcers:		
Baseline:	\multicolumn{2}{l	}{Have student read a sentence. When finished, ask a simple question about the sentence. Wait 5 seconds for a response. A correct response is scored (+) if student correctly answers question about the sentence- do not reinforce. Move to next trial. An incorrect response is scored (-) if student does not correctly answer question about the sentence- do not prompt. Move to next trial.}
Teaching Procedures:	\multicolumn{2}{l	}{Have student read a sentence. When finished, ask a simple question about the sentence. Wait 5 seconds for a response. If student correctly answers question about the sentence, praise and provide reinforcer. If student does not answer question about the sentence, ask the question again as you point to the answer in the sentence. Wait 5 seconds for a response. If student correctly answers question about the sentence, praise and provide reinforcer. If student does not correctly answer question about the sentence, physically guide student to point to the correct answer in the sentence as you say the answer. Score V if correct response followed verbal prompt. Score M if correct response followed model prompt. Score P if physical guidance was used.}
Additional Targets:		

CHAPTER 17

ABA Programs Compatible with

ABLLS®-R Domain R

"Math Skills"

Count To 10
Compatible with ABLLS®-R Code R1

Student's Name:	Start Date:	
Objective:	When teacher says, "Count to 10" student will count from 1 to 10.	
Person Implementing Objective:		
Setting/Environment:		
Materials:		
Reinforcers:		
Baseline:	Say, "Count to 10." Wait 5 seconds for a response. A correct response is scored (+) if student counts from 1 to 10- <u>do not reinforce</u>. Move to next trial. An incorrect response is scored (-) if student does not count from 1 to 10- <u>do not prompt</u>. Move to next trial.	
Teaching Procedures:	Say, "Count to 10." Wait 5 seconds for a response. If student counts from 1 to 10, praise and provide a reinforcer. If student does not count from 1 to 10, say, "Count to 10" as you begin the counting 1… 2….. Wait 5 seconds for a response. If student counts to 10, praise and provide reinforcer. If student does not count to 10, physically guide student to count by touching student's mouth as you count to 10. Score V if correct response followed verbal prompt. Score M if correct response followed model prompt. Score P if physical guidance was used.	
Additional Targets:		

Count Up To 100
Compatible with ABLLS®-R Code R2

Student's Name:	Start Date:

Objective:	When teacher says, "Count to ____ (say number from 1 to 100)" student will count to the given number.
Person Implementing Objective:	
Setting/Environment:	
Materials:	
Reinforcers:	
Baseline:	Say, "Count to ____ (say number 1 to 100)." Wait 5 seconds for a response. A correct response is scored (+) if student counts to named number- <u>do not reinforce</u>. Move to next trial. An incorrect response is scored (-) if student does not count to named number- <u>do not prompt</u>. Move to next trial.
Teaching Procedures:	Say, "Count to____ (say number 1 to 100)." Wait 5 seconds for a response. If student counts to named number, praise and provide reinforcer. If student does not count to named number, say, "Count to ____ (say number from 1 to 100)" as you begin counting 1… 2….. Wait 5 seconds for a response. If student counts to named number, praise and provide reinforcer. If student does not count to named number, physically guide student to count by touching student's mouth as you count to named number. Score V if correct response followed verbal prompt. Score M if correct response followed model prompt. Score P if physical guidance was used.
Additional Targets:	

Count Items When Counting Is Started For Student
Compatible with ABLLS®-R Code R3

Student's Name:	Start Date:
Objective:	When teacher presents items to student, says "Count the items" and then begins the counting sequence, "1... (touches one item) 2.... (touches second item)" student will continue counting all items.
Person Implementing Objective:	
Setting/Environment:	
Materials:	
Reinforcers:	
Baseline:	Present items to student. Say, "Count the ____ (items)" and touch items as you begin counting, "1... 2...." Wait 5 seconds for a response. A correct response is scored (+) if student continues counting all items- <u>do not reinforce</u>. Move to next trial. An incorrect response is scored (-) if student does not continue counting all items- <u>do not prompt</u>. Move to next trial.
Teaching Procedures:	Present items to student. Say, "Count the ____ (items)" and touch items as you begin counting, "1... 2...." Wait 5 seconds for a response. If student continues counting all items, praise and provide reinforcer. If student does not continue counting all items, say, "Count the items" as you begin counting 1... 2..... Wait 5 seconds for a response. If student continues counting all items, praise and provide reinforcer. If student does not continue counting all items, physically guide student to touch the items as you finish counting all items. Score V if correct response followed verbal prompt. Score M if correct response followed model prompt. Score P if physical guidance was used.
Additional Targets:	

Count Items
Compatible with ABLLS®-R Code R4

Student's Name:	Start Date:
Objective:	When teacher presents items to student and says "Count the items" student will count the items.
Person Implementing Objective:	
Setting/Environment:	
Materials:	
Reinforcers:	
Baseline:	Present items to student and say, "Count the items." Wait 5 seconds for a response. A correct response is scored (+) if student counts the items- <u>do not reinforce</u>. Move to next trial. An incorrect response is scored (-) if student does not count the items- <u>do not prompt</u>. Move to next trial.
Teaching Procedures:	Present items to student and say, "Count the items." Wait 5 seconds for a response. If student counts the items, praise and provide reinforcer. If student does not count the items, say, "Count the items" as you begin counting 1… 2….. Wait 5 seconds for a response. If student counts the items, praise and provide reinforcer. If student does not count the items, physically guide student to touch the items as you count the items. Score V if correct response followed verbal prompt. Score M if correct response followed model prompt. Score P if physical guidance was used.
Additional Targets:	

The BIG Book of ABA Programs

Count Items From A Larger Group Of Items
Compatible with ABLLS®-R Code R5

Student's Name:	Start Date:	
Objective:	When teacher presents items to student and says "Give me ____ (say a number of items less than the total number presented)" student will give teacher the number of items named. For example, if 10 counting bears are presented, say, "Give me 6 bears."	
Person Implementing Objective:		
Setting/Environment:		
Materials:		
Reinforcers:		
Baseline:	Present items to student and say, "Give me ____ (say a number of items less than the total number of items present)." Wait 5 seconds for a response. A correct response is scored (+) if student gives teacher correct number of items- <u>do not reinforce</u>. Move to next trial. An incorrect response is scored (-) if student does not give teacher correct number of items- <u>do not prompt</u>. Move to next trial.	
Teaching Procedures:	Present items to student and say, "Give me ____ (say a number of items less than the total number of items present)." Wait 5 seconds for a response. If student gives teacher correct number of items, praise and provide reinforcer. If student does not give teacher correct number of items, say, "Give me ____ (say a number of items less than the total number of items present)" as you gesture to the items. If student gives teacher correct number of items, praise and provide reinforcer. If student does not give teacher correct number of items, physically guide student to give correct number of items. Score V if correct response followed verbal prompt. Score M if correct response followed model prompt. Score P if physical guidance was used.	
Additional Targets:		

Expressive Identification Of Numbers Presented On A Number Line
Compatible with ABLLS®-R Code R6

Student's Name:		Start Date:	
Objective:	When teacher presents a number line containing the numbers 1 to 10 and says, "Read the numbers" student will say the numbers in order from 1 to 10.		
Person Implementing Objective:			
Setting/Environment:			
Materials:			
Reinforcers:			
Baseline:	Present a number line with numbers 1 to 10 to student and say, "Read the numbers." Wait 5 seconds for a response. A correct response is scored (+) if student reads the numbers in order from 1 to 10- <u>do not reinforce</u>. Move to next trial. An incorrect response is scored (-) if student does not read numbers in order from 1 to 10- <u>do not prompt</u>. Move to next trial.		
Teaching Procedures:	Present a number line with numbers 1 to 10 to student and say, "Read the numbers." Wait 5 seconds for a response. If student reads the numbers in order from 1 to 10, praise and provide reinforcer. If student does not read the numbers in order from 1 to 10, say, "Read the numbers" as you gesture to the number line. If student reads the numbers in order from 1 to 10, praise and provide reinforcer. If student does not read the numbers in order from 1 to 10, physically guide student to touch each number as you say them from 1 to 10. Score V if correct response followed verbal prompt. Score M if correct response followed model prompt. Score P if physical guidance was used.		
Additional Targets:			

The BIG Book of ABA Programs

Expressive Identification Of Numbers
Compatible with ABLLS®-R Code R7

Student's Name:	Start Date:	
Objective:	When teacher presents a number to student and says, "What number?" student will correctly name the number presented.	
Person Implementing Objective:		
Setting/Environment:		
Materials:		
Reinforcers:		
Baseline:	Present a number to student and say, "What number?" Wait 5 seconds for a response. A correct response is scored (+) if student says the name of the number presented- <u>do not reinforce</u>. Move to next trial. An incorrect response is scored (-) if student does not say the name of the number presented- <u>do not prompt</u>. Move to next trial.	
Teaching Procedures:	Present a number to student and say, "What number?" Wait 5 seconds for a response. If student says the name of the number presented, praise and provide reinforcer. If student does not say the name of the number presented, say, "What number?" as you gesture to the number. Wait 5 seconds for a response. If student says the name of the number presented, praise and provide reinforcer. If student does not say the name of the number presented, physically guide student to touch the number as you say "This is the number ____ (name number)." Score V if correct response followed verbal prompt. Score M if correct response followed model prompt. Score P if physical guidance was used.	
Additional Targets:		

www.stimuluspublications.com   The Autism Skill Acquisition Program™

Matching Written Numbers To Number of Items
Compatible with ABLLS®-R Code R8

Student's Name:		Start Date:
Objective:		When teacher presents a group of items and several number cards to student and says, "Match" student will correctly match the number card with the number corresponding to the number of items in the group. For example, teacher presents a group of 5 items to student and then presents number cards containing the numbers 4, 5, 6, and 7. Student should match the "5" number card to the group of 5 items.
Person Implementing Objective:		
Setting/Environment:		
Materials:		
Reinforcers:		
Baseline:		Present a group of items to student. Present number cards and say, "Match." Wait 5 seconds for a response. A correct response is scored (+) if student matches the correct number card to the group of items - do not reinforce. Move to next trial. An incorrect response is scored (-) if student does not match the correct number card to the group of items- do not prompt. Move to next trial.
Teaching Procedures:		Present a group of items to student. Present number cards and say, "Match." Wait 5 seconds for a response. If student matches the correct number card to the group of items, praise and provide reinforcer. If student does not match the correct number card to the group of items, say, "Match" as you gesture to the correct number card. Wait 5 seconds for a response. If student matches the correct number card to the group of items, praise and provide reinforcer. If student does not match the correct number card to the group of items, physically guide student to match the correct number card to the group of items. Score V if correct response followed verbal prompt. Score M if correct response followed model prompt. Score P if physical guidance was used.
Additional Targets:		

Number Concepts – "More"
Compatible with ABLLS®-R Code R9

Student's Name:	Start Date:
Objective:	When teacher presents student with two small groups of items, one group having more than the other and says, "Which one has more?" student will identify the group containing more items.
Person Implementing Objective:	
Setting/Environment:	
Materials:	
Reinforcers:	
Baseline:	Present two unequal groups of items to student and say, "Which one has more?" Wait 5 seconds for a response. A correct response is scored (+) if student identifies the group containing more items - <u>do not reinforce</u>. Move to next trial. An incorrect response is scored (-) if student does not identify the group containing more items- <u>do not prompt</u>. Move to next trial.
Teaching Procedures:	Present two unequal groups of items to student and say, "Which one has more?" Wait 5 seconds for a response. If student identifies the group containing more items, praise and provide reinforcer. If student does not identify the group containing more items, say, "Which one has more?" as you gesture to the group containing more items. Wait 5 seconds for a response. If student identifies the group containing more items, praise and provide reinforcer. If student does not identify the group containing more items, physically guide student to touch the group containing more items. Score V if correct response followed verbal prompt. Score M if correct response followed model prompt. Score P if physical guidance was used.
Additional Targets:	

Number Concepts – "Less"
Compatible with ABLLS®-R Code R10

Student's Name:	Start Date:
Objective:	When teacher presents student with two small groups of items, one group having fewer items than the other and says, "Which one has less?" student will identify the group containing fewer items.
Person Implementing Objective:	
Setting/Environment:	
Materials:	
Reinforcers:	
Baseline:	Present two unequal groups of items to student and say, "Which one has less?" Wait 5 seconds for a response. A correct response is scored (+) if student identifies the group containing fewer items - <u>do not reinforce</u>. Move to next trial. An incorrect response is scored (-) if student does not identify the group containing fewer items- <u>do not prompt</u>. Move to next trial.
Teaching Procedures:	Present two unequal groups of items to student and say, "Which one has less?" Wait 5 seconds for a response. If student identifies the group containing fewer items, praise and provide reinforcer. If student does not identify the group containing fewer items, say, "Which one has less?" as you gesture to the group containing fewer items. Wait 5 seconds for a response. If student identifies the group containing fewer items, praise and provide reinforcer. If student does not identify the group containing fewer items, physically guide student to touch the group containing fewer items. Score V if correct response followed verbal prompt. Score M if correct response followed model prompt. Score P if physical guidance was used.
Additional Targets:	

The BIG Book of ABA Programs

Number Concepts – "Some"
Compatible with ABLLS®-R Code R11

Student's Name:	Start Date:	
Objective:	When teacher presents small cups of items, one cup contains one item and the other cup contains at least three items and says, "Which one has *some* in it?" student will identify the group containing some items.	
Person Implementing Objective:		
Setting/Environment:		
Materials:		
Reinforcers:		
Baseline:	Present two cups of items, one cup contains one item and the other cup contains at least three items. Say, "Which cup has some in it?" Wait 5 seconds for a response. A correct response is scored (+) if student identifies the cup containing at least three items - <u>do not reinforce</u>. Move to next trial. An incorrect response is scored (-) if student does not identify the cup containing at least three items- <u>do not prompt</u>. Move to next trial.	
Teaching Procedures:	Present two cups of items, one cup contains one item and the other cup contains at least three items. Say, "Which cup has some in it?" Wait 5 seconds for a response. If student identifies the cup containing at least three items, praise and provide reinforcer. If student does not identify the cup containing at least three items, say, "Which one has some in it?" as you gesture to the cup containing at least three items. Wait 5 seconds for a response. If student identifies the cup containing at least three items, praise and provide reinforcer. If student does not identify the cup containing at least three items, physically guide student to touch the cup containing at least three items. Score V if correct response followed verbal prompt. Score M if correct response followed model prompt. Score P if physical guidance was used.	
Additional Targets:		

www.stimuluspublications.com · The Autism Skill Acquisition Program™

Number Concepts – "All"
Compatible with ABLLS®-R Code R12

Student's Name:	Start Date:
Objective:	When teacher presents small cups to student, one cup has no items in it and the other cup has at least three items in it and says, "Which one has *all* the items in it?" student will identify the cup containing at least three items.
Person Implementing Objective:	
Setting/Environment:	
Materials:	
Reinforcers:	
Baseline:	Present two cups to student, one cup contains no items and the other cup contains at least three items. Say, "Which cup has all the items in it?" Wait 5 seconds for a response. A correct response is scored (+) if student identifies the cup containing at least three items - <u>do not reinforce</u>. Move to next trial. An incorrect response is scored (-) if student does not identify the cup containing at least three items- <u>do not prompt</u>. Move to next trial.
Teaching Procedures:	Present two cups to student, one cup contains no items and the other cup contains at least three items. Say, "Which cup has all the items in it?" Wait 5 seconds for a response. If student identifies the cup containing at least three items, praise and provide reinforcer. If student does not identify the cup containing at least three items, say, "Which cup has all the items in it?" as you gesture to the cup containing at least three items. Wait 5 seconds for a response. If student identifies the cup containing at least three items, praise and provide reinforcer. If student does not identify the cup containing at least three items, physically guide student to touch the cup containing at least three items. Score V if correct response followed verbal prompt. Score M if correct response followed model prompt. Score P if physical guidance was used.
Additional Targets:	

The BIG Book of ABA Programs

Number Concepts – "None"
Compatible with ABLLS®-R Code R13

Student's Name:	Start Date:	
Objective:	When teacher presents small cups to student, one cup contains no items and the other cup contains at least three items and says, "Which one has *none* in it?" student will identify the cup containing no items.	
Person Implementing Objective:		
Setting/Environment:		
Materials:		
Reinforcers:		
Baseline:	Present two cups to student, one cup contains no items and the other cup contains at least three items. Say, "Which cup has none in it?" Wait 5 seconds for a response. A correct response is scored (+) if student identifies the cup containing no items - <u>do not reinforce</u>. Move to next trial. An incorrect response is scored (-) if student does not identify the cup containing no items- <u>do not prompt</u>. Move to next trial.	
Teaching Procedures:	Present two cups to student, one cup contains no items and the other cup contains at least three items. Say, "Which cup has none in it?" Wait 5 seconds for a response. If student identifies the cup containing no items, praise and provide reinforcer. If student does not identify the cup containing no items, say, "Which cup has none in it?" as you gesture to the cup containing no items. Wait 5 seconds for a response. If student identifies the cup containing no items, praise and provide reinforcer. If student does not identify the cup containing no items, physically guide student to touch the cup containing no items. Score V if correct response followed verbal prompt. Score M if correct response followed model prompt. Score P if physical guidance was used.	
Additional Targets:		

Make Larger Group Of Objects
Compatible with ABLLS®-R Code R14

Student's Name:	Start Date:
Objective:	When teacher presents student with small group of objects and makes additional objects within available and says, "You have ___ (say number of objects presented to student) you need to make a group of ___ (say larger number of objects)" student will combine the correct number of additional objects to make the named amount. For example, student is given 3 bears and is told, "You have 3 bears; you need to make a group of 8 bears." Student adds 5 bears to existing group of 3 bears.
Person Implementing Objective:	
Setting/Environment:	
Materials:	
Reinforcers:	
Baseline:	Present a small group of objects to student and make additional objects available. Say, "You have ____ (say number of objects presented to student) you need to make a group of ____ (say larger number of objects)." Wait 5 seconds for a response. A correct response is scored (+) if student combines correct number of additional objects to form named number of objects - do not reinforce. Move to next trial. An incorrect response is scored (-) if student does not combine correct number of additional objects to form named number of objects - do not prompt. Move to next trial.
Teaching Procedures:	Present a small group of objects to student and make additional objects available. Say, "You have ____ (say number of objects presented to student) you need to make a group of ____ (say larger number of objects)." Wait 5 seconds for a response. If student combines correct number of additional objects to existing objects to form the named number of objects, praise and provide reinforcer. If student does not combine correct number of additional objects to existing objects to form the named number of objects, say, "You have ____ (say number of objects presented to student) you need to make a group of ____ (say larger number)" as you gesture to the additional objects. Wait 5 seconds for a response. If student combines correct number of additional objects to existing objects to form the named number of objects, praise and provide reinforcer. If student does not combine correct number of additional objects to existing objects to form the named number of objects, physically guide student to combine correct number of additional objects to existing objects to form the named number of objects. Score V if correct response followed verbal prompt. Score M if correct response followed model prompt. Score P if physical guidance was used.
Additional Targets:	

Expressing Number Concepts – "Same"
Compatible with ABLLS®-R Code R15 (Expressive)

Student's Name:		Start Date:	
Objective:		When teacher presents two groups containing the same number of items to student and asks, "Are these groups the same or different?" student will answer "Same."	
Person Implementing Objective:			
Setting/Environment:			
Materials:			
Reinforcers:			
Baseline:		Present two groups containing the same number of items to student and say, "Are these groups the same or different?" Wait 5 seconds for a response. A correct response is scored (+) if student says, "Same" - <u>do not reinforce</u>. Move to next trial. An incorrect response is scored (-) if student does not say "Same" - <u>do not prompt</u>. Move to next trial.	
Teaching Procedures:		Present two groups containing the same number of items to student and say, "Are these groups the same or different?" Wait 5 seconds for a response. If student says "Same," praise and provide reinforcer. If student does not say, "Same," say, "Are these groups the same of different?" as you gesture to the groups. Wait 5 seconds for a response. If student says, "Same," praise and provide reinforcer. If student does not say, "Same" physically guide student to touch both groups as you say, "These groups are the same." Score V if correct response followed verbal prompt. Score M if correct response followed model prompt. Score P if physical guidance was used.	
Additional Targets:			

Expressing Number Concepts – "Same"
Compatible with ABLLS®-R Code R15 (Receptive)

Student's Name:	Start Date:

Objective:	When teacher presents two sets of groups, one set containing the same number of items in each group and one set containing a different number of items in each group to the student and points to the group with the same number of items in each group and says, "Point to the ones that are the same" student will point to the set containing the same number of items in the groups.
Person Implementing Objective:	
Setting/Environment:	
Materials:	
Reinforcers:	
Baseline:	Present two sets of groups, one set containing the same number of items in each group and one set containing a different number of items in each group and say, "Point to the ones that are the same." Wait 5 seconds for a response. A correct response is scored (+) if student points to set containing same number of items- do not reinforce. Move to next trial. An incorrect response is scored (-) if student does not point to set containing the same number of items- do not prompt. Move to next trial.
Teaching Procedures:	Present two sets of groups, one set containing the same number of items in each group and one set containing a different number of items in each group and say, "Point to the ones that are the same." Wait 5 seconds for a response. If student points to set containing same number of items, praise and provide reinforcer. If student does not point to the set containing the same number of items, say, "Point to the ones that are the same" as you gesture to the set containing the same number of items. Wait 5 seconds for a response. If student points to set containing the same number of items, praise and provide reinforcer. If student does not point to set containing the same number of items, physically guide student to point to set containing the same number of items as you say, "These are the same." Score V if correct response followed verbal prompt. Score M if correct response followed model prompt. Score P if physical guidance was used.
Additional Targets:	

Expressing Number Concepts – "Different"
Compatible with ABLLS®-R Code R16 (Expressive)

Student's Name:	Start Date:

Objective:	When teacher presents two groups containing a different number of items to student and asks, "Are these groups the same of different?" student will answer "Different."
Person Implementing Objective:	
Setting/Environment:	
Materials:	
Reinforcers:	
Baseline:	Present two groups containing a different number of items to student and say, "Are these groups the same or different?" Wait 5 seconds for a response. A correct response is scored (+) if student says, "Different" - <u>do not reinforce</u>. Move to next trial. An incorrect response is scored (-) if student does not say "Different" - <u>do not prompt</u>. Move to next trial.
Teaching Procedures:	Present two groups containing a different number of items to student and ask, "Are these groups the same or different?" Wait 5 seconds for a response. If student says "Different," praise and provide reinforcer. If student does not say, "Different," say, "Are these groups the same of different?" as you gesture to the groups. Wait 5 seconds for a response. If student says, "Different," praise and provide reinforcer. If student does not say, "Different," physically guide student to touch both groups as you say, "These groups are different." Score V if correct response followed verbal prompt. Score M if correct response followed model prompt. Score P if physical guidance was used.
Additional Targets:	

Expressing Number Concepts – "Different"
Compatible with ABLLS®-R Code R16 (Receptive)

Student's Name:		Start Date:	
Objective:		When teacher presents two sets of groups, one set containing the same number of items in each group and one set containing a different number of items in each group to student and says, "Point to the ones that are different" student will point to the set containing a different number of items in the groups.	
Person Implementing Objective:			
Setting/Environment:			
Materials:			
Reinforcers:			
Baseline:		Present two sets of groups, one set containing the same number of items in each group and one set containing a different number of items in each group and say, "Point to the ones that are different." Wait 5 seconds for a response. A correct response is scored (+) if student points to set containing a different number of items- <u>do not reinforce</u>. Move to next trial. An incorrect response is scored (-) if student does not point to set containing a different number of items- <u>do not prompt</u>. Move to next trial.	
Teaching Procedures:		Present two sets of groups, one set containing the same number of items in each group and one set containing a different number of items in each group and say, "Point to the ones that are different." Wait 5 seconds for a response. If student points to set containing a different number of items in each group, praise and provide reinforcer. If student does not point to the set containing different number of items, say, "Point to the ones that are different" as you gesture to the set containing a different number of items. Wait 5 seconds for a response. If student points to set containing a different number of items, praise and provide reinforcer. If student does not point to set containing a different number of items, physically guide student to point to set containing a different number of items as you say, "These are different." Score V if correct response followed verbal prompt. Score M if correct response followed model prompt. Score P if physical guidance was used.	
Additional Targets:			

Number Concepts – "Greater"
Compatible with ABLLS®-R Code R17 (Expressive)

Student's Name:	Start Date:
Objective:	When teacher presents to student two small groups of items, one group containing more than the other, points to the group containing more items and asks, "Is this one greater or less than?" student will say, "Greater."
Person Implementing Objective:	
Setting/Environment:	
Materials:	
Reinforcers:	
Baseline:	Present two unequal groups of items to student. Point to the one containing more items and say, "Is this one greater or less than?" Wait 5 seconds for a response. A correct response is scored (+) if student says, "Greater" - <u>do not reinforce</u>. Move to next trial. An incorrect response is scored (-) if student does not say, "Greater" - <u>do not prompt</u> Move to next trial.
Teaching Procedures:	Present two unequal groups of items to student. Point to the one containing more items and say, "Is this one greater or less than?" Wait 5 seconds for a response. If student says, "Greater," praise and provide reinforcer. If student does not say, "Greater," say, "Is this greater or less than?" as you gesture to the group containing more items. Wait 5 seconds for a response. If student says, "Greater," praise and provide reinforcer. If student does not say, "Greater," physically guide student to touch the group containing more items as you say, "This one is greater." Score V if correct response followed verbal prompt. Score M if correct response followed model prompt. Score P if physical guidance was used.
Additional Targets:	

Number Concepts – "Greater"
Compatible with ABLLS®-R Code R17 (Receptive)

Student's Name:	Start Date:

Objective:	When teacher presents to student two small groups of items, one group containing more than the other and says, "Which one is greater?" student will identify the group containing more items.
Person Implementing Objective:	
Setting/Environment:	
Materials:	
Reinforcers:	
Baseline:	Present two unequal groups of items to student and say, "Which one is greater?" Wait 5 seconds for a response. A correct response is scored (+) if student identifies the group containing more items - <u>do not reinforce</u>. Move to next trial. An incorrect response is scored (-) if student does not identify the group containing more items- <u>do not prompt</u>. Move to next trial.
Teaching Procedures:	Present two unequal groups of items to student and say, "Which one is greater?" Wait 5 seconds for a response. If student identifies the group containing more items, praise and provide reinforcer. If student does not identify the group containing more items, say, "Which one is greater?" as you gesture to the group containing more items. Wait 5 seconds for a response. If student identifies the group containing more items, praise and provide reinforcer. If student does not identify the group containing more items, physically guide student to touch the group containing more items. Score V if correct response followed verbal prompt. Score M if correct response followed model prompt. Score P if physical guidance was used.
Additional Targets:	

Number Concepts – "Addition"
Compatible with ABLLS®-R Code R18 (Expressive)

Student's Name:	Start Date:	
Objective:	When teacher has a cup of items and is placing additional items one by one into the cup and asks, "What is this called?" student will say, "Adding."	
Person Implementing Objective:		
Setting/Environment:		
Materials:		
Reinforcers:		
Baseline:	Place a cup with a few items in it in front of you. Slowly place additional items one by one into the cup as you say, "What is this called?" Wait 5 seconds for a response. A correct response is scored (+) if student says, "Adding" - <u>do not reinforce</u>. Move to next trial. An incorrect response is scored (-) if student does not say, "Adding" - <u>do not prompt</u>. Move to next trial.	
Teaching Procedures:	Place a cup with a few items in it in front of you. Slowly place additional items one by one into the cup as you say, "What is this called?" Wait 5 seconds for a response. If student says, "Adding", praise and provide reinforcer. If student does not say, "Adding", place more items in the cup and say, "This is called adding; What is this called?" Wait 5 seconds for a response. If student says, "Adding", praise and provide reinforcer. If student does not say, "Adding", physically guide by touching student's mouth as you say, "This is called adding." Score V if correct response followed verbal prompt. Score M if correct response followed model prompt. Score P if physical guidance was used.	
Additional Targets:		

Number Concepts – "Addition"
Compatible with ABLLS®-R Code R18 (Receptive)

Student's Name:	Start Date:
Objective:	When teacher presents a cup of items with additional items within reach to student and says, "Add ____ (say a number) more" student will place the correct number of additional items into the cup.
Person Implementing Objective:	
Setting/Environment:	
Materials:	
Reinforcers:	
Baseline:	Present a cup containing a few items to student. Place additional items within student's reach. Say, "Add ____ (say a number) more." Wait 5 seconds for a response. A correct response is scored (+) if student places the correct number of additional items into the cup - <u>do not reinforce</u>. Move to next trial. An incorrect response is scored (-) if student does not place the correct number of additional items into the cup- <u>do not prompt</u>. Move to next trial.
Teaching Procedures:	Present a cup containing a few items to student. Place additional items within student's reach. Say, "Add ____ (say a number) more." Wait 5 seconds for a response. If student places the correct number of additional items into the cup, praise and provide reinforcer. If student does not place the correct number of additional items into the cup, say, "Add ____ (say a number) more" as you gesture to the additional items. Wait 5 seconds for a response. If student places the correct number of additional items into the cup, praise and provide reinforcer. If student does not place the correct number of additional items into the cup, physically guide student to place the correct number of additional items into the cup. Score V if correct response followed verbal prompt. Score M if correct response followed model prompt. Score P if physical guidance was used.
Additional Targets:	

The BIG Book of ABA Programs

Object Retrieval
Compatible with ABLLS®-R Code R19

Student's Name:	Start Date:	
Objective:	When teacher tells student to retrieve a certain number of objects from a certain location, student will walk to named location and retrieve correct number of objects. For example, "Go to the desk and bring back 5 pencils."	
Person Implementing Objective:		
Setting/Environment:		
Materials:		
Reinforcers:		
Baseline:	Ensure a group of objects are placed a few feet away from student. Say, "Go to the ____ (name location) and bring back ____ (name a number of objects) ____ (name objects)." Wait 5 seconds for a response. A correct response is scored (+) if student retrieves the correct number of objects - <u>do not reinforce</u>. Move to next trial. An incorrect response is scored (-) if student does not retrieve the correct number of objects- <u>do not prompt</u>. Move to next trial.	
Teaching Procedures:	Ensure a group of objects are placed a few feet away from student. Say, "Go to the ____ (name location) and bring back ____ (name a number of objects) ____ (name objects)." Wait 5 seconds for a response. If student retrieves the correct number of objects, praise and provide reinforcer. If student does not retrieve the correct number of objects, say, "Go to the ____ (name location) and bring back ____ (name a number of objects) ____ (name objects)" as you gesture to the location of the objects. Wait 5 seconds for a response. If student retrieves the correct number of objects, praise and provide reinforcer. If student does not retrieve the correct number of objects, physically guide student to retrieve the correct number of objects. Score V if correct response followed verbal prompt. Score M if correct response followed model prompt. Score P if physical guidance was used.	
Additional Targets:		

www.stimuluspublications.com   The Autism Skill Acquisition Program™

Addition With Carrying
Compatible with ABLLS®-R Code R20

Student's Name:		Start Date:
Objective:	When teacher presents to student a written addition problem that involves carrying and says, "Solve this" student will write the correct answer to the problem.	
Person Implementing Objective:		
Setting/Environment:		
Materials:		
Reinforcers:		
Baseline:	Present student with a written addition problem that involves carrying and say, "Solve this." Wait 5 seconds for a response. A correct response is scored (+) if student writes the correct answer - <u>do not reinforce</u>. Move to next trial. An incorrect response is scored (-) if student does not write correct answer- <u>do not prompt</u>. Move to next trial.	
Teaching Procedures:	Present student with a written addition problem that involves carrying and say, "Solve this." Wait 5 seconds for a response. If student writes the correct answer, praise and provide reinforcer. If student does not write the correct answer, say, "Solve this like this" as you model the correct steps on an identical problem next to student's problem. Wait 5 seconds for a response. If student writes the correct answer, praise and provide reinforcer. If student does not write the correct answer, physically guide student to write the correct answer. Score V if correct response followed verbal prompt. Score M if correct response followed model prompt. Score P if physical guidance was used.	
Additional Targets:		

Telling Time On An Analog Clock
Compatible with ABLLS®-R Code R21

Student's Name:		Start Date:	
Objective:	When teacher shows student an analog clock and says, "What time is it?" student will say the correct time.		
Person Implementing Objective:			
Setting/Environment:			
Materials:			
Reinforcers:			
Baseline:	Present an analog clock to student and say, "What time is it?" Wait 5 seconds for a response. A correct response is scored (+) if student says correct time - <u>do not reinforce</u>. Move to next trial. An incorrect response is scored (-) if student does not say correct time- <u>do not prompt</u>. Move to next trial.		
Teaching Procedures:	Present an analog clock to student and say, "What time is it?" Wait 5 seconds for a response. If student says correct time, praise and provide reinforcer. If student does not say correct time, say, "The little hand is the hour and the big hand is the minutes. So, the time is (for example) 8:15" as you point to the hands on the clock. Say, "What time is it?" Wait 5 seconds for a response. If student says correct time, praise and provide reinforcer. If student does not say correct time, physically guide student's hand to touch the hands on the clock as you say the correct time. Score V if correct response followed verbal prompt. Score M if correct response followed model prompt. Score P if physical guidance was used.		
Additional Targets:			

The BIG Book of ABA Programs

Telling Time On A Digital Clock
Compatible with ABLLS®-R Code R21

Student's Name:		Start Date:
Objective:	When teacher shows student a digital clock and says, "What time is it?" student will say the correct time.	
Person Implementing Objective:		
Setting/Environment:		
Materials:		
Reinforcers:		
Baseline:	Present a digital clock to student and say, "What time is it?" Wait 5 seconds for a response. A correct response is scored (+) if student says correct time - <u>do not reinforce</u>. Move to next trial. An incorrect response is scored (-) if student does not say correct time- <u>do not prompt</u>. Move to next trial.	
Teaching Procedures:	Present a digital clock to student and say, "What time is it?" Wait 5 seconds for a response. If student says correct time, praise and provide reinforcer. If student does not say correct time, say, "The first number is the hour. The numbers on this side are the minutes. So, the time is (for example) 4:20" as you point to the clock." Say, "What time is it?" Wait 5 seconds for a response. If student says correct time, praise and provide reinforcer. If student does not say correct time, physically guide student's hand to touch the numbers as you say the correct time. Score V if correct response followed verbal prompt. Score M if correct response followed model prompt. Score P if physical guidance was used.	
Additional Targets:		

The BIG Book of ABA Programs

Coin Names
Compatible with ABLLS®-R Code R22

Student's Name:		Start Date:
Objective:	\multicolumn{2}{l	}{When teacher presents a coin to student and says, "What coin is this?" student will say the correct coin name.}
Person Implementing Objective:		
Setting/Environment:		
Materials:		
Reinforcers:		
Baseline:	\multicolumn{2}{l	}{Present coin to student and say, "What coin is this?" Wait 5 seconds for a response. A correct response is scored (+) if student says correct coin name - <u>do not reinforce</u>. Move to next trial. An incorrect response is scored (-) if student does not say correct coin name- <u>do not prompt</u>. Move to next trial.}
Teaching Procedures:	\multicolumn{2}{l	}{Present coin to student and say, "What coin is this?" Wait 5 seconds for a response. If student says correct coin name, praise and provide reinforcer. If student does not say correct coin name, say, "This is a ____ (name the coin)" as you point to the coin. Say, "What coin is this?" Wait 5 seconds for a response. If student says correct coin name, praise and provide reinforcer. If student does not say correct coin name, physically guide student's hand to touch the coin as you say, "This is a ____ (name coin). Score V if correct response followed verbal prompt. Score M if correct response followed model prompt. Score P if physical guidance was used.}
Additional Targets:		

Coin Values
Compatible with ABLLS®-R Code R23

Student's Name:		Start Date:	
Objective:	When teacher presents a coin to student and says, "How much is this worth?" student will say the correct coin value.		
Person Implementing Objective:			
Setting/Environment:			
Materials:			
Reinforcers:			
Baseline:	Present coin to student and say, "How much is this worth?" Wait 5 seconds for a response. A correct response is scored (+) if student says correct coin value - do not reinforce. Move to next trial. An incorrect response is scored (-) if student does not say correct coin value- do not prompt. Move to next trial.		
Teaching Procedures:	Present coin to student and say, "How much is this worth?" Wait 5 seconds for a response. If student says correct coin value, praise and provide reinforcer. If student does not say correct coin value, say, "This is worth ____ (name coin value) cents" as you point to the coin. Say, "How much is this worth?" Wait 5 seconds for a response. If student says correct coin value, praise and provide reinforcer. If student does not say correct coin value, physically guide student's hand to touch the coin as you say, "This is worth ____ (name coin value) cents." Score V if correct response followed verbal prompt. Score M if correct response followed model prompt. Score P if physical guidance was used.		
Additional Targets:			

The BIG Book of ABA Programs

Adding Coins
Compatible with ABLLS®-R Code R24

Student's Name:	Start Date:	
Objective:	When teacher presents several coins to student and says, "Give me ____ (name amount) cents?" student will give teacher coins that equal the named value.	
Person Implementing Objective:		
Setting/Environment:		
Materials:		
Reinforcers:		
Baseline:	Present several coins to student and say, "Give me ____ (name amount) cents?" Wait 5 seconds for a response. A correct response is scored (+) if student gives coins equaling the named value - <u>do not reinforce</u>. Move to next trial. An incorrect response is scored (-) if student does not give coins equaling the named value- <u>do not prompt</u>. Move to next trial.	
Teaching Procedures:	Present several coins to student and say, "Give me ____ (name amount) cents?" Wait 5 seconds for a response. If student gives coins equaling the named value, praise and provide reinforcer. If student does not give coins equaling the named value, say, "Give me ____ (name amount) cents?" as you gesture to the coins. Wait 5 seconds for a response. If student gives coins equaling the named value, praise and provide reinforcer. If student does not give coins equaling the named value, physically guide student to give coins equaling the named value as you say the cumulative value of each coin being added to the named value. Score V if correct response followed verbal prompt. Score M if correct response followed model prompt. Score P if physical guidance was used.	
Additional Targets:		

Expressing Number Concepts – "Equal"
Compatible with ABLLS®-R Code R25 (Expressive)

Student's Name:	Start Date:
Objective:	When teacher presents two groups containing the same number of items to student and asks, "Are these groups equal or unequal?" student will answer, "Equal."
Person Implementing Objective:	
Setting/Environment:	
Materials:	
Reinforcers:	
Baseline:	Present two groups containing the same number of items to student and say, "Are these groups equal or unequal?" Wait 5 seconds for a response. A correct response is scored (+) if student says, "Equal" - <u>do not reinforce</u>. Move to next trial. An incorrect response is scored (-) if student does not say, "Equal" - <u>do not prompt</u>. Move to next trial.
Teaching Procedures:	Present two groups containing the same number of items to student and say, "Are these groups equal or unequal?" Wait 5 seconds for a response. If student says "Equal," praise and provide reinforcer. If student does not say, "Equal," say, "Are these groups equal or unequal?" as you gesture to the groups. Wait 5 seconds for a response. If student says, "Equal," praise and provide reinforcer. If student does not say, "Equal" physically guide student to touch both groups as you say, "These groups are equal." Score V if correct response followed verbal prompt. Score M if correct response followed model prompt. Score P if physical guidance was used.
Additional Targets:	

Expressing Number Concepts – "Equal"
Compatible with ABLLS®-R Code R25 (Receptive)

Student's Name:		Start Date:	
Objective:		When teacher presents two sets of groups, one set containing the same number of items in each group and one set containing a different number of items in each group and says, "Point to the ones that are equal" student will point to the set containing the same number of items in the groups.	
Person Implementing Objective:			
Setting/Environment:			
Materials:			
Reinforcers:			
Baseline:		Present two sets of groups, one set containing the same number of items in each group and one set containing a different number of items in each group. Say, "Point to the ones that are equal." Wait 5 seconds for a response. A correct response is scored (+) if student points to set containing same number of items in each group- do not reinforce. Move to next trial. An incorrect response is scored (-) if student does not point to set containing same number of items in each group- do not prompt. Move to next trial.	
Teaching Procedures:		Present two sets of groups, one set containing the same number of items in each group and one set containing a different number of items in each group. Say, "Point to the ones that are equal." Wait 5 seconds for a response. If student points to set containing an equal number of items in each group, praise and provide reinforcer. If student does not point to the set containing an equal number of items in each group, say, "Point to the ones that are equal" as you gesture to the set containing the same number of items in each group. Wait 5 seconds for a response. If student points to set containing an equal number of items in each group, praise and provide reinforcer. If student does not point to set containing an equal number of items in each group, physically guide student to point to correct set as you say, "These are equal." Score V if correct response followed verbal prompt. Score M if correct response followed model prompt. Score P if physical guidance was used.	
Additional Targets:			

Expressing Number Concepts – "Unequal"
Compatible with ABLLS®-R Code R26 (Expressive)

Student's Name:		Start Date:	
Objective:		When teacher presents two groups containing a different number of items to student and asks, "Are these groups equal or unequal?" student will answer "Unequal."	

Person Implementing Objective:	
Setting/Environment:	
Materials:	
Reinforcers:	
Baseline:	Present two groups containing a different number of items to student and say, "Are these groups equal or unequal?" Wait 5 seconds for a response. A correct response is scored (+) if student says, "Unequal" - <u>do not reinforce</u>. Move to next trial. An incorrect response is scored (-) if student does not say "Unequal" - <u>do not prompt</u>. Move to next trial.
Teaching Procedures:	Present two groups containing a different number of items to student and say, "Are these groups equal or unequal?" Wait 5 seconds for a response. If student says "Unequal," praise and provide reinforcer. If student does not say, "Unequal," say, "Are these groups equal or unequal?" as you gesture to the groups. Wait 5 seconds for a response. If student says, "Unequal," praise and provide reinforcer. If student does not say, "Unequal" physically guide student to touch both groups as you say, "These groups are unequal." Score V if correct response followed verbal prompt. Score M if correct response followed model prompt. Score P if physical guidance was used.
Additional Targets:	

The BIG Book of ABA Programs

Expressing Number Concepts – "Unequal"
Compatible with ABLLS®-R Code R26 (Receptive)

Student's Name:		Start Date:	
Objective:			

Student's Name:	Start Date:
Objective:	When teacher presents two sets of groups, one set containing the same number of items in each group and one set containing a different number of items in each group to student and says, "Point to the ones that are unequal" student will point to the set containing a different number of items in the groups.
Person Implementing Objective:	
Setting/Environment:	
Materials:	
Reinforcers:	
Baseline:	Present two sets of groups, one set containing the same number of items in each group and one set containing a different number of items in each group. Say, "Point to the ones that are unequal." Wait 5 seconds for a response. A correct response is scored (+) if student points to set containing a different number of items in each group- <u>do not reinforce</u>. Move to next trial. An incorrect response is scored (-) if student does not point to set containing a different number of items in each group- <u>do not prompt</u>. Move to next trial.
Teaching Procedures:	Present two sets of groups, one set containing the same number of items in each group and one set containing a different number of items in each group. Say, "Point to the ones that are unequal." Wait 5 seconds for a response. If student points to set containing a different number of items in each group, praise and provide reinforcer. If student does not point to the set containing different number of items in each group, say, "Point to the ones that are unequal" as you gesture to the set containing a different number of items in each group. Wait 5 seconds for a response. If student points to set containing a different number of items in each group, praise and provide reinforcer. If student does not point to set containing a different number of items, physically guide student to point to set containing a different number of items as you say, "These are unequal." Score V if correct response followed verbal prompt. Score M if correct response followed model prompt. Score P if physical guidance was used.
Additional Targets:	

Number Concepts – "Minus"
Compatible with ABLLS®-R Code R27 (Expressive)

Student's Name:		Start Date:
Objective:	When teacher presents a minus sign to student and asks, "What sign is this?" student will say, "Minus."	
Person Implementing Objective:		
Setting/Environment:		
Materials:		
Reinforcers:		
Baseline:	Present a minus sign to student and say, "What sign is this?" Wait 5 seconds for a response. A correct response is scored (+) if student says, "Minus" - <u>do not reinforce</u>. Move to next trial. An incorrect response is scored (-) if student does not say, "Minus" - <u>do not prompt</u> Move to next trial.	
Teaching Procedures:	Present a minus sign to the student and say, "What sign is this?" Wait 5 seconds for a response. If student says, "Minus," praise and provide reinforcer. If student does not say, "Minus," gesture to minus sign and say, "What sign is this?" Wait 5 seconds for a response. If student says, "Minus," praise and provide reinforcer. If student does not say, "Minus," physically guide student to touch the minus sign as you say, "This is minus." Score V if correct response followed verbal prompt. Score M if correct response followed model prompt. Score P if physical guidance was used.	
Additional Targets:		

Number Concepts – "Minus"
Compatible with ABLLS®-R Code R27 (Receptive)

Student's Name:	Start Date:
Objective:	When teacher presents a plus sign and a minus sign to student and says, "Which one is minus" student will point to the minus sign.
Person Implementing Objective:	
Setting/Environment:	
Materials:	
Reinforcers:	
Baseline:	Present a plus and a minus sign to student and say, "Which one is minus?" Wait 5 seconds for a response. A correct response is scored (+) if student points to the minus sign - <u>do not reinforce</u>. Move to next trial. An incorrect response is scored (-) if student does not point to the minus sign- <u>do not prompt</u>. Move to next trial.
Teaching Procedures:	Present a plus and a minus sign to student and say, "Which one is minus?" Wait 5 seconds for a response. If student points to the minus sign, praise and provide reinforcer. If student does not point to the minus sign, say, "Which one is minus" as you point to the minus sign. Wait 5 seconds for a response. If student points to the minus sign, praise and provide reinforcer. If student does not point to the minus sign, physically guide student to point to the minus sign. Score V if correct response followed verbal prompt. Score M if correct response followed model prompt. Score P if physical guidance was used.
Additional Targets:	

Number Concepts – "Plus"
Compatible with ABLLS®-R Code R28 (Expressive)

Student's Name:		Start Date:	
Objective:	When teacher presents a plus sign to student and asks, "What sign is this?" student will say, "Plus."		
Person Implementing Objective:			
Setting/Environment:			
Materials:			
Reinforcers:			
Baseline:	Present a plus sign to student and say, "What sign is this?" Wait 5 seconds for a response. A correct response is scored (+) if student says, "Plus" - <u>do not reinforce</u>. Move to next trial. An incorrect response is scored (-) if student does not say, "Plus" - <u>do not prompt</u> Move to next trial.		
Teaching Procedures:	Present a plus sign to student and say, "What sign is this?" Wait 5 seconds for a response. If student says, "Plus," praise and provide reinforcer. If student does not say, "Plus," gesture to the plus sign and say, "What sign is this?" Wait 5 seconds for a response. If student says, "Plus," praise and provide reinforcer. If student does not say, "Plus," physically guide student to touch the plus sign as you say, "This is plus." Score V if correct response followed verbal prompt. Score M if correct response followed model prompt. Score P if physical guidance was used.		
Additional Targets:			

Number Concepts – "Plus"
Compatible with ABLLS®-R Code R28 (Receptive)

Student's Name:		Start Date:	
Objective:	When teacher presents a plus sign and a minus sign to student and says, "Which one is plus" student will point to the plus sign.		
Person Implementing Objective:			
Setting/Environment:			
Materials:			
Reinforcers:			
Baseline:	Present a plus and a minus sign to student and say, "Which one is plus?" Wait 5 seconds for a response. A correct response is scored (+) if student points to the plus sign - <u>do not reinforce</u>. Move to next trial. An incorrect response is scored (-) if student does not point to the plus sign- <u>do not prompt</u>. Move to next trial.		
Teaching Procedures:	Present a plus and a minus sign to student and say, "Which one is plus?" Wait 5 seconds for a response. If student points to the plus sign, praise and provide reinforcer. If student does not point to the plus sign, say, "Which one is plus" as you point to the plus sign. Wait 5 seconds for a response. If student points to the plus sign, praise and provide reinforcer. If student does not point to the plus sign, physically guide student to point to the plus sign. Score V if correct response followed verbal prompt. Score M if correct response followed model prompt. Score P if physical guidance was used.		
Additional Targets:			

Number Concepts – "Subtraction"
Compatible with ABLLS®-R Code R29 (Expressive)

Student's Name:		Start Date:	
Objective:	When teacher has a cup of items and is taking out items one by one from the cup and asks student, "What is this called?" student will say, "Subtracting."		
Person Implementing Objective:			
Setting/Environment:			
Materials:			
Reinforcers:			
Baseline:	Place a cup containing several items in front of you. Slowly take out items one by one as you say, "What is this called?" Wait 5 seconds for a response. A correct response is scored (+) if student says, "Subtracting" - <u>do not reinforce</u>. Move to next trial. An incorrect response is scored (-) if student does not say, "Subtracting" - <u>do not prompt</u>. Move to next trial.		
Teaching Procedures:	Place a cup containing several items in front of you. Slowly take out items one by one as you say, "What is this called?" Wait 5 seconds for a response. If student says, "Subtracting," praise and provide reinforcer. If student does not say, "Subtracting," take out more items and say, "This is called subtracting; What is this called?" Wait 5 seconds for a response. If student says, "Subtracting," praise and provide reinforcer. If student does not say, "Subtracting," physically guide by touching student's mouth as you say, "This is called subtracting." Score V if correct response followed verbal prompt. Score M if correct response followed model prompt. Score P if physical guidance was used.		
Additional Targets:			

The BIG Book of ABA Programs

Number Concepts – "Subtracting"
Compatible with ABLLS®-R Code R29 (Receptive)

Student's Name:		Start Date:	
Objective:	When teacher presents a cup of items to student and says, "Subtract ____ (say a number)" student will remove the correct number of items from the cup.		
Person Implementing Objective:			
Setting/Environment:			
Materials:			
Reinforcers:			
Baseline:	Present a cup with several items to student and say, "Subtract ____ (say a number)." Wait 5 seconds for a response. A correct response is scored (+) if student removes the correct number of items from the cup - <u>do not reinforce</u>. Move to next trial. An incorrect response is scored (-) if student does not remove the correct number of items from the cup- <u>do not prompt</u>. Move to next trial.		
Teaching Procedures:	Present a cup with several items to student and say, "Subtract ____ (say a number)." Wait 5 seconds for a response. If student removes the correct number of items from the cup, praise and provide reinforcer. If student does not remove the correct number of items from the cup, say, "Subtract ____ (say a number)" as you make a motion as if taking items from the cup. Wait 5 seconds for a response. If student removes the correct number of items from the cup, praise and provide reinforcer. If student does not remove the correct number of items from the cup, physically guide student to remove the correct number of items from the cup. Score V if correct response followed verbal prompt. Score M if correct response followed model prompt. Score P if physical guidance was used.		
Additional Targets:			

CHAPTER 18

ABA Programs Compatible with ABLLS®-R Domain S "Writing Skills"

Write On Paper
Compatible with ABLLS®-R Code S1

Student's Name:		Start Date:	
Objective:	When teacher says, "Write on paper" student will make a visible mark on the paper.		

Person Implementing Objective:	
Setting/Environment:	
Materials:	
Reinforcers:	
Baseline:	Give student a writing utensil and a piece of paper. Say, "Write on paper." Wait 5 seconds for a response. A correct response is scored (+) if student makes a mark on the paper- <u>do not reinforce</u>. Move to next trial. An incorrect response is scored (-) if student does not make mark on the paper- <u>do not prompt</u>. Move to next trial.
Teaching Procedures:	Give student a writing utensil and a piece of paper. Say, "Write on paper." Wait 5 seconds for a response. If student makes a mark on the paper, praise and provide reinforcer. If student does not make a mark on the paper, say, "Write on paper" as you gesture to the paper. Wait 5 seconds for a response. If student makes a mark on the paper, praise and provide reinforcer. If student does not make a mark on the paper, physically guide student to make a mark on the paper. Score V if correct response followed verbal prompt. Score M if correct response followed model prompt. Score P if physical guidance was used.
Additional Targets:	

Coloring
Compatible with ABLLS®-R Code S2

Student's Name:	Start Date:
Objective:	When teacher says, "Color in the shape" student will color inside the shape without going outside the lines.
Person Implementing Objective:	
Setting/Environment:	
Materials:	
Reinforcers:	
Baseline:	Give student a writing utensil and a piece of paper containing an outlined shape. Say, "Color in the shape." Wait 5 seconds for a response. A correct response is scored (+) if student colors inside the shape without going outside the lines- <u>do not reinforce</u>. Move to next trial. An incorrect response is scored (-) if student colors outside the shape- <u>do not prompt</u>. Move to next trial.
Teaching Procedures:	Give student a writing utensil and a piece of paper containing an outlined shape. Say, "Color in the shape." Wait 5 seconds for a response. If student colors inside the shape without going outside the lines, praise and provide reinforcer. If student colors outside the shape, say, "Color in the shape" as you gesture to the inside of the shape. Wait 5 seconds for a response. If student colors inside the shape without going outside the lines, praise and provide reinforcer. If student colors outside the shape, physically guide student to colors inside the shape. Score V if correct response followed verbal prompt. Score M if correct response followed model prompt. Score P if physical guidance was used.
Additional Targets:	

Tracing
Compatible with ABLLS®-R Code S3

Student's Name:		Start Date:
Objective:	When teacher presents a line or shape on a piece of paper and says, "Trace the ____ (name what student is to trace)" student will accurately trace the named shape or line.	
Person Implementing Objective:		
Setting/Environment:		
Materials:		
Reinforcers:		
Baseline:	Give student a writing utensil and a piece of paper containing lines or shapes. Say, "Trace the ____ (name what student is to trace)." Wait 5 seconds for a response. A correct response is scored (+) if student accurately traces named line or shape- <u>do not reinforce</u>. Move to next trial. An incorrect response is scored (-) if student does not accurately trace named line or shape- <u>do not prompt</u>. Move to next trial.	
Teaching Procedures:	Give student a writing utensil and a piece of paper containing lines or shapes. Say, "Trace the ____ (name what student is to trace)." Wait 5 seconds for a response. If student accurately traces named line or shape, praise and provide reinforcer. If student does not accurately trace named line or shape, say, "Trace the ____ (name what student is to trace)" as you gesture to the line/shape. Wait 5 seconds for a response. If student accurately traces named line or shape, praise and provide reinforcer. If student does not accurately trace named line or shape, physically guide student to accurately trace named line or shape. Score V if correct response followed verbal prompt. Score M if correct response followed model prompt. Score P if physical guidance was used.	
Additional Targets:		

Tracing Numbers Or Letters
Compatible with ABLLS®-R Code S4

Student's Name:		Start Date:	
Objective:		When teacher presents a number or letter on a piece of paper and says, "Trace the ____ (letter/number)" student will accurately trace the letter/number.	
Person Implementing Objective:			
Setting/Environment:			
Materials:			
Reinforcers:			
Baseline:		Give student a writing utensil and a piece of paper containing letters or numbers. Say, "Trace the ____ (letter/number)." Wait 5 seconds for a response. A correct response is scored (+) if student accurately traces the letter/number- <u>do not reinforce</u>. Move to next trial. An incorrect response is scored (-) if student does not accurately trace named letter/number- <u>do not prompt</u>. Move to next trial.	
Teaching Procedures:		Give student a writing utensil and a piece of paper containing letters or numbers. Say, "Trace the ____ (letter/number)." Wait 5 seconds for a response. If student accurately traces the letter/number, praise and provide reinforcer. If student does not accurately trace the letter/number, say, "Trace the ____ (letter/number)" as you gesture to the letter/number. Wait 5 seconds for a response. If student accurately traces the letter/number, praise and provide reinforcer. If student does not accurately trace the letter/number, physically guide student to accurately trace the letter/number. Score V if correct response followed verbal prompt. Score M if correct response followed model prompt. Score P if physical guidance was used.	
Additional Targets:			

The BIG Book of ABA Programs

Copying – Straight Lines
Compatible with ABLLS®-R Code S5

Student's Name:	Start Date:
Objective:	When teacher gives student a piece of paper containing a straight line and says, "Draw the line" student will draw a line similar in length to the one on the paper.
Person Implementing Objective:	
Setting/Environment:	
Materials:	
Reinforcers:	
Baseline:	Give student a writing utensil and a piece of paper containing a straight line. Say, "Draw the line." Wait 5 seconds for a response. A correct response is scored (+) if student accurately draws a line similar in length to the line on the paper- do not reinforce. Move to next trial. An incorrect response is scored (-) if student does not accurately draw a line similar in length to the line on the paper - do not prompt. Move to next trial.
Teaching Procedures:	Give student a writing utensil and a piece of paper containing a straight line. Say, "Draw the line." Wait 5 seconds for a response. If student accurately draws a line similar in length to the line on the paper, praise and provide reinforcer. If student does not accurately draw a line similar in length to the line on the paper, say, "Draw the line" as you gesture to the line. Wait 5 seconds for a response. If student accurately draws a line similar in length to the line on the paper, praise and provide reinforcer. If does not accurately draw a line similar in length to the line on the paper, physically guide student to accurately draw a line similar in length to the line on the paper. Score V if correct response followed verbal prompt. Score M if correct response followed model prompt. Score P if physical guidance was used.
Additional Targets:	

Copying – Curved Lines
Compatible with ABLLS®-R Code S6

Student's Name:		Start Date:	
Objective:	When teacher gives student a piece of paper containing a curved line and says, "Draw the line" student will draw a line similar in shape to the one on the paper.		
Person Implementing Objective:			
Setting/Environment:			
Materials:			
Reinforcers:			
Baseline:	Give student a writing utensil and a piece of paper containing a curved line. Say, "Draw the line." Wait 5 seconds for a response. A correct response is scored (+) if student accurately draws a line similar in shape to the line on the paper- <u>do not reinforce</u>. Move to next trial. An incorrect response is scored (-) if student does not draw a line similar in shape to the line on the paper- <u>do not prompt</u>. Move to next trial.		
Teaching Procedures:	Give student a writing utensil and a piece of paper containing a curved line. Say, "Draw the line." Wait 5 seconds for a response. If student accurately draws a line similar in shape to the line on the paper, praise and provide reinforcer. If student does not accurately draw a line similar in shape to the line on the paper, say, "Draw the line" as you gesture to the line. Wait 5 seconds for a response. If student accurately draws a line similar in shape to the line on the paper, praise and provide reinforcer. If student does not accurately draw a line similar in shape to the line on the paper, physically guide student to accurately draw a line similar in shape to the line on the paper. Score V if correct response followed verbal prompt. Score M if correct response followed model prompt. Score P if physical guidance was used.		
Additional Targets:			

Copying – Letters
Compatible with ABLLS®-R Code S7

Student's Name:		Start Date:	
Objective:	When teacher gives student a piece of paper containing a letter and says, "Draw the letter" student will draw a letter like the one on the paper.		
Person Implementing Objective:			
Setting/Environment:			
Materials:			
Reinforcers:			
Baseline:	Give student a writing utensil and a piece of paper containing a letter. Say, "Draw the letter." Wait 5 seconds for a response. A correct response is scored (+) if student accurately draws the letter- <u>do not reinforce</u>. Move to next trial. An incorrect response is scored (-) if student does not accurately draw the letter- <u>do not prompt</u>. Move to next trial.		
Teaching Procedures:	Give student a writing utensil and a piece of paper containing a letter. Say, "Draw the letter." Wait 5 seconds for a response. If student accurately draws the letter, praise and provide reinforcer. If student does not accurately draw the letter, say, "Draw the letter" as you gesture to the letter. Wait 5 seconds for a response. If student accurately draws the letter, praise and provide reinforcer. If student does not accurately draw the letter, physically guide student to accurately draw the letter. Score V if correct response followed verbal prompt. Score M if correct response followed model prompt. Score P if physical guidance was used.		
Additional Targets:			

Copying – Numbers
Compatible with ABLLS®-R Code S8

Student's Name:		Start Date:	
Objective:		When teacher gives student a piece of paper containing a number and says, "Draw the number" student will draw a number like the one on the paper.	
Person Implementing Objective:			
Setting/Environment:			
Materials:			
Reinforcers:			
Baseline:		Give student a writing utensil and a piece of paper containing a number. Say, "Draw the number." Wait 5 seconds for a response. A correct response is scored (+) if student accurately draws the number - <u>do not reinforce</u>. Move to next trial. An incorrect response is scored (-) if student does not accurately draw the number- <u>do not prompt</u>. Move to next trial.	
Teaching Procedures:		Give student a writing utensil and a piece of paper containing a number. Say, "Draw the number." Wait 5 seconds for a response. If student accurately draws the number, praise and provide reinforcer. If student does not accurately draw the number, say, "Draw the number" as you gesture to the number. Wait 5 seconds for a response. If student accurately draws the number, praise and provide reinforcer. If student does not accurately draw the number, physically guide student to accurately draw the number. Score V if correct response followed verbal prompt. Score M if correct response followed model prompt. Score P if physical guidance was used.	
Additional Targets:			

Writing Letters
Compatible with ABLLS®-R Code S9

Student's Name:	Start Date:

Objective:	When teacher gives student a piece of paper and says, "Write the letter ____ (name letter)" student will write the named letter.
Person Implementing Objective:	
Setting/Environment:	
Materials:	
Reinforcers:	
Baseline:	Give student a writing utensil and a piece of paper. Say, "Write the letter ____ (name letter)." Wait 5 seconds for a response. A correct response is scored (+) if student accurately writes the letter - <u>do not reinforce</u>. Move to next trial. An incorrect response is scored (-) if student does not accurately write the letter- <u>do not prompt</u>. Move to next trial.
Teaching Procedures:	Give student a writing utensil and a piece of paper. Say, "Write the letter ____ (name letter)." Wait 5 seconds for a response. If student accurately writes the letter, praise and provide reinforcer. If student does not accurately write the letter, say, "Write the letter ____ (name letter)" as you gesture to the paper. Wait 5 seconds for a response. If student accurately writes the letter, praise and provide reinforcer. If student does not accurately write the letter, physically guide student to accurately write the letter. Score V if correct response followed verbal prompt. Score M if correct response followed model prompt. Score P if physical guidance was used.
Additional Targets:	

Writing Numbers
Compatible with ABLLS®-R Code S10

Student's Name:		Start Date:	
Objective:	When teacher gives student a piece of paper and says, "Write the number ____ (name number)" student will write the named number.		
Person Implementing Objective:			
Setting/Environment:			
Materials:			
Reinforcers:			
Baseline:	Give student a writing utensil and a piece of paper. Say, "Write the number ____ (name number)." Wait 5 seconds for a response. A correct response is scored (+) if student accurately writes the number - <u>do not reinforce</u>. Move to next trial. An incorrect response is scored (-) if student does not accurately write the number- <u>do not prompt</u>. Move to next trial.		
Teaching Procedures:	Give student a writing utensil and a piece of paper. Say, "Write the number ____ (name number)." Wait 5 seconds for a response. If student accurately writes the number, praise and provide reinforcer. If student does not accurately write the number, say, "Write the number ____ (name number)." as you gesture to the paper. Wait 5 seconds for a response. If student accurately writes the number, praise and provide reinforcer. If student does not accurately write the number, physically guide student to accurately write the number. Score V if correct response followed verbal prompt. Score M if correct response followed model prompt. Score P if physical guidance was used.		
Additional Targets:			

CHAPTER 19

ABA Programs Compatible with

ABLLS®-R Domain T

"Spelling"

The BIG Book of ABA Programs

Match Letters To Letters In A Word
Compatible with ABLLS®-R Code T1

Student's Name:	Start Date:	
Objective:	When teacher presents a word card and all the individual letters in the word to student and says, "Match" student will place the individual letters on the identical letters in the word card.	
Person Implementing Objective:		
Setting/Environment:		
Materials:		
Reinforcers:		
Baseline:	Present a word card to student and then present all the individual letters in the word. Say, "Match." Wait 5 seconds for a response. A correct response is scored (+) if student places all the individual letters on the identical letters in the word card- do not reinforce. Move to next trial. An incorrect response is scored (-) if student does not place all the individual letters on the identical letters in the word card- do not prompt. Move to next trial.	
Teaching Procedures:	Present a word card to student and then present all the individual letters in the word. Say, "Match." Wait 5 seconds for a response. If student places all the individual letters on the identical letters in the word card, praise and provide reinforcer. If student does not place all the individual letters on the identical letters in the word card, say, "Match" as you model placing one letter on its identical letter in the word card. Wait 5 seconds for a response. If student places all the individual letters on the identical letters in the word card, praise and provide reinforcer. If student does not place all the individual letters on the identical letters in the word card, physically guide student to place all the individual letters on the identical letters in the word card. Score V if correct response followed verbal prompt. Score M if correct response followed model prompt. Score P if physical guidance was used.	
Additional Targets:		

Word Completion
Compatible with ABLLS®-R Code T2

Student's Name:		Start Date:	
Objective:		When teacher presents a picture of a three letter word (for example, dog, mop, can, cat, bat), a word card containing the printed word of the picture with one letter missing (for example D _ G), individual letters, one of which is the missing letter from the word card and says, "Complete the word" student will move the correct individual letter to the missing space in the word card completing the word.	
Person Implementing Objective:			
Setting/Environment:			
Materials:			
Reinforcers:			
Baseline:		Present a picture of a three letter word to student. Present a word card containing the printed word of the picture with one letter missing. Present individual letters, one of which is the missing letter from the word card, and say, "Complete the word." Wait 5 seconds for a response. A correct response is scored (+) if student places correct letter into the space on the word card- <u>do not reinforce</u>. Move to next trial. An incorrect response is scored (-) if student does not place correct letter into the space on the word card- <u>do not prompt</u>. Move to next trial.	
Teaching Procedures:		Present a picture of a three letter word to student. Present a word card containing the printed word of the picture with one letter missing. Present individual letters, one of which is the letter from the word card, and say, "Complete the word." Wait 5 seconds for a response. If student places correct letter into the missing space on the word card, praise and provide reinforcer. If student does not place correct letter into the space on the word card, say, "Complete the word" as you point to the correct letter and the space. Wait 5 seconds for a response. If student places correct letter into the space on the word card, praise and provide reinforcer. If student does not place correct letter into the space on the word card, physically guide student to place the correct letter into the space on the word card. Score V if correct response followed verbal prompt. Score M if correct response followed model prompt. Score P if physical guidance was used.	
Additional Targets:			

Copying Words
Compatible with ABLLS®-R Code T3

Student's Name:		Start Date:	

Objective:	When teacher gives student a piece of paper containing a word and says, "Copy the word" student will write the word.
Person Implementing Objective:	
Setting/Environment:	
Materials:	
Reinforcers:	
Baseline:	Give student a writing utensil and a piece of paper containing a word. Say, "Copy the word." Wait 5 seconds for a response. A correct response is scored (+) if student accurately writes the word- <u>do not reinforce</u>. Move to next trial. An incorrect response is scored (-) if student does not accurately write the word- <u>do not prompt</u>. Move to next trial.
Teaching Procedures:	Give student a writing utensil and a piece of paper containing a word. Say, "Copy the word." Wait 5 seconds for a response. If student accurately writes the word, praise and provide reinforcer. If student does not accurately write the word, say, "Copy the word" as you gesture to the word. Wait 5 seconds for a response. If student accurately writes the word, praise and provide reinforcer. If student does not accurately write the word, physically guide student to accurately write the word. Score V if correct response followed verbal prompt. Score M if correct response followed model prompt. Score P if physical guidance was used.
Additional Targets:	

Word Completion
Compatible with ABLLS®-R Code T4

Student's Name:	Start Date:
Objective: When teacher presents a writing utensil, a picture of a three letter word (for example, dog, mop, can, cat, bat), a word card containing the printed word of the picture with one letter missing (for example D _ G), and says, "Complete the word" student will write the correct letter to complete the word.	
Person Implementing Objective:	
Setting/Environment:	
Materials:	
Reinforcers:	
Baseline:	Present a writing utensil and a picture of a three letter word to student. Present a word card containing the printed word of the picture with one letter missing. Say, "Complete the word." Wait 5 seconds for a response. A correct response is scored (+) if student writes the correct letter into the space on the word card- <u>do not reinforce</u>. Move to next trial. An incorrect response is scored (-) if student does not write correct letter into the space on the word card- <u>do not prompt</u>. Move to next trial.
Teaching Procedures:	Present a writing utensil and a picture of a three letter word to student. Present a word card containing the printed word of the picture with one letter missing. Say, "Complete the word." Wait 5 seconds for a response. If student writes correct letter into the space on the word card, praise and provide reinforcer. If student does not write correct letter into the space on the word card, say, "Complete the word" as you point to the space in the word card. Wait 5 seconds for a response. If student writes correct letter into the space on the word card, praise and provide reinforcer. If student does not write correct letter into the space on the word card, physically guide student to write the correct letter into the space on the word card. Score V if correct response followed verbal prompt. Score M if correct response followed model prompt. Score P if physical guidance was used.
Additional Targets:	

The BIG Book of ABA Programs

Spelling
Compatible with ABLLS®-R Code T5

Student's Name:		Start Date:
Objective:	When teacher says, "Spell the word ____ (name word)" student will correctly spell the word.	
Person Implementing Objective:		
Setting/Environment:		
Materials:		
Reinforcers:		
Baseline:	Say, "Spell the word ____ (name word)." Wait 5 seconds for a response. A correct response is scored (+) if student correctly spells the word- <u>do not reinforce</u>. Move to next trial. An incorrect response is scored (-) if student does not correctly spell the word- <u>do not prompt</u>. Move to next trial.	
Teaching Procedures:	Say, "Spell the word ____ (name word)." Wait 5 seconds for a response. If student correctly spells the word, praise and provide reinforcer. If student does not correctly spell the word, say, "Spell the word ____ (name word). It starts with a ____ (name first letter of word)." Wait 5 seconds for a response. If student correctly spells the word, praise and provide reinforcer. If student does not correctly spell the word, physically guide student by touching student's mouth as you spell the word. Score V if correct response followed verbal prompt. Score M if correct response followed model prompt. Score P if physical guidance was used.	
Additional Targets:		

Spelling Words On Paper
Compatible with ABLLS®-R Code T6

Student's Name:	Start Date:
Objective:	When teacher gives student a writing utensil, a piece of paper, and says, "Write the word ____ (name word)" student will write the named word.
Person Implementing Objective:	
Setting/Environment:	
Materials:	
Reinforcers:	
Baseline:	Give student a writing utensil and a piece of paper. Say, "Write the word ____ (name word)." Wait 5 seconds for a response. A correct response is scored (+) if student accurately writes the word - <u>do not reinforce</u>. Move to next trial. An incorrect response is scored (-) if student does not accurately write the word- <u>do not prompt</u>. Move to next trial.
Teaching Procedures:	Give student a writing utensil and a piece of paper. Say, "Write the word ____ (name word)." Wait 5 seconds for a response. If student accurately writes the word, praise and provide reinforcer. If student does not accurately write the word, say, "Write the word ____ (name word)" as you gesture to the paper. Wait 5 seconds for a response. If student accurately writes the word, praise and provide reinforcer. If student does not accurately write the word, physically guide student to accurately write the word. Score V if correct response followed verbal prompt. Score M if correct response followed model prompt. Score P if physical guidance was used.
Additional Targets:	

The BIG Book of ABA Programs

Spelling Student's Name On Paper
Compatible with ABLLS®-R Code T7

Student's Name:	Start Date:
Objective:	When teacher gives student a piece of paper and says, "Write your name" student will write his/her name.
Person Implementing Objective:	
Setting/Environment:	
Materials:	
Reinforcers:	
Baseline:	Give student a writing utensil and a piece of paper. Say, "Write your name." Wait 5 seconds for a response. A correct response is scored (+) if student accurately writes name - <u>do not reinforce</u>. Move to next trial. An incorrect response is scored (-) if student does not accurately write name- <u>do not prompt</u>. Move to next trial.
Teaching Procedures:	Give student a writing utensil and a piece of paper. Say, "Write your name." Wait 5 seconds for a response. If student accurately writes name, praise and provide reinforcer. If student does not accurately write name, say, "Write your name" as you gesture to the paper. Wait 5 seconds for a response. If student accurately writes name, praise and provide reinforcer. If student does not accurately write name, physically guide student to accurately write name. Score V if correct response followed verbal prompt. Score M if correct response followed <u>model</u> prompt. Score P if physical guidance was used.
Additional Targets:	

CHAPTER 20

ABA Programs Compatible with

ABLLS®-R Domain U

"Dressing Skills"

Pull Pants Down
Compatible with ABLLS®-R Code U1

Student's Name:		Start Date:	
Objective:	When student's pants are pulled up and teacher says, "Pull down pants" student will completely pull down pants.		
Person Implementing Objective:			
Setting/Environment:			
Materials:			
Reinforcers:			
Baseline:	When student's pants are pulled up say, "Pull down pants." Wait 5 seconds for a response. A correct response is scored (+) if student completely pulls down pants- <u>do not reinforce</u>. Move to next trial. An incorrect response is scored (-) if student does not completely pull down pants- <u>do not prompt</u>. Move to next trial.		
Teaching Procedures:	When student's pants are pulled up say, "Pull down pants." Wait 5 seconds for a response. If student completely pulls down pants, provide praise and reinforcer. If student does not completely pull down pants, say, "Pull down pants" as you gesture to the pants. Wait 5 seconds for a response. If student completely pulls down pants, praise and provide reinforcer. If student does not completely pull down pants, physically guide student to completely pull down pants. Score V if correct response followed verbal prompt. Score M if correct response followed model prompt. Score P if physical guidance was used.		
Additional Targets:			

Pull Pants Up
Compatible with ABLLS®-R Code U1

Student's Name:		Start Date:	
Objective:	\multicolumn{3}{l	}{When student's pants are around ankles and teacher says, "Pull up pants" student will completely pull up pants.}
Person Implementing Objective:			
Setting/Environment:			
Materials:			
Reinforcers:			
Baseline:	\multicolumn{3}{l	}{When student's pants are around ankles say, "Pull up pants." Wait 5 seconds for a response. A correct response is scored (+) if student completely pulls up pants- <u>do not reinforce</u>. Move to next trial. An incorrect response is scored (-) if student does not completely pull up pants- <u>do not prompt</u>. Move to next trial.}
Teaching Procedures:	\multicolumn{3}{l	}{When student's pants are around ankles say, "Pull up pants." Wait 5 seconds for a response. If student completely pulls up pants, provide praise and reinforcer. If student does not completely pull up pants, say, "Pull up pants" as you gesture to the pants. Wait 5 seconds for a response. If student completely pulls up pants, praise and provide reinforcer. If student does not completely pull up pants, physically guide student to completely pull up pants. Score V if correct response followed verbal prompt. Score M if correct response followed model prompt. Score P if physical guidance was used.}
Additional Targets:			

The BIG Book of ABA Programs

Put Shoes On
Compatible with ABLLS®-R Code U2

Student's Name:		Start Date:	
Objective:	When student's shoes are off and teacher says, "Put shoes on" student will put shoes on.		

Person Implementing Objective:	
Setting/Environment:	
Materials:	
Reinforcers:	
Baseline:	When student's shoes are off say, "Put shoes on." Wait 5 seconds for a response. A correct response is scored (+) if student puts shoes on- <u>do not reinforce</u>. Move to next trial. An incorrect response is scored (-) if student does not put shoes on- <u>do not prompt</u>. Move to next trial.
Teaching Procedures:	When student's shoes are off say, "Put shoes on." Wait 5 seconds for a response. If student puts shoes on, provide praise and reinforcer. If student does not put shoes on, say, "Put shoes on" as you gesture to the shoes. Wait 5 seconds for a response. If student puts shoes on, praise and provide reinforcer. If student does not put shoes on, physically guide student to put shoes on. Score V if correct response followed verbal prompt. Score M if correct response followed model prompt. Score P if physical guidance was used.
Additional Targets:	

www.stimuluspublications.com   The Autism Skill Acquisition Program™

Take Shoes Off
Compatible with ABLLS®-R Code U2

Student's Name:		Start Date:	
Objective:	When student's shoes are on and teacher says, "Take shoes off" student will take shoes off.		
Person Implementing Objective:			
Setting/Environment:			
Materials:			
Reinforcers:			
Baseline:	When student's shoes are on say, "Take shoes off." Wait 5 seconds for a response. A correct response is scored (+) if student takes shoes off- do not reinforce. Move to next trial. An incorrect response is scored (-) if student does not take shoes off- do not prompt. Move to next trial.		
Teaching Procedures:	When student's shoes are on say, "Take shoes off." Wait 5 seconds for a response. If student takes shoes off, provide praise and reinforcer. If student does not take shoes off, say, "Take shoes off" as you gesture to the shoes. Wait 5 seconds for a response. If student takes shoes off, praise and provide reinforcer. If student does not take shoes off, physically guide student to take shoes off. Score V if correct response followed verbal prompt. Score M if correct response followed model prompt. Score P if physical guidance was used.		
Additional Targets:			

Put T-Shirt On
Compatible with ABLLS®-R Code U3

Student's Name:		Start Date:	
Objective:	When student's t-shirt is off and teacher says, "Put shirt on" student will put t-shirt on.		
Person Implementing Objective:			
Setting/Environment:			
Materials:			
Reinforcers:			
Baseline:	When student's t-shirt is off say, "Put shirt on." Wait 5 seconds for a response. A correct response is scored (+) if student puts shirt on- <u>do not reinforce</u>. Move to next trial. An incorrect response is scored (-) if student does not put shirt on- <u>do not prompt</u>. Move to next trial.		
Teaching Procedures:	When student's t-shirt is off say, "Put shirt on." Wait 5 seconds for a response. If student puts shirt on, provide praise and reinforcer. If student does not put shirt on, say, "Put shirt on" as you gesture to the shirt. Wait 5 seconds for a response. If student puts shirt on, praise and provide reinforcer. If student does not put shirt on, physically guide student to put shirt on. Score V if correct response followed verbal prompt. Score M if correct response followed model prompt. Score P if physical guidance was used.		
Additional Targets:			

Take T-Shirt Off
Compatible with ABLLS®-R Code U3

Student's Name:		Start Date:
Objective:	When student's t-shirt is on and teacher says, "Take shirt off" student will take t-shirt off.	
Person Implementing Objective:		
Setting/Environment:		
Materials:		
Reinforcers:		
Baseline:	When student's t-shirt is on say, "Take shirt off." Wait 5 seconds for a response. A correct response is scored (+) if student takes shirt off- <u>do not reinforce</u>. Move to next trial. An incorrect response is scored (-) if student does not take shirt off- <u>do not prompt</u>. Move to next trial.	
Teaching Procedures:	When student's t-shirt is on say, "Take shirt off." Wait 5 seconds for a response. If student takes shirt off, provide praise and reinforcer. If student does not take shirt off, say, "Take shirt off" as you gesture to the shirt. Wait 5 seconds for a response. If student takes shirt off, praise and provide reinforcer. If student does not take shirt off, physically guide student to take shirt off. Score V if correct response followed verbal prompt. Score M if correct response followed model prompt. Score P if physical guidance was used.	
Additional Targets:		

Take Buttoning Shirt Off
Compatible with ABLLS®-R Code U4

Student's Name:	Start Date:
Objective:	When student's buttoning shirt is on and teacher says, "Take shirt off" student will take buttoning shirt off.
Person Implementing Objective:	
Setting/Environment:	
Materials:	
Reinforcers:	
Baseline:	When student's buttoning shirt is on say, "Take shirt off." Wait 5 seconds for a response. A correct response is scored (+) if student takes shirt off- <u>do not reinforce</u>. Move to next trial. An incorrect response is scored (-) if student does not take shirt off- <u>do not prompt</u>. Move to next trial.
Teaching Procedures:	When student's buttoning shirt is on say, "Take shirt off." Wait 5 seconds for a response. If student takes shirt off, provide praise and reinforcer. If student does not take shirt off, say, "Take shirt off" as you gesture to the shirt. Wait 5 seconds for a response. If student takes shirt off, praise and provide reinforcer. If student does not take shirt off, physically guide student to take shirt off. Score V if correct response followed verbal prompt. Score M if correct response followed model prompt. Score P if physical guidance was used.
Additional Targets:	

Put Buttoning Shirt On
Compatible with ABLLS®-R Code U4

Student's Name:		Start Date:	
Objective:	When student's buttoning shirt is off and teacher says, "Put shirt on" student will put buttoning shirt on.		
Person Implementing Objective:			
Setting/Environment:			
Materials:			
Reinforcers:			
Baseline:	When student's buttoning shirt is off say, "Put shirt on." Wait 5 seconds for a response. A correct response is scored (+) if student puts shirt on- <u>do not reinforce</u>. Move to next trial. An incorrect response is scored (-) if student does not put shirt on- <u>do not prompt</u>. Move to next trial.		
Teaching Procedures:	When student's buttoning shirt is off say, "Put shirt on." Wait 5 seconds for a response. If student puts shirt on, provide praise and reinforcer. If student does not put shirt on, say, "Put shirt on" as you gesture to the shirt. Wait 5 seconds for a response. If student puts shirt on, praise and provide reinforcer. If student does not put shirt on, physically guide student to put shirt on. Score V if correct response followed verbal prompt. Score M if correct response followed model prompt. Score P if physical guidance was used.		
Additional Targets:			

The BIG Book of ABA Programs

Put Pants On
Compatible with ABLLS®-R Code U5

Student's Name:		Start Date:	
Objective:	When student's pants are off and teacher says, "Put pants on" student will put pants on.		
Person Implementing Objective:			
Setting/Environment:			
Materials:			
Reinforcers:			
Baseline:	When student's pants are off say, "Put pants on." Wait 5 seconds for a response. A correct response is scored (+) if student puts pants on- <u>do not reinforce</u>. Move to next trial. An incorrect response is scored (-) if student does not put pants on- <u>do not prompt</u>. Move to next trial.		
Teaching Procedures:	When student's pants are off say, "Put pants on." Wait 5 seconds for a response. If student puts pants on, provide praise and reinforcer. If student does not put pants on, say, "Put pants on" as you gesture to the pants. Wait 5 seconds for a response. If student puts pants on, praise and provide reinforcer. If student does not put pants on, physically guide student to put pants on. Score V if correct response followed verbal prompt. Score M if correct response followed model prompt. Score P if physical guidance was used.		
Additional Targets:			

Take Pants Off
Compatible with ABLLS®-R Code U5

Student's Name:	Start Date:
Objective:	When student's pants are on and teacher says, "Take pants off" student will take pants off.

Person Implementing Objective:	
Setting/Environment:	
Materials:	
Reinforcers:	
Baseline:	When student's pants are on say, "Take pants off." Wait 5 seconds for a response. A correct response is scored (+) if student takes pants off- <u>do not reinforce</u>. Move to next trial. An incorrect response is scored (-) if student does not take pants off- <u>do not prompt</u>. Move to next trial.
Teaching Procedures:	When student's pants are on say, "Take pants off." Wait 5 seconds for a response. If student takes pants off, provide praise and reinforcer. If student does not take pants off, say, "Take pants off" as you gesture to the pants. Wait 5 seconds for a response. If student takes pants off, praise and provide reinforcer. If student does not take pants off, physically guide student to take pants off. Score V if correct response followed verbal prompt. Score M if correct response followed model prompt. Score P if physical guidance was used.
Additional Targets:	

The BIG Book of ABA Programs

Put Socks On
Compatible with ABLLS®-R Code U6

Student's Name:		Start Date:
Objective:		When student's socks are off and teacher says, "Put socks on" student will put socks on.
Person Implementing Objective:		
Setting/Environment:		
Materials:		
Reinforcers:		
Baseline:		When student's socks are off say, "Put socks on." Wait 5 seconds for a response. A correct response is scored (+) if student puts socks on- <u>do not reinforce</u>. Move to next trial. An incorrect response is scored (-) if student does not put socks on- <u>do not prompt</u>. Move to next trial.
Teaching Procedures:		When student's socks are off say, "Put socks on." Wait 5 seconds for a response. If student puts socks on, provide praise and reinforcer. If student does not put socks on, say, "Put socks on" as you gesture to the socks. Wait 5 seconds for a response. If student puts socks on, praise and provide reinforcer. If student does not put socks on, physically guide student to put socks on. Score V if correct response followed verbal prompt. Score M if correct response followed model prompt. Score P if physical guidance was used.
Additional Targets:		

www.stimuluspublications.com   468   The Autism Skill Acquisition Program™

Take Socks Off
Compatible with ABLLS®-R Code U6

Student's Name:		Start Date:
Objective:	When student's socks are on and teacher says, "Take socks off" student will take socks off.	
Person Implementing Objective:		
Setting/Environment:		
Materials:		
Reinforcers:		
Baseline:	When student's socks are on say, "Take socks off." Wait 5 seconds for a response. A correct response is scored (+) if student takes socks off- <u>do not reinforce</u>. Move to next trial. An incorrect response is scored (-) if student does not take socks off- <u>do not prompt</u>. Move to next trial.	
Teaching Procedures:	When student's socks are on say, "Take socks off." Wait 5 seconds for a response. If student takes socks off, provide praise and reinforcer. If student does not take socks off, say, "Take socks off" as you gesture to the socks. Wait 5 seconds for a response. If student takes socks off, praise and provide reinforcer. If student does not take socks off, physically guide student to take socks off. Score V if correct response followed verbal prompt. Score M if correct response followed model prompt. Score P if physical guidance was used.	
Additional Targets:		

Put Coat On
Compatible with ABLLS®-R Code U7

Student's Name:		Start Date:
Objective:	When student's coat is off and teacher says, "Put coat on" student will put coat on.	
Person Implementing Objective:		
Setting/Environment:		
Materials:		
Reinforcers:		
Baseline:	When student's coat is off say, "Put coat on." Wait 5 seconds for a response. A correct response is scored (+) if student puts coat on- <u>do not reinforce</u>. Move to next trial. An incorrect response is scored (-) if student does not put coat on- <u>do not prompt</u>. Move to next trial.	
Teaching Procedures:	When student's coat is off say, "Put coat on." Wait 5 seconds for a response. If student puts coat on, praise and provide reinforcer. If student does not put coat on, say, "Put coat on" as you gesture to the coat. Wait 5 seconds for a response. If student puts coat on, praise and provide reinforcer. If student does not put coat on, physically guide student to put coat on. Score V if correct response followed verbal prompt. Score M if correct response followed model prompt. Score P if physical guidance was used.	
Additional Targets:		

Take Coat Off
Compatible with ABLLS®-R Code U7

Student's Name:		Start Date:	
Objective:	\multicolumn{3}{l}{When student's coat is on and teacher says, "Take coat off" student will take coat off.}

Person Implementing Objective:	
Setting/Environment:	
Materials:	
Reinforcers:	
Baseline:	When student's coat is on say, "Take coat off." Wait 5 seconds for a response. A correct response is scored (+) if student takes coat off- <u>do not reinforce</u>. Move to next trial. An incorrect response is scored (-) if student does not take coat off- <u>do not prompt</u>. Move to next trial.
Teaching Procedures:	When student's coat is on say, "Take coat off." Wait 5 seconds for a response. If student takes coat off, provide praise and reinforcer. If student does not take coat off, say, "Take coat off" as you gesture to the coat. Wait 5 seconds for a response. If student takes coat off, praise and provide reinforcer. If student does not take coat off, physically guide student to take coat off. Score V if correct response followed verbal prompt. Score M if correct response followed model prompt. Score P if physical guidance was used.
Additional Targets:	

Unzipping
Compatible with ABLLS®-R Code U8

Student's Name:		Start Date:	
Objective:	When student's zipper is up on a non-clothing item and teacher says, "Unzip the zipper" student will unzip the zipper.		
Person Implementing Objective:			
Setting/Environment:			
Materials:			
Reinforcers:			
Baseline:	When student's zipper is up on a non-clothing item say, "Unzip the zipper." Wait 5 seconds for a response. A correct response is scored (+) if student completely unzips zipper- <u>do not reinforce</u>. Move to next trial. An incorrect response is scored (-) if student does not completely unzip zipper- <u>do not prompt</u>. Move to next trial.		
Teaching Procedures:	When student's zipper is up on a non-clothing item say, "Unzip the zipper." Wait 5 seconds for a response. If student completely unzips zipper, provide praise and reinforcer. If student does not completely unzip zipper, say, "Unzip the zipper" as you gesture to the zipper. Wait 5 seconds for a response. If student completely unzips zipper, praise and provide reinforcer. If student does not completely unzip zipper, physically guide student to completely unzip zipper. Score V if correct response followed verbal prompt. Score M if correct response followed model prompt. Score P if physical guidance was used.		
Additional Targets:			

Zipping
Compatible with ABLLS®-R Code U9

Student's Name:		Start Date:	
Objective:		When student's zipper is completely unzipped on a non-clothing item and teacher says, "Zip the zipper" student will completely zip the zipper.	
Person Implementing Objective:			
Setting/Environment:			
Materials:			
Reinforcers:			
Baseline:		When student's zipper is completely unzipped on a non-clothing item say, "Zip the zipper." Wait 5 seconds for a response. A correct response is scored (+) if student completely zips zipper- <u>do not reinforce</u>. Move to next trial. An incorrect response is scored (-) if student does not completely zip zipper- <u>do not prompt</u>. Move to next trial.	
Teaching Procedures:		When student's zipper is completely unzipped on a non-clothing item say, "Zip the zipper." Wait 5 seconds for a response. If student completely zips zipper, praise and provide reinforcer. If student does not completely zip zipper, say, "Zip the zipper" as you gesture to the zipper. Wait 5 seconds for a response. If student completely zips zipper, praise and provide reinforcer. If student does not completely zip zipper, physically guide student to completely zip zipper. Score V if correct response followed verbal prompt. Score M if correct response followed model prompt. Score P if physical guidance was used.	
Additional Targets:			

Unzipping Clothing
Compatible with ABLLS®-R Code U10

Student's Name:		Start Date:	
Objective:	When student's zipper is up on a clothing item and teacher says, "Unzip the zipper" student will unzip the zipper.		
Person Implementing Objective:			
Setting/Environment:			
Materials:			
Reinforcers:			
Baseline:	When student's zipper is up on a clothing item say, "Unzip the zipper." Wait 5 seconds for a response. A correct response is scored (+) if student completely unzips zipper- <u>do not reinforce</u>. Move to next trial. An incorrect response is scored (-) if student does not completely unzip zipper- <u>do not prompt</u>. Move to next trial.		
Teaching Procedures:	When student's zipper is up on a clothing item say, "Unzip the zipper." Wait 5 seconds for a response. If student completely unzips zipper, provide praise and reinforcer. If student does not completely unzip zipper, say, "Unzip the zipper" as you gesture to the zipper. Wait 5 seconds for a response. If student completely unzips zipper, praise and provide reinforcer. If student does not completely unzip zipper, physically guide student to completely unzip zipper. Score V if correct response followed verbal prompt. Score M if correct response followed model prompt. Score P if physical guidance was used.		
Additional Targets:			

Zipping Clothing
Compatible with ABLLS®-R Code U10

Student's Name:	Start Date:	
Objective:	When student's zipper is completely unzipped on a clothing item and teacher says, "Zip the zipper" student will completely zip the zipper.	
Person Implementing Objective:		
Setting/Environment:		
Materials:		
Reinforcers:		
Baseline:	When student's zipper is completely unzipped on a clothing item say, "Zip the zipper." Wait 5 seconds for a response. A correct response is scored (+) if student completely zips zipper- <u>do not reinforce</u>. Move to next trial. An incorrect response is scored (-) if student does not completely zip zipper- <u>do not prompt</u>. Move to next trial.	
Teaching Procedures:	When student's zipper is completely unzipped on a clothing item say, "Zip the zipper." Wait 5 seconds for a response. If student completely zips zipper, praise and provide reinforcer. If student does not completely zip zipper, say, "Zip the zipper" as you gesture to the zipper. Wait 5 seconds for a response. If student completely zips zipper, praise and provide reinforcer. If student does not completely zip zipper, physically guide student to completely zip zipper. Score V if correct response followed verbal prompt. Score M if correct response followed model prompt. Score P if physical guidance was used.	
Additional Targets:		

Buttoning
Compatible with ABLLS®-R Code U11

Student's Name:		Start Date:	
Objective:	When student's buttons are unbuttoned and teacher says, "Button the buttons" student will button the buttons.		
Person Implementing Objective:			
Setting/Environment:			
Materials:			
Reinforcers:			
Baseline:	When student's buttons are unbuttoned say, "Button the buttons." Wait 5 seconds for a response. A correct response is scored (+) if student buttons the buttons- do not reinforce. Move to next trial. An incorrect response is scored (-) if student does not button the buttons- do not prompt. Move to next trial.		
Teaching Procedures:	When student's buttons are unbuttoned say, "Button the buttons." Wait 5 seconds for a response. If student buttons the buttons, provide praise and reinforcer. If student does not button the buttons, say, "Button the buttons" as you gesture to the buttons. Wait 5 seconds for a response. If student buttons the buttons, praise and provide reinforcer. If student does not button the buttons, physically guide student to button the buttons. Score V if correct response followed verbal prompt. Score M if correct response followed model prompt. Score P if physical guidance was used.		
Additional Targets:			

Snapping
Compatible with ABLLS®-R Code U12

Student's Name:	Start Date:
Objective:	When student's snaps are unsnapped and teacher says, "Snap the snaps" student will snap the snaps.
Person Implementing Objective:	
Setting/Environment:	
Materials:	
Reinforcers:	
Baseline:	When student's snaps are unsnapped say, "Snap the snaps." Wait 5 seconds for a response. A correct response is scored (+) if student snaps the snaps- <u>do not reinforce</u>. Move to next trial. An incorrect response is scored (-) if student does not snap the snaps- <u>do not prompt</u>. Move to next trial.
Teaching Procedures:	When student's snaps are unsnapped say, "Snap the snaps." Wait 5 seconds for a response. If student snaps the snaps, provide praise and reinforcer. If student does not snap the snaps, say, "Snap the snaps" as you gesture to the snaps. Wait 5 seconds for a response. If student snaps the snaps, praise and provide reinforcer. If student does not snap the snaps, physically guide student to snap the snaps. Score V if correct response followed verbal prompt. Score M if correct response followed model prompt. Score P if physical guidance was used.
Additional Targets:	

Unsnapping
Compatible with ABLLS®-R Code U12

Student's Name:		Start Date:	
Objective:	When student's snaps are snapped and teacher says, "Unsnap the snaps" student will unsnap the snaps.		
Person Implementing Objective:			
Setting/Environment:			
Materials:			
Reinforcers:			
Baseline:	When student's snaps are snapped say, "Unsnap the snaps." Wait 5 seconds for a response. A correct response is scored (+) if student unsnaps the snaps- <u>do not reinforce</u>. Move to next trial. An incorrect response is scored (-) if student does not unsnap the snaps- <u>do not prompt</u>. Move to next trial.		
Teaching Procedures:	When student's snaps are snapped say, "Unsnap the snaps." Wait 5 seconds for a response. If student unsnaps the snaps, provide praise and reinforcer. If student does not unsnap the snaps, say, "Unsnap the snaps" as you gesture to the snaps. Wait 5 seconds for a response. If student unsnaps the snaps, praise and provide reinforcer. If student does not unsnap the snaps, physically guide student to unsnap the snaps. Score V if correct response followed verbal prompt. Score M if correct response followed model prompt. Score P if physical guidance was used.		
Additional Targets:			

Belt Fastening
Compatible with ABLLS®-R Code U13

Student's Name:		Start Date:	
Objective:	When student's belt is unfastened and teacher says, "Fasten your belt" student will fasten the belt.		
Person Implementing Objective:			
Setting/Environment:			
Materials:			
Reinforcers:			
Baseline:	When student's belt is unfastened say, "Fasten your belt." Wait 5 seconds for a response. A correct response is scored (+) if student fastens belt- <u>do not reinforce</u>. Move to next trial. An incorrect response is scored (-) if student does not fasten belt- <u>do not prompt</u>. Move to next trial.		
Teaching Procedures:	When student's belt is unfastened say, "Fasten your belt." Wait 5 seconds for a response. If student fastens belt, provide praise and reinforcer. If student does not fasten belt, say, "Fasten your belt" as you gesture to belt. Wait 5 seconds for a response. If student fastens belt, praise and provide reinforcer. If student does not fasten belt, physically guide student to fasten belt. Score V if correct response followed verbal prompt. Score M if correct response followed model prompt. Score P if physical guidance was used.		
Additional Targets:			

Unfastening Belt
Compatible with ABLLS®-R Code U13

Student's Name:		Start Date:	
Objective:	When student's belt is fastened and teacher says, "Unfasten your belt" student will unfasten belt.		
Person Implementing Objective:			
Setting/Environment:			
Materials:			
Reinforcers:			
Baseline:	When student's belt is fastened say, "Unfasten your belt." Wait 5 seconds for a response. A correct response is scored (+) if student unfastens belt- <u>do not reinforce</u>. Move to next trial. An incorrect response is scored (-) if student does not unfasten belt- <u>do not prompt</u>. Move to next trial.		
Teaching Procedures:	When student's belt is fastened say, "Unfasten your belt." Wait 5 seconds for a response. If student unfastens belt, provide praise and reinforcer. If student does not unfasten belt, say, "Unfasten your belt" as you gesture to belt. Wait 5 seconds for a response. If student unfastens belt, praise and provide reinforcer. If student does not unfasten belt, physically guide student to unfasten belt. Score V if correct response followed verbal prompt. Score M if correct response followed model prompt. Score P if physical guidance was used.		
Additional Targets:			

Clothing Adjustment
Compatible with ABLLS®-R Code U14

Student's Name:	Start Date:
Objective:	When an item of student's clothing is not worn properly and teacher says, "Fix your ____ (name item of clothing)" student will adjust named clothing item.
Person Implementing Objective:	
Setting/Environment:	
Materials:	
Reinforcers:	
Baseline:	When an item of student's clothing is not worn properly say, "Fix your ____ (name item of clothing)." Wait 5 seconds for a response. A correct response is scored (+) if student adjusts the named item of clothing- <u>do not reinforce</u>. Move to next trial. An incorrect response is scored (-) if student does not adjust named item of clothing- <u>do not prompt</u>. Move to next trial.
Teaching Procedures:	When an item of student's clothing is not worn properly say, "Fix your ____ (name item of clothing)." Wait 5 seconds for a response. If student adjusts the named item of clothing, provide praise and reinforcer. If student does not adjust the named item of clothing, say, "Fix your ____ (name item of clothing)" as you gesture to the item of clothing. Wait 5 seconds for a response. If student adjusts the named item of clothing, praise and provide reinforcer. If student does not adjust the named item of clothing, physically guide student to adjust the named item of clothing. Score V if correct response followed verbal prompt. Score M if correct response followed model prompt. Score P if physical guidance was used.
Additional Targets:	

Shoe Tying
Compatible with ABLLS®-R Code U15

Student's Name:		Start Date:	
Objective:	When student's shoe is untied and teacher says, "Tie your shoe" student will tie the shoe.		

Person Implementing Objective:	
Setting/Environment:	
Materials:	
Reinforcers:	
Baseline:	When student's shoe is untied say, "Tie your shoe." Wait 5 seconds for a response. A correct response is scored (+) if student ties shoe- <u>do not reinforce</u>. Move to next trial. An incorrect response is scored (-) if student does not tie shoe- <u>do not prompt</u>. Move to next trial.
Teaching Procedures:	When student's shoe is untied say, "Tie your shoe." Wait 5 seconds for a response. If student ties shoe, provide praise and reinforcer. If student does not tie shoe, say, "Tie your shoe" as you slowly model the step of shoe tying that student is currently on. Wait 5 seconds for a response. If student ties shoe, praise and provide reinforcer. If student does not tie shoe, physically guide student to tie shoe. Score V if correct response followed verbal prompt. Score M if correct response followed model prompt. Score P if physical guidance was used.
Additional Targets:	

CHAPTER 21

ABA Programs Compatible with

ABLLS®-R Domain V

"Eating Skills"

The BIG Book of ABA Programs

Using Fingers To Eat
Compatible with ABLLS®-R Code V1

Student's Name:		Start Date:	
Objective:	When teacher gives student a preferred food and says, "Take a bite" student will use fingers to deliver food from plate to mouth.		
Person Implementing Objective:			
Setting/Environment:			
Materials:			
Reinforcers:			
Baseline:	Give student a preferred food and say, "Take a bite." Wait 5 seconds for a response. A correct response is scored (+) if student uses fingers to deliver food from plate to mouth - do not reinforce. Move to next trial. An incorrect response is scored (-) if student does not use fingers to deliver food from plate to mouth- do not prompt. Move to next trial.		
Teaching Procedures:	Give student a preferred food and say, "Take a bite." Wait 5 seconds for a response. If student uses fingers to deliver food from plate to mouth, praise and provide reinforcer. If student does not use fingers to deliver food from plate to mouth, say, "Take a bite" as you model raising a bite to your mouth. Wait 5 seconds for a response. If student uses fingers to deliver food from plate to mouth, praise and provide reinforcer. If student does not use fingers to deliver food from plate to mouth, physically guide student to deliver food from plate to mouth with fingers. Score V if correct response followed verbal prompt. Score M if correct response followed model prompt. Score P if physical guidance was used.		
Additional Targets:			

Straw Drinking
Compatible with ABLLS®-R Code V2

Student's Name:		Start Date:	
Objective:	When teacher gives student a preferred liquid in a cup with a straw and says, "Take a drink" student will drink from straw without spilling.		
Person Implementing Objective:			
Setting/Environment:			
Materials:			
Reinforcers:			
Baseline:	Give student a preferred liquid in a cup with straw and say, "Take a drink." Wait 5 seconds for a response. A correct response is scored (+) if student drinks from straw without spilling - <u>do not reinforce</u>. Move to next trial. An incorrect response is scored (-) if student does not drink from straw without spilling- <u>do not prompt</u>. Move to next trial.		
Teaching Procedures:	Give student a preferred liquid in a cup with straw and say, "Take a drink." Wait 5 seconds for a response. If student drinks from straw without spilling, praise and provide reinforcer. If student does not drink from straw without spilling, say, "Take a drink" as you model putting a straw up to your mouth. Wait 5 seconds for a response. If student drinks from straw without spilling, praise and provide reinforcer. If student does not drink from straw without spilling, physically guide student to raise straw to mouth. Score V if correct response followed verbal prompt. Score M if correct response followed model prompt. Score P if physical guidance was used.		
Additional Targets:			

Cup Drinking
Compatible with ABLLS®-R Code V3

Student's Name:	Start Date:
Objective:	When teacher gives student a preferred liquid in an open-faced cup and says, "Take a drink" student will drink from cup without spilling.
Person Implementing Objective:	
Setting/Environment:	
Materials:	
Reinforcers:	
Baseline:	Give student a preferred liquid in an open-faced cup and say, "Take a drink." Wait 5 seconds for a response. A correct response is scored (+) if student drinks without spilling - <u>do not reinforce</u>. Move to next trial. An incorrect response is scored (-) if student does not drink without spilling- <u>do not prompt</u>. Move to next trial.
Teaching Procedures:	Give student a preferred liquid in an open-faced cup and say, "Take a drink." Wait 5 seconds for a response. If student drinks without spilling, praise and provide reinforcer. If student does not drink without spilling, say, "Take a drink" as you model a drinking motion. Wait 5 seconds for a response. If student drinks without spilling, praise and provide reinforcer. If student does not drink without spilling, physically guide student to raise cup to mouth. Score V if correct response followed verbal prompt. Score M if correct response followed model prompt. Score P if physical guidance was used.
Additional Targets:	

Using A Fork Or Spoon
Compatible with ABLLS®-R Code V4

Student's Name:	Start Date:
Objective:	When teacher gives student a preferred food (that can be eaten with a fork or a spoon), provides a fork or a spoon, and says, "Take a bite" student will use fork or spoon to deliver food from plate to mouth.
Person Implementing Objective:	
Setting/Environment:	
Materials:	
Reinforcers:	
Baseline:	Give student a preferred food (that can be eaten with a fork or spoon), a fork or a spoon, and say, "Take a bite." Wait 5 seconds for a response. A correct response is scored (+) if student uses fork or spoon to deliver food from plate to mouth - do not reinforce. Move to next trial. An incorrect response is scored (-) if student does not use fork or spoon to deliver food from plate to mouth- do not prompt. Move to next trial.
Teaching Procedures:	Give student a preferred food (that can be eaten with a fork or spoon), a fork or a spoon, and say, "Take a bite." Wait 5 seconds for a response. If student uses fork or spoon to deliver food from plate to mouth, praise and provide reinforcer. If student does not use fork or spoon to deliver food from plate to mouth, say, "Take a bite" as you gesture to the fork or spoon. Wait 5 seconds for a response. If student uses fork or spoon to deliver food from plate to mouth, praise and provide reinforcer. If student does not use fork or spoon to deliver food from plate to mouth, physically guide student to deliver food from plate to mouth. Score V if correct response followed verbal prompt. Score M if correct response followed model prompt. Score P if physical guidance was used.
Additional Targets:	

Spreading
Compatible with ABLLS®-R Code V5

Student's Name:		Start Date:	
Objective:	\multicolumn{3}{l	}{When teacher gives student a spreadable condiment, a piece of bread, a dull knife, and says, "Spread the ____ (name spreadable condiment)" student will use dull knife to spread condiment on bread.}

Person Implementing Objective:	
Setting/Environment:	
Materials:	
Reinforcers:	
Baseline:	Give student a spreadable condiment, a piece of bread, a dull knife, and say, "Spread the ____ (name spreadable condiment)." Wait 5 seconds for a response. A correct response is scored (+) if student uses dull knife to spread condiment on bread - <u>do not reinforce</u>. Move to next trial. An incorrect response is scored (-) if student does not use dull knife to spread condiment on bread- <u>do not prompt</u>. Move to next trial.
Teaching Procedures:	Give student a spreadable condiment, a piece of bread, a dull knife, and say, "Spread the ____ (name spreadable condiment)." Wait 5 seconds for a response. If student uses dull knife to spread condiment on bread, provide praise and reinforcer. If student does not use dull knife to spread condiment on bread, say, "Spread the ____ (name spreadable condiment)" as you gesture to the knife and the bread. Wait 5 seconds for a response. If student uses dull knife to spread condiment on bread, praise and provide reinforcer. If student does not use dull knife to spread condiment on bread, physically guide student to spread condiment on bread. Score V if correct response followed verbal prompt. Score M if correct response followed model prompt. Score P if physical guidance was used.
Additional Targets:	

Pouring
Compatible with ABLLS®-R Code V6

Student's Name:	Start Date:

Objective:	When teacher gives student a container of liquid, an empty cup, and says, "Pour some into your cup" student will pour liquid from container into cup.
Person Implementing Objective:	
Setting/Environment:	
Materials:	
Reinforcers:	
Baseline:	Give student a container of liquid and an empty cup and say, "Pour some into the cup." Wait 5 seconds for a response. A correct response is scored (+) if student pours liquid into cup without spilling - <u>do not reinforce</u>. Move to next trial. An incorrect response is scored (-) if student does not pour liquid into cup without spilling- <u>do not prompt</u>. Move to next trial.
Teaching Procedures:	Give student a container of liquid and an empty cup and say, "Pour some into the cup." Wait 5 seconds for a response. If student pours liquid into cup without spilling, provide praise and reinforcer. If student does not pour liquid into cup without spilling, say, "Pour some into the cup" as you gesture to the cup. Wait 5 seconds for a response. If student pours liquid into cup without spilling, praise and provide reinforcer. If student does not pour liquid into cup without spilling, physically guide student to pour liquid into cup. Score V if correct response followed verbal prompt. Score M if correct response followed model prompt. Score P if physical guidance was used.
Additional Targets:	

Cutting
Compatible with ABLLS®-R Code V7

Student's Name:		Start Date:	
Objective:	\multicolumn{3}{l	}{When teacher gives student a soft food item and a knife and says, "Cut a bite" student will cut a bite-sized portion of the food with the knife.}

Person Implementing Objective:	
Setting/Environment:	
Materials:	
Reinforcers:	
Baseline:	Give student a soft food item and a knife and say, "Cut a bite." Wait 5 seconds for a response. A correct response is scored (+) if student cuts a small amount from the food item- <u>do not reinforce</u>. Move to next trial. An incorrect response is scored (-) if student does not cut a small amount from the food item- <u>do not prompt</u>. Move to next trial.
Teaching Procedures:	Give student a soft food item and a knife and say, "Cut a bite." Wait 5 seconds for a response. If student cuts a small amount from the food item, praise and provide reinforcer. If student does not cut a small amount from the food item, say, "Cut a bite" as you gesture to the knife. Wait 5 seconds for a response. If student cuts a small amount from the food item, praise and provide reinforcer. If student does not cut a small amount from the food item, physically guide student to cut a small amount from the food item. Score V if correct response followed verbal prompt. Score M if correct response followed model prompt. Score P if physical guidance was used.
Additional Targets:	

Bring Lunch To Lunchroom Seat
Compatible with ABLLS®-R Code V8

Student's Name:	Start Date:
Objective:	When teacher gives student a tray of food and says, "Take your food to your seat" student will carry tray to seat without spilling food.
Person Implementing Objective:	
Setting/Environment:	
Materials:	
Reinforcers:	
Baseline:	Give student a tray of food and say, "Take your food to your seat." Wait 5 seconds for a response. A correct response is scored (+) if student carries food to seat without spilling food- <u>do not reinforce</u>. Move to next trial. An incorrect response is scored (-) if student does not carry food to seat without spilling food- <u>do not prompt</u>. Move to next trial.
Teaching Procedures:	Give student a tray of food and say, "Take your food to your seat." Wait 5 seconds for a response. If student carries food to seat without spilling food, provide praise and reinforcer. If student does not carry food to seat without spilling food, say, "Take your food to your seat" as you gesture to the seat. Wait 5 seconds for a response. If student carries food to seat without spilling food, praise and provide reinforcer. If student does not carry food to seat without spilling food, physically guide student to take food to seat. Score V if correct response followed verbal prompt. Score M if correct response followed model prompt. Score P if physical guidance was used.
Additional Targets:	

Clean Area Following A Meal
Compatible with ABLLS®-R Code V9

Student's Name:		Start Date:	
Objective:	\multicolumn{3}{l	}{Following a meal, when teacher says, "Clean up your area" student will throw away garbage and wipe table so that no excess food or drink remains.}

Person Implementing Objective:	
Setting/Environment:	
Materials:	
Reinforcers:	
Baseline:	Following a meal say, "Clean up your area." Wait 5 seconds for a response. A correct response is scored (+) if student throws away garbage and wipes table so that no excess food or drink remains- <u>do not reinforce</u>. Move to next trial. An incorrect response is scored (-) if student does not throw away garbage and wipe table so that no excess food or drink remains- <u>do not prompt</u>. Move to next trial.
Teaching Procedures:	Following a meal say, "Clean up your area." Wait 5 seconds for a response. If student throws away garbage and wipes table so that no excess food or drink remains, provide praise and reinforcer. If student does not throw away garbage and wipe table so that no excess food or drink remains, say, "Clean up your area" as you gesture to the table. Wait 5 seconds for a response. If student throws away garbage and wipes table so that no excess food or drink remains, praise and provide reinforcer. If student does not throw away garbage and wipe table so that no excess food or drink remains, physically guide student to throw away garbage and wipe table so that no excess food or drink remains. Score V if correct response followed verbal prompt. Score M if correct response followed model prompt. Score P if physical guidance was used.
Additional Targets:	

Clean Area During A Meal
Compatible with ABLLS®-R Code V10

Student's Name:		Start Date:	
Objective:	\multicolumn{3}{l	}{During a meal, when student spills, drops crumbs, or allows garbage to fall to the floor, and teacher says, "Clean up your mess" student will throw away garbage and wipe table so that no excess food or drink remains.}
Person Implementing Objective:			
Setting/Environment:			
Materials:			
Reinforcers:			
Baseline:	\multicolumn{3}{l	}{During a meal when student spills, drops crumbs, or allows garbage to fall to the floor, say, "Clean up your mess." Wait 5 seconds for a response. A correct response is scored (+) if student throws away garbage and wipes table so that no excess food or drink remains- do not reinforce. Move to next trial. An incorrect response is scored (-) if student does not throw away garbage and wipe table so that no excess food or drink remains- do not prompt. Move to next trial.}
Teaching Procedures:	\multicolumn{3}{l	}{During a meal when student spills, drops crumbs, or allows garbage to fall to the floor, say, "Clean up your mess." Wait 5 seconds for a response. If student throws away garbage and wipes table so that no excess food or drink remains, praise and provide reinforcer. If student does not throw away garbage and wipe table so that no excess food or drink remains, say, "Clean up your mess" as you gesture to the table or floor. Wait 5 seconds for a response. If student throws away garbage and wipes table so that no excess food or drink remains, praise and provide reinforcer. If student does not throw away garbage and wipe table so that no excess food or drink remains, physically guide student to throw away garbage and wipe table so that no excess food or drink remains. Score V if correct response followed verbal prompt. Score M if correct response followed model prompt. Score P if physical guidance was used.}
Additional Targets:			

CHAPTER 22

ABA Programs Compatible with

ABLLS®-R Domain W

"Grooming"

Hand Washing
Compatible with ABLLS®-R Code W1

Student's Name:		Start Date:	
Objective:	When teacher says, "Wash hands" student will wash hands.		

Person Implementing Objective:	
Setting/Environment:	
Materials:	
Reinforcers:	
Baseline:	When student is in front of sink, say, "Wash hands." Wait 5 seconds for a response. A correct response is scored (+), if student washes hands-<u>do not reinforce</u>. Move to next trial. An incorrect response is scored (-) if student does not wash hands - <u>do not prompt</u>. Move to next trial.
Teaching Procedures:	When student is in front of sink, say, "Wash hands." Wait 5 seconds for a response. If student washes hands, praise and provide reinforcer. If student does not wash hands, say, "Wash hands" as you model hand washing. Wait 5 seconds for a response. If student washes hands, praise and provide reinforcer. If student does not wash hands, physically guide student to wash hands. Score V for correct response that followed verbal prompt. Score M if the correct response followed the model prompt. Score P if physical guidance was used.
Additional Targets:	

Hand Drying
Compatible with ABLLS®-R Code W2

Student's Name:		Start Date:
Objective:	When teacher says, "Dry hands" student will dry hands.	

Person Implementing Objective:	
Setting/Environment:	
Materials:	
Reinforcers:	
Baseline:	After student washes hands, provide towel/paper towels. Say, "Dry hands." Wait 5 seconds for a response. A correct response is scored (+), if student wipes all water off hands-<u>do not reinforce</u>. Move to next trial. An incorrect response is scored (-) if student does not wipe all water off hands - <u>do not prompt</u>. Move to next trial.
Teaching Procedures:	After student washes hands, provide towel/paper towels. Say, "Dry hands." Wait 5 seconds for a response. If student wipes all water off hands, praise and provide reinforcer. If student does not wipe all water off hands, say, "Dry hands" as you gesture to the towel/paper towels. Wait 5 seconds for a response. If student wipes all water off hands, praise and provide reinforcer. If student does not wipe all water off hands, physically guide student to wipe all water off hands. Score V for correct response that followed verbal prompt. Score M if the correct response followed the model prompt. Score P if physical guidance was used.
Additional Targets:	

Face Washing
Compatible with ABLLS®-R Code W3

Student's Name:		Start Date:	
Objective:	When teacher says, "Wash face" student will wash face.		

Person Implementing Objective:	
Setting/Environment:	
Materials:	
Reinforcers:	
Baseline:	When student is in front of sink, say, "Wash face." Wait 5 seconds for a response. A correct response is scored (+), if student washes face- <u>do not reinforce</u>. Move to next trial. An incorrect response is scored (-) if student does not wash face- <u>do not prompt</u>. Move to next trial.
Teaching Procedures:	When student is in front of sink, say, "Wash face." Wait 5 seconds for a response. If student washes face, praise and provide reinforcer. If student does not wash face, say, "Wash face" as you model face washing. Wait 5 seconds for a response. If student washes face, praise and provide reinforcer. If student does not wash face, physically guide student to wash face. Score V for correct response that followed verbal prompt. Score M if the correct response followed the model prompt. Score P if physical guidance was used.
Additional Targets:	

Face Drying
Compatible with ABLLS®-R Code W4

Student's Name:		Start Date:	
Objective:	When student is given towel/paper towels and teacher says, "Dry face" student will dry face.		
Person Implementing Objective:			
Setting/Environment:			
Materials:			
Reinforcers:			
Baseline:	After student washes face, provide towel/paper towels. Say, "Dry face." Wait 5 seconds for a response. A correct response is scored (+), if student wipes all water off face- <u>do not reinforce</u>. Move to next trial. An incorrect response is scored (-) if student does not wipe all water off face- <u>do not prompt</u>. Move to next trial.		
Teaching Procedures:	After student washes face, provide towel/paper towels. Say, "Dry face." Wait 5 seconds for a response. If student wipes all water off face, praise and provide reinforcer. If student does not wipe all water off face, say "Dry face" as you gesture to the towel/paper towels. Wait 5 seconds for a response. If student wipes all water off face, praise and provide reinforcer. If student does not wipe all water off face, physically guide student to wipe all water off face. Score V for correct response that followed verbal prompt. Score M if the correct response followed the model prompt. Score P if physical guidance was used.		
Additional Targets:			

Hair Brushing
Compatible with ABLLS®-R Code W5

Student's Name:	Start Date:
Objective:	When teacher provides a hair brush and says, "Brush hair" student will run brush through hair.
Person Implementing Objective:	
Setting/Environment:	
Materials:	
Reinforcers:	
Baseline:	Provide student with a hair brush and say, "Brush hair." Wait 5 seconds for a response. A correct response is scored (+), if student runs brush through hair- <u>do not reinforce</u>. Move to next trial. An incorrect response is scored (-) if student does not run brush through hair- <u>do not prompt</u>. Move to next trial.
Teaching Procedures:	Provide student with a hair brush and say, "Brush hair." Wait 5 seconds for a response. If student runs brush through hair, praise and provide reinforcer. If student does not run brush through hair, say, "Brush hair" as you model hair brushing. Wait 5 seconds for a response. If student runs brush through hair, praise and provide reinforcer. If student does not run brush through hair, physically guide student to run brush through hair. Score V for correct response that followed verbal prompt. Score M if the correct response followed the model prompt. Score P if physical guidance was used.
Additional Targets:	

Tooth Brushing
Compatible with ABLLS®-R Code W6

Student's Name:	Start Date:

Objective:	When teacher provides a toothbrush, toothpaste, and sink and says, "Brush teeth" student will brush teeth.
Person Implementing Objective:	
Setting/Environment:	
Materials:	
Reinforcers:	
Baseline:	Provide student with a toothbrush, toothpaste, and sink and say, "Brush teeth." Wait 5 seconds for a response. A correct response is scored (+), if student brushes teeth- <u>do not reinforce</u>. Move to next trial. An incorrect response is scored (-) if student does not brush teeth- <u>do not prompt</u>. Move to next trial.
Teaching Procedures:	Provide student with a toothbrush, toothpaste, and sink and say, "Brush teeth." Wait 5 seconds for a response. If student brushes teeth, praise and provide reinforcer. If student does not brush teeth, say, "Brush teeth" as you gesture to the toothbrush. Wait 5 seconds for a response. If student brushes teeth, praise and provide reinforcer. If student does not brush teeth, physically guide student to brush teeth. Score V for correct response that followed verbal prompt. Score M if the correct response followed the model prompt. Score P if physical guidance was used.
Additional Targets:	

Nose Blowing
Compatible with ABLLS®-R Code W7

Student's Name:		Start Date:
Objective:	\multicolumn{2}{l	}{When student needs to blow nose (nose is running, student is sniffling, etc.) and teacher says, "Blow your nose" student will use a tissue to blow nose.}
Person Implementing Objective:		
Setting/Environment:		
Materials:		
Reinforcers:		
Baseline:	\multicolumn{2}{l	}{Provide student with a tissue and say, "Blow your nose." Wait 5 seconds for a response. A correct response is scored (+), if student blows nose- <u>do not reinforce</u>. Move to next trial. An incorrect response is scored (-) if student does not blow nose- <u>do not prompt</u>. Move to next trial.}
Teaching Procedures:	\multicolumn{2}{l	}{Provide student with a tissue and say, "Blow your nose." Wait 5 seconds for a response. If student blows nose, praise and provide reinforcer. If student does not blow nose, say, "Blow your nose" as you model nose blowing with your own tissue. Wait 5 seconds for a response. If student blows nose, praise and provide reinforcer. If student does not blow nose, physically guide student to blow nose. Score V for correct response that followed verbal prompt. Score M if the correct response followed the model prompt. Score P if physical guidance was used.}
Additional Targets:		

CHAPTER 23

ABA Programs Compatible with

ABLLS®-R Domain X

"Toileting Skills"

Urinate In Toilet (Boys)
Compatible with ABLLS®-R Code X1

Student's Name:		Start Date:	
Objective:	When student is in front of toilet, pants unbuttoned/unzipped/unsnapped, etc. and teacher says, "Pee in the potty" student will urinate into toilet.		
Person Implementing Objective:			
Setting/Environment:			
Materials:			
Reinforcers:			
Baseline:	When student is in front of toilet, pants unbuttoned/unzipped/unsnapped, etc., say, "Pee in the potty." Wait 5 seconds for a response. A correct response is scored (+) if student urinates in toilet- <u>do not reinforce</u>. Move to next trial. An incorrect response is scored (-) if student does not urinate in toilet- <u>do not prompt</u>. Move to next trial.		
Teaching Procedures:	When student is in front of toilet, pants unbuttoned/unzipped/unsnapped, etc., say, "Pee in the potty." Wait 5 seconds for a response. If student urinates in toilet, praise and provide reinforcer. If student does not urinate in toilet, reposition student so student is more likely to urinate in toilet as you say, "Pee in potty." Wait 5 seconds for a response. If student urinates in toilet, praise and provide reinforcer. If student does not urinate in toilet, physically guide student to urinate in toilet. Score V for correct response that followed verbal prompt. Score M if the correct response followed the model prompt. Score P if physical guidance was used.		
Additional Targets:			

Urinate In Toilet (Girls)
Compatible with ABLLS®-R Code X1

Student's Name:		Start Date:	
Objective:		When student is sitting on toilet, pants unbuttoned/unzipped/unsnapped, etc. and teacher says, "Pee in the potty" student will urinate into toilet.	
Person Implementing Objective:			
Setting/Environment:			
Materials:			
Reinforcers:			
Baseline:		When student is sitting on toilet, pants unbuttoned/unzipped/unsnapped, etc., say, "Pee in the potty." Wait 5 seconds for a response. A correct response is scored (+) if student urinates in toilet- <u>do not reinforce</u>. Move to next trial. An incorrect response is scored (-) if student does not urinate in toilet- <u>do not prompt</u>. Move to next trial.	
Teaching Procedures:		When student is sitting on toilet, pants unbuttoned/unzipped/unsnapped, etc., say, "Pee in the potty." Wait 5 seconds for a response. If student urinates in toilet, praise and provide reinforcer. If student does not urinate in toilet, reposition student so student is more likely to urinate in toilet as you say, "Pee in potty." Wait 5 seconds for a response. If student urinates in toilet, praise and provide reinforcer. If student does not urinate in toilet, physically guide student to urinate in toilet. Score V for correct response that followed verbal prompt. Score M if the correct response followed the model prompt. Score P if physical guidance was used.	
Additional Targets:			

The BIG Book of ABA Programs

Ask To Use Bathroom
Compatible with ABLLS®-R Code X4

Student's Name:		Start Date:
Objective:	When teacher sees student needs to use the bathroom (grabbing self, standing by door, etc.) and asks if student needs to go, student will say, "I need to go potty."	
Person Implementing Objective:		
Setting/Environment:		
Materials:		
Reinforcers:		
Baseline:	Say, "If you need to go potty you have to tell me." Wait 5 seconds for a response. A correct response is scored (+), if student says "I have to go potty"- <u>do not reinforce</u>. Move to next trial. An incorrect response is scored (-) if student does not say, "I have to go potty"- <u>do not prompt</u>. Move to next trial.	
Teaching Procedures:	Say, "If you need to go potty you have to tell me." Wait 5 seconds for a response. If student says "I have to go potty" praise, provide reinforcer, and take student to the bathroom. If student does not say "I have to go potty" say, "If you need to go potty you have to tell me" as you gesture towards the bathroom. Wait 5 seconds for a response. If student says, "I have to go potty," praise, provide reinforcer, and take to the bathroom. If student does not say, "I have to go potty," physically guide student by touching student's mouth as you say "I have to go to the potty" and then guide student to bathroom Score V for correct response that followed verbal prompt. Score M if the correct response followed the model prompt. Score P if physical guidance was used.	
Additional Targets:		

www.stimuluspublications.com   The Autism Skill Acquisition Program™

Wipe Following Urination (Girls)
Compatible with ABLLS®-R Code X5

Student's Name:		Start Date:	
Objective:	After student urinates and teacher says, "Wipe" student will wipe self.		
Person Implementing Objective:			
Setting/Environment:			
Materials:			
Reinforcers:			
Baseline:	After student urinates, say, "Wipe." Wait 5 seconds for a response. A correct response is scored (+), if student wipes excess urine- <u>do not reinforce</u>. Move to next trial. An incorrect response is scored (-) if student does not wipe excess urine- <u>do not prompt</u>. Move to next trial.		
Teaching Procedures:	After student urinates, say, "Wipe." Wait 5 seconds for a response. If student wipes excess urine, praise and provide reinforcer. If student does not wipe excess urine, say, "Wipe like this" as you gesture towards excess urine. Wait 5 seconds for a response. If student wipes excess urine, praise and provide reinforcer. If student does not wipe excess urine, physically guide student to wipe excess urine. Score V for correct response that followed verbal prompt. Score M if the correct response followed the model prompt. Score P if physical guidance was used.		
Additional Targets:			

Wipe Following Bowel Movement
Compatible with ABLLS®-R Code X8

Student's Name:	Start Date:
Objective:	After student has bowel movement and teacher says, "Wipe your bottom" student will wipe self.
Person Implementing Objective:	
Setting/Environment:	
Materials:	
Reinforcers:	
Baseline:	After student has bowel movement, say, "Wipe your bottom." Wait 5 seconds for a response. A correct response is scored (+), if student wipes excess feces from buttocks- <u>do not reinforce</u>. Move to next trial. An incorrect response is scored (-) if student does not wipe excess feces from buttocks- <u>do not prompt</u>. Move to next trial.
Teaching Procedures:	After student has bowel movement, say, "Wipe your bottom." Wait 5 seconds for a response. If student wipes excess feces from buttocks, praise and provide reinforcer. If student does not wipe excess feces from buttocks, say, "Wipe your bottom" as you gesture to student's buttocks. Wait 5 seconds for a response. If student wipes excess feces from buttocks, praise and provide reinforcer. If student does not wipe excess feces from buttocks, physically guide student to wipe excess feces from buttocks. Score V for correct response that followed verbal prompt. Score M if the correct response followed the model prompt. Score P if physical guidance was used.
Additional Targets:	

CHAPTER 24

ABA Programs Compatible with

ABLLS®-R Domain Y

"Gross Motor Skills"

Walk Towards Teacher
Compatible with ABLLS®-R Code Y1

Student's Name:		Start Date:	
Objective:	When teacher is standing in front of student and says, "Walk" student will walk towards teacher.		
Person Implementing Objective:			
Setting/Environment:			
Materials:			
Reinforcers:			
Baseline:	Stand in front of student. Say, "Walk." Wait 5 seconds for a response. A correct response is scored (+) if student walks towards you- <u>do not reinforce</u>. Move to next trial. An incorrect response is scored (-) if the student does not walk towards you, or walks on his/her toes or with inappropriate gait- <u>do not prompt</u>. Move to next trial.		
Teaching Procedures:	Stand in front of student. Say, "Walk." Wait 5 seconds for a response. If student walks towards you, praise and provide reinforcer. If student does not walk towards you, say, "Walk," and motion with hands for student to come to you. Wait 5 seconds for a response. If student walks to you, praise and provide reinforcer. If student does not walk to you, physically guide student to walk to you. Score V for correct response that followed verbal prompt. Score M if correct response followed model prompt. Score P if physical guidance was used.		
Additional Targets:			

Kneeling
Compatible with ABLLS®-R Code Y2

Student's Name:		Start Date:
Objective:	When teacher says, "Kneel" student will go from a standing to a kneeling position.	
Person Implementing Objective:		
Setting/Environment:		
Materials:		
Reinforcers:		
Baseline:	When student is standing, say, "Kneel." Wait 5 seconds for a response. A correct response is scored (+) if student kneels with both feet under body- <u>do not reinforce</u>. Move to next trial. An incorrect response is scored (-) if student does not kneel with both feet under body - <u>do not prompt</u>. Move to next trial.	
Teaching Procedures:	When student is standing, say, "Kneel." Wait 5 seconds for a response. If student kneels with both feet under body, praise and provide reinforcer. If student does not kneel with both feet under body, say, "Kneel," and model correct kneeling. Wait 5 seconds for a response. If student kneels with both feet under body, praise and provide reinforcer. If student does not kneel with both feet under body, physically guide student into a kneeling position. Score V for correct response that followed verbal prompt. Score M if correct response followed model prompt. Score P if physical guidance was used.	
Additional Targets:		

Run Towards Teacher
Compatible with ABLLS®-R Code Y3

Student's Name:		Start Date:	
Objective:	When teacher is at least 15 feet (5 meters) from student and says, "Run" student will run towards teacher.		
Person Implementing Objective:			
Setting/Environment:			
Materials:			
Reinforcers:			
Baseline:	Stand 15 feet (5 meters) in front of student. Say, "Run." A correct response is scored (+) if student runs towards you- <u>do not reinforce</u>. Move to next trial. An incorrect response is scored (-) if student does not run towards you- <u>do not prompt</u>. Move to next trial.		
Teaching Procedures:	Stand 15 feet (5 meters) in front of student. Say, "Run." Wait 5 seconds for a response. If student runs towards you, praise and provide reinforcer. If student does not run towards you, say, "Run to me," and motion with hands for student to run to you. Wait 5 seconds for a response. If student runs to you, praise and provide reinforcer. If student does not run to you, physically guide student to run to you. Score V for correct response that followed verbal prompt. Score M if correct response followed model prompt. Score P if physical guidance was used.		
Additional Targets:			

Rolling
Compatible with ABLLS®-R Code Y4

Student's Name:		Start Date:	
Objective:		When student is lying on the ground and teacher says "Roll" student will roll to the side.	

Person Implementing Objective:	
Setting/Environment:	
Materials:	
Reinforcers:	
Baseline:	While student is lying on the ground, say, "Roll." Wait 5 seconds for a response. A correct response is scored (+) if student rolls to the side- <u>do not reinforce</u>. Move to next trial. An incorrect response is scored (-) if student does not roll to the side- <u>do not prompt</u>. Move to next trial.
Teaching Procedures:	While student is lying on the ground, say, "Roll." Wait 5 seconds for a response. If student rolls to the side, praise and provide reinforcer. If student does not roll to the side, say, "Roll," and model rolling. Wait 5 seconds for a response. If student rolls to the side, praise and provide reinforcer. If student does not roll to the side, physically guide student to roll to the side. Score V for correct response that followed verbal prompt. Score M if correct response followed model prompt. Score P if physical guidance was used.
Additional Targets:	

Jump Towards Teacher
Compatible with ABLLS®-R Code Y5

Student's Name:	Start Date:
Objective:	When student is standing on the ground and the teacher says, "Jump to me" student will jump towards teacher.
Person Implementing Objective:	
Setting/Environment:	
Materials:	
Reinforcers:	
Baseline:	Stand in front of student and say, "Jump to me." Wait 5 seconds for a response. A correct response is scored (+) if student jumps towards you- <u>do not reinforce</u>. Move to next trial. An incorrect response is scored (-) if student does not jump towards you- <u>do not prompt</u>. Move to next trial.
Teaching Procedures:	Stand in front of student and say, "Jump to me." Wait 5 seconds for a response. If student jumps towards you, praise and provide reinforcer. If student does not jump towards you, say, "Jump to me," and model jumping forward. Wait 5 seconds for a response. If student jumps towards you, praise and provide reinforcer. If student does not jump towards you, physically guide student to jump towards you. Score V for correct response that followed verbal prompt. Score M if correct response followed model prompt. Score P if physical guidance was used.
Additional Targets:	

Jump From Elevated Location
Compatible with ABLLS®-R Code Y6

Student's Name:		Start Date:	
Objective:	When student is standing on an elevated object (for example, stairs, small table, chair, etc.) and teacher says, "Jump off" student will jump from elevated object to the floor.		
Person Implementing Objective:			
Setting/Environment:			
Materials:			
Reinforcers:			
Baseline:	When student is on elevated object, stand in front of student and say, "Jump off." Wait 5 seconds for a response. A correct response is scored (+) if student jumps off of elevated object- do not reinforce. Move to next trial. An incorrect response is scored (-) if student does not jump off elevated object- do not prompt. Move to next trial.		
Teaching Procedures:	When student is on elevated object, stand in front of student and say, "Jump off." Wait 5 seconds for a response If student jumps from elevated object, praise and provide reinforcer. If student does not jump off elevated object, say, "Jump off," and use hands to wave student to you. Wait 5 seconds for a response. If student jumps off elevated object, praise and provide reinforcer. If student does not jump off elevated object, physically guide student to jump off. Score V for correct response that followed verbal prompt. Score M if correct response followed model prompt. Score P if physical guidance was used.		
Additional Targets:			

Walk Away From Teacher
Compatible with ABLLS®-R Code Y7

Student's Name:		Start Date:	
Objective:	When teacher is standing in front of student and says, "Walk backwards" student will walk backwards away from teacher.		
Person Implementing Objective:			
Setting/Environment:			
Materials:			
Reinforcers:			
Baseline:	Stand in front of student. Say, "Walk backwards." Wait 5 seconds for a response. A correct response is scored (+) if student walks backwards away from you- <u>do not reinforce</u>. Move to next trial. An incorrect response is scored (-) if the student does not walk backwards away from you- <u>do not prompt</u>. Move to next trial.		
Teaching Procedures:	Stand in front of student. Say, "Walk backwards." Wait 5 seconds for a response. If student walks backwards away from you, praise and provide reinforcer. If student does not walk backwards away from you, say, "Walk backwards," and motion with your hands for student to back up. Wait 5 seconds for a response. If student walks backwards away from you, praise and provide reinforcer. If student does not walk backwards away from you, physically guide student to walk backwards away from you. Score V for correct response that followed verbal prompt. Score M if correct response followed model prompt. Score P if physical guidance was used.		
Additional Targets:			

Jump In Place
Compatible with ABLLS®-R Code Y8

Student's Name:		Start Date:	
Objective:	When teacher says, "Jump" student will jump up in the air.		

Person Implementing Objective:	
Setting/Environment:	
Materials:	
Reinforcers:	
Baseline:	Stand in front of student. Say, "Jump." Wait 5 seconds for a response. A correct response is scored (+) if student jumps up in the air- <u>do not reinforce</u>. Move to next trial. An incorrect response is scored (-) if student does not jump up in the air-<u>do not prompt</u>. Move to next trial.
Teaching Procedures:	Stand in front of student. Say, "Jump." Wait 5 seconds for a response. If student jumps up in air, praise and provide reinforcer. If student does not jump up in the air, say, "Jump," and model jumping. Wait 5 seconds for a response. If student jumps up in air, praise and provide reinforcer. If student does not jump up in air, physically guide student to jump. Score V for correct response that followed verbal prompt. Score M if correct response followed model prompt. Score P if physical guidance was used.
Additional Targets:	

Throwing
Compatible with ABLLS®-R Code Y9

Student's Name:		Start Date:	
Objective:	\multicolumn{3}{l	}{When student has ball and teacher is standing in front of student and says, "Throw the ball" student will throw ball to teacher.}

Student's Name:	Start Date:
Objective:	When student has ball and teacher is standing in front of student and says, "Throw the ball" student will throw ball to teacher.
Person Implementing Objective:	
Setting/Environment:	
Materials:	
Reinforcers:	
Baseline:	Stand in front of student when student has a ball. Say, "Throw the ball." Wait 5 seconds for a response. A correct response is scored (+) if student throws the ball towards you- <u>do not reinforce</u>. Move to next trial. An incorrect response is scored (-) if student does not throw the ball towards you- <u>do not prompt</u>. Move to next trial.
Teaching Procedures:	Stand in front of student when student has a ball. Say, "Throw the ball." Wait 5 seconds for a response. If student throws the ball towards you, praise and provide reinforcer. If student does not throw the ball towards you, say, "Throw the ball," and wave/gesture with your hands for student to throw the ball to you. Wait 5 seconds for a response. If student throws the ball towards you, praise and provide reinforcer. If student does not throw the ball towards you, physically guide student to throw the ball. Score V for correct response that followed verbal prompt. Score M if correct response followed model prompt. Score P if physical guidance was used.
Additional Targets:	

Ball Rolling
Compatible with ABLLS®-R Code Y10

Student's Name:	Start Date:
Objective:	When teacher is standing in front of student and says, "Roll the ball" student will roll the ball to teacher.
Person Implementing Objective:	
Setting/Environment:	
Materials:	
Reinforcers:	
Baseline:	Stand in front of student when student has a ball. Say, "Roll the ball." Wait 5 seconds for a response. A correct response is scored (+) if student rolls the ball towards you- do not reinforce. Move to next trial. An incorrect response is scored (-) if the student does not roll the ball towards you-do not prompt. Move to next trial.
Teaching Procedures:	Stand in front of student when student has a ball. Say, "Roll the ball." Wait 5 seconds for a response. If student rolls the ball towards you, praise and provide reinforcer. If student does not roll the ball towards you, say, "Roll the ball," and wave/gesture with your hands for student to roll the ball to you. Wait 5 seconds for a response. If student rolls the ball towards you, praise and provide reinforcer. If student does not roll the ball towards you physically guide student to roll the ball. Score V for correct response that followed verbal prompt. Score M if correct response followed model prompt. Score P if physical guidance was used.
Additional Targets:	

Ladder Climbing
Compatible with ABLLS®-R Code Y11

Student's Name:	Start Date:
Objective:	When student is standing in front of a small ladder and teacher says, "Climb the ladder" student will climb the ladder.
Person Implementing Objective:	
Setting/Environment:	
Materials:	
Reinforcers:	
Baseline:	With student in front of ladder say, "Climb the ladder." Wait 5 seconds for a response. A correct response is scored (+) if student climbs the ladder- <u>do not reinforce</u>. Move to next trial. An incorrect response is scored (-) if the student does not climb the ladder- <u>do not prompt</u>. Move to next trial.
Teaching Procedures:	With student in front of ladder say, "Climb the ladder." Wait 5 seconds for a response. If student climbs the ladder, praise and provide reinforcer. If student does not climb the ladder, say, "Climb the ladder" and gesture to the top of the ladder. Wait 5 seconds for a response. If student climbs the ladder, praise and provide reinforcer. If student does not climb the ladder, physically guide student to climb the ladder. Score V for correct response that followed verbal prompt. Score M if correct response followed model prompt. Score P if physical guidance was used.
Additional Targets:	

Student Will Crawl On Stomach
Compatible with ABLLS®-R Code Y12

Student's Name:		Start Date:	
Objective:	When student is lying on the ground and teacher says, "Crawl" student will crawl forward towards teacher.		
Person Implementing Objective:			
Setting/Environment:			
Materials:			
Reinforcers:			
Baseline:	Ensure student is lying prone on floor. Say, "Crawl." Wait 5 seconds for a response. A correct response is scored (+) if student crawls forward on stomach- do not reinforce. Move to next trial. An incorrect response is scored (-) if student does not crawl on stomach-do not prompt. Move to next trial.		
Teaching Procedures:	Ensure student is lying prone on floor. Say, "Crawl." Wait 5 seconds for a response. If student crawls on stomach praise and provide reinforcer. If student does not crawl on stomach, get on your stomach and model crawling as you again say, "Crawl." Wait 5 seconds for a response. If student crawls praise and provide reinforcer. If student does not crawl on stomach, physically guide student to crawl. Score M for correct response following initial prompt. Score P if physical guidance was used.		
Additional Targets:			

Deep Knee Bends
Compatible with ABLLS®-R Code Y13

Student's Name:	Start Date:
Objective:	When teacher is standing in front of student and says, "Crouch down" student will bend knees far enough so that student's buttocks are close to the floor.
Person Implementing Objective:	
Setting/Environment:	
Materials:	
Reinforcers:	
Baseline:	Stand in front of student. Say, "Crouch down." Wait 5 seconds for a response. A correct response is scored (+) if student bends knees so that buttocks are close to the floor- <u>do not reinforce</u>. Move to next trial. An incorrect response is scored (-) if student does not bend knees far enough so that buttocks are close to the floor- <u>do not prompt</u>. Move to next trial.
Teaching Procedures:	Stand in front of student. Say, "Crouch down." Wait 5 seconds for a response. If student bends knees so far that buttocks are close to the floor, praise and provide reinforcer. If student does not bend knees so far that buttocks are close to the floor, say, "Crouch down" as you model the crouching movement. Wait 5 seconds for a response. If student bends knees so far that buttocks are close to the floor, praise and provide reinforcer. If student does not bend knees so far that buttocks are close to the floor physically guide student to crouch down. Score M for correct response following initial prompt. Score P if physical guidance was used.
Additional Targets:	

Walking Heel To Toe
Compatible with ABLLS®-R Code Y14

Student's Name:	Start Date:

Objective:	When student is standing in front of a taped line on the floor, balance beam, or other narrow strip and teacher says, "Walk" student will walk heel to toe on narrow strip.
Person Implementing Objective:	
Setting/Environment:	
Materials:	
Reinforcers:	
Baseline:	When student is standing in front of a narrow strip, say, "Walk." Wait 5 seconds for a response. A correct response is scored (+) if student walks forward heel to toe- <u>do not reinforce</u>. Move to next trial. An incorrect response is scored (-) if student does not walk forward heel to toe- <u>do not prompt</u>. Move to next trial.
Teaching Procedures:	When student is standing in front of a narrow strip, say, "Walk." Wait 5 seconds for a response. If student walks forward heel to toe on narrow strip, praise and provide reinforcer. If student does not walk forward heel to toe on narrow strip, say "Walk," and gesture to the strip. Wait 5 seconds for a response. If student walks forward heel to toe on narrow strip, praise and provide reinforcer. If student does not walk forward heel to toe on narrow strip, physically guide walking. Score V for correct response that followed verbal prompt. Score M if correct response followed model prompt. Score P if physical guidance was used.
Additional Targets:	

Ball Catching
Compatible with ABLLS®-R Code Y15

Student's Name:		Start Date:	
Objective:	When teacher says, "Catch" and throws ball to student, student will catch the ball.		
Person Implementing Objective:			
Setting/Environment:			
Materials:			
Reinforcers:			
Baseline:	Stand in front of student and say, "Catch" as you throw the ball to student. A correct response is scored (+) if student catches the ball - <u>do not reinforce</u>. Move to next trial. An incorrect response is scored (-) if the student does not catch the ball- <u>do not prompt</u>. Move to next trial.		
Teaching Procedures:	Stand in front of student and say, "Catch" as you throw the ball to student. If student catches the ball, praise and provide reinforcer If student does not catch the ball, throw ball again as you say, "Catch." If student catches ball, praise and provide reinforcer. If student does not catch the ball, physically guide catching the ball by either placing ball in student's hands, or by throwing the ball in the air and guiding student to catch the ball. Score V for correct response that followed verbal prompt. Score M if correct response followed model prompt. Score P if physical guidance was used.		
Additional Targets:			

Tricycle Riding
Compatible with ABLLS®-R Code Y16

Student's Name:		Start Date:	
Objective:	When teacher provides a tricycle, an open space for which to ride it, and says, "Ride" student will ride the tricycle.		
Person Implementing Objective:			
Setting/Environment:			
Materials:			
Reinforcers:			
Baseline:	Seat student on tricycle. Say, "Ride." Wait 5 seconds for a response. A correct response is scored (+) if student pedals and steers the tricycle - <u>do not reinforce</u>. Move to next trial. An incorrect response is scored (-) if student does not pedal and steer the tricycle- <u>do not prompt</u>. Move to next trial.		
Teaching Procedures:	Seat student on tricycle. Say, "Ride." Wait 5 seconds for a response. If student pedals and steers tricycle, praise and provide reinforcer. If student does not pedal and steer tricycle, say, "Ride" and give student a little push to help student get moving. Wait 5 seconds for a response. If student pedals and steers tricycle, praise and provide reinforcer. If student does not pedal and steer tricycle physically guide riding the tricycle. Score V for correct response that followed verbal prompt. Score P if physical guidance was used.		
Additional Targets:			

Sideways Walking
Compatible with ABLLS®-R Code Y17

Student's Name:		Start Date:
Objective:	When teacher says, "Walk sideways" student will walk sideways.	
Person Implementing Objective:		
Setting/Environment:		
Materials:		
Reinforcers:		
Baseline:	Stand in front of student and say, "Walk sideways." Wait 5 seconds for a response. A correct response is scored (+) if student walks sideways - <u>do not reinforce</u>. Move to next trial. An incorrect response is scored (-) if student does not walk sideways- <u>do not prompt</u>. Move to next trial.	
Teaching Procedures:	Stand in front of student and say, "Walk sideways." Wait 5 seconds for a response. If student walks sideways, praise and provide reinforcer. If student does not walk sideways, say, "Walk sideways," and model walking sideways. Wait 5 seconds for a response. If student walks sideways, praise and provide reinforcer. If student does not walk sideways, physically guide student to walk sideways. Score V for correct response that followed verbal prompt. Score M if correct response followed model prompt. Score P if physical guidance was used.	
Additional Targets:		

The BIG Book of ABA Programs

Galloping Like A Horse
Compatible with ABLLS®-R Code Y18

Student's Name:		Start Date:
Objective:	When teacher says, "Gallop" student will gallop like a horse.	
Person Implementing Objective:		
Setting/Environment:		
Materials:		
Reinforcers:		
Baseline:	Stand in front of student and say, "Gallop." Wait 5 seconds for a response. A correct response is scored (+) if student gallops like a horse - <u>do not reinforce</u>. Move to next trial. An incorrect response is scored (-) if student does not gallop like a horse- <u>do not prompt</u>. Move to next trial.	
Teaching Procedures:	Stand in front of student and say, "Gallop." Wait 5 seconds for a response. If student gallops like a horse, praise and provide reinforcer. If student does not gallop like a horse say, "Gallop," and model galloping like a horse. Wait 5 seconds for a response. If student gallops like a horse, praise and provide reinforcer. If student does not gallop like a horse, physically guide student to gallop like a horse. Score V for correct response that followed verbal prompt. Score M if correct response followed model prompt. Score P if physical guidance was used.	
Additional Targets:		

Stand On One Foot
Compatible with ABLLS®-R Code Y19

Student's Name:		Start Date:
Objective:	When teacher says, "Stand on your left/right foot" student will stand on named foot.	

Person Implementing Objective:	
Setting/Environment:	
Materials:	
Reinforcers:	
Baseline:	Say, "Stand on left/right foot." Wait 5 seconds for a response. A correct response is scored (+) if student stands on named foot- <u>do not reinforce</u>. Move to next trial. An incorrect response is scored (-) if student does not stand on named foot- <u>do not prompt</u>. Move to next trial.
Teaching Procedures:	Say, "Stand on left/right foot." Wait 5 seconds for a response. If student stands on named foot, praise and provide reinforcer. If student does not stand on named foot, say, "Stand on left/right foot," and gesture to the named foot. Wait 5 seconds for a response. If student stands on named foot, praise and provide reinforcer. If student does not stand on named foot, physically guide student to stand on named foot. Score V for correct response that followed verbal prompt. Score M if correct response followed model prompt. Score P if physical guidance was used.
Additional Targets:	

Ball Kicking
Compatible with ABLLS®-R Code Y20

Student's Name:		Start Date:	
Objective:	When teacher stands in front of student when student has a ball and says, "Kick it to me" student will kick the ball to teacher.		
Person Implementing Objective:			
Setting/Environment:			
Materials:			
Reinforcers:			
Baseline:	When student has a ball, stand in front of student and say, "Kick it to me." Wait 5 seconds for a response. A correct response is scored (+) if student kicks the ball to you - <u>do not reinforce</u>. Move to next trial. An incorrect response is scored (-) if the student does not kick the ball to you- <u>do not prompt</u>. Move to next trial.		
Teaching Procedures:	When student has a ball, stand in front of student and say, "Kick it to me." Wait 5 seconds for a response. If student kicks the ball to you, praise and provide reinforcer. If student does not kick the ball to you, say, "Kick it to me," and make a kicking motion with your leg. Wait 5 seconds for a response. If student kicks the ball to you, praise and provide reinforcer. If student does not kick the ball to you, physically guide student to kick the ball. Score V for correct response that followed verbal prompt. Score M if correct response followed model prompt. Score P if physical guidance was used.		
Additional Targets:			

The BIG Book of ABA Programs

Hang With Two Hands From Monkey Bars
Compatible with ABLLS®-R Code Y21

Student's Name:		Start Date:	
Objective:	When teacher raises student to monkey bars and says, "Hang" student will hang with both hands from the monkey bars.		
Person Implementing Objective:			
Setting/Environment:			
Materials:			
Reinforcers:			
Baseline:	Raise student to monkey bars and say, "Hang." Wait 5 seconds for a response. A correct response is scored (+) if student hangs from monkey bars- <u>do not reinforce</u>. Move to next trial. An incorrect response is scored (-) if student does not hang from monkey bars- <u>do not prompt</u>. Move to next trial.		
Teaching Procedures:	Raise student to monkey bars and say, "Hang." Wait 5 seconds for a response. If student hangs from monkey bars, praise and provide reinforcer. If student does not hang from monkey bars, say, "Hang" as you model hanging. Wait 5 seconds for a response. If student hangs from monkey bars, praise and provide reinforcer. If student does not hang from monkey bars, physically guide student to hang from monkey bars. Score V for correct response that followed verbal prompt. Score M if correct response followed model prompt. Score P if physical guidance was used.		
Additional Targets:			

Ball Catching
Compatible with ABLLS®-R Code Y22

Student's Name:		Start Date:	
Objective:	\multicolumn{3}{l}{When teacher stands in front of student with a ball and says, "Catch" and then throws the ball to student, student will catch the ball only using student's hands.}
Person Implementing Objective:			
Setting/Environment:			
Materials:			
Reinforcers:			
Baseline:	\multicolumn{3}{l}{Stand in front of student with a ball. Say, "Catch." Throw the ball to student. A correct response is scored (+) if student catches the ball using hands only- <u>do not reinforce</u>. Move to next trial. An incorrect response is scored (-) if the student does not catch the ball using hands only- <u>do not prompt</u>. Move to next trial.}
Teaching Procedures:	\multicolumn{3}{l}{Stand in front of student with a ball. Say, "Catch." Throw the ball to student. If student catches the ball with hands only, praise and provide reinforcer. If student does not catch the ball with hands only, say, "Catch it like this," and place the ball in student's hands. Stand in front of student with a ball. Say, "Catch." Throw the ball to student. If student catches the ball with hands only, praise and provide reinforcer. If student does not catch the ball with hands only, physically guide student to catch the ball. Score V for correct response that followed verbal prompt. Score M if correct response followed model prompt. Score P if physical guidance was used.}
Additional Targets:			

Ball Throwing
Compatible with ABLLS®-R Code Y23

Student's Name:		Start Date:	
Objective:	When teacher stands in front of student when student has a ball and says, "Throw it to me" student will throw the ball to teacher.		
Person Implementing Objective:			
Setting/Environment:			
Materials:			
Reinforcers:			
Baseline:	When student has a ball, stand in front of student and say, "Throw it to me." Wait 5 seconds for a response. A correct response is scored (+) if student throws the ball to teacher - <u>do not reinforce</u>. Move to next trial. An incorrect response is scored (-) if student does not throw the ball to teacher- <u>do not prompt</u>. Move to next trial.		
Teaching Procedures:	When student has a ball, stand in front of student and say, "Throw it to me." Wait 5 seconds for a response. If student throws the ball to you, praise and provide reinforcer. If student does not throw the ball to you, say, "Throw it to me," and hold hands out ready to catch the ball. Wait 5 seconds for a response. If student throws the ball to you, praise and provide reinforcer. If student does not throw the ball to you, physically guide student to throw the ball. Score V for correct response that followed verbal prompt. Score M if correct response followed model prompt. Score P if physical guidance was used.		
Additional Targets:			

Throw And Catch Ball By Self
Compatible with ABLLS®-R Code Y24

Student's Name:	Start Date:

Objective:	When student has a ball and teacher says, "Throw it up and catch it" student will throw the ball into the air and catch it by self.
Person Implementing Objective:	
Setting/Environment:	
Materials:	
Reinforcers:	
Baseline:	When student has a ball, stand in front of student and say, "Throw it up and catch it." Wait 5 seconds for a response. A correct response is scored (+) if student throws the ball in the air and catches the ball by self- do not reinforce. Move to next trial. An incorrect response is scored (-) if student does not throw the ball in air and catch it by self- do not prompt. Move to next trial.
Teaching Procedures:	When student has a ball, stand in front of student and say, "Throw it up and catch it." Wait 5 seconds for a response. If student throws the ball in the air and catches the ball by self, praise and provide reinforcer. If student does not throw the ball in the air and catch the ball by self, say, "Throw it up and catch it like this," as you model the throw and catch. Wait 5 seconds for a response. If student throws the ball in the air and catches the ball by self, praise and provide reinforcer. If student does not throw the ball in the air and catch the ball by self, physically guide student to throw the ball in the air and catch the ball by self. Score V for correct response that followed verbal prompt. Score M if correct response followed model prompt. Score P if physical guidance was used.
Additional Targets:	

Ball Bouncing
Compatible with ABLLS®-R Code Y25

Student's Name:		Start Date:	
Objective:	When student has a ball and teacher says, "Bounce the ball" student will bounce the ball on the ground.		
Person Implementing Objective:			
Setting/Environment:			
Materials:			
Reinforcers:			
Baseline:	When student has a ball, say, "Bounce the ball." Wait 5 seconds for a response. A correct response is scored (+) if student bounces the ball on the ground - <u>do not reinforce</u>. Move to next trial. An incorrect response is scored (-) if student does not bounce the ball on the ground- <u>do not prompt</u>. Move to next trial.		
Teaching Procedures:	When student has a ball, say, "Bounce the ball." Wait 5 seconds for a response. If student bounces the ball on the ground, praise and provide reinforcer. If student does not bounce the ball on the ground, say, "Bounce the ball," and make a motion as if you are bouncing the ball. Wait 5 seconds for a response. If student bounces the ball on the ground, praise and provide reinforcer. If student does not bounce the ball, physically guide student to bounce the ball. Score V for correct response that followed verbal prompt. Score M if correct response followed model prompt. Score P if physical guidance was used.		
Additional Targets:			

Kicking
Compatible with ABLLS®-R Code Y26

Student's Name:		Start Date:	
Objective:	When teacher rolls a ball to student and says, "Kick it" student will kick the rolling ball.		

Person Implementing Objective:	
Setting/Environment:	
Materials:	
Reinforcers:	
Baseline:	Roll a ball to student and say, "Kick it." Wait 5 seconds for a response. A correct response is scored (+) if student kicks the rolling ball- <u>do not reinforce</u>. Move to next trial. An incorrect response is scored (-) if student does not kick the rolling ball-<u>do not prompt</u>. Move to next trial.
Teaching Procedures:	Roll a ball to student and say, "Kick it." Wait 5 seconds for a response. If student kicks the rolling ball, praise and provide reinforcer. If student does not kick the rolling ball, say, "Kick it," as you model kicking the ball. Roll ball again. Wait 5 seconds for a response. If student kicks the rolling ball, praise and provide reinforcer. If student does not kick the rolling ball, physically guide student to kick the rolling ball. Score V for correct response that followed verbal prompt. Score M if correct response followed model prompt. Score P if physical guidance was used.
Additional Targets:	

Swinging
Compatible with ABLLS®-R Code Y27

Student's Name:	Start Date:

Objective:	When student is on a swing and teacher gives student a little push to start student swinging and says, "Swing by yourself" student will pump legs to maintain momentum.
Person Implementing Objective:	
Setting/Environment:	
Materials:	
Reinforcers:	
Baseline:	Place student on a swing and give a little push so that student begins swinging. Say, "Swing by yourself." Wait 5 seconds for a response. A correct response is scored (+) if student pumps legs to maintain momentum- <u>do not reinforce</u>. Move to next trial. An incorrect response is scored (-) if student does not pump legs to maintain momentum- <u>do not prompt</u>. Move to next trial.
Teaching Procedures:	Place student on a swing and give a little push so that student begins swinging. Say, "Swing by yourself." Wait 5 seconds for a response. If student pumps legs to maintain momentum, praise and provide reinforcer. If student does not pump legs to maintain momentum, say, "Swing by yourself, pump your legs," as you gesture to student's legs. Wait 5 seconds for a response. If student pumps legs to maintain momentum, praise and provide reinforcer. If student does not pump legs to maintain momentum, physically guide student to pumps legs. Score V for correct response that followed verbal prompt. Score M if correct response followed model prompt. Score P if physical guidance was used.
Additional Targets:	

Skipping
Compatible with ABLLS®-R Code Y28

Student's Name:		Start Date:	
Objective:	When teacher is standing in front of student and says, "Skip" student will skip.		

Person Implementing Objective:	
Setting/Environment:	
Materials:	
Reinforcers:	
Baseline:	Stand in front of student and say, "Skip." Wait 5 seconds for a response. A correct response is scored (+) if student skips - do not reinforce. Move to next trial. An incorrect response is scored (-) if student does not skip- do not prompt. Move to next trial.
Teaching Procedures:	Stand in front of student and say, "Skip." Wait 5 seconds for a response. If student skips, praise and provide reinforcer. If student does not skip, say, "Skip," and model skipping. Wait 5 seconds for a response. If student skips, praise and provide reinforcer. If student does not skip, physically guide student to skip. Score V for correct response that followed verbal prompt. Score M if correct response followed model prompt. Score P if physical guidance was used.
Additional Targets:	

Jump And Claps
Compatible with ABLLS®-R Code Y29

Student's Name:		Start Date:	
Objective:	When teacher is standing in front of student and says, "Do jumping jacks" student will jump up in the air, spread legs, and clap hands above head.		
Person Implementing Objective:			
Setting/Environment:			
Materials:			
Reinforcers:			
Baseline:	Stand in front of student and say, "Do jumping jacks." Wait 5 seconds for a response. A correct response is scored (+) if student jumps up in the air, spreads legs, and claps hands above head- <u>do not reinforce</u>. Move to next trial. An incorrect response is scored (-) if student does not jump up in the air, spread legs, and clap hands above head- <u>do not prompt</u>. Move to next trial.		
Teaching Procedures:	Stand in front of student and say, "Do jumping jacks." Wait 5 seconds for a response. If student jumps up in the air, spreads legs, and claps hands above head, praise and provide reinforcer. If student does not jump up in the air, spread legs, and clap hands above head, say "Do jumping jacks," as you model jumping jacks. Wait 5 seconds for a response. If student jumps up in the air, spreads legs, and claps hands above head, praise and provide reinforcer. If student does not jump up in the air, spread legs, and clap hands above head, physically guide student to do jumping jacks. Score V for correct response that followed verbal prompt. Score M if correct response followed model prompt. Score P if physical guidance was used.		
Additional Targets:			

Bicycle Riding
Compatible with ABLLS®-R Code Y30

Student's Name:		Start Date:	
Objective:	When teacher provides a bicycle, an open space for which to ride it, and says, "Ride" student will ride the bicycle.		
Person Implementing Objective:			
Setting/Environment:			
Materials:			
Reinforcers:			
Baseline:	Seat student on bicycle and say, "Ride." Wait 5 seconds for a response. A correct response is scored (+) if student pedals and steers the bicycle - <u>do not reinforce</u>. Move to next trial. An incorrect response is scored (-) if student does not pedal and steer the bicycle-<u>do not prompt</u>. Move to next trial.		
Teaching Procedures:	Seat student on bicycle and say, "Ride." Wait 5 seconds for a response. If student pedals and steers bicycle, praise and provide reinforcer. If student does not pedal and steer bicycle, say, "Ride" and give student a little push to help get moving. Wait 5 seconds for a response. If student pedals and steers bicycle, praise and provide reinforcer. If student does not pedal and steer bicycle, physically guide student to ride the bicycle. Score V for correct response that followed verbal prompt. Score P if physical guidance was used.		
Additional Targets:			

CHAPTER 25

ABA Programs Compatible with

ABLLS®-R Domain Z

"Fine Motor Skills"

Write On Paper
Compatible with ABLLS®-R Code Z1

Student's Name:		Start Date:	
Objective:	When student is given a writing utensil, a piece of paper, and teacher says, "Write on paper" student will write on paper.		
Person Implementing Objective:			
Setting/Environment:			
Materials:			
Reinforcers:			
Baseline:	Present paper and writing utensil to student. Say, "Write on paper." Wait 5 seconds for a response. A correct response is scored (+) if student writes on paper- do not reinforce. Move to next trial. An incorrect response is scored (-) if student does not write on paper-do not prompt. Move to next trial.		
Teaching Procedures:	Present paper and writing utensil to student. Say, "Write on paper." Wait 5 seconds for a response. If student writes on paper, praise and provide reinforcer. If student does not write on paper, say "Write on paper" as you gesture towards the paper. Wait 5 seconds for a response. If student writes on paper, praise and provide reinforcer. If student does not write on paper, physically guide student to write on paper. Score V for correct response that followed verbal prompt. Score M if correct response followed model prompt. Score P if physical guidance was used.		
Additional Targets:			

Shape Sorter
Compatible with ABLLS®-R Code Z2

Student's Name:		Start Date:	
Objective:	When presented with shapes, a shape sorter, and teacher says, "Put in" student will put shapes through corresponding holes in a shape sorter.		
Person Implementing Objective:			
Setting/Environment:			
Materials:			
Reinforcers:			
Baseline:	Place shape sorter box and corresponding shapes in front of student. Say, "Put in." Wait 5 seconds for a response. A correct response is scored (+) if student puts shapes in the correct holes- do not reinforce. Move to next trial. An incorrect response is scored (-) if the student does not put shapes into correct holes- do not prompt. Move to next trial.		
Teaching Procedures:	Place shape sorter box and corresponding shapes in front of student. Say, "Put in." Wait 5 seconds for a response. If student places shapes in correct holes, praise and provide reinforcer. If student does not place shapes in correct holes, model placing correct shapes into correct holes. Say, "Put in." Wait 5 seconds for a response. If student places shapes in correct holes, praise and provide reinforcer. If student does not place shapes in correct holes, physically guide student to place shapes in correct holes. Score V for correct response that followed verbal prompt. Score M if correct response followed model prompt. Score P if physical guidance was used.		
Additional Targets:			

The BIG Book of ABA Programs

Puzzle- Single Piece Inset
Compatible With ABLLS®-R Code Z3

Student's Name:		Start Date:	
Objective:		When student is presented with a single piece inset-type puzzle and teacher says, "Put in" student will place piece into correct location.	
Person Implementing Objective:			
Setting/Environment:			
Materials:			
Reinforcers:			
Baseline:		Present puzzle frame to student. Present puzzle piece to student and say, "Put in." Wait 5 seconds for a response. A correct response is scored (+) if student places piece into correct location - <u>do not reinforce</u>. Move to next trial. An incorrect response is scored (-) if student does not place piece into correct location- <u>do not prompt</u>. Move to next trial.	
Teaching Procedures:		Present puzzle frame to student. Present puzzle piece to student and say, "Put in." Wait 5 seconds for a response. If student places piece into correct location, praise and provide reinforcer. If student does not place piece into correct location, say, "Put in" while gesturing to the correct location. Wait 5 seconds for a response. If student places piece into correct location, praise and provide reinforcer. If student does not place piece into correct location, physically guide student to place piece into correct location. Score V for correct response that followed verbal prompt. Score M if correct response followed model prompt. Score P if physical guidance was used.	
Additional Targets:			

www.stimuluspublications.com   The Autism Skill Acquisition Program™

Puzzle- Multiple Piece Inset
Compatible With ABLLS®-R Code Z4

Student's Name:		Start Date:
Objective:	Given a single piece inset-type puzzle and teacher says, "Put in" student will place pieces into correct locations	
Person Implementing Objective:		
Setting/Environment:		
Materials:		
Reinforcers:		
Baseline:	Present puzzle frame to student. Present puzzle pieces to student and say, "Put in." Wait 5 seconds for a response. A correct response is scored (+) if student places pieces into correct locations - <u>do not reinforce</u>. Move to next trial. An incorrect response is scored (-) if student does not place pieces into correct locations- <u>do not prompt</u>. Move to next trial.	
Teaching Procedures:	Present puzzle frame to student. Present puzzle pieces to student and say, "Put in." Wait 5 seconds for a response. If student places pieces into correct locations, praise and provide reinforcer. If student does not place pieces into correct locations, say, "Put in" while gesturing to correct locations. Wait 5 seconds for a response. If student places pieces into correct locations, praise and provide reinforcer. If student does not place pieces into correct locations, physically guide student to place pieces into correct locations. Score V for correct response that followed verbal prompt. Score M if correct response followed model prompt. Score P if physical guidance was used.	
Additional Targets:		

Pattern Cards
Compatible with ABLLS®-R Code Z5

Student's Name:	Start Date:
Objective:	When presented with blocks, a pattern card, and teacher says, "Match" student will place blocks on pattern card in correct locations.
Person Implementing Objective:	
Setting/Environment:	
Materials:	
Reinforcers:	
Baseline:	Present pattern card and corresponding blocks to student. Say, "Match." Wait 5 seconds for a response. A correct response is scored (+) if student puts blocks on the correct locations on the pattern card- <u>do not reinforce</u>. Move to next trial. An incorrect response is scored (-) if student does not place blocks on the correct locations on the pattern card- <u>do not prompt</u>. Move to next trial.
Teaching Procedures:	Present pattern card and corresponding blocks to student. Say, "Match." Wait 5 seconds for a response. If student places blocks in correct locations on the card, praise and provide reinforcer. If student does not place blocks on correct locations on the pattern card, model placing a block on the card as you say, "Match." Wait 5 seconds for a response. If student places blocks on correct locations on the pattern card, praise and provide reinforcer. If student does not place blocks on correct locations on the pattern card, physically guide student to place blocks on the correct locations on the pattern card. Score V for correct response that followed verbal prompt. Score M if correct response followed model prompt. Score P if physical guidance was used.
Additional Targets:	

Move Items From Hand To Hand
Compatible with ABLLS®-R Code Z6

Student's Name:	Start Date:
Objective:	When student holds an item in hand and teacher says, "Switch hands" student will move the item from one hand to other hand.
Person Implementing Objective:	
Setting/Environment:	
Materials:	
Reinforcers:	
Baseline:	Place an item in student's hand and say, "Switch hands." Wait 5 seconds for a response. A correct response is scored (+) if student moves the item to the other hand- <u>do not reinforce</u>. Move to next trial. An incorrect response is scored (-) if student does not move the item to the other hand- <u>do not prompt</u>. Move to next trial.
Teaching Procedures:	Place an item in student's hand. Say, "Switch hands." Wait 5 seconds for a response. If student moves item to other hand, praise and provide reinforcer. If student does not move item to other hand, model moving an item from one hand to the other as you say, "Switch hands." Wait 5 seconds for a response. If student moves item to other hand, praise and provide reinforcer. If student does not move item to other hand, physically guide student to move the item from one hand to the other. Score V for correct response that followed verbal prompt. Score M if correct response followed model prompt. Score P if physical guidance was used.
Additional Targets:	

Peg Board
Compatible with ABLLS®-R Code Z7

Student's Name:		Start Date:	
Objective:	When student has a peg board and pegs and teacher says, "Put in" student will insert pegs into the peg board.		
Person Implementing Objective:			
Setting/Environment:			
Materials:			
Reinforcers:			
Baseline:	Present peg board and pegs to student. Say, "Put in." Wait 5 seconds for a response. A correct response is scored (+) if student inserts pegs into the board- <u>do not reinforce</u>. Move to next trial. An incorrect response is scored (-) if student does not insert pegs into board- <u>do not prompt</u>. Move to next trial.		
Teaching Procedures:	Present peg board and pegs to student. Say, "Put in." Wait 5 seconds for a response. If student inserts pegs into board, praise and provide reinforcer. If student does not insert pegs into board, model inserting a peg into the board as you say, "Put in." Wait 5 seconds for a response. If student inserts pegs into board, praise and provide reinforcer. If student does not insert pegs into board, physically guide student to insert pegs into board. Score V for correct response that followed verbal prompt. Score M if correct response followed model prompt. Score P if physical guidance was used.		
Additional Targets:			

Turn Book Pages
Compatible with ABLLS®-R Code Z8

Student's Name:		Start Date:
Objective:	When student is holding an open book and teacher says, "Turn the page" student will turn from one page to the next.	
Person Implementing Objective:		
Setting/Environment:		
Materials:		
Reinforcers:		
Baseline:	When student is holding an open book, say, "Turn the page." Wait 5 seconds for a response. A correct response is scored (+) if student turns from one page to the next- <u>do not reinforce</u>. Move to next trial. An incorrect response is scored (-) if student does not turn from one page to the next- <u>do not prompt</u>. Move to next trial.	
Teaching Procedures:	When student is holding an open book, say, "Turn the page." Wait 5 seconds for a response. If student turns from one page to the next, praise and provide reinforcer. If student does not turn from one page to the next, say, "Turn the page" as you gesture towards the page. Wait 5 seconds for a response. If student turns from one page to the next, praise and provide reinforcer. If student does not turn from one page to the next, physically guide student to turn the page. Score V for correct response that followed verbal prompt. Score M if correct response followed model prompt. Score P if physical guidance was used.	
Additional Targets:		

Put Clothespin On A String
Compatible with ABLLS®-R Code Z9

Student's Name:		Start Date:	
Objective:	When student has clothespins, string, and teacher says, "Put on" student will place clothespins on string.		
Person Implementing Objective:			
Setting/Environment:			
Materials:			
Reinforcers:			
Baseline:	Present clothespins and string to student. Say, "Put on." Wait 5 seconds for a response. A correct response is scored (+) if student places clothespins on string- <u>do not reinforce</u>. Move to next trial. An incorrect response is scored (-) if student does not place clothespins on string- <u>do not prompt</u>. Move to next trial.		
Teaching Procedures:	Present clothespins and string to student. Say, "Put on." Wait 5 seconds for a response. If student places clothespins on string, praise and provide reinforcer. If student does not place clothespin on string, model placing a clothespin on string. Say, "Put on." Wait 5 seconds for a response. If student places clothespin on string, praise and provide reinforcer. If student does not place clothespin on string, physically guide student to place clothespins on string. Score V for correct response that followed verbal prompt. Score M if correct response followed model prompt. Score P if physical guidance was used.		
Additional Targets:			

The BIG Book of ABA Programs

Student Will Color Inside The Lines
Compatible with ABLLS®-R Code Z10

Student's Name:	Start Date:
Objective:	When provided with a crayon, a piece of paper containing the outline of a shape, and teacher says, "Color" student will color in the shape.
Person Implementing Objective:	
Setting/Environment:	
Materials:	
Reinforcers:	
Baseline:	Present crayon and paper containing the outline of a shape to student. Say, "Color." Wait 5 seconds for a response. A correct response is scored (+) if student colors in shape staying inside the lines - <u>do not reinforce</u>. Move to next trial. An incorrect response is scored (-) if student does not color in shape staying inside the lines -<u>do not prompt</u>. Move to next trial.
Teaching Procedures:	Present crayon and paper containing the outline of a shape to student. Say, "Color." Wait 5 seconds for a response. If student colors in shape staying inside the lines, praise and provide reinforcer. If student does not color in shape staying inside the lines, say, "Color" as you gesture towards the inside of the shape. Wait 5 seconds for a response. If student colors in shape staying inside the lines, praise and provide reinforcer. If student does not color in shape staying inside the lines, physically guide student to color in shape staying inside the lines. Score V for correct response that followed verbal prompt. Score M if correct response followed model prompt. Score P if physical guidance was used.
Additional Targets:	

Open Zipper Style Bags
Compatible with ABLLS®-R Code Z11

Student's Name:		Start Date:	
Objective:	When teacher gives student a zipper style bag containing preferred edibles and says, "Open the bag" student will unzip the bag.		
Person Implementing Objective:			
Setting/Environment:			
Materials:			
Reinforcers:			
Baseline:	Present a sealed zipper style bag containing a preferred edible to student. Say "Open the bag." Wait 5 seconds for a response. A correct response is scored (+) if student opens the bag- <u>do not reinforce</u>. Move to next trial. An incorrect response is scored (-) if student does not open the bag- <u>do not prompt</u>. Move to next trial.		
Teaching Procedures:	Present a sealed zipper style bag containing a preferred edible to student. Say "Open the bag." Wait 5 seconds for a response. If student opens the bag, praise and allow access to the edible. If student does not open the bag, say, "Open the bag" as you gesture towards the zipper. Wait 5 seconds for a response. If student opens the bag, praise and allow access to edible. If student does not open the bag, physically guide student to open the bag. Score V for correct response that followed verbal prompt. Score M if correct response followed model prompt. Score P if physical guidance was used.		
Additional Targets:			

Cut With Scissors
Compatible with ABLLS®-R Code Z12

Student's Name:		Start Date:	
Objective:	When provided with a pair of scissors and a piece of paper and teacher says, "Cut paper" student will cut the paper.		
Person Implementing Objective:			
Setting/Environment:			
Materials:			
Reinforcers:			
Baseline:	Present scissors and paper to student. Say, "Cut paper." Wait 5 seconds for a response. A correct response is scored (+) if student cuts paper- <u>do not reinforce</u>. Move to next trial. An incorrect response is scored (-) if student does not cut paper- <u>do not prompt</u>. Move to next trial.		
Teaching Procedures:	Present scissors and paper to student. Say, "Cut paper." Wait 5 seconds for a response. If student cuts paper, praise and provide reinforcer If student does not cut paper, say, "Cut paper" as you gesture to scissors and paper. Wait 5 seconds for a response. If student cuts paper, praise and provide reinforcer. If student does not cut paper, physically guide student to cut paper. Score V for correct response that followed verbal prompt. Score M if correct response followed model prompt. Score P if physical guidance was used.		
Additional Targets:			

Block Stacking
Compatible with ABLLS®-R Code Z13

Student's Name:	Start Date:
Objective:	When given several blocks and teacher says, "Stack the blocks" student will place blocks on top of one another.
Person Implementing Objective:	
Setting/Environment:	
Materials:	
Reinforcers:	
Baseline:	Present blocks to student and say, "Stack the blocks." Wait 5 seconds for a response. A correct response is scored (+) if student stacks blocks- <u>do not reinforce</u>. Move to next trial. An incorrect response is scored (-) if student does not stack blocks- <u>do not prompt</u>. Move to next trial.
Teaching Procedures:	Present blocks to student and say, "Stack the blocks." Wait 5 seconds for a response. If student stacks blocks, praise and provide reinforcer. If student does not stack blocks, model stacking blocks. Say, "Stack the blocks." Wait 5 seconds for a response. If student stacks blocks, praise and provide reinforcer. If student does not stack blocks, physically guide student to stack blocks. Score V for correct response that followed verbal prompt. Score M if correct response followed model prompt. Score P if physical guidance was used.
Additional Targets:	

The BIG Book of ABA Programs

Bead Stringing
Compatible with ABLLS®-R Code Z14

Student's Name:		Start Date:	
Objective:		When given string, beads, and teacher says "String beads" student will place the string through the beads.	
Person Implementing Objective:			
Setting/Environment:			
Materials:			
Reinforcers:			
Baseline:		Present string and beads to student. Say, "String beads." Wait 5 seconds for a response. A correct response is scored (+) if student places string through the beads- <u>do not reinforce</u>. Move to next trial. An incorrect response is scored (-) if student does not place string through the beads- <u>do not prompt</u>. Move to next trial.	
Teaching Procedures:		Present string and beads to student. Say, "String beads." Wait 5 seconds for a response. If student places string through beads, praise and provide reinforcer. If student does not place string through beads, model bead stringing. Say, "String beads." Wait 5 seconds for a response. If student places string through beads, praise and provide reinforcer. If student does not place string through beads, physically guide student to place string through beads. Score V for correct response that followed verbal prompt. Score M if correct response followed model prompt. Score P if physical guidance was used.	
Additional Targets:			

www.stimuluspublications.com   The Autism Skill Acquisition Program™

The BIG Book of ABA Programs

Unscrewing Lid From Jar
Compatible with ABLLS®-R Code Z15

Student's Name:		Start Date:	
Objective:		When given a jar with a lid screwed down and teacher says, "Take off the lid" student will unscrew the lid from the jar.	
Person Implementing Objective:			
Setting/Environment:			
Materials:			
Reinforcers:			
Baseline:		Present student with a jar with the lid screwed on. Say, "Take off the lid." Wait 5 seconds for a response. A correct response is scored (+) if student unscrews the lid- <u>do not reinforce</u>. Move to next trial. An incorrect response is scored (-) if student does not unscrew the lid- <u>do not prompt</u>. Move to next trial.	
Teaching Procedures:		Present student with a jar with the lid screwed on. Say, "Take off the lid." Wait 5 seconds for a response. If student unscrews the lid, praise and provide reinforcer. If student does not unscrew the lid, model a screwing motion with your hands as you say, "Take off the lid." Wait 5 seconds for a response. If student unscrews the lid, praise and provide reinforcer. If student does not unscrew the lid, physically guide student to unscrew the lid. Score V for correct response that followed verbal prompt. Score M if correct response followed model prompt. Score P if physical guidance was used.	
Additional Targets:			

Cut Paper In Half With Scissors
Compatible with ABLLS®-R Code Z16

Student's Name:		Start Date:	
Objective:	When student has a sheet of paper, scissors, and the teacher says, "Cut in half" student will cut all the way across the sheet of paper.		
Person Implementing Objective:			
Setting/Environment:			
Materials:			
Reinforcers:			
Baseline:	Present scissors and paper to student. Say, "Cut in half." Wait 5 seconds for a response. A correct response is scored (+) if student cuts all the way across paper- <u>do not reinforce</u>. Move to next trial. An incorrect response is scored (-) if student does not cut all the way across paper- <u>do not prompt</u>. Move to next trial.		
Teaching Procedures:	Present scissors and paper to student. Say, "Cut in half." Wait 5 seconds for a response. If student cuts all the way across paper, praise and provide reinforcer. If student does not cut all the way across paper, gesture with your hand across the paper as you say, "Cut in half." Wait 5 seconds for a response. If student cuts all the way across paper, praise and provide reinforcer. If student does not cut all the way across paper physically guide student to cut across paper. Score V for correct response that followed verbal prompt. Score M if correct response followed model prompt. Score P if physical guidance was used.		
Additional Targets:			

The BIG Book of ABA Programs

Tracing With Finger
Compatible with ABLLS®-R Code Z17

Student's Name:		Start Date:	
Objective:	When given a sheet of paper with a line drawn on it and teacher says, "Trace with finger" student will trace the line with finger.		

Person Implementing Objective:	
Setting/Environment:	
Materials:	
Reinforcers:	
Baseline:	Present a piece of paper with a line drawn on it to student. Say, "Trace with finger." Wait 5 seconds for a response. A correct response is scored (+) if student uses a finger to trace the line - do not reinforce. Move to next trial. An incorrect response is scored (-) if student does not use a finger to trace the line- do not prompt. Move to next trial.
Teaching Procedures:	Present a piece of paper with a line drawn on it to student. Say, "Trace with finger." Wait 5 seconds for a response. If student traces line with a finger, praise and provide reinforcer. If student does not trace line with a finger, model tracing with your own finger. Say, "Trace with finger." Wait 5 seconds for a response. If student traces line with a finger, praise and provide reinforcer. If student does not trace line with a finger, physically guide student to trace line with a finger. Score V for correct response that followed verbal prompt. Score M if correct response followed model prompt. Score P if physical guidance was used.
Additional Targets:	

Gluing
Compatible with ABLLS®-R Code Z18

Student's Name:		Start Date:
Objective:	When given a piece of paper and a glue bottle and teacher says, "Put glue on paper" student will squeeze glue onto paper.	
Person Implementing Objective:		
Setting/Environment:		
Materials:		
Reinforcers:		
Baseline:	Present paper and glue bottle to student. Say, "Put glue on paper." Wait 5 seconds for a response. A correct response is scored (+) if student squeezes glue onto the paper- <u>do not reinforce</u>. Move to next trial. An incorrect response is scored (-) if student does not squeeze glue onto paper- <u>do not prompt</u>. Move to next trial.	
Teaching Procedures:	Present paper and glue bottle to student. Say, "Put glue on paper." Wait 5 seconds for a response. If student squeezes glue onto paper, praise and provide reinforcer. If student does not squeeze glue onto paper, model turning the glue bottle upside down and squeezing. Say, "Put glue on paper. Wait 5 seconds for a response. If student squeezes glue onto paper, praise and provide reinforcer. If student does not squeeze glue onto paper, physically guide student to squeeze glue onto paper. Score V for correct response that followed verbal prompt. Score M if correct response followed model prompt. Score P if physical guidance was used.	
Additional Targets:		

Open Wrapped Snacks
Compatible with ABLLS®-R Code Z19

Student's Name:		Start Date:	
Objective:	When student is provided with a preferred snack and teacher says, "Open your snack" student will unwrap snack.		
Person Implementing Objective:			
Setting/Environment:			
Materials:			
Reinforcers:			
Baseline:	Present wrapped snack to student. Say, "Open your snack." Wait 5 seconds for a response. A correct response is scored (+) if student opens wrapper and removes snack- <u>do not reinforce</u>. Move to next trial. An incorrect response is scored (-) if student does not open wrapper and remove snack- <u>do not prompt</u>. Move to next trial.		
Teaching Procedures:	Present wrapped snack to student. Say, "Open your snack." Wait 5 seconds for a response. If student opens wrapper and removes snack, praise and allow student to consume snack. If student does not open wrapper and remove snack, model pulling the wrapper open. Say, "Open your snack." Wait 5 seconds for a response. If student opens wrapper and removes snack, praise and allow student to consume snack. If student does not open wrapper and remove snack physically guide student to open wrapper and remove snack. Score V for correct response that followed verbal prompt. Score M if correct response followed model prompt. Score P if physical guidance was used.		
Additional Targets:			

Draw Shapes Given A Model
Compatible with ABLLS®-R Code Z20

Student's Name:		Start Date:	
Objective:		When student has a writing utensil and a piece of paper containing a shape to use as a model and teacher says, "Draw ____ (name of shape)" student will draw the shape.	
Person Implementing Objective:			
Setting/Environment:			
Materials:			
Reinforcers:			
Baseline:		Present a writing utensil and a piece of paper containing a shape to student. Say, "Draw ____ (name of shape)." Wait 5 seconds for a response. A correct response is scored (+) if student draws the shape- <u>do not reinforce</u>. Move to next trial. An incorrect response is scored (-) if student does not draw the shape- <u>do not prompt</u>. Move to next trial.	
Teaching Procedures:		Present a writing utensil and a piece of paper containing a shape to student. Say, "Draw ____ (name of shape)." Wait 5 seconds for a response. If student draws shape, praise and provide reinforcer. If student does not draw shape, gesture to the shape on the paper and say, "Draw ____ (name of shape)." Wait 5 seconds for a response. If student draws shape, praise and provide reinforcer. If student does not draw shape, physically guide student to draw shape. Score V for correct response that followed verbal prompt. Score P if physical guidance was used.	
Additional Targets:			

The BIG Book of ABA Programs

Gluing Things To Paper
Compatible with ABLLS®-R Code Z21

Student's Name:		Start Date:
Objective:	When given small pieces of paper, a full sheet of paper, a bottle of glue, and teacher says, "Glue the pieces to the paper" student will place a small amount of glue onto small pieces of paper and stick them on the full sheet of paper.	
Person Implementing Objective:		
Setting/Environment:		
Materials:		
Reinforcers:		
Baseline:	Present full sheet of paper, cut pieces of papers, and glue to student. Say, "Glue the pieces to the paper." Wait 5 seconds for a response. A correct response is scored (+) if student places small amount of glue on cut pieces and sticks cut pieces onto full sheet- <u>do not reinforce</u>. Move to next trial. An incorrect response is scored (-) if student does not place small amount of glue on cut pieces and stick cut pieces onto full sheet- <u>do not prompt</u>. Move to next trial.	
Teaching Procedures:	Present full sheet of paper, cut pieces of papers, and glue to student. Say, "Glue the pieces to the paper." Wait 5 seconds for a response. If student places small amount of glue on cut pieces and sticks cut pieces onto full sheet, praise and provide reinforcer. If student does not place small amount of glue on cut pieces and stick cut pieces onto full sheet, gesture to the cut pieces, the glue, and the full sheet of paper and say, "Glue the pieces on the paper." Wait 5 seconds for a response. If student places small amount of glue on cut pieces and sticks cut pieces onto full sheet, praise and provide reinforcer. If student does not place small amount of glue on cut pieces and stick cut pieces onto full sheet, physically guide student to place small amount of glue on cut pieces and stick cut pieces onto full sheet. Score V for correct response that followed verbal prompt. Score M if correct response followed model prompt. Score P if physical guidance was used.	
Additional Targets:		

Gluing Things On Paper To Match A Model
Compatible with ABLLS®-R Code Z22

Student's Name:		Start Date:
Objective:	When given a sheet of paper with a model picture, small pieces of paper, a full sheet of paper, a bottle of glue, and teacher says, "Glue the pieces to the paper to make the picture" student will place a small amount of glue onto cut pieces of paper and stick them on the full sheet of paper to approximate the model.	
Person Implementing Objective:		
Setting/Environment:		
Materials:		
Reinforcers:		
Baseline:	Present model picture, full sheet of paper, cut pieces of papers and glue to student. Say, "Glue the pieces to the paper to make the picture." Wait 5 seconds for a response. A correct response is scored (+) if student places small amount of glue on cut pieces and sticks cut pieces onto full sheet so that pieces resemble the model- <u>do not reinforce</u>. Move to next trial. An incorrect response is scored (-) if student does not place small amount of glue on cut pieces and stick cut pieces onto full sheet so that the pieces resemble the model- <u>do not prompt</u>. Move to next trial.	
Teaching Procedures:	Present model picture, full sheet of paper, cut pieces of papers and glue to student. Say, "Glue the pieces to the paper to make the picture." Wait 5 seconds for a response. If student places small amount of glue on cut pieces and sticks cut pieces onto full sheet so that the pieces resemble the model, praise and provide reinforcer. If student does not place small amount of glue on cut pieces and stick cut pieces onto full sheet so that they resemble the model, gesture to the model and say, "Glue the pieces on the paper to make the picture." Wait 5 seconds for a response. If student places small amount of glue on cut pieces and sticks cut pieces onto full sheet so that the pieces resemble the model, praise and provide reinforcer. If student does not place small amount of glue on cut pieces and stick cut pieces onto full sheet so that they resemble the model, physically guide student to not place small amount of glue on cut pieces and stick cut pieces onto full sheet so that they resemble the model. Score V for correct response that followed verbal prompt. Score M if correct response followed model prompt. Score P if physical guidance was used.	
Additional Targets:		

Put Rings On Stake
Compatible with ABLLS®-R Code Z23

Student's Name:		Start Date:	
Objective:	When given rings and a stake and teacher says, "Put on" student will place rings onto stake.		
Person Implementing Objective:			
Setting/Environment:			
Materials:			
Reinforcers:			
Baseline:	Present rings and stake to student. Say, "Put on." Wait 5 seconds for a response. A correct response is scored (+) if student places rings on the stake- <u>do not reinforce</u>. Move to next trial. An incorrect response is scored (-) if student does not place rings on stake- <u>do not prompt</u>. Move to next trial.		
Teaching Procedures:	Present rings and stake to student. Say, "Put on." Wait 5 seconds for a response. If student places rings on stake, praise and provide reinforcer. If student does not place rings on stake, model placing a ring on the stake. Say, "Put on." Wait 5 seconds for a response. If student places rings on stake, praise and provide reinforcer. If student does not place rings on stake, physically guide student to place rings on the stake. Score V for correct response that followed verbal prompt. Score M if correct response followed model prompt. Score P if physical guidance was used.		
Additional Targets:			

Screw Lid On Jar
Compatible with ABLLS®-R Code Z24

Student's Name:		Start Date:	
Objective:	When given a jar, a lid, and teacher says, "Put the lid on" student will screw the lid onto the jar.		
Person Implementing Objective:			
Setting/Environment:			
Materials:			
Reinforcers:			
Baseline:	Give student a jar and a lid. Say, "Put the lid on." Wait 5 seconds for a response. A correct response is scored (+) if the student screws the lid onto the jar- <u>do not reinforce</u>. Move to next trial. An incorrect response is scored (-) if the student does not screw the lid onto the jar- <u>do not prompt</u>. Move to next trial.		
Teaching Procedures:	Give student a jar and a lid. Say, "Put the lid on." Wait 5 seconds for a response. If student screws lid onto jar, praise and provide reinforcer. If student does not screw lid onto jar, model a screwing motion with your hands as you say, "Put the lid on." Wait 5 seconds for a response. If student screws lid onto jar, praise and provide reinforcer. If student does not screw lid onto jar, physically guide student to screw lid onto jar. Score V for correct response that followed verbal prompt. Score M if correct response followed model prompt. Score P if physical guidance was used.		
Additional Targets:			

Use Thumb And Index Finger To Pick Up Small Items
Compatible with ABLLS®-R Code Z25

Student's Name:		Start Date:	
Objective:	\multicolumn{3}{l	}{When a small item is placed in front of student and teacher says, "Pick up the ____ (name item)" student will use thumb and index finger to pick up the named item.}

Person Implementing Objective:	
Setting/Environment:	
Materials:	
Reinforcers:	
Baseline:	Present small object to student. Say, "Pick up the ____ (name item)." Wait 5 seconds for a response. A correct response is scored (+) if student picks up item using thumb and index finger- <u>do not reinforce</u>. Move to next trial. An incorrect response is scored (-) if student does not pick up item using thumb and index finger- <u>do not prompt</u>. Move to next trial.
Teaching Procedures:	Present small object to student. Say, "Pick up the ____ (name item)." Wait 5 seconds for a response. If student picks up item using thumb and index finger, praise and provide reinforcer. If student does not pick up item using thumb and index finger, model picking up item with thumb and index finger. Say, "Pick up the ____ (name item)." Wait 5 seconds for a response. If student picks up item using thumb and index finger, praise and provide reinforcer. If student does not pick up item using thumb and index finger, physically guide student to use thumb and index finger to pick up the item. Score V for correct response that followed verbal prompt. Score M if correct response followed model prompt. Score P if physical guidance was used.
Additional Targets:	

Paper Folding
Compatible with ABLLS®-R Code Z26

Student's Name:	Start Date:
Objective:	When given a piece of paper and teacher says, "Fold in half" student will fold the paper in half.
Person Implementing Objective:	
Setting/Environment:	
Materials:	
Reinforcers:	
Baseline:	Present paper to student. Say, "Fold in half." Wait 5 seconds for a response. A correct response is scored (+) if student folds paper in half- <u>do not reinforce</u>. Move to next trial. An incorrect response is scored (-) if student does fold paper in half- <u>do not prompt</u>. Move to next trial.
Teaching Procedures:	Present paper to student. Say, "Fold in half." Wait 5 seconds for a response. If student folds paper in half, praise and provide reinforcer. If student does not fold paper in half, model paper folding. Say, "Fold in half." Wait 5 seconds for a response. If student folds paper in half, praise and provide reinforcer. If student does not fold paper in half, physically guide student to fold paper in half. Score M for correct response following initial prompt. Score P if physical guidance was used.
Additional Targets:	

Student Will Cut Shapes With Scissors
Compatible with ABLLS®-R Code Z27

Student's Name:		Start Date:
Objective:	When given a pair of scissors, a sheet of paper containing the outlines of shapes, and teacher says "Cut out the ____ (name shape)" student will cut out the named shape on the lines.	
Person Implementing Objective:		
Setting/Environment:		
Materials:		
Reinforcers:		
Baseline:	Present scissors and paper containing the outline of shapes to student. Say, "Cut out ____ (name shape)." Wait 5 seconds for a response. A correct response is scored (+) if student cuts the out shape- <u>do not reinforce</u>. Move to next trial. An incorrect response is scored (-) if student does not cut out shape- <u>do not prompt</u>. Move to next trial.	
Teaching Procedures:	Present scissors and paper containing the outline of shapes to student. Say, "Cut out ____ (name shape)." Wait 5 seconds for a response. If student cuts out the shape, praise and provide reinforcer. If student does not cut out shape, gesture to the outline of shape and say, "Cut out the ____ (name shape)." Wait 5 seconds for a response. If student cuts out shape, praise and provide reinforcer. If student does not cut out shape, physically guide student to cut out the shape. Score V for correct response that followed verbal prompt. Score M if correct response followed model prompt. Score P if physical guidance was used.	
Additional Targets:		

The BIG Book of ABA Programs

Drawing Shapes
Compatible with ABLLS®-R Code Z28

Student's Name:	Start Date:	
Objective:	When given a writing utensil, piece of paper, and teacher says, "Draw a ____ (name shape)" student will draw named shape.	
Person Implementing Objective:		
Setting/Environment:		
Materials:		
Reinforcers:		
Baseline:	Present paper and writing utensil to student. Say, "Draw a ____ (name shape)." Wait 5 seconds for a response. A correct response is scored (+) if student draws named shape- <u>do not reinforce</u>. Move to next trial. An incorrect response is scored (-) if student does draw named shape- <u>do not prompt</u>. Move to next trial.	
Teaching Procedures:	Present paper and writing utensil to student. Say, "Draw a ____ (name shape)." Wait 5 seconds for a response. If student draws named shape, praise and provide reinforcer. If student does not draw named shape, gesture to the paper and say, "Draw a ____ (name shape)." Wait 5 seconds for a response. If student draws named shape, praise and provide reinforcer. If student does not draw named shape, physically guide student to draw named shape. Score V for correct response that followed verbal prompt. Score P if physical guidance was used.	
Additional Targets:		